Engineering the Human–Computer Interface

ESSEX SERIES IN TELECOMMUNICATION AND INFORMATION SYSTEMS

Series editors

Andy Downton
Ed Jones

Forthcoming Titles

Computer Communication Networks
Image Processing
Speech Processing
Satellite and Mobile Radio Systems

ENGINEERING THE HUMAN–COMPUTER INTERFACE

Edited by
Andy Downton
Department of Electronic Systems Engineering
University of Essex

McGRAW-HILL BOOK COMPANY

London · New York · St Louis · San Francisco · Auckland
Bogotá · Caracas · Hamburg · Lisbon · Madrid · Mexico · Milan
Montreal · New Delhi · Panama · Paris · San Juan · São Paulo
Singapore · Sydney · Tokyo · Toronto

Published by
McGRAW-HILL Book Company (UK) Limited
SHOPPENHANGERS ROAD · MAIDENHEAD · BERKSHIRE · ENGLAND
TEL: 0628 23432
FAX: 0628 770224

British Library Cataloguing in Publication Data

Engineering the human–computer interface. – (Essex series in
  telecommunication and information systems).
  1. Man. Interactions with computer systems
  I. Downton, Andy   II. Series
  004.019

  ISBN 0-07-707321-5

Library of Congress Cataloging-in-Publication Data

Engineering the human–computer interface/editor, Andy Downton.
    p.   cm.—(Essex series in telecommunication and information systems)
  Includes bibliographical references and index.
  ISBN 0-07-707321-5
  1. Human–computer interaction.   2. User interfaces (Computer systems)
  I. Downton, A. C.   II. Series.
  QA76.9.H85E53   1991
  005.1—dc20   90-24975 CIP

1234 CUP 94321

Typeset by Computape (Pickering) Ltd, Pickering, North Yorkshire
and printed and bound in Great Britain at the University Press, Cambridge

Contents

Notes on the contributors

Bruce Anderson, MA, MSc, worked at Stanford University's Artificial Intelligence Laboratory before coming to Essex University as a lecturer. He is a consultant to industry on training and software engineering, and is interested in effective interaction for problem solving, in object-oriented programming, and in learning methods.

Gary Ashworth, BA, works in the Human Factors Division of British Telecom Research Laboratories at Martlesham. He acted as a consultant on the development of the BTRL text-to-speech synthesizer used in the Alvey VODIS project.

Phil Barnard, BSc, PhD, CPsychol, FBPsS, is a senior member of the research staff at the MRC Applied Psychology Unit in Cambridge, where he has worked since 1972. He has published over 80 papers, principally on cognitive aspects of human–computer interaction. He is the 1990 holder of the Ergonomics Society's Otto Edholm award for distinguished basic research contributions to ergonomics.

Peter Boucherat has spent his career working at British Telecom Research Laboratories at Martlesham, and was initially in the Telephone Instruments Division, where he was involved in subjective assessment tests. More recently he has worked in the Human Factors Division, where he was responsible for much of the evaluation work carried out by BT as part of the Alvey Adaptive Intelligent Dialogues project.

Andy Downton, BSc, PhD, CEng, MIEE, is a Senior Lecturer in the Department of Electronic Systems Engineering at Essex University, and was previously a lecturer in the Department of Electronics at Southampton University from 1978 to 1986. He has extensive research experience within the fields of human–computer systems and pattern recognition, and has been involved in developing and evaluating several commercial products involving significant HCI design problems.

Hilary Johnson, BSc, PhD, worked as a research psychologist at the

MRC's development unit for four years before moving to the Computer Science Department at Queen Mary and Westfield College as a post-doctoral research fellow in 1986. She is currently working on an ESPRIT Basic Research Action looking at 'Interactive dialogues for explanation and learning'.

Peter Johnson, BSc, PhD, Reader in Computer Science, Queen Mary and Westfield College, London, has a background in cognitive psychology, and was previously with the Ergonomics Unit at University College, London. His research interests are in cognitive ergonomics, user modelling, and evaluation methodologies. He presently leads the HCI research laboratories at QMW. He has been involved in a number of Alvey, IED and Esprit research projects, and with the development of the London HCI centre.

Peter Jones, BSc, MSc, is currently a lecturer in the Department of Electrical Engineering at the University of Western Australia, and was previously a lecturer in the Department of Electronic Systems Engineering at the University of Essex from 1981 to 1989. He was an academic partner in the Alvey Adaptive Intelligent Dialogues project, the largest MMI project run as part of the Alvey programme. His research interests are in interactive computer systems design.

Simon Jones, BSc, PhD, is a research engineer at British Telecom Research Laboratories at Martlesham, and was previously a lecturer in the Department of Electronic Systems Engineering at Essex University from 1984 to 1989. His interests are in user interfaces for broadband networks and distributed systems.

Graham Leedham, BSc, MSc, PhD, CEng, MIEE, spent the early part of his career with GEC, and has been a lecturer in the Department of Electronic Systems Engineering at the University of Essex since 1984. His research interests are in human–computer interaction and the automatic recognition of handwriting.

Series preface

This book is part of a series, the *Essex Series in Telecommunication and Information Systems*, which has developed from a set of short courses run by the Department of Electronic Systems Engineering at the University of Essex since 1987. The courses are presented as one-week modules of the Department's MSc in Telecommunication and Information Systems, and are offered simultaneously as industry short courses. To date, a total of over 600 industrial personnel have attended the courses, in addition to the 70 or so postgraduate students registered each year for the MSc. The flexibility of the short-course format means that the contents both of individual courses and the courses offered from year to year have been able to develop to reflect current industrial and academic demand.

The aim of the book series is to provide readable yet authoritative coverage of key topics within the field of telecommunication and information systems. Being derived from a highly regarded university postgraduate course, the books are well suited to use in advanced taught courses at universities and polytechnics, and as a starting point and background reference for researchers. Equally, the industrial orientation of the courses ensures that both the content and presentation style are suited to the needs of the professional engineer in mid-career.

The books in the series are based largely on the course notes circulated to students, and so have been 'class-tested' several times before publication. Though primarily authored and edited by academic staff at Essex, where appropriate each book includes chapters contributed by acknowledged experts from other universities, research establishments and industry (originally presented as seminars on the courses). Our colleagues at British Telecom Research Laboratories, Martlesham, have also provided advice and assistance in developing course syllabuses and ensuring that the material included correctly reflects industry practice as well as academic principles.

As series editors, we would like to acknowledge the tremendous support we have had in developing the concept of the series from the original idea through to the publication of the first group of books. The successful completion of this project would not have been possible without the substantial commitment shown not only by individual authors but by the Department of Electronic Systems Engineering as a whole to this project. Particular thanks go to the editors of the individual books, each of whom, in addition to authoring several chapters, was responsible for integrating the various contributors' chapters of his or her book into a coherent whole.

July 1990

Andy Downton
Ed Jones

Preface

Over the past two decades, the development of the microprocessor has changed the status of the computer from being a specialized system for commercial data processing and scientific research into a ubiquitous part of everyday life. Its manifestations include not only 'conventional' computing systems such as personal computers and workstations, but also embedded applications where the microprocessor acts as an intelligent controller, for example in a video recorder or a washing machine. We all now expect to use many computer systems in our daily lives, ranging from domestic equipment through office computers to bank cash machines. Despite their variety, what all these systems have in common is the user: in almost every case, some kind of interface is required to mediate the user's intentions and translate them into functional control of the system. Thus, designing the interface with regard to the potential users of a system should be a significant aspect of the design of the whole system.

Human–computer interaction is therefore an area with which every electronic engineer, computer scientist and programmer ought to be familiar. Yet the bibliography of HCI is currently dominated by authors from the human sciences; texts written by technologists are relatively rare. When the authors of this book first prepared a short course on human–computer interaction four years ago, we were dismayed to find that there was no single textbook we could recommend as covering the syllabus we wanted to teach from an appropriately technological viewpoint. As we were already preparing comprehensive printed notes for our course, the solution seemed obvious, and the concept of *Engineering the Human–Computer Interface* was born.

This book provides an overview of human factors in general and the human information processor in particular, based on research in the human sciences. It shows how this knowledge can be used to infer guidelines and develop methodologies and techniques for designing appropriate user interfaces. We have tried to show how a layered approach to user interface design and design tools is emerging, but we have not emphasized the practical software and hardware construction aspects of HCI, as these are covered in depth in mainstream literature. Our experience from the course and from our own research has been that most mistakes are made and difficulties encountered at the earlier, more abstract stages of specification and analysis.

As authors, we have benefited from the advice of colleagues and students too numerous to mention in preparing this book. In addition, as editor, I would like to acknowledge the assistance of Mark Corbett and David Crowther at McGraw-Hill, Dominic Recaldin (who originally suggested the idea of a book series based on the courses), and particularly Alistair Sutcliffe for his detailed and constructive suggestions for improvements based on reading the first draft manuscript. Most of his suggestions have been incorporated with considerable advantage to the clarity and structure of the book. Finally, I would like to thank my co-authors with whom it has been a pleasure to collaborate.

July 1990   Andy Downton

PART I

User psychology and applied psychological research

1 Engineering the human–computer interface: an overview

ANDY DOWNTON

1.1 Introduction

Interaction between users and systems has been with us ever since man invented the wheel. However, since the introduction of computers the potential and need has existed to design complex dialogues in which the relationship between the user's input and the functional output of a system has become ever more sophisticated. Human–computer interaction has crept up on electronic and software design engineers with great stealth: once upon a time a `writeln` (Pascal) or `printf` (C) statement was simply a method of outputting data from a computer program; now it is often the sharp end of a complex dialogue between human and system.

But whereas design methods for conventional engineering and computer science problems are for the most part well developed and documented, effective communication with users seems to present an intractable and intangible problem whose solution is clouded in the indeterminacy of human behaviour. The limited nature of experimental evidence and primitive level of formal theories in the human sciences contrast starkly with well-proven, elegant and concise formal methods which are widespread in engineering and computer science. As a result, human–computer interaction receives very little attention from many system designers, even though it is perhaps the most pervasive of all areas of system design. This pervasiveness provides the justification for this book: no system designer can consider their skills complete without some understanding of the issues involved in human–computer interaction, yet many 'design' human–computer interfaces in complete ignorance of these issues. In effect, they are relying on the resilience and adaptability of the human to compensate for deficiencies in their design.

In this book, we start by assuming that most engineering systems are tools: workshop tools are used to magnify and refine the mechanical skills of the human hand; transport is a tool for moving humans around in a comfortable and speedy manner; domestic equipment provides support for a variety of activities within the house; computer systems are a tool to support information processing. With all of these systems, the design objective is to optimize the performance of the person and the machine together as a system.

In very simple cases, optimizing the machine itself is equivalent to optimizing the human–machine system; for example, improving the design of a lathe may improve the accuracy of work which can be accomplished using it. Increasingly, however, there is a need to optimize the human–machine system as a whole: in the case of the lathe, poor design of the controls (gearing) can lead to poor-quality work even though the basic capabilities of the machine have been enhanced.

Traditionally, this optimization has been achieved by means of (informal) evaluation and long-term feedback from users. Thus, over several decades the horseless carriage evolved into the modern motor car as various aspects of control and ergonomic design were progressively refined in the light of experience. Unfortunately, these traditional methods are impractical in most computer-based systems owing to their very short life-cycle and complex interface: hence we now urgently need to develop revised design strategies which can be applied within the framework of current design practice.

1.2 Fields of study

A major problem in human–computer interaction, and a distinctive difference compared with other subject areas, is the sheer breadth of knowledge required. Even acknowledged experts in the field are generally expert only within a restricted problem domain. The coverage of this book is substantially wider than the knowledge of any of its individual contributors. The main areas relevant to the study of human–computer interaction can be classified as follows:

Electronic engineering; computer science

These disciplines provide the technological framework for human–computer system design.

Psychology

Behavioural and cognitive psychology are concerned with understanding human behaviour, perception, cognitive processing and motor control skills, and propose models of these processes which give useful insights into methods of matching machines to the human user. Experimental psychology provides the basis of formal evaluation techniques for measuring objective performance and subjective opinions of human–computer systems.

Ergonomics

Ergonomics is concerned with the more physical aspects of matching machines to humans, and has established a wealth of anthropometric data which provides guidance in the design of the workplace and its environment, computer keyboards and VDUs, and the physical aspects of any interface device between human and machine.

Linguistics

Human–computer communication by definition involves the use of some type of language, whether that language is 'natural language', a concise command language, menu-based, form-filling, or a graphical language. Linguistics is the study of language, and aspects such as computational linguistics and formal language theory overlap into the formalisms of computer science, and are widely used in the formal specification of human–computer dialogues. Mathematical communication theories, such as Shannon's (1948) work, and Zipf's (1949) 'principle of least human effort', also bridge the gap between linguistics, computer science and electronic engineering.

Sociology

Sociology in this context is concerned with study of the impact of human–computer systems on the structure of society.

Anthropology

Anthropology (the science of man) is in part concerned with the study of human–computer interaction. Where this interaction is influenced by the presence of technology (for example in the office), anthropology can provide valuable insights into activities such as team interaction with computer systems, for example design team work, typing pools, etc.

Graphic design and typography

The aesthetic skills of graphic design and typography are increasingly important to human–computer systems design as user interfaces become more flexible and powerful. Few, however, can yet claim to have mastered the new media of textual and graphic displays.

Evidently, no individual can expect to have formal training in all these areas, though demand is high for people with multidisciplinary backgrounds combining computer systems expertise with some human science skills. A more realistic alternative is to aim for an 'awareness' level understanding over all of the relevant subject areas, perhaps combined with specialist detailed knowledge in one or more areas. This 'awareness' level of knowledge is particularly essential for engineers and computer scientists, who by default are expected to design user–system interfaces as part of the overall system design process.

To support this need, the chapters of this book present the subject of human–computer interface design in a layered way. The lowest layer, covered in Chapters 1, 2, 4 and 8 and the first part of Chapter 12, can be viewed as an 'awareness' level: material presented in these chapters is intended to provide basic design guidelines derived from established characteristics of users and the systems they interact with, and to be directly usable by design engineers. The intermediate layer is designated the 'practitioner' level, and is covered in Chapters 5, 6, 7 and 12–14: here, emphasis is placed upon the higher levels of the design process, such as system analysis and specification at the start, and evaluation methodologies throughout the design process. Typically, such activities will require a multidisciplinary design team, including both technical and human science skills. Finally, the 'specialist' level (Chapters 3, 9, 10 and 11) covers specialist applied psychological research and engineering topics which are of increasing importance in human–computer systems design. This structure is reviewed within the context of the conventional engineering development life-cycle below.

1.3 HCI in the engineering development life-cycle

Figure 1.1 shows the traditional view of engineering development as a process of successive refinement from an initial specification. The various design stages proceed (at least nominally) sequentially, although iteration is expected in the implementation and debugging stages and may also involve system analysis and development and production if serious design defects are uncovered. Documentation of all stages of the project is essential to ensure smooth transition from one stage to the next, and normally constitutes a major component of the project as a whole.

Figure 1.2 shows how an awareness of HCI design guidelines can be exploited at various stages in this development cycle.

An *awareness of basic human characteristics* (perceptual, cognitive and motor skills—Chapter 2) allows additional human factors issues to be taken into account at the feasibility analysis and system analysis and development stages. In addition, it can be used to hypothesize *dialogue guidelines* (Chapter 4) on which user interface designs can be based. Many of these guidelines have been reaffirmed by extensive empirical

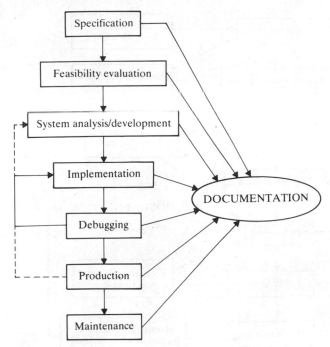

Figure 1.1 Typical engineering development life-cycle

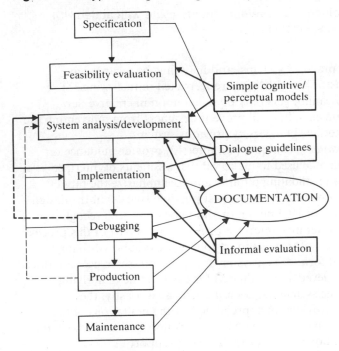

Figure 1.2 Engineering development life-cycle with added HCI awareness

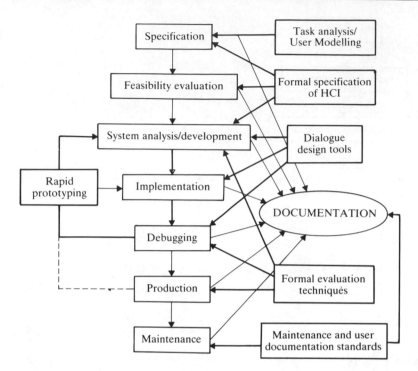

Figure 1.3 Engineering development life-cycle with added HCI practitioners and specialists

evaluation with practical systems, and may thus be regarded as reasonably robust. The guidelines are restricted in their range of application, and cannot generally be relied upon in creative new interface environments, but will prevent designers from reinventing the worst human interface blunders of previous systems.

Informal evaluation techniques (Chapter 12) provide guidance on methods which can be used to make valid assessments of interface designs, to avoid invalidating pitfalls, and to emphasize the rapid extraction of information at the earliest possible stage(s) in the design cycle. A key aspect of HCI design methodology has been recognition of the importance of iterative interface prototyping as part of this process. Although specialist software support tools are available, with many simple menu- and form-driven systems, simulation of the user interface can readily be achieved and evaluated long before the underlying functionality of the system has been implemented. Lastly, the 'awareness' level provides an appreciation of the limitations of the guidelines and techniques presented, and pointers indicating how to invoke the 'practitioner' level of HCI design support.

Figure 1.3 shows a variety of ways in which practitioner and specialist level knowledge can be applied to the development life-cycle. These techniques are usually best applied within multidisciplinary project groups which include specialist expertise in the human sciences as well as personnel with computer science and engineering backgrounds. Such groups are well established in large North American companies such as IBM, Xerox and AT&T, but are less frequently encountered in the UK, where the HCI discipline seems more heavily based in academia. Initiatives such as the establishment of three national HCI Centres (in Glasgow, Loughborough and London) under the UK Alvey programme do, however, enable companies to access specialist skills on a consultancy basis where there is insufficient demand to justify the establishment of a permanent multidisciplinary group.

Within the conventional development life-cycle, *task analysis and user modelling* (Chapter 5) can be applied at the earliest level of system specification to model the user's activity in undertaking a task, to analyse and generalize their activities, and to define a framework for modelling the task within the system.

Formal specification techniques (some of which are reviewed in Chapter 3), an amalgam of ideas from computer science, linguistics, and psychology, provide the basis of a number of methods of modelling human–computer dialogues and tasks formally. Many *dialogue systems* which have been constructed as research vehicles (Chapter 7) are also based upon formal dialogue specification techniques, and in some cases these systems have been further developed to provide *dialogue design tools* for *rapid prototyping* of interfaces (Chapter 6). An important feature of these dialogue design tools has been their incorporation of automatic mechanisms for monitoring user interaction, to allow subsequent review and evaluation of user performance.

Formal evaluation techniques (Chapters 12–14), originating from experimental psychology, provide a methodology for evaluating human–computer systems in terms of both objective performance measures (e.g., time to complete tasks, error performance) and subjective opinions (user satisfaction ratings, etc.). Their emphasis is upon carrying out small-scale structured experiments as early as possible in the design cycle to provide early user feedback, minimize evaluation costs and maximize the number of possible prototyping iterations. At this level, the only valid benchmark for a system is the target application itself.

Finally, in recognition of the importance of *documentation* for users and for system maintenance, there is considerable research activity in defining *documentation techniques* (both on- and offline). This area is beyond the scope of this book, but guidelines are well documented elsewhere (e.g., Bailey, 1982; Shneiderman, 1987), and research in areas such as hypertext for online documentation, technical and maintenance manuals is mushrooming (Conklin, 1987).

Providing these additional methods over and above the basic 'awareness' level offers an increased opportunity for creativity in the

HCI design process. Designers can now investigate more unusual solutions to their problems armed with techniques which enable them to evaluate and compare alternative solutions, and to establish whether appropriate performance standards and criteria are met. In summary, the awareness level provides the basis for a 'first-guess' design; the 'practitioner' level provides support for formalizing, iterating and evaluating this design to produce an optimum solution.

1.4 An HCI syllabus

From the outline of HCI activities which can be applied to the development life-cycle given above, the following HCI syllabus, broken down into major topic areas, can be derived. The order of the topics outlined below corresponds broadly with the order in which the topics are presented in this book, and also the order in which the subject areas are encountered in the design process.

Knowledge of human function mechanisms

Cognitive psychology provides the underlying basis for this aspect of HCI, which is based upon current theories of human perception, cognitive processing, problem solving and memory. *Perception* covers the characteristics of the human senses, of which sight and hearing are of primary concern in HCI. The human senses may be viewed as inputs to the human information processor. Information processing (*cognition*) may be broken down into a number of distinct areas, of which the two most important, for HCI purposes, are *memory* and *problem solving/decision making*, both of which are heavily used in human–machine interaction. At the output end of the human information processor, *motor skills* are used to translate the brain's intentions into physical actions, i.e., hand, arm, head or eye movements, or speech output.

Design guidelines for man–machine interfaces

Guidelines concerning a large range of dialogue characteristics such as dialogue styles, structures, textual and graphic content, response times and display rates can be derived from a variety of sources. The *human function model* provides an insight into how to match user and system; extensive *empirical guidelines* have been established from experimental evaluation work carried out on a wide range of interfaces; *long-term feedback* and experience have demonstrated that particular dialogue styles work effectively in specific situations. 'Common sense' is often used as the basis of user interface design, but it is dangerous to rely on this, since all the evidence suggests that what may be common sense to the designer is seldom consistent with the views of users, or even those of other designers.

Rapid prototyping techniques

Rapid prototyping techniques are based upon the use of *formal dialogue specification methods* and software tools for translating from specification to *simulations* or *implementations* of the user interface component of a system. At a higher level, simulation can be used to explore the practical usefulness of a system, and answer questions about its viability long before implementation is feasible. For example, millions of pounds continue to be spent towards realizing a 'speech dictation machine': how such a machine can be used, the nature of the dialogue required to control the machine, and indeed whether such a machine would actually prove useful are already being explored at quite modest cost using simulations based upon machine shorthand transcription by shorthand reporters (see Section 9.4.4).

Rapid evaluation techniques

Evaluation techniques can be broadly subdivided into four categories: *analytic methods*, based upon analysing dialogue transactions such as keystrokes; *empirical methods* such as formal experiments and less formal observation of users; *user feedback*, as provided by interviews and questionnaires, and *expert analysis*, where human factors experts provide objective assessment of an interface. In all cases the objective is to generate unbiased information concerning the acceptability (or otherwise) of an interface design. Many of the techniques have their origins in the methods of experimental psychology.

1.5 Summary

Human interaction with computers is an open-ended subject area, whose scope extends from computer science and engineering into human sciences such as psychology, linguistics and ergonomics. It also encompasses more subjective elements, such as aesthetic design quality. As an 'open' subject area, it is impractical for individuals to become expert in all aspects of the field, and most HCI practitioners therefore specialize in specific areas.

To ensure high-quality, appealing and satisfying user interfaces to products, support for HCI design is needed at two levels. At the 'awareness' level, all engineers and designers should be introduced to a simple model of the human information processor and the implications which result from this model; they should be aware of basic dialogue styles and guidelines and be able to apply these in straightforward interface designs; and they should have some knowledge of prototyping and evaluation techniques, and be able to evaluate interface designs informally with reasonable objectivity. At the 'practitioner' level, multidisciplinary teams comprising engineers, computer scientists and human scientists are able to undertake much more rigorous HCI design and evaluation work, using more formal methods derived from all these areas.

This book is intended primarily to provide 'awareness' level knowledge for system designers with technological backgrounds. It provides sufficient coverage of the field to enable simple design problems to be undertaken with confidence, and pointers indicating where more detailed knowledge can be obtained when necessary. Finally, it is intended to sensitize designers to the contribution which specialists in a range of fields can make to the process of human–computer interface design.

References

Bailey, R. W. (1982) *Human Performance Engineering: a Guide for System Designers*, Prentice-Hall, Englewood Cliffs, NJ.
Conklin, J. (1987) 'Hypertext: an introduction and survey', *IEEE Computer*, **20**, 17–41.
Shannon, C. E. (1948) 'A mathematical theory of communication', *Bell System Technical Journal*, **27**, 3.
Shneiderman, B. (1987) *Designing the User Interface: Strategies for Effective Human–Computer Interaction*, Addison-Wesley, Reading, Mass.
Zipf, G. K. (1949) *Human Behaviour and the Principle of Least Effort*, Hafner (facsimile reprint 1972), New York.

2 Human aspects of human–computer interaction

ANDY DOWNTON and GRAHAM LEEDHAM

2.1 Introduction

Effective design of human–computer systems requires the designer to have an understanding not only of the technical components of the system, but also of the human components. As an aid to understanding, computers are conventionally modelled as a combination of a central processor and its associated memory along with an input/output controller to communicate with the peripheral components and the outside world. The operation of the computer and its components are fully understood and the model can therefore be fully defined.

Ideally, for the purposes of engineering design, it would be desirable to model the human part of the overall system in the same way. Unfortunately, humans are much less predictable, consistent and deterministic than computers, and thus defining a general model for the human part of the system is not possible given the current understanding which exists of the human processor's operation.

Instead, a number of more fragmentary and incomplete models of the human as an information processor have been proposed, each of which can be applied in restricted circumstances. These models have been derived from hypotheses proposed by cognitive psychologists and reinforced by empirical exploration within the field of experimental psychology. Over a period of time, their robustness and range of application has been established, with the result that they now form useful predictive tools in the design of human–computer systems. However, although the models accurately depict first-order effects, analysis at a more detailed level usually reveals limitations and inconsistencies. The models are therefore primarily useful in predicting gross behaviour, but suppress detail.

In general, the most accurate, detailed and specific models relate to those aspects of human performance which can be most easily tested. Thus the characteristics of the human senses (particularly vision and hearing) are well established, whereas those aspects of the human processor which can only be observed indirectly (such as short- and long-term memory) are less clearly understood. In the following sections, the various components of the human processor are considered in more detail, and their principal capabilities and limitations presented.

2.2 Human senses

The main human senses are vision, hearing, touch, smell and taste. In interactive computer systems vision and hearing are by far the most frequently used, while touch, smell and taste are used to a lesser extent but may be useful in input/output devices for the handicapped where the primary senses are missing or impaired. In Sections 2.3–2.6 the human senses are reviewed individually in terms of their relevance to human–computer interface design.

2.3 Vision

For the normally sighted person, vision is by far the most powerful sense. Psychologists have argued that the human visual system is designed to produce organized perception in terms of motion, size, shape, distance, relative position and texture. Because we are used to viewing three-dimensional objects, the visual system attempts to interpret all stimulation reaching the eyes as if it were reflected from a real scene in three dimensions even when we are viewing a flat, two-dimensional surface.

Before discussing the implications of vision in the human–computer interface, we need to define a few terms in vision and visual science.

2.3.1 Luminance

Luminance is the light reflected from the surface of an object and is measured in candelas per square metre. As the luminance of an object becomes greater, the eye's visual acuity or ability to discern small detail also increases. The pupil diameter decreases and therefore increases the depth of focus in the same way as in a standard camera lens when the aperture is adjusted. An increase in luminance of an object or display will also make the eye more sensitive to flicker.

2.3.2 Contrast

Contrast, as the term suggests, describes the relationship between light emitted from an object and light emitted from the background

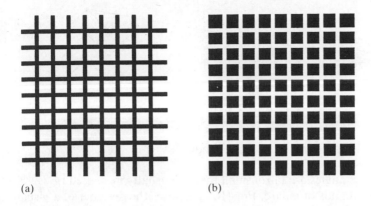

(a)   (b)

Figure 2.1 The Hermann grid

surrounding the object. Contrast is defined as the difference between the luminance of the object and its background divided by the luminance of the background. This will produce a positive number if the object is emitting more light than the background or a negative number if the background is emitting more light than the object. Objects can therefore be described as having positive or negative contrast.

2.3.3 Brightness

Brightness is a subjective response to light. There is no real means of measuring absolute levels of brightness as there is of measuring luminance and contrast, but in general a high luminance from an object implies a high brightness. It is possible to experience odd effects around areas of high-to-low brightness boundaries. For example, in the Hermann grid shown in Figure 2.1 most people 'see' white dots at the intersections of the black lines and black dots at the intersections of the white lines but the dots 'disappear' at an intersection when that intersection is viewed directly. This type of effect is quite frequently observed, and designers should be wary of creating it on a display screen.

2.3.4 Visual angle and visual acuity

Visual angle is defined as the angle subtended by an object at the eye. *Visual acuity* defines the minimum visual angle which can be resolved. For example, in the diagram shown in Figure 2.2 an object, which is L metres high and D metres from an observer, produces an angle ϕ minutes of arc at the eye as approximated below:

$$\phi = 120 \tan^{-1}\frac{L}{2D}$$

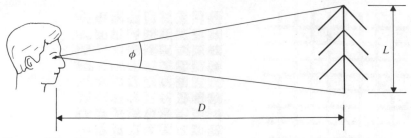

Figure 2.2 The definition of visual angle

Because these angles are fairly small they are usually measured in minutes or seconds of an arc. For HCI purposes the designer of a visual display should note that in good viewing conditions a minimal perceptible visual angle of about 15 min of arc should be maintained and in poor viewing conditions this should be increased to 21 min. These correspond to a 4.3-mm object and a 6.1-mm object respectively viewed from 1 m.

2.3.5 Visual field

By *visual field* we mean the area discernible to the average person. This field of view obviously varies depending on whether the head and eyes are stationary, whether the eyes are allowed to move while the head remains stationary or whether both the head and eyes are allowed to move. The diagrams in Figure 2.3 show the typical fields of view in the three cases indicated above. In Figure 2.3(a) the head and eyes are both stationary and the field of view for both eyes (binocular vision) is restricted to between 62 ° and 70 ° about the straight-ahead position. Monocular vision is possible round to between 94 ° and 104 ° of the straight-ahead position but the region beyond that is a blind spot

If the eyes are allowed to move but the head remains stationary then the visual field changes as shown in Figure 2.3(b). In this case the visual field for binocular vision still remains between 62 ° and 70 ° about the straight-ahead position because the bridge of the nose restricts the field of view in one direction for each eye. Monocular vision is increased to approximately 166 ° and consequently the blind spot is reduced in size. Although binocular vision up to ± 70 ° from the straight-ahead position is possible, the recommended maximum is ± 30 ° of the straight-ahead position.

Having the eyes or the head fixed are rather severe constraints when using interactive computer equipment, though they may occur for pilots in aircraft, for example. The usual situation is as shown in Figure 2.3(c), where both head and eyes are allowed to move. In this case, depending upon the flexibility of the neck, binocular vision can be achieved round to between 100 ° and 120 ° of the straight-ahead position and monocular

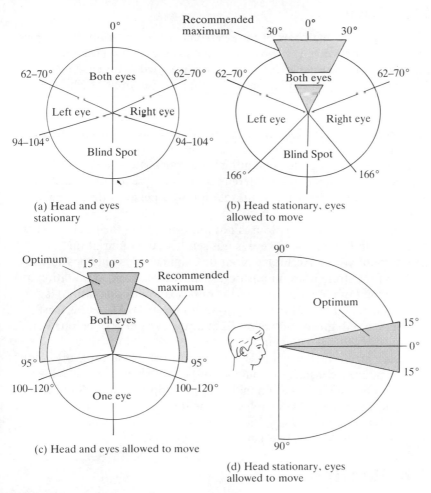

Figure 2.3 Field of view

vision achieved through the whole 360 °, thus removing any blind spot. The recommended maximum field of view in this situation is ±95 ° but the recommended optimum for detailed interactive work is ±15 ° of the straight-ahead position.

In Figure 2.3(a)–(c) the view looking down on top of the head has been considered. Figure 2.3(d) shows the side elevation and indicates that, with the head and eyes allowed to move, the field of view is ±90 ° about the straight-ahead position. However, as with the plan view, the optimum range of view for detailed interactive work is recommended to be ±15 ° about the straight-ahead position.

The visual field is a very important factor in defining the size of a particular display screen or the layout of displays and control equipment. The above information provides some guidelines on the size and position of displays to achieve optimum usability.

2.3.6 Colour

Visible light is a small part of the electromagnetic spectrum. It occupies the 400–700 nm wavelength region which extends from ultraviolet to infrared. If the wavelength of visible light is varied between 400 and 700 nm and constant luminance and saturation (amount of white light added) are maintained, a person with normal colour vision is able to distinguish approximately 128 distinct differences in colour. If luminance and saturation are varied in addition to the wavelength of the light, approximately 8000 distinct differences in colour can be detected. Although up to 8000 different colours can be distinguished comparatively, only 8 to 10 different colours can be identified accurately without training when viewed in isolation by a person with normal colour vision.

People's sensitivity to colour is not uniform across their field of view. As shown in Figure 2.4, the eye is not sensitive to colour at the periphery of vision. Accurate colour discrimination is only possible to ± 60 ° of the straight-ahead position (with the head and eyes stationary) and the limit of colour awareness (as opposed to discrimination) is approximately ± 90 ° of the straight-ahead position. The eye is least sensitive to red, green and yellow light at the periphery of colour vision and most sensitive to blue light.

An important fact which must be remembered when using any colour coding is that a considerable number of people have defective colour vision. Published information indicates that approximately 8 per cent of men and 1 per cent of women have some form of colour blindness.

More information about vision can be found in Bailey (1982), Wagner (1988), Monk (1984) and Sutcliffe (1988).

2.4 Hearing

For normally sighted and hearing people hearing is the most important sense after vision in any computer interaction. Most people can detect

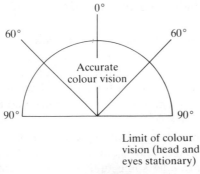

Figure 2.4 Field of view for accurate colour vision

sound in the frequency range 20 Hz up to 20 000 Hz but both the upper and lower frequency limits tends to deteriorate with age and health. Hearing is more sensitive within the range 1000–4000 Hz, which in musical terms corresponds approximately to the top two octaves of the piano keyboard.

As well as frequency variation, sound can also have loudness variation. Defining the threshold of hearing as 0 dB, then a whisper registers as 20 dB and normal conversation registers between 50 dB and 70 dB. Ear damage is likely to occur if the sound exceeds 140 dB. The ear is insensitive to frequency changes below about 20 dB (that is, below a whisper). The sensitivity to both frequency and loudness varies from person to person and indeed from the same person from time to time, depending upon what level of sound they have been exposed to in the very recent past. For example, when a person has been subjected to a fairly high level of constant background noise (as often occurs in factory environments) their sensitivity to changes in frequency and loudness is reduced for a while after they leave the noisy environment. The duration of this deterioration depends on the magnitude and duration of the initial exposure.

Hearing impairment is a relatively common problem which is often underestimated as it is not always as apparent as vision impairment, but is estimated to affect around 10 per cent of the population overall. It is particularly prevalent among the old.

Although sound is the second most important medium for conveying information to the user from a computer system, it can also be a cause of great distraction and annoyance. Because sound is such an invasive medium, it should be used sparingly and with a great deal of caution in the design of human–computer systems. This issue is reconsidered in Chapter 9 in the context of speech input and output systems.

2.5 Touch

For computer interaction purposes, the sense of touch ranks third after vision and hearing. However, for the blind it has a higher importance and is therefore useful in aids for the disabled. It is also useful in areas of high auditory or visual noise where an additional channel is needed to attract the user's attention. For example, there are paging systems which vibrate to attract the wearer's attention. The fingertips are very sensitive to changes in pressure but as with any physical contact this pressure sensation diminishes with constant application (as long as the pressure sensation is below the pain threshold).

Although touch is not used a great deal consciously in human–computer interaction, tactile feedback conveys important subconscious information. Touch is also closely associated with ergonomic design aspects of a system. For example, when using a keyboard or switch it is very disconcerting if there is no obvious tactile or audible sensation that the switch has been operated. It is not uncommon for computer operators to complain that they do not like the 'feel' of a particular keyboard. These complaints çan be associated with the position and shape of the keys but are also directed at keyboards which require too much or too little pressure to operate the keys or have a 'soggy' feel to the key action. If there is no obvious visual or auditory indication of the switch being operated then touch is the next most likely means of providing that feedback.

2.6 Taste and smell

Taste and smell are not particularly useful in human–computer interface design and because they are not among our primary senses they are poorly developed and not very accurate in most people. In addition, taste and smell are highly dependent upon health. However, these senses can be trained, and there are a number of people who have very highly developed taste and smell.

2.7 Modelling the human processing system

Figure 2.5 shows one attempt to model the interface between the human and the computer. On the right of the diagram is a simple model of a conventional computer system and on the left is a model of the human user. Input devices, such as a keyboard, allow the user to input data to the computer, and output devices, such as a display screen, enable the results of operations from the computer to be presented to the user. Output from the computer is monitored by the user's sensors (normally eyes and ears) and this input is passed to the human cognitive processing system, which generates a suitable response from the user's responders (for example fingers). These operate an input device to dictate the next operation of the computer.

The human processing system is very complex and poorly understood and therefore cannot be accurately or fully represented by a model. However, as a first approximation a model can be proposed which consists essentially of three parts: perceptual processing, intellectual (or cognitive) processing, and motor control, all of which interact with human memory. This model has many similarities with models of conventional computers in terms of processors, memories and interaction between them by paths similar to busses. These similarities are purely for modelling purposes and do not necessarily represent the true operation of the human processing system. In reality, the brain is a massively parallel network of neurones. However, despite its limitations the model provides useful insights into human processing.

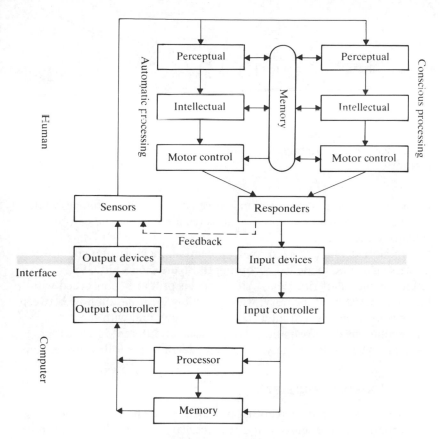

Figure 2.5   Model of the human processing system

2.7.1 Conscious and automatic processing

As can be seen in Figure 2.5, the three subsystems of the human
processing system are split into two parts: conscious and automatic
processing. Conscious processing occurs where all the responses to
incoming stimuli on the senses are considered and time is taken in the
intellectual part of the processing to decide on a suitable response. This
form of processing is associated with new or infrequent actions and
therefore produces slow, considered responses. Human processing can
also take place at the automatic or subconscious level. In automatic
processing all responses are of a reflex nature, as very little time is spent
on intellectual processing. Automatic processing relates to frequent
actions which have become automatic through practice and are
therefore relatively fast responses.

All actions begin as consciously processed or considered actions but
with practice and experience they become automatic or reflex actions
with occasional conscious observation. Once an action has become

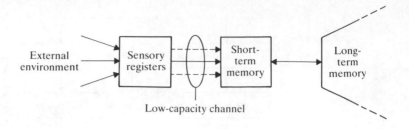

Figure 2.6 A simple model of human perception, cognition and memory

automatic it becomes relatively inflexible and difficult to change, while actions which remain conscious actions remain flexible and can be changed quite easily.

At a more detailed level, human perception, memory and cognitive processing can be modelled according to Figure 2.6 (Kidd, 1982; Atkinson and Schiffrin, 1968). This model is primarily concerned with the characteristics of memory, with modelling information flow between the sensors, memory and intellectual processing, and with the representations of information that are used at different levels within the brain. The model is analysed in more detail in the following sections.

2.7.2 Sensory registers

The outermost level or perceptual processing, which provides the connection from the sensory organs (eyes, ears, etc.) to the brain can be viewed as a set of temporary buffer registers. Information is stored in these registers before being passed on for subsequent perceptual processing (see below), and is represented in an unprocessed or uncoded state. Thus the information is stored directly in its physical form, rather than in the corresponding symbolic form, which may be used at a later stage of cognitive processing. For example, a letter would be represented in the sensory registers by its shape, whereas subsequently it would be represented as the symbol itself. As a result, sensory information at this level is unrecognized and not meaningful.

It has been shown experimentally that the visual sensory registers have a persistence of about 0.2 seconds, whereas auditory persistence is somewhat longer, about 2 seconds. Most people will be well aware of the effects of visual persistence, which are of course exploited in film and TV to make a series of discrete images appear as a continuous moving image. Auditory persistence is less easily demonstrated, but is thought to be necessary in the sequential processing of speech by the brain.

There is very limited subconscious control of the sensory organs through direct feedback at this level. For example, saccadic eye movements ensure continuous stimulation of the rods and cones to static visual input, which in turn maintains the flow of information for perceptual processing; in the absence of these movements the optic output would gradually decay.

2.7.3 Low-capacity channel

The channel between the sensory registers and the short-term memory has been shown to have a low capacity, which in practical terms is observed as limiting the ability of a person to pay attention to all sensory input simultaneously. Under conscious and subconscious control, the channel can be directed to concentrate on a particular part of the visual field (fixation), and within this there is a relatively low conscious data input rate (a typical reading rate is 300 words per minute, for example). Subconsciously however, a very much higher data rate occurs: thus in a task such as driving, conscious fixation may be upon the road and vehicle ahead, but subconsciously the driver can still detect and respond to sudden movements in the peripheral visual field (e.g., a car pulling out from a side road), or significant sounds (e.g., an ambulance or police siren).

Within the short-term memory (see below) it has been demonstrated that information is stored in a symbolically coded form. In the model of Figure 2.6 it is therefore postulated that the channel also performs a conversion from the physical representation of the sensory registers to the symbolic representation of the short-term memory. The limited coding speed of this conversion then provides an explanation of the limited bandwidth of the channel. For practical human–computer system design purposes, the key point to observe is the need for a limited data presentation rate, to avoid overloading the channel capacity.

2.7.4 Short-term memory

In the model of Figure 2.6, the short-term memory (STM) and long-term memory (LTM) are shown as separate and discrete. Of course, in practice no such demarcation exists in the brain, and the concept of STM and LTM is merely a convenient way of modelling two different types of cognitive activity. However, for practical reasons of ease of observation, very much more investigation has taken place of STM than of LTM. As a result, understanding of the characteristics of STM is relatively stable and developed, whereas the characteristics of LTM are much less well understood.

Short-term memory, like the sensory registers, can be viewed as a temporary storage buffer, but here the information is represented symbolically rather than physically. Miller (1956) demonstrated in a classic paper that the STM has a capacity of 7 ± 2 'chunks' of information. The 'chunks' can correspond to anything which the person perceives as a meaningful entity: they could be individual letters or numbers, but equally a single chunk could correspond to a word, a phrase or some larger semantic unit. For example, where a telephone number is specified merely as a string of digits 012401871, it may be difficult for someone to remember each of the 9 individual digits; however if the number is specified as several groups, e.g., 01 240 1871, each group may be encoded as a single chunk, reducing the overall memory requirement. A more impressive example occurs in memorizing chess piece positions on a board: non-chess players can normally only remember the position of about 7 individual pieces, but experts can remember the position of every piece on the board. They achieve this by recognizing groups of pieces as conforming to standard playing patterns, and encoding each of these groups as a single chunk rather than each piece. Thus the number of chunks which can be stored in STM appears to be independent of the amount of information per chunk (or bits/chunk in conventional computing terms).

Other experimental work has shown that the STM has a limited storage time of 20–30 seconds, although overt or covert rehearsal can increase this. More important however is the fact that this same memory appears also to be used as the equivalent of working registers for cognitive processing. Thus STM appears to be used both for storage and decision making.

It is apparent from this model that the STM represents a major bottleneck in human information processing and communication, and in interaction with a computer there is a constant danger of overload. This problem is particularly severe for naive users, since these users rely predominantly on information stored in STM, whereas more experienced users will have committed much of their knowledge about a system to LTM. To minimize this problem, the system designer should maximize the ability of the user to recode information as 1 chunk (thereby reducing STM load) and use meaningful and familiar chunks wherever possible. Since decision making and STM interact, loading can also be reduced by simplifying decision making, and by minimizing STM storage requirements where problem solving and decision making are required simultaneously.

2.7.5 STM to LTM channel

The main characteristics of the channel between short- and long-term memory are that it is indirect (there is no conscious way of forcing an item to be transferred from STM to LTM) and asymmetric. Items can be retrieved rapidly from LTM once stored there, but the storage process requires rehearsal and practice and is thus very slow. It follows from these characteristics that the LTM cannot be used as working memory for cognitive processing. However, where storage of items is transferred from STM to LTM as a task becomes more familiar, advantage is gained in reducing the interference between storage and decision making in STM.

2.7.6 Long-term memory

Information is transferred from short-term to long-term memory by conscious effort to 'learn' or by unconscious repeated exposure. The LTM is semantically based and is accessed associatively. No limits to its size have yet been discovered, and it would appear that information, once stored in LTM, is never actually forgotten. Information which is most recently and most frequently used is also most readily retrieved, but the associative nature of access means that as more information is stored, new associations interfere with existing similar associations and have the effect of masking previously stored information, which then becomes irretrievable and apparently forgotten.

Most strategies for improving long-term memory (as sometimes advertised in newspapers) rely principally on building more and better associative links to the information, combined with practice.

2.7.7 Closure

The limited capacity of the STM produces a strong subconscious desire for the computer system user to 'close' the current task; once the task is complete, information relating to it which is held in the STM can be discarded, and the STM becomes available for new information or cognitive processing. This process is known as *closure*, and is particularly apparent among inexperienced users of a system who rely more heavily upon STM. Thus inexperienced users in general prefer a system which offers multiple small operations to complete a task (e.g., multiple menu selection), whereas experienced users may be able to manage larger operations.

2.7.8 User attitude and anxiety

Studies of user attitude have shown that a negative attitude towards a system can inhibit both learning and performance and that anxiety may reduce STM, resulting in slower learning (Shneiderman, 1980). Unfortunately, anxiety is often promoted by a user's fear of failure in using an unfamiliar system, and may be exacerbated by repeated errors, overloading of the STM with details of the system, and perceived external pressure to use the system. A vicious circle can easily be established where anxiety inhibits performance, which in turn produces a negative attitude towards the system, and further slows down the process of learning to use the system.

It is thus important that the system design should appear friendly and forgiving to the user and that its introduction should be non-stressful and supportive if learning time is to be minimized.

2.8 Motor control

The main responders of the human operator are two hands, consisting of four fingers and one thumb on each hand, two feet and one voice. It is interesting to consider what the physical limitations of the human are in operating input and output devices. For instance, using hands only it is possible for the average user to produce approximately 1000 key or button presses per minute using alternate fingers (as in piano playing). Alternatively, if one finger is used repetitively to press the same button or key then the maximum rate which can be achieved is approximately 400 presses per minute. If alternate feet are used a typical user can produce 600 presses per minute but if a single foot is used around 300 presses per minute is a comfortable maximum speed. Dexterity of the feet is fairly restricted and a great deal of practice is required to achieve a high level of competence (e.g., organists acquire this skill).

Voice output is one of the most natural forms of human communication and normal speech occurs at between 180 and 400 words per minute (see Chapter 9 for a detailed discussion).

2.9 Conclusions

Human senses, perception, cognition and motor control are important components of any human–computer system, and contribute substantially to the efficiency and effectiveness of the system as a whole. Their characteristics and performance have been established primarily by empirical testing. Performance characteristics of the most readily observable components, the human senses, are accurately known and well understood, but our understanding of the underlying processes of perception and cognition is much more fragmentary. Nevertheless, a variety of useful (though incomplete) models which describe human performance exist, and these models prove valuable in predicting some of the gross problems which occur in specific types of human–computer interaction.

References

Atkinson, R. C. and Schiffrin R. M. (1968) 'Human memory: a proposed system and its control processes', *The Psychology of Learning and Motivation*, **2**, 89–195.
Bailey, R. W. (1982) *Human Performance Engineering: a Guide for System Designers*, Prentice-Hall, Englewood Cliffs, NJ.
Kidd, A. L. (1982) *Man–machine Dialogue Design*, Research study v.1, No.1,

Martlesham Consultancy Services, British Telecom Research Laboratories, Ipswich.

Miller, G. A. (1956) 'The magical number seven plus or minus two: some limits on our capacity for processing information', *Psychological Reviews*, **63** 81–97.

Monk, A. (1984) *Fundamentals of Human–Computer Interaction*, Academic Press, London.

Shneiderman, B. (1980) *Software Psychology*, Winthrop, Cambridge, Mass.

Sutcliffe, A. (1988) *Human–Computer Interface Design*, Macmillan Education, Basingstoke.

Wagner, E. (1988) *The Computer Display Designer's Handbook*, Chartwell-Bratt, Lund, Sweden.

Further reading

Card, S. K., Moran, T. P. and Newell, A. (1983) *The Psychology of Human–Computer Interaction*, Lawrence Erlbaum Associates, Hillsdale, NJ, 23–97.

Foley, J. D., Wallace, V. L. and Chan P. (1984) 'The Human Factors of Computer Graphics Interaction Techniques', *IEEE Computer Graphics and Applications*, **4**(11), 13–48.

3 Applied cognitive psychology: research for human–computer interaction

PHIL BARNARD

3.1 Introduction

3.1.1 Cognitive psychology

Since its rapid evolution in the 1960s (e.g., see Neisser, 1967) cognitive psychology has sought to improve our scientific understanding of the fundamental properties of the human information processing mechanism. Its primary emphases have been upon developing and testing theories concerning the ways in which that mechanism constructs, manipulates and acts upon mental representations. Individual theories cover *perception, language understanding and production, memory, problem solving, consciousness, intention and the control of action*, and many more. These areas of concern are all potentially relevant to the ways in which users will behave in the course of interacting with a computer.

Applying cognitive psychology directly to the problems of human–computer interaction is far from straightforward. Typically, individual theories are tested and evolve in the context of rather abstract laboratory tasks. These seek to isolate the influences upon behaviour of the component processes and mental representations which underlie cognition. Although substantial progress has been made towards defining and characterizing important cognitive phenomena, there is little consensus concerning the theoretical concepts and principles that best explain them.

Laboratory experiments typically focus upon repeated measurement of relatively 'local' episodes of behaviour—as when subjects respond to discretely presented stimulus material. The basic phenomena obtained in these settings and the theories developed to account for them do not readily generalize beyond the confines of particular experimental conditions. Also, it is often far from clear how the phenomena and theories can be extended to more complex human–computer systems where the component processes of cognition are integrated to control extended and purposeful sequences of behaviour (e.g., see Barnard, 1987).

3.1.2 Applied cognitive psychology

Applied cognitive psychology attempts to bridge the gap between the properties of cognition as studied in the more abstract laboratory tasks and those phenomena that are characteristic of cognition in the tasks of everyday life. There is considerable conceptual and methodological overlap between the core discipline of cognitive psychology and its applied counterpart. There are also differences. In the laboratory, hotly debated theoretical issues may focus upon predictions concerning relatively small differences in behaviour whose detection requires carefully controlled experimental conditions. The variables that give rise to those effects may be contributing relatively little to the overall ease or difficulty of carrying out the tasks of everyday life. As Landauer (1987) has remarked: 'The point of applied research is to understand what matters in realistic contexts.'

Predicting what is likely to matter in advance can be extremely difficult. In the context of HCI, for example, there are many different ways in which an interface design may prove problematic. It might have an elegant and consistent command language: users may nevertheless err when the command structures are incompatible with the organization of information on the VDU (e.g., see Barnard et al., 1981). Alternatively, the command language may prove problematic because it requires frequent use of shift key combinations on the keyboard (e.g., see Hammond et al., 1980). Empirical evaluation may of course identify such problems. They nevertheless invite theoretical and practical analysis.

From a theoretical perspective this may require taking an integrated approach to the analysis of perception, cognition and action. This in turn may mean that our basic theoretical approaches need rethinking. Their scope may need to be substantially increased and this may require the development of concepts and techniques that enable us to generate approximate, but applicable, characterizations of cognition (e.g., see Card, et al., 1983; Norman, 1986; Young and Barnard, 1987). From a more practical perspective, an integrated analysis of contributory factors may focus upon the various trade-offs that need to be taken into account in the actual process of system design (e.g., see Norman, 1983, 1986). Enhancing one attribute of an interface (e.g., displaying more helpful information) may have associated costs (it takes time to present and occupies VDU space). From this point of view there may be no clear resolution of a design problem, only trade-offs among alternative options.

Given the diversity of methods and theoretical concepts, as well as the broad range of practical issues associated with human–computer interaction, there are many different ways of pursuing research in applied cognitive psychology. The potential pay-offs are substantial. Sophisticated empirical methods, principled knowledge of the characteristics of user–system interactions and applicable models of user cognition could do much to enhance system designs and streamline their development. In moving towards these practical objectives, significant insights may also emerge concerning more fundamental theoretical issues, thereby also enhancing the core discipline of cognitive psychology itself.

3.1.3 Key questions for this chapter

The primary purpose of this chapter is to assess the contributions that can be and are being made by applied cognitive psychology to the study of human–computer interaction. This is a field in which there is currently a vast amount of research activity: hence, the assessment is restricted to illustrations of the key types of contribution, and, in addition, simultaneously focuses upon the use of interactive systems by those who are not specialists in a computer discipline. In justifying the contribution applied cognitive psychology can make to the study of HCI, answers to two core questions must be provided:

1   What progress is being made within applied cognitive psychology towards contributing a principled understanding of the phenomena of system use?

2   What are the prospects for the systematic application of that principled understanding?

Many of the issues raised in this chapter are also covered elsewhere: an extensive examination of the subject is provided by Carroll (1987); see in particular the editor's preface and the chapters by Landauer and by Whiteside and Wixon. The role of cognitive psychology in system design is also the topic of a chapter by Hammond *et al.* (1987). Another critical appraisal of progress is provided by Newell and Card (1985).

3.2 The visions

3.2.1 Alternative objectives

Cognitive psychologists actually turned their attention to the problems of human–computer interaction almost as soon as the technology became available to them. Over and above the immediate objectives of a particular study, most of the researchers had some broader vision concerning the potential of their concepts and methods.

Some concentrated upon the traditional goals of human factors. The *measurement of performance* with an appropriately sampled population of users could help choose among alternative interfaces with considerably better reliability than a designer's intuitions (e.g., see Ledgard *et al.*, 1980). Others were concerned with using behavioural evidence to formulate *guidelines and principles* which could be more generally applied early in the design process (e.g., see Black and Sebrechts, 1981).

Systematic analysis also offered the prospect of potentially powerful alternatives to traditional emphases on empiricism and guidelines. Such alternatives included the use of *formal methods* to represent alternative interface designs in a way that would reveal their overall complexity or the presence of internal inconsistencies (e.g., Reisner, 1982). Others advocated using specific psychological assumptions to *model and predict* key attributes of user.behaviour—such as the time it would take users to learn a system or to perform specific tasks (e.g., Card *et al.*, 1983).

For many of these approaches to apply, system and task specifications had to be predefined and thus the visions remained essentially evaluative in nature. For others the vision included a more creative component, where the understanding supplied by cognitive concepts and methods could be used much more directly, to 'invent' new types of interfaces that resolve the problems (e.g., see Landauer, 1985). Representative samples of each of these approaches will be examined in subsequent sections.

3.2.2 An organizing schema

Before considering research achievements, it is helpful to have some kind of organizing scheme that can encompass key points of the different visions. In very general terms, applied cognitive psychology can be viewed as bringing an empirical and conceptual 'toolkit' to bear on the problems of human–computer interaction. Like any toolkit, its constituent elements fulfil different functions. One way of organizing these elements into a broader research strategy is illustrated in Figure 3.1 (from Hammond and Barnard, 1984).

Some of the empirical methods focus upon observation and the acquisition of problem-defining data (cf. the 'field' studies of Figure 3.1). They enable key phenomena of system use or user cognition to be charted. The problems associated with existing systems are, for example, frequently studied by obtaining session protocols of users attempting a realistic sample of tasks, supplemented by measures of user-perceived difficulties as assessed from their verbal comments or via assessment of their preferences (see Chapters 12–14). Such techniques are equally well

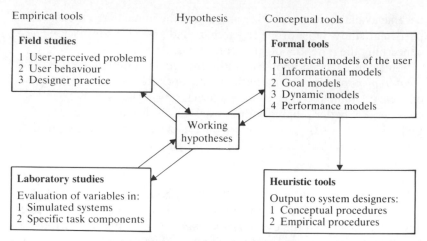

Figure 3.1 The toolkit organized into a research strategy (adapted from Hammond and Barnard, 1984)

suited to the exploration of the problems faced by designers as well as those faced by users. Alternatively, issues may initially be explored by studying users' basic conceptualizations within a task domain (see Chapter 5).

Explorational data of this type can fulfil both practical and research functions. They can be used to provide feedback to designers concerning usability. They can also provide a rich hunting ground for ideas and insight concerning the more basic causes of difficulties. Gradual accumulation of patterns of difficulties provides important signposts as to 'what really matters' in human–computer interaction. This in turn helps to formulate hypotheses and to frame the requirements that our analytic and conceptual methods must meet (the 'formal' tools of Figure 3.1).

Many of the more formal analytic methods, such as task analysis, can also have an exploratory character. However, once such analyses are initially framed, or preliminary hypotheses formed on the basis of observational evidence, their ramifications can be tested in the laboratory using more classic experimental procedures and designs. Tests may involve truly interactive systems or simulations of them. Alternatively, they may take key variables and study their consequences in tasks closely allied to those that might be accomplished with a computer system. If closely modelled upon a particular application, these studies can furnish a direct input to the design process. However, where variables are systematically manipulated they primarily serve to help define and delineate relationships between attributes of users, tasks and systems and attributes of performance. In short, such studies help us to understand the phenomena of system use.

Equally, those studies provide a basis for evaluating whether or not our more conceptual and analytic methods are accurately capturing and predicting what users are likely to do. Once such relationships are validated, the wider enterprise can really talk about heuristic engineering tools: conceptual and empirical procedures that can actually be used in system design and development. Naturally, the scheme shown in Figure 3.1 does not accurately capture all the different research visions. The elements of the toolkit can be structured and used in a variety of ways. Research achievements can nevertheless be considered in terms of how our working hypotheses have been shaped (1) by exploratory studies; (2) by more conceptual analyses; (3) by experimental investigations of potential principles; and (4) in terms of the prospects for translating the products of the research into truly applicable tools.

In the following sections, each of these points will be considered in turn. The achievements will be presented in terms of the progress being made by the different kinds of activities. Since they all represent developing rather than mature research topics, there are many possible criticisms of the various studies and ideas. A subsequent section (3.7) will therefore consider some of the general criticisms that apply to the field as a whole.

3.3 Exploratory empiricism

In the context of longer-term research programmes, exploratory studies have served to shape working hypotheses in a number of specific ways. For example, hypotheses may be shaped towards the *reformulation of a design issue*, towards further scientific *clarification of cognitive issues*, or towards the more methodological concern of clarifying the properties of particular *methods and measures*. The Telecom Gold exemplar reported as the first phase of the Adaptive Intelligent Dialogues (AID) project (which forms the 'case study' of Chapter 13) exhibits elements of all of these issues.

3.3.1 Reformulations of design issues

Work carried out by a group currently at Bell Communications Research (e.g., see Furnas *et al.*, 1982, 1983; Gomez and Lochbaum, 1984; Landauer, 1987) provides an excellent example of the reformulation of a design issue. One problem on which this group focused involved the way in which people name and categorize things: a problem of central importance to the design of information retrieval systems and command languages. The problem of naming and categorizing was explored using a range of empirical methods such as name/descriptor generation, category assignment and sorting tasks. These techniques were applied across such diverse domains as text-editing, the contents of Yellow Page directories, cooking, and 'goods wanted and for sale'.

The common theme to emerge across studies, users and domains concerned the inherent variability in the way in which people name things. People can and do use a variety of different names or descriptions when referring to the same concept. The empirical data obtained in these studies added more than the simple identification of the problem. First, the variability could be quantified. The likelihood of any two people using the same name to refer spontaneously to the same concept ranged from a paltry 0.07 to a meagre 0.18. This reveals the likely extent of the problems for standard keyword retrieval systems, which rely on the user generating one or only a few names that are the same as those chosen by the original designer of the system.

Second, statistical simulations based upon the data were used to explore the probable success of alternative accessing schemes. Where target information could be referred to only by a single name, the probability of first try success was low (10–20 per cent). However, the simulated probability of retrieval success could be dramatically improved (e.g., to 75–85 per cent) by multiple 'aliasing'—where the system accepts many, not necessarily unique, names for target information (Furnas et al., 1983).

The same research group then went on to examine experimentally the issue of whether or not such enriched search vocabularies would actually enhance performance without an unacceptable cost in terms of the system retrieving many non-target items. Gomez and Lochbaum (1984) reported a study in which they systematically manipulated the richness of the search vocabulary with a database of 188 recipes drawn from cookbooks. As the size of the vocabulary was increased, so successful retrieval increased from 12 to 73 per cent. Furthermore, the enriched vocabularies required fewer entries on average to reach the target than did the leaner vocabularies.

Another example of exploratory research with similar properties is provided by an IBM research group. Here the general problems of learning to use word processing systems were the focus of concern (e.g., see Mack et al., 1983; Carroll, 1984). In this case an initial study was conducted to identify the kinds of problems that first-time users encountered. A small sample of users were asked to learn basic text entry and revision tasks by following a self-study training manual. While carrying out the tasks, users were asked to 'think aloud'—to verbalize what they were trying to do and what they thought was going on. Records were preserved of both the explicit user–system exchanges and the users' verbal commentary.

On the basis of these qualitative data, the investigators provide a rough taxonomy of the problems. Many of the difficulties could be attributed to a lack of very basic knowledge and the consequential difficulties of interpreting what the concepts and jargon mean. They report one user thinking that she might be 'the printer'. Similarly, users often did not appear to know what was relevant; they made *ad hoc* interpretations and inferences on the basis of very limited information; they generalized knowledge from their experience of typewriting; they assumed consistency of similar operations; they had trouble following directions and in gaining benefit from the help system, and so on. Carroll (1984) concludes. 'Learning in this situation appears to be very frustrating. System interfaces are inscrutable to the novice and the accompanying training materials provide little help in penetrating these mysteries.'

The more general picture concerning user cognition during learning is evident from the taxonomic descriptions themselves. These make frequent reference to interpretation, assumptions, inference, and generalization. Users were not slavishly following instructions: they were highly active participants in the learning process. Neither the training manual nor the interface provided appropriate support for active learners. In consequence, the researchers went on to explore ways of achieving more effective support.

In one series of studies, they examined alternatives to conventional documentation. The alternatives included 'guided exploration cards' and 'minimal manuals' (see Carroll, 1984). For example, the minimal manual drastically cut the amount of information presented; oriented the instructional material towards real tasks (rather than exercising facilities or functions); provided for more learner initiative (e.g., learners are left to explore deletions and insertions in a letter 'on their own'); and provided greater error recovery information. Empirical verification of this approach showed that such manuals could be considerably more effective than their more conventional counterparts both in terms of acquiring basic skills and in terms of transfer to more advanced skills.

In a related series of studies, this same research group also examined a possibility for reducing initial learning difficulties. One way of protecting active, exploratory users from making errors and getting into difficulties is to reduce the number of ways in which they can go wrong. This was achieved in a 'training wheels' word processing system by initially disabling a whole range of functions required to carry out the more sophisticated tasks. In this system, the 'first-time' user has access only to very basic functionality. The more complex functions remained in the interface itself—as menu items in their appropriate contexts. However, if selected, the user was advised that that function was not available. Experimental studies were conducted in which basic tasks were learned on the training wheels system or on the complete commercial system. As with the minimal manual, the data suggested that the training wheels approach saved time and facilitated learning (again, see Carroll, 1984).

The achievements of this general approach are very real, whether applied to enriched keyword vocabularies, training manuals, or systems tailored for first-time users. In each case, a mismatch between current design practice and users' natural predispositions has been identified and represented in terms of a general property of user cognition, i.e. variability in naming, or the active nature of human learning. In each case, the design problem is reformulated from the perspective of user cognition and the potential advantages of a possible solution are supported by empirical evidence. The 'solutions' actually evaluated are not, of course, commercial products. They nevertheless stand in marked contrast to design 'intuition' and constitute a clear demonstration of the potential benefits that could accrue were such solutions to be actively pursued in development projects.

3.3.2 Clarification of cognitive issues

Exploratory research has also helped to shape hypotheses primarily concerned with the further clarification of specific cognitive issues. For example, Hammond *et al.* (1980) studied users of an early relational database system which relied upon a highly notational command language. As with the Mack *et al.* (1983) study, the initial methodology involved obtaining session logs and 'thinking aloud' protocols while users tried to solve a series of preset problems. Again, the investigators developed a taxonomy of errors and difficulties. Users frequently had problems with the form and content of the command language. One specific exchange was:

```
user types:        *t < - avg (age, people)
system responds:   age is an unset block
```

In this case, the command language required the arguments to be specified in a particular order—the block of data referred to had to be specified before the attribute over which the averaging was to be done. This kind of error could potentially have been due to users simply converting a natural language representation of the problem (I want the average age of the people) into a command string. However, such errors occur in the context of a set of command argument structures and in the context of other representations relevant to the particular instance of command entry (e.g., information on the VDU).

Having identified possible factors that could contribute to this class of error, Barnard *et al.* (1981) went on to explore experimentally their respective contributions to learning and performance in general. Several schemes for sequencing arguments were compared. In two schemes a pivotal argument always occurred in a constant position. In two other schemes the position of that pivotal argument varied. In these schemes the arguments were ordered in such a way as to be compatible or incompatible with users' natural language biases.

Three of these schemes led to roughly equivalent overall performance across initial learning. One scheme enhanced performance. That scheme involved placing the pivotal argument in a particular position (the first element) within the argument string. Positional consistency did not demonstrably enhance performance with the pivotal argument elsewhere in the string (i.e. the second element). Incompatibilities with natural language biases did not appear to retard learning and only contributed to argument reversal errors when the position of the pivotal argument varied from command to command. Irrespective of the particular scheme for ordering arguments, performance was adversely affected when an information field presented argument identities on the VDU in an order that was incompatible with their ordering in command entry. A subsequent experimental study (Hammond *et al.*, 1987) went on to show that the learning of argument structures was also influenced by the explicit prompting of command operations and by properties of the names used to refer to those operations.

The achievements and potential benefits of exploratory research of this kind are more indirect than those of the two preceding illustrations. These more factorial studies provide indications of the conditions under which particular variables can influence performance. They also provide some clues as to the relative magnitude of influences on user behaviour. However, the link to full-blown designs with much greater functionality and richer tasks is often unclear. With larger command sets or different detailed constraints for argument ordering users may well behave differently.

What such studies achieve is twofold. First, knowing about the boundary conditions under which particular phenomena occur provides constraints for our working hypotheses concerning user cognition. As such constraints emerge over a series of studies they help us refine and reformulate our ideas as to what really contributes to error or ease of learning. Second, the nature of the phenomena enable us to pinpoint and illustrate how and why very general principles, such as maintaining consistency or natural language compatibility, may not necessarily be expected to provide the kinds of benefit often assumed by designers.

3.3.3 Methods and measures

The broader value of exploratory research clearly depends upon the properties of the methods used and upon the way in which qualitative and quantitative data are interpreted. The collection of 'thinking aloud' protocols in conjunction with session logs, which played a part in two of the illustrations given above, is now a popular exploratory methodology. Its use, however, is highly laborious. In consequence, data are usually collected only for a relatively small number of tasks and users. This raises issues about the representativeness of such qualitative data. In addition, when users are reporting their thoughts verbally, they may not be performing the tasks in the same way as they would without concurrent verbalization (e.g., Ericsson and Simon, 1980).

These methodological concerns have led investigators to refine the techniques either to reduce the overall amount of effort involved (e.g., Hammond *et al.*, 1984), or to acquire other forms of verbal protocols. For example, O'Malley *et al.* (1984) asked pairs of users openly to discuss problems during interactive sessions. This kind of technique provides enriched qualitative data concerning users' current concepts, rationales and explanations of system functioning. In contrast, Barnard *et al.* (1986) discouraged verbalization during actual interactive performance. What users could verbalize about the system was separately and quantitatively assessed using a different technique in which users described and explained pictures of system states to an experimenter.

In the Barnard *et al.* study, all users were queried on the same system states at two stages of experience. The contents of the protocols were quantified using techniques from the text memory literature in cognitive psychology. In this way the development of users' articulatable knowledge could be assessed and related to performance. As learning progressed the measures indicated that users' descriptions contained an increasing number of true statements about the system. Furthermore, this correlated with performance. Those users who performed well also verbalized a greater number of true statements about system operation. In marked contrast, the number of false statements about system operation did not decrease over the course of learning studied. Although apparently unrelated to overall improvements in performance, the pattern of false statements did appear related to the errors made during interactive performance. This led the authors to conjecture different relations between user knowledge and performance measures.

Other relationships among different 'measures' have also been the subject of exploratory research. One major problem in relating design issues to research information is that alternative behavioural measures can tell different stories. This is often the case with measures of performance and measures of preference.

In one recent example, user preference and performance was explored in the context of different methods for entering data into a spreadsheet (MacLean *et al.*, 1985). One method for entering data relied entirely upon the use of a mouse to point to each successive cell into which data had to be entered. An alternative method enabled the cursor to move automatically from cell to cell in a row or column. This method required a number of menu selections to determine the mode of cursor movement. This latter method required time and effort to set up but then saved on the number of mouse movements required during row or column entry. On this basis it would be efficient for entering large tables of data. However, for small tables the time cost of the additional menu selections should not be worthwhile.

MacLean *et al.* asked a sample of users to practise each method and then allowed them to make their own choice. This was done across tables of increasing size. To accrue maximum benefit from the alternative methods available, users should switch from the mouse method to the menu method when it becomes temporally efficient to do so. However, when the trade-off function was plotted, it was found that users tended to choose the menu method for the smaller sizes of table in spite of the fact that they were actually faster with the mouse method.

As with factorial studies aimed at clarifying cognitive issues, the potential benefits of exploratory studies of methods and measures are indirect. They are nevertheless of crucial importance: they help us to understand the nature of evidence and how it may relate to design issues. As with the uncovering of different relations among articulatable knowledge, overall performance and error (Barnard *et al.* 1986), novel methodological techniques can provide a new perspective on an otherwise unclear problem. Likewise, understanding the relationship between performance and preference can help assess the validity of particular assumptions concerning, for example, user modelling. The MacLean *et al.* data query the safeness of the assumption (Card *et al.*, 1983) that users will choose temporally efficient methods.

3.3.4 Exploratory empiricism: conclusions

As is emphasized elsewhere in this book, empirical methods can be applied throughout the design process, and not just at its end. Exploratory empiricism provides a vital mechanism for reformulating design issues into a tractable form, for clarifying interacting cognitive issues, and for defining appropriate experimental methods and measures at an early stage in product research and development.

However, as is illustrated by the examples, effective exploitation of the potential of exploratory empiricism requires significant creativity, judgement and experience in order to maximize results for the minimum input of effort. Asking the right questions in the right way is the issue that distinguishes the most valuable and original research.

3.4 Analytic approaches

Empirical explorations of user performance help to define 'what matters' in human–computer interactions; to delineate phenomena; and to strengthen methodologies. However, the systematization of our empirical knowledge requires conceptual analyses of the properties of systems, tasks and users. Many 'conceptual frameworks' are currently under development (e.g., see Olson, 1987). Here, a distinction will be made between those frameworks that focus on the knowledge requirement of tasks and those that focus on the cognitive processes that occur during the execution of tasks. In a richly interdisciplinary context, broad distinctions obviously oversimplify the true state of affairs. Individual frameworks typically differ in their detailed objectives and in the precise way in which concepts are used. The distinction between knowledge- and process-based approaches nevertheless enables some of the major contrasts and similarities to be drawn out.

3.4.1 Knowledge-based analyses

Since early systems more often than not made use of artificial command languages, several investigators made use of linguistic techniques to describe the ideal knowledge that a user would require to operate a system without error. Among the pioneers in this area were Reisner (1981), (1982), Moran (1981) and Payne and Green (1983).

The actual notations proposed by these investigators have very different properties. Reisner (1982), for example, proposed a kind of 'psychological' BNF (Backus–Naur Form). This distinguished overt actions that a user must perform ('input' actions) and mental operations ('cognitive' actions) associated with their execution. Key characteristics of user performance were assumed to be related to the number of terminal symbols in the 'sentences' of the grammar and the overall number of grammatical rules required to describe dialogues.

Similar assumptions were made by Payne and Green (1983) in the development of their task action grammar (TAG). They argued that the kind of BNF form adopted by Reisner failed to capture high-level regularities in command languages that users were likely to abstract. They therefore proposed a two-level grammatical model that distinguished sets and rules. The sets represented entities with common properties in the relevant domain, while the rules determined how sets of elements could legally be combined into sequences. The authors argued that this was not only more realistic from a cognitive viewpoint but also that it was technically more economical. Systems could generally be described with fewer rules than would be required in a BNF grammar.

Moran's 1981 command language grammar (CLG) was developed to enable designers to separate different levels of system knowledge and their relationships. It distinguishes three components. The first is a conceptual component which represents task and semantic levels of description. A communications component distinguishes a syntactic level and an interaction level; while a physical component distinguishes low-level considerations such as spatial layout and device requirements. The grammar specifies how symbols at one level of description are mapped onto lower-level symbols. In this framework it is not assumed that users necessarily require all these levels to operate a system—they could rely on knowledge at an interaction level. However, without an elaborated conceptual component users would get into difficulties when something goes wrong.

Other notational techniques with similar characteristics have been developed to analyse the properties of tasks. Moran (1983) has himself proposed another form of analysis (ETIT) in which notations are used to represent an external task space (e.g., in terms of entities in documents such as paragraphs and words) and an internal task space (in system internal terms such as lines and character strings). The complexity of the mapping from one form of representation to the other is presumed to be related to ease of learning or of transfer from one system to another. In a different vein, Johnson and his colleagues (Johnson et al. 1984; Johnson, 1985; and this volume, Chapter 5) have utilized a form of action–object grammar to describe what people need to know about computer-related tasks.

Perhaps the most influential form of task notation for human–computer interaction is the GOMS (goals, operators, methods and selection rules) approach proposed by Card, et al. (1983). In this approach, high-level goals, such as 'edit manuscript', are decomposed into lower-level goals, such as 'delete word'. Operators are elementary perceptual, motor or cognitive acts, which change the task environment or a user's mental state. Methods are the procedures that must be followed to achieve individual goals. Selection rules are heuristics for resolving conflicts where more than one method is available. Explicit specification of these elements can be used to model how long it will take an expert to perform the tasks. As with the hierarchy of rules in CLG, GOMS models can be constructed at several levels of detail.

This general approach has recently been developed into production system simulations of the knowledge users need to acquire to support error-free expert performance (e.g., Kieras and Polson, 1985; Polson, 1987). As with other approaches, properties of the set of production rules required to simulate a user's how-to-do-it knowledge are utilized to predict learning and transfer effects (e.g., see Polson et al., 1986). Ease of learning is viewed in terms of the 'cognitive complexity' of the production rule representations that need to be 'acquired'; while ease of transfer can be assessed in terms of the number of common elements shared by pre- and post-transfer knowledge.

As representations designed to predict key aspects of usability, their main limitation is their tendency to assume relatively simple relations between 'knowledge' and user 'behaviour'. They also tend to focus upon rather idealized, error-free, expert knowledge. Typically, the analyses make little reference to the kinds of mental activities involved in task execution—such as interpretation or problem solving. Likewise, very real constraints on human cognition, such as memory retrieval and the limited capacity of mental processing, tend to play only a minor part in the derivation of predictions. These aspects are the focus of attention for process-based approaches.

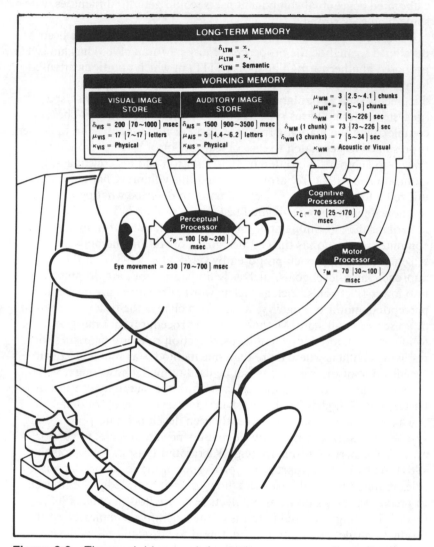

Figure 3.2 The model human information processor (from Card *et al.*, 1983). © 1983 Lawrence Erlbaum Associates

3.4.2 Process-based approaches

As a part of their general effort to provide a scientific basis for the study of human–computer interaction, Card *et al.* (1983) adopted a particular perspective on the constraints on human information processing. This they encapsulated in their 'model human information processor'. The model distinguished different processors and memory systems (see Figure 3.2). Each was assigned relevant quantitative parameters such as cycle times or capacities. These parameters were abstracted from the relevant psychological literature.

The model provided a general background against which their calculational methods could be developed. Indeed, these investigators gave a number of simple illustrations of the ways in which such parameter estimates could be used to work through fragmentary components of user behaviour. It is not difficult to see how a framework of this sort can be used to guide the construction of performance models concerning the temporal attributes of expert skills. However, it is difficult to relate it directly to more qualitative aspects of cognition, such as how users manipulate their representations of knowledge. In fact, subsequent developments of the GOMS approach have tended to carry over only the more general assumptions concerning limited-capacity working memory (e.g., Polson and Kieras, 1984) or the kinds of parameters required in memory access (e.g., John and Newell, 1987).

A rather different perspective is advocated by Norman (1986). His analysis focuses on the kinds of mental activities that occur in the control of action at an interface. Seven stages of activity are currently distinguished (Figure 3.3). In common with most other approaches, goals serve a pivotal role. Once a goal is formed, three further stages are involved in generating an action: forming an intention to act; specifying the action sequence; and executing it. The effect of that action is also assessed through three stages: perceiving the system state, interpreting that state; and evaluating the interpretation in relation to the original goal. These stages are viewed as approximations and need not be strictly seriated.

Norman's framework is not quantitatively predictive. Rather, it provides a basis for representing and understanding the cognitive consequences of particular designs. Menus, for example, can be thought of as devices that assist intention formation and action specification. Requirements for successive menu selections may nevertheless slow down execution in comparison with direct command entry. Likewise, it provides a clear conceptualization of the potential benefits of direct manipulation interfaces. The use of iconic representations and pointing devices serve to reduce 'the gulfs' between the system and the user. Users are directly acting upon representations of concepts in the task domain without requirements in action specification for command names or indirect menu selections. Similarly, where the consequences of an action are directly visible, interpretation and evaluation are facilitated.

A framework that combines basic features of the two process-based approaches outlined above has recently been proposed by Barnard (1987). This approach assumes a distributed architecture for human cognition with substantial capabilities for parallel processing of information (Figure 3.4). In this view, different subsystems of cognition

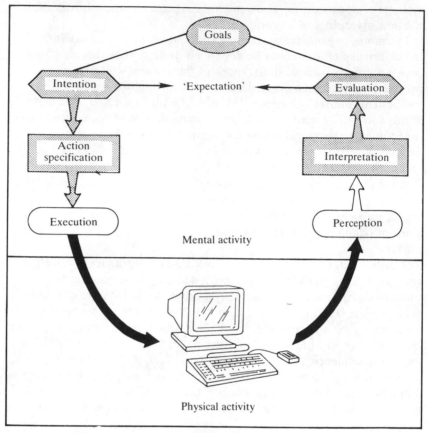

Figure 3.3 Norman's seven stages of user activity (from Norman, 1986). © 1986 Lawrence Erlbaum Associates

contain explicit processes that map from one kind of mental code to another (e.g., from a raw visual representation to an object-based code). These processes embody the procedural knowledge required to execute the mapping. They also have access to declarative representations of information stored in 'image records' (episodic memory structures) associated with each subsystem; hence there is no general-purpose working memory. Cognition is viewed as being dynamically controlled via representations passed among subsystems.

The explicit decomposition of the memory and processing resources of cognition enabled Barnard to define a form of cognitive task analysis. It was assumed that key attributes of user behaviour could be inferred from a description of the way in which cognitive resources would function during task execution. The description incorporates components that refer both to knowledge and to information-processing constraints:

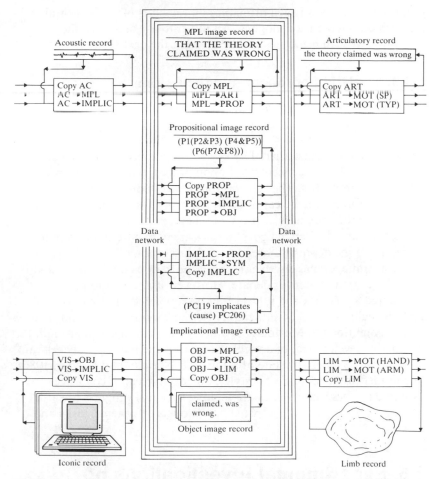

Figure 3.4 The interacting cognitive subsystems framework (from Barnard, 1987)

```
User Behaviour<-Fn(Process Configuration & Procedural
Knowledge & Record Contents & Dynamic Control)
```

In addition, different phases of cognitive activity, such as command entry or the interpretation of system states, are viewed as drawing upon different process configurations and memory resources. As with other approaches, this implies a family of models. In this case, members of the family describe the phases of activity that occur during task execution in a manner not dissimilar from Norman's overall view.

This approach is also intended to be predictive. Common patterns of mental activity are assumed to give rise to similar patterns of user behaviour. Such prediction requires principled relationships to be defined among the elements of the analysis and Barnard (1987) has proposed a number of such principles on the basis of experimental research on interactive dialogues. An illustrative example of the derivation of such principles will be given in the next section.

3.4.3 Analytic approaches: conclusions

The process-based approaches illustrated here all attempt to capture, in an approximate manner, one or more aspects of what is going on in the user's head. In this respect, they complement the knowledge-based approaches described earlier. The key assumptions concerning user behaviour tend to be concentrated upon processes and their temporal or substantive properties. The assumptions concerning knowledge representation tend to be captured in a far more approximate way than is the case with grammars or production system representations. In effect, the individual analytic techniques are committed to different trade-offs in the depth and breadth of their coverage.

The advantages and disadvantages of the various different trade-offs are, of course, a matter for debate. However, user cognition is undoubtedly complex and it has often been pointed out that no single analytic technique will be sufficiently rich to capture all relevant features of user cognition (cf. Morton et al., 1979). Against this background, the systematic development of a whole range of principled approaches can be regarded as a healthy state of affairs (cf. Norman and Draper, 1986). In contrast to the more classic style of theory typical of cognitive psychology, these approaches are making very real progress towards finding ways of specifying approximate models of systems, tasks and users.

3.5 Experimental investigations of principles

The experimental literature on human–computer interaction is now substantial. A significant proportion of this work has been directed at evaluating general issues associated with design alternatives. One example of an empirical 'issue' is whether a few menus with many items are more effective than many menus each involving a few items (e.g., see Miller, 1981; Snowberry et al., 1983). Earlier, Section 3.3 outlined other examples where experimental techniques were used to evaluate potential design alternatives (Gomez and Lochbaum, 1984; Carroll, 1984); as well as one example of experimental techniques being used to explore more cognitive-oriented issues (Barnard et al., 1981).

If our understanding of user behaviour is to advance in a systematic manner, then experimental research must go beyond the empirical facts to explicit statements of principles that can be generalized to new settings. For this to occur prototype principles and models need to be tested. Since the emphasis of the previous section was on the general properties of the different frameworks, experimental assessments of their predictions were not discussed. Indeed, as yet, the empirical ramifications of only some of those frameworks have been explored. The largest concentration of these concern various derivatives of the GOMS family of models (e.g., see Card et al., 1983; Polson, 1987; John and Newell, 1987). There is also some data for the more grammatical formulations (e.g., see Payne and Green, 1983; Payne, 1984).

Where such assessments have been carried out, it is generally reported that the data fit the predictions of the model with reasonable accuracy. However, it is important to note that most of this type of empirical work is carried out by the originators of the model under test—and they get to choose the 'testing ground'. Where models have been evaluated by third parties, the fits can be less than impressive. Such was the case with an independent assessment (Allen and Scerbo, 1983) of the 'keystroke level model' of Card et al. (1983).

As the various models evolve, it can be expected that many debates will focus upon concerns with the predictive accuracy and scope of the various modelling approaches. Rather than pursuing such detailed issues here, this section will simply provide two illustrations in which experimental research is focused on an issue of principle. In the first illustration, classic principles from experimental psychology are applied to a setting in human–computer interaction. In the second illustration, evidence obtained in human–computer interaction is itself used to derive a principle.

3.5.1 An application of classic principles

In the opening sections of this chapter, it was pointed out that links between classic laboratory psychology and complex applied problems can be difficult to establish. Although they are relatively rare, there are clear cases where known principles of behaviour have been found to have utility in analysing problems in human–computer interaction. One such instance concerns principles that govern human choice and movement time. Indeed, such principles play a substantial role in the kinds of analyses advocated by Card et al. (1983). The present illustration concerns the application of principles to the 'depth/breadth' issue in menu searches (Landauer and Nachbar, 1985).

In selecting items from a menu, users are making a choice among a specific number of alternatives. They must also carry out a movement to execute that choice. Hick's law governs the relationship between choice time and the number of alternatives, while Fitts' law governs movement time as a function of target size and movement distance. Both of these laws have a logarithmic form:

Hick's law (choice reaction time)
$$T = c + k \log 2b$$

where b is the number of equally likely alternatives and c and k represent constants;

Fitts' law (movement time)

$$T = c' + k' \log 2d/w$$

where d represents the distance, w the width of the target and c' and k' are again constants.

Landauer and Nachbar examined the applicability of these laws for menu choice where users made a selection by pointing at a touch-sensitive screen. This is an ingenious setting because the application of Fitts' law can be directly related to the number of menu options. The distance from the screen (d) is a constant under these circumstances and as the number of menu options available on the screen increases so the space available for each response-sensitive area will reduce. Thus, both movement time and decision time could be expected to be a logarithmic function of the number of alternatives—or, more conventionally, the branching factor in menu search.

Landauer and Nachbar report two experiments in which the depth and breadth menu searches were examined for a database of 4096 items. In the experiments, each menu contained 2, 4, 8 or 16 choices. In one case the targets were integer numbers; in the other they were alphabetically organized words. Pre-terminal choices were made by touching a sensitive band on the screen in which either an integer or an alphabetic range was specified. In both cases the mean touch time per screen proved to be a linear function of the logarithm of the number of alternatives in each panel. Their data are reproduced in Figure 3.5.

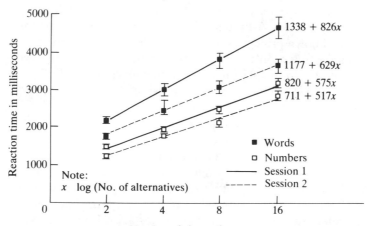

Mean response time per touch

Figure 3.5 The logarithmic fit obtained by Landauer and Nachbar (1985) (reproduced with permission from ACM)

Thus, in this setting, both laws applied. There must have been no substantial contribution from other processes, such as perceptual scanning, that was other than a constant or a logarithmic function of the number of alternatives. In terms of both mean and total search times the depth/breadth trade-off could be resolved in favour of breadth. Of course, in this instance there could be no ambiguity in the assignment of a target digit or word to a particular range. With fuzzier categories of information (such as those characteristic of viewdata systems) other decisional processes may come into play. The generality of such results therefore requires further empirical examination.

3.5.2 From experimental evidence to principles

Demonstrations of the application of known principles seem unlikely to form a basis for resolving many of the issues in human–computer interaction. Novel approximate principles need to be sought. In developing an approach to cognitive task analysis (see Section 3.4.2), Barnard (1987) attempted to define principled relationships between cognitive activity and overt performance on the basis of experimental evidence. Some of the principles were motivated on the basis of a particular experiment concerned with the learning of command name sets.

The experiment (Grudin and Barnard, 1984) examined the learning of five different namesets for text-editing tasks. The namesets involved semantically specific names (e.g., delete); abbreviations of those names (dlt); known words whose meaning was unrelated to their function in the text editing context (e.g., parole); novel 'pseudowords' (e.g., ragole); and random consonant strings (e.g., FNM). Over the course of initial learning, the specific names were learned relatively efficiently. The abbreviations and unrelated words incurred some performance costs; while the pseudowords and consonant strings incurred even greater costs. Representative learning data are reproduced in Figure 3.6.

Barnard (1987) considered these data in relation to the demands placed upon the individual mental processes incorporated within his theoretical framework (see Figure 3.4). In order to issue a command name, separate processes must be recruited to map a semantic representation of the command operation onto its surface structure form (i.e., the name to be entered) and that surface structure form must be mapped onto motor actions for the control of keystroking. It was assumed that if individual processes do not embody appropriate procedural knowledge for effecting these mappings, then the dynamic control of action requires access to memory representations or inferential processing. These require additional information-processing transactions among the subsystems of cognition. These extra transactions take time and increase the cognitive workload.

The Grudin and Barnard data suggested that the extra load could be

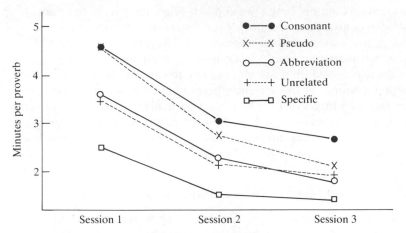

Figure 3.6 The mean editing times for learning the five command name sets (from Grudin and Barnard, 1984)

approximated by assuming a principled relationship between the number of processes for which new procedural knowledge needed to be acquired and the complexity of dynamic control required within the human information-processing mechanism. For the specific command names, it could reasonably be assumed that users would possess appropriate procedural knowledge both for the mapping from meaning to form and for the mapping from form to the required keystroke sequence.

With the abbreviations and unrelated words, procedural knowledge would be absent for one processing component. In the case of abbreviations, procedural knowledge would be in place for mapping from meaning to the form of the full command word, but not for the precise sequence of characters to be keystroked. In contrast, with the unrelated words, the mapping from meaning to form would not be proceduralized. However, since the actual lexical items were known, the mapping from form to keystroke sequence would be proceduralized. With the pseudowords and consonant strings neither form of mental mapping would be known.

The resulting principles were specified in terms of general relationships between process configurations, procedural knowledge, record contents and the dynamic control of human processing activity (see Section 3.4.2). Namely, if all elements in a configuration of processes required to support a phase of cognitive activity are fully proceduralized, then output can be controlled relatively automatically from the contents of a single image record. Where one process within a required configuration does not embody appropriate procedural knowledge then output cannot be controlled automatically and extra information-processing transactions are required to control action.

Where two (or more) processes are unproceduralized then many extra information-processing transactions will be required.

These principles essentially account for the differences in initial performance depicted in Figure 3.6. However, performance with the pseudoword vocabulary improves faster than that for the consonant strings. In order to account for this pattern it is necessary to call upon another principle through which memory retrieval is enhanced by structural descriptions of possible lexical forms. The kinds of command names actually studied by Grudin and Barnard can be regarded as somewhat archaic when compared with more recent text-editing systems. However, the important point is that the principles proposed are not restricted to that form of dialogue. They are stated in a very general form that can equally well be applied to the analysis of iconic interfaces or to forms of dialogue style as yet undeveloped.

3.5.3 Experimental investigations of principles: conclusions

Whereas exploratory empiricism has been characterized by the use of empirical methods to reformulate design issues and clarify existing principles, by contrast the class of research illustrated in this section has had as its objective the derivation or statement of new principles and proof of their generality. The origin of such principles derives in some cases from classic work in experimental psychology, and in others directly from experimental evidence from observation of human–computer interaction.

The two approaches are thus distinguished by their philosophy: exploratory empiricism is primarily concerned with refining principles and demarcating issues in more detail; investigations of principles seek to generate the widest possible generality of the proposed principles.

3.6 Theory as a means to pragmatic tools

In moving towards an applicable cognitive science, the various research projects described in this chapter have utilized very different tactics for calling upon principles and psychological theory. Some tactics have called for only the weakest form of synthesis. In problem-based solutions derived from exploratory research (Section 3.3), such as the use of multiple aliasing or minimal manuals, theories were not systematically used. Rather, a psychological description of a usability issue was used to motivate a form of design. In these instances a general-purpose application tool is not proposed. The gap between research and application is bridged by practical demonstration. This directly displays the plausibility of the idea to its target audience, system designers.

In other cases cognitive theory plays a direct role. In some instances, the application of the theory is best viewed in terms of a tool for thought rather than a tool for prediction. Such is the case with Norman's (1986) stages of mental activity. The kinds of subdivision proposed by Norman do not require a great deal of psychological expertise to understand. Accordingly, the distinctions themselves can have direct utility when supported by a few examples of how they relate to particular designs. They can help human factors practitioners, or even software designers, to conceptualize the nature of a design issue from the perspective of user cognition. Indeed, such conceptualizations are often felt to convey what is important about cognitive issues in a more relevant and digestible form than highly focused and technically presented models (e.g., see Whiteside and Wixon, 1987).

Much of the analytic emphasis in the study of human–computer interaction has been directed at stronger forms of synthesis. In strong synthesis, models based upon psychological principles are used to predict aspects of user behaviour in learning and performance. The intention here is generally to create tools that can be used to supplement empirical assessments, rather than to replace them. There are powerful arguments (e.g., see Reisner, 1987; Whiteside and Wixon, 1987) against any proposal to abandon empirical evaluations of designs and simply replace them with user modelling.

The encouraging feature of modelling activities in human–computer interaction research is the emphasis upon a rapid transition from theoretical discussion to exploration of possible pragmatic tools. What research programmes have often strived to achieve is a practical demonstration of the utility of a tool and a methodology for its use. Representing a system dialogue in a formal grammar is, for example, a methodology in its own right. Although early examples tended to have an illustrative form, the potential utility of such techniques is now being demonstrated with significant coverage of the features of commercial products (e.g., see Green *et al.*, 1988).

The work of Card *et al.* (1983) also demonstrated a rapid transition from a theoretical representation (the model human information processor), to approximate engineering tools with very different methodological characteristics from grammars. In their case, the tools demonstrated were akin to mathematical methods employed in engineering disciplines. Task analysis and empirical estimates of relevant parameters could be used in mathematical modelling to predict key aspects of user performance, such as task execution times. The authors illustrate how such modelling could assist in design decisions concerning, for example, the range of different methods to incorporate into a system or the relative efficiency of different forms of input devices.

Although initially based upon the GOMS framework of Card *et al.*, the work of Kieras and Polson has involved the demonstration of a different type of tool for use in an evaluative methodology (e.g., see Polson, 1987). In this case, a theory of cognitive complexity is explicitly realized in a working production system. This production system formalism is carried out with a real or envisaged system. Likewise, the way in which that system actually works is represented in a generalized transition network (GTN). The explicit representation of how to do it and how-it-works knowledge enables both the user and the system to be simulated. Such simulations can then be applied iteratively both to explore properties of designs and to provide quantitative predictions concerning ease of learning and use.

The actual simulation of user knowledge means that some of the effort of a design team must be devoted to representing user knowledge. In order to do this, it is clear that someone on that team must have specialist how-to-do-it knowledge of cognitive complexity theory and how to implement it. Approaches that seek to avoid a requirement for specialist knowledge of cognitive theory are also under development. One possibility is to simulate theoretical constraints on human cognition, such as a programmable model of the user (Young and Green, 1986; Runciman and Hammond, 1986).

Operating within such a cognitive constrained architecture, designers would 'program' user tasks that they have in mind for their envisaged system. If the designer finds it difficult to program the task, then, by implication, users are also likely to find the task difficult. This kind of methodology involves designers using their own specialist skills to identify potential usability issues. By uncovering and exploring the nature of the problem for themselves, they should gain insight into how to create an alternative design that would avoid the problem.

A rather different kind of tool has been developed from Barnard's (1987) cognitive task analysis. In this analysis, a theoretical decomposition of cognitive resources (see Section 3.4.2 and Figure 3.4) is used as a language to describe mental processing. Principles governing cognitive activity were then inferred from empirical studies and represented in this resource-based language (e.g., see Section 3.4.2). These were then supplemented by explicit rules for mapping from the principles to specific types of software application and to specific properties of user behaviour. These principles and mapping rules were then represented in the knowledge base of an expert system. A demonstrator system has been implemented for a restricted range of issues associated with command names, command sequences and menu sequencing (e.g., see Barnard et al., 1987).

This expert system builds approximate models of the way in which the human information-processing mechanism will cope with the demands of a particular interface. On the basis of these models, the system draws principled inferences about both quantitative and qualitative aspects of user behaviour. Use of this tool does not require detailed specialist knowledge of the modelling process. The tool is aimed at human factors practitioners or designers with some knowledge of cognitive science. In addition, it does not require extensive formal specification of the interface. An analyst can approach the expert system with a specific design issue in mind. The system will elicit just that information it needs in order to build an appropriate 'cognitive task model'. Once that model is built, the system issues a textual report on the likely properties of user behaviour. If need be, the analyst can use the 'what if' capability of the expert system to explore the consequences of modifying design features.

3.6.1 Theory as a means to pragmatic tools: conclusions

The example above perhaps illustrates the most desirable objective of all that can be contributed to human–computer interface design by applied cognitive psychology: the development of mechanized tools to assist system designers in predicting users' problems in interacting with interfaces. Ideally, such tools should be incorporated within the framework of appropriate interface-prototyping tools (see Chapters 6 and 7) to provide feedback and insight to the designer concerning user performance and attitudes to the interface, in an environment that supports rapid prototyping, and without the need for extensive experimental evaluation.

3.7 The realities of achievement

In the introduction to this chapter two key questions were posed. These concerned the extent to which applied cognitive psychology was contributing a principled understanding of the phenomena of system use and the prospects of that understanding being applied. There is a great deal of research activity, many empirical methods, a plethora of conceptual frameworks, a lot of evidence, and some prototype tools based upon theory. The ultimate value of research achievements in applied science must rest on the use of that science in design.

Obviously, much remains to be done by way of developing the various visions into a mature discipline that is routinely incorporated into system development. For such visions to be fully realized it is important to have a firm grasp of practical realities and to be in a position to respond in a positive way to more critical appraisals of the progress being made. From a purely scientific perspective, it is clear that there are many difficulties with our ideas, methodologies and evidence.

Exploratory methodologies have been used to great advantage and are being improved (Section 3.3). However, as Landauer (1987) has pointed out, the core discipline of experimental psychology has not been particularly productive in evolving the kinds of sophisticated exploratory paradigms that are really needed. It is also necessary to learn more about how to gain maximum benefit from those paradigms. In the case of exploratory studies using protocol methodologies, it is easy enough to collect the data. Then, much depends upon the skill and insight of a particular researcher in abstracting interesting or salient issues. Doing this successfully, particularly in relation to applicable theory, is often a matter of experience and judgement. Indeed, applied psychologists who are good at doing it may not be able to articulate how they do it.

Similarly, the different conceptual frameworks (3.4) can all be regarded as capturing something important about cognition. However, they do make different trade-offs in modelling and in relation to the issues they address. The contrast between knowledge-based approaches (3.4.1) and process-based approaches (3.4.2) illustrates the kinds of trade-offs made. Most of the approaches remain partial and as yet have only been worked through for very restricted sets of circumstances. In this context, relatively little theoretical progress has made towards dealing with all the different facets of interface use in an integrated way.

There are also problems with the kinds of assumptions made by the individual conceptual approaches. Predictions are usually based not on a single simple assumption but on a combination of assumptions. Under such circumstances a great deal has to be taken on trust. Sometimes constituent assumptions are open to debate. Most process-based approaches outlined earlier assume that human cognition is constrained by a central working memory of limited capacity. At least one makes a fundamentally different assumption. Barnard (1987) assumes that the restricted capability of the human cognitive mechanism to handle information in the short term is related to the coordination and control of distributed processes.

On other occasions, assumptions are implicit or only informally stated. This can make it difficult for people to agree on the content of a particular form of analysis. Such considerations can have profound consequences. To take just one example, the production system notation advocated by Polson (1987) enforces explicitness in the representation of user knowledge. However, the complete predictive mechanism assumes that productions are written in a particular 'style'. Variation in the style of writing individual production rules could in principle alter the outcome of the simulation (e.g., see Green et al., 1988).

Uncovering and validating principles on the basis of experimental evidence (3.5) can also be a difficult and lengthy process. The accuracy and generality of particular findings are a constant cause for concern. Furthermore, in some instances different pieces of evidence relating to a common topic can show markedly different patterns. Such has been the case with two of the topics considered earlier. Different experiments on the 'naturalness' of command names for text editing have yielded superficially different results, sometimes coming down in favour of natural terminology (e.g., Ledgard *et al.*, 1980), sometimes in favour of computer-oriented terminology (Scapin, 1981) and sometimes showing that choice of terminology makes relatively little difference to overall performance (Landauer *et al.*, 1983).

Likewise, some studies of the breadth/depth issue in menu search have come out in favour of breadth (e.g., Landauer and Nachbar, 1985), while others have come down in favour of intermediate branching factors (Kiger, 1984; Miller, 1981). To the non-expert user of behavioural evidence these differences can be perplexing. However, it is frequently the case that factors other than the central topic of concern, such as the technique of assessment or the materials employed, are also varying from study to study. The real problem for the derivation of principles is to establish how all the relevant factors interact to determine the phenomena of system use. Such principles are unlikely to emerge from isolated or fragmentary pieces of evidence on any given topic.

In many respects, applied research occupies the uncomfortable position of being squarely placed between the deep blue sea of science and the devil of practical application. There are equally powerful general criticisms from the perspective of those concerned with the practicalities of design and development. Many of the salient points have been recently discussed by Newell and Card (1985). They reinforce the general point that the theoretical contribution of applied science is too limited in scope. They also point out that there tends to be not enough knowledge to answer real design issues of current concern; and that when the researchers have obtained appropriate knowledge, its input is too late to be of real value. Thus, by the time scientific data for line editors is understood and accurately modelled, designers are building display editors; and by the time behaviour with these is understood, design attention is focused upon iconic interfaces and so on.

There are also plenty of more detailed questions concerning the kinds of design tools that are under development (3.6). One issue is the extent to which they are actually capturing the things that really matter in interface design. There is an argument, for example, that models of error-free performance times for expert users are deficient in this respect. A substantial proportion of the variance in real performance times may be caused by a very small number of highly costly errors (Landauer, 1987). Similarly, these models do not capture the real context in which users are likely to interact with a system. Whiteside and Wixon (1987) point out that modelling the complexity of the procedure for inserting a diskette is unlikely to predict very relevant problems in the context of system use. They report a user who physically inserted a diskette into a seam on the machine's plastic case rather than into the actual drive.

Another issue is the extent to which the kinds of tools being proposed actually mesh with the politics, schedules and practicalities of development teamwork (again, see Whiteside and Wixon, 1987). Theoretically motivated modelling may be all very well in principle, but it may call upon too many resources for too little gain in the context of a hard-pressed development team. The kinds of theoretical models being developed are also primarily evaluative. With the possible exception of the idea of programmable user models (Young and Green, 1986), they do little to support creative design.

3.8 The future

Many of the critical points raised in the previous section can be answered sensibly. User cognition is complex. Although our scientific knowledge of the principles that govern these complexities is insufficient, enough is known to be of immediate conceptual and empirical value. The intuitions of system designers often display quite erroneous beliefs about user cognition (e.g., see Hammond et al., 1983). In addition, the various criticisms and weaknesses are grounds, not for ignoring the progress that is being made towards an applied science of human computer interaction, but for improving the discipline.

Thus, much can be done to address the problems of complexity, restricted scope, and the tendency for research to lag behind design (e.g., see Newell and Card, 1985). Issues associated with the complexity of cognition and the scope of our theories can be tackled by developing new forms of approximate cognitive modelling that have generalizable and cumulative properties. It may also be possible to speed up that process by making use of new methodologies for assessing the scope of models. For example, Young and Barnard (1987) have recently proposed a technique that involves a preliminary assessment of a model's scope by exploring how it copes with a range of scenarios describing different types of user–system interactions. This kind of assessment is itself approximate and could reduce our dependence upon lengthy experimental tests.

The particular issues raised by considering research achievements and their limitations also have implications for where future effort needs to be concentrated. In the present chapter the coverage has necessarily been selective. No reference has been made to popular concepts such as mental models (e.g., see Young, 1981; Halasz and Moran, 1983) or to the use of design 'metaphors' (e.g., see Carroll and Thomas, 1982). On the basis of the issues that have served as illustrations here, three topics would seem to merit considerable future attention.

In order to deal with the many different things that can go wrong with an interface design, models are needed that integrate over the various perceptual, cognitive and motor resources of human cognition (e.g., see Barnard, 1987). In order to deal with the inherent variability of user behaviour, concepts are required to deal with the properties of individual differences and strategic variations in cognition (e.g., see Egan and Gomez, 1985). In order to develop our prospective design tools, it is necessary to improve our understanding of the ways in which designers make decisions and to find out what tools they really need (e.g., see Rosson *et al.*, 1987).

References

Allen, R. B. and M. W. Scerbo (1983) 'Details of command-language keystrokes', *ACM Transactions on Office Information Systems*, **1**, 159–178.

Barnard, P. J. (1987) 'Cognitive resources and the learning of human-computer dialogs', in *Interfacing Thought: Cognitive Aspects of Human–Computer Interaction*, J. M. Carroll (ed.), MIT Press, Cambridge, Mass, Chapter 11, 112–158.

Barnard, P. J., N. V. Hammond, J. Morton, J. Long and I. A. Clark (1981) 'Consistency and compatibility in human–computer dialogue', *International Journal of Man–Machine Studies*, **15**, 87–134.

Barnard, P. J., M. W. Wilson and A. MacLean (1986) 'The elicitation of system knowledge by picture probes', in *Proceedings, CHI '86, Human Factors in Computer Systems*, ACM, New York, 235–240.

Barnard, P. J., M. W. Wilson and A. MacLean (1987) 'Approximate modelling of cognitive activity: towards an expert system design aid', in *Proceedings CHI + GI '87, Human Factors in Computing Systems*, ACM, New York, 21–26.

Black, J. and M. Sebrechts (1981) 'Facilitating human–computer communication', *Applied Psycholinguistics*, **2**, 146–177.

Card, S. K., T. P. Moran and A. Newell (1983) *The Psychology of Human–Computer Interaction*, Lawrence Erlbaum Associates, Hillsdale, NJ.

Carroll, J. M. (1984) 'Minimalist design for active users', in *Human–Computer Interaction—Interact '84*, B. Shackel (ed.), North-Holland, Amsterdam, 39–44.

Carroll, J. M. (1987) *Interfacing Thought: Cognitive Aspects of Human–Computer Interaction*, MIT Press, Cambridge, Mass, preface, ix–xv.

Carroll, J. M. and J. C. Thomas (1982) 'Metaphor and the cognitive representation of computing systems', *IEEE Transactions on Systems, Man and Cybernetics*, **12**, 107–116.

Egan, D. E. and L. M. Gomez (1985) 'Assaying, isolating and accommodating individual differences in learning a complex skill', in *Individual Differences in Cognition*, R. F. Dillon (ed.), vol. 2, Academic Press, London, 174–217.

Ericsson, K. and H. Simon (1980) 'Verbal reports as data', *Psychological Review*, **87**, 215–251.

Furnas, G. W., L. M. Gomez, T. K. Landauer and S. M. Dumais (1982) 'Statistical semantics: How can a computer use what people name things to guess what things people mean when they name things?', in *Proceedings, Human Factors in Computer Systems*, ACM, New York, 251–253.

Furnas, G. W., T. K. Landauer, L. M. Gomez and S. T. Dumas (1983) 'Statistical semantics: analysis of the potential performance of key-word information systems', *Bell System Technical Journal*, 1753–1806.

Gomez, L. M. and C. C. Lochbaum (1984) 'People can retrieve more objects with enriched keyword vocabularies. But is there a performance cost', in *Human–Computer Interaction—Interact '84*, B. Shackel (ed.), North-Holland, Amsterdam, 257–261.

Green, T. R. G., F. Schiele, and S. J. Payne (1988) 'Formalisable models of user knowledge in human–computer interaction', in *Working with Computers: Theory Versus Outcome*, G. C. van der Veer, T. R. G. Green, J. M. Hoc and D. Murray (eds), Academic Press, London, 3–46.

Grudin, J. T. and P. J. Barnard (1984) 'The cognitive demands of learning command names for text editing', *Human Factors*, **26**, 407–422.

Halasz, F. G. and T. P. Moran (1983) 'Mental models and problem solving in using a calculator', in *Proceedings CHI '83, Human Factors in Computer Systems*, ACM, 212–216.

Hammond, N. V. and P. J. Barnard (1984) 'Dialogue design: characteristics of user knowledge', in *Fundamentals of Human–Computer Interaction*, A. Monk (ed.), Academic Press, London, Chapter 9, 127–164.

Hammond, N. V., B. Christie and C. Marshall (1987) 'The role of cognitive psychology in user–interface design', in *Applying Cognitive Psychology to User Interface Design*, B. Christie and M. Gardiner (eds), Wiley, Chichester, Chapter 2, 13–53.

Hammond, N. V., J. B. Long, I. A. Clark, P. J. Barnard and J. Morton (1980) 'Documenting human–computer mismatch in interactive systems', in *Proceedings, Ninth International Symposium on Human Factors in Telecommunications*, Red Bank, NJ, 17–24.

Hammond, N. V., A. K. Jorgensen, A. MacLean, P. J. Barnard and J. Long (1983) 'Design practice and interface usability: evidence from interviews with designers', in *Proceedings CHI '83, Human Factors in Computer Systems*, ACM, New York, 40–44.

Hammond, N. V., G. Hinton, P. J. Barnard, A. MacLean and A. Whitefield (1984) 'Evaluating the interface of a document processor: a comparison of expert judgement and user observation', in *Human–Computer Interaction—Interact '84*, B. Shackel (ed.), North-Holland, Amsterdam, 725–729.

Hammond, N. V., P. J. Barnard, J. Morton, J. Long and I. A. Clark (1987) 'Characterising user performance in command driven dialogue', *Behaviour and Information Technology*, **6**, 159–205.

John, B. E. and A. Newell (1987) 'Predicting the time to recall computer command abbreviations', in *Proceedings, CHI + GI '87, Human Factors in Computing Systems*, ACM, New York, 33–39.

Johnson, P. (1985) 'Towards a task model of messaging', in *People and Computers: Designing the Interface*, P. Johnson and S. Cooke (eds), Cambridge University Press, Cambridge, 46–62.

Johnson, P., D. Diaper and J. Long (1984) Tasks, skills and knowledge: task analysis for knowledge description', in *Human–Computer Interaction—Interact '84*, B. Shackel (ed.), North-Holland, Amsterdam, 499–503.

Kieras, D. E. and P. G. Polson (1985) 'An approach to formal analysis of user complexity', *International Journal of Man–Machine Studies*, **22**, 365–94.

Kiger, J. I. (1984) 'The depth/breadth trade-off in the design of menu driven user interfaces', *International Journal of Man–Machine Studies*, **20**, 201–13.

Landauer, T. K. (1985) 'Psychological research as a mother of invention', in *Proceedings, CHI '85, Human Factors in Computer Systems*, ACM, New York, 44.

Landauer, T. K. (1987) 'Relations between cognitive psychology and computer systems design', in *Interfacing Thought: Cognitive Aspects of Human–Computer Interaction*, J. M. Carroll (ed.), MIT Press, Cambridge, Mass, Chapter 1, 1–25.

Landauer, T. K. and D. W. Nachbar (1985) 'Selection from alphabetic and numeric menu trees using a touch screen: depth, breadth and width', in

Proceedings, CHI '85, Human Factors in Computing Systems, ACM, New York, 73–77.

Landauer, T. K., K. M. Galotti, and S. Hartwell (1983) 'Natural command names and initial learning: a study of text editing terms', *Communications of the ACM*, **26**, 495–503.

Ledgard, H., J. Whiteside, A. Singer and W. Seymour (1980) 'The natural language of interactive systems', *Communications of the ACM*, **23**, 556–563.

Mack, R. L., C. H. Lewis and J. M. Carroll (1983) 'Learning to use word processors: problems and prospects', *ACM Transactions on Office Information Systems*, **1**, 254–271.

MacLean, A., P. J. Barnard and M. W. Wilson (1985) 'Evaluating the human interface of a data entry system: user choice and performance measures yield different trade-off functions', in *People and Computers: Designing the Interface*, P. Johnson and S. Cook (eds), Cambridge University Press, Cambridge, 172–185.

Miller, D. P. (1981) 'The depth/breadth trade-off in hierarchical computer menus', *Proceedings of the Human Factors Society*, 296–300.

Moran, T. P. (1981) 'The command language grammar, a representation for the user interface of interactive computer systems', *International Journal of Man–Machine Studies*, **15**, 3–50.

Moran, T. P. (1983) 'Getting into a system: external–internal task mapping analysis', in *Proceedings, CHI '83, Human Factors in Computing Systems*, ACM, New York, 45–49.

Morton, J., P. J. Barnard, N. V. Hammond and J. Long (1979) 'Interacting with the computer: a framework', in *Teleinformatics '79*, E. J. Boutmy and A. Danthine (eds), North-Holland, Amsterdam, 201–208.

Neisser, U. (1967) *Cognitive Psychology*, Appleton-Century-Crofts, New York.

Newell, A. and S. K. Card (1985) 'The prospects for psychological science in human–computer interaction', *Human–Computer Interaction*, **1**, 209–242.

Norman, D. A. (1983) 'Design principles for human–computer interaction', in *Proceedings, CHI '83, Human Factors in Computing Systems*, ACM, New York, 1–10.

Norman, D. A. (1986) 'Cognitive engineering', in *User Centred System Design*, D. A. Norman and S. W. Draper (eds), Lawrence Erlbaum Associates, Hillsdale, NJ, 31–62.

Norman, D. A. and S. W. Draper (1986) *User Centred System Design*, D. A. Norman and S. W. Draper (eds), Lawrence Erlbaum Associates, Hillsdale, NJ, Introduction, 1–5.

O'Malley, C., S. W. Draper and M. S. Riley (1984) 'Constructive interaction: a method for studying human–computer interaction', in *Human–Computer Interaction—Interact '84*, B. Shackel (ed.), North-Holland, Amsterdam, 269–274.

Olson, J. R. (1987) 'Cognitive analysis of people's use of software', in *Interfacing Thought: Cognitive Aspects of Human–Computer Interaction*, J. M. Carroll (ed.), MIT Press, Cambridge, Mass, Chapter 10, 260–293.

Payne, S. J. (1984) 'Task action grammars', in *Human–Computer Interaction—Interact '84*, B. Shackel (ed.), North-Holland, Amsterdam, 527–532.

Payne, S. J. and T. R. G. Green (1983) 'The user's perception of the interaction language: a two-level model', in *Proceedings, CHI '83, Human Factors in Computing Systems*, ACM, New York, 202–206.

Polson, P. G. (1987) 'A quantitative theory of human–computer interaction', in *Interfacing Thought: Cognitive Aspects of Human–Computer Interaction*, J. M. Carroll (ed.), MIT Press, Cambridge, Mass, Chapter 8, 184–235.

Polson, P. G. and D. E. Kieras (1984) 'A formal description of users' knowledge of how to operate a device and user complexity', *Behaviour Research Methods, Instruments and Computers*, **16**, 249–255.

Polson, P. G., E. Muncher and G. Engelbeck (1986) 'A test of a common elements theory of transfer', in *Proceedings, CHI '86, Human Factors in Computing Systems*, ACM, New York, 78–83.

Reisner, P. (1981) 'Formal grammar and human factors design of an interactive graphics system', *IEEE Transactions on Software Engineering*, SE 7, 229–240.

Reisner, P. (1982) 'Further developments towards using formal grammar as a design tool', in *Proceedings, Human Factors in Computer Systems*, ACM, New York, 304–308.

Reisner, P. (1987) 'Human–computer interaction: what is it and what research is needed', in *Interfacing Thought: Cognitive Aspects of Human–Computer Interaction*, J. M. Carroll (ed.), MIT Press, Cambridge, Mass, 337–352.

Rosson, M. B., S. Maass and W. Kellogg (1987) 'Designing for designers: an analysis of design practice in the real world', in *Proceedings, CHI + GI '87, Human Factors in Computing Systems*, ACM, New York,

Runciman, C. and N. V. Hammond (1986) 'User programs: a way to match computer systems and human cognition', in *People and Computers: Designing for Usability*, M. D. Harrison and A. F. Monk (eds), Cambridge University Press, Cambridge, 464–481.

Scapin, D. L. (1981) 'Computer commands in restricted natural language: some aspects of memory of experience', *Human Factors*, **23**, 365–375.

Snowberry, K., S. R. Parkinson, and N. Sisson (1983) 'Computer display menus', *Ergonomics*, **26**, 699–712.

Whiteside, J. and D. Wixon (1987) 'Improving human–computer interaction: a quest for cognitive science', in *Interfacing Thought: Cognitive Aspects of Human–Computer Interaction*, J. M. Carroll (ed.), MIT Press, Cambridge, Mass, 353–365.

Young, R. M. (1981) 'The machine inside the machine: users' models of pocket calculators', *International Journal of Man–Machine Studies*, **15**, 51–85.

Young, R. M. and P. J. Barnard (1987) 'The use of scenarios in human–computer interaction research: turbocharging the tortoise of cumulative science', in *Proceedings, CHI + GI '87, Human Factors in Computing Systems*, ACM, New York, 291–296.

Young, R. M. and T. R. G. Green (1986) 'Towards programmable user models', in *Alvey Programme Annual Report 1986 Poster Supplement*, Alvey Directorate, London, project MMI/112, p. 319.

PART II

Human–computer dialogue design

4 Dialogue styles: basic techniques and guidelines

ANDY DOWNTON

4.1 Introduction

4.1.1 History

Computer dialogue styles have been transformed over the last twenty-five years by the introduction of first minicomputers and then microprocessors. The introduction of the first minicomputer (the DEC PDP8), though primarily viewed as a breakthrough in dedicated real-time computing, also represented a landmark in human–computer interaction. Whereas mainframes had typically been run in a batch mode, minicomputers were used interactively, introducing for the first time the need to provide a programmed interface between the user and the computer.

Since the early 1970s the microprocessor has become a ubiquitous part of most electronic systems. The widespread availability of microcomputers based upon microprocessor technology has accelerated the trends first begun by minicomputers, by putting significant raw computing power in the hands of inexperienced users for the first time. System performance in this case is clearly dependent upon maximizing the *usability* of the computer rather than using its processing power efficiently, and thus much of the processing power of personal computers is now expended not in processing data but in facilitating communication with the user. Even where the basic level of communication (via the operating system) is rather traditional (typically, a terse command line dialogue where the user is expected to know the names of commands acceptable to the machine), applications such as word processors, database managers, spreadsheets, etc., overlay this with simpler menu-selection command mechanisms.

Increasingly, machines like the Apple Macintosh model their user interface upon familiar metaphors such as the office desk, and use a pointer device (the mouse) to select and manipulate objects. This example illustrates the close interrelationship between the capabilities of the technology and the style of the user interface, because the WIMP (variously an acronym for windows, icons, mouse, pull-down menus, or windows, icons, menus, pointers) style of user interaction was fully explored and evaluated in the early 1970s at the Xerox Palo Alto Research Center using dedicated minicomputer workstations. In spite of their apparent visual appeal and friendliness, however, the software complexity of such graphics-oriented interfaces is high, and thus it was not until 16- and 32-bit microprocessors were introduced that sufficient processing power was available to enable such systems to become practicable at low cost.

4.1.2 Application areas

Although the archetypal concept of a human–computer dialogue conjures up images of the user sitting in front of a terminal interacting with a keyboard and video display, the expression admits a much wider range of interpretations than this. Many familiar home, office and entertainment systems now contain embedded microcontrollers with which dialogues of a sort are conducted.

A minimal example of such a system is the familiar digital watch (Figure 4.1). Typically, this incorporates, in addition to clock, day and date functions, a stopwatch with lap timer, a presettable countdown timer, and one or more alarms. It may seem natural and obvious with hindsight that all these functions can be readily controlled and initialized with only four pushbuttons, but in the absence of a known solution the problem would be much more taxing. Furthermore, given only the specification of the required functionality, and the availability of a single four-bit input, it is clear that many possible solutions could be generated, varying widely in simplicity, consistency, flexibility and ease of use.

Other examples of domestic equipment containing a microcontroller are now commonplace: video cassette recorders, teletext TV sets, microwave and conventional ovens, and automatic washing machines

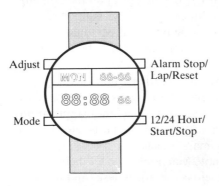

Figure 4.1 The digital watch—a minimal example of human–computer dialogue

all enable the mode of operation to be programmed using a rudimentary pushbutton dialogue, typically augmented by feedback from a display panel. Such dialogues can generally be categorized as simple forms of menu selection, and are readily formalized using state transition diagram techniques (see Sections 6.5 and 7.5.1).

In the office, business and industrial environment, too, examples of embedded systems abound: photocopiers, intelligent VDU terminals, telephones, PABXs, machine tools and industrial process controllers are all controlled using dialogues of greater or lesser sophistication. Word processors, video games and personal computers running databases, spreadsheets, graphics and communication packages represent the conventional concept of computers and provide a more versatile and flexible potential for human–computer interaction. The availability of video displays, keyboards and graphic input devices opens up opportunities for much richer, more powerful and more extensive dialogues using menus, form-filling, command languages and /or direct manipulation to specify commands.

4.1.3 Dialogue design objectives

In all these application areas, the concept of developing the engineering design using top-down techniques starting from systems analysis and specification is well understood: what is often overlooked is that exactly the same process of step-wise refinement should and can be applied to the process of interface and dialogue design. Instead, the user–interface design is often based upon unsupported implicit assumptions made by the design engineer about the nature of the task, the user's model of the task, and the characteristics of the users.

As part of the design process, the designer needs to be armed with a comprehensive understanding of the types of interfaces and dialogue styles available, their appropriateness for different categories of users, and their system implications in terms of display, input device and processing power requirements. The objective of this chapter is to provide an overview and taxonomy of different dialogue styles; Chapters 6 and 7 then discuss some of the techniques and tools available to support different human–computer dialogue models and illustrate the models and dialogue styles using some example research systems. Chapter 5, on knowledge analysis of tasks, is concerned with ways of eliciting knowledge of user models and methods which can provide a specification for the required dialogue.

4.2 Dialogue properties

Before reviewing specific styles of dialogue in detail, it is worth while considering some desirable generic characteristics of these dialogues. Alison Kidd (1982) cites five important properties:

- initiative;
- flexibility;
- complexity;
- power;
- information load;

to which can also be added:

- consistency;
- feedback;
- observability;
- controllability;
- efficiency;
- balance.

These properties are considered in more detail below.

4.2.1 Initiative

Initiative is the most fundamental property of any dialogue, since it defines the overall style of communication and thus, to a large extent, the type of user for whom the system is intended. The two most common styles are computer-initiated and user-initiated. In *computer-initiated* dialogues, the user responds to explicit prompts from the computer to input commands or command parameters: typically, (s)he will be presented with a series of options from which a selection must be made (menu selection), or a number of boxes into which parameters must be inserted (form-filling), or questions to which answers must be specified in a more or less restricted way (for example yes/no vs. natural language). The key characteristic is that the dialogue consists of a closed set of options defined by the computer.

By contrast, *user-initiated* dialogues are open-ended in nature: the user is expected to know a valid set of command words and their allowable syntax, and possibly a semantic structure for the system if operation in several different modes is possible. A typical example of a user-initiated dialogue would be the command language of a computer operating system; superimposed upon this could be the semantic structure of a variety of other command language-driven programs such as editors and debuggers, each with their own distinct style of dialogue.

Dialogues need not be purely computer-initiated or user-initiated. *Variable-initiative* dialogues are becoming more common, particularly in systems intended for wide ranges of users. In many current systems, the level of user initiative required is chosen by the users themselves (for example by selecting between user-initiated and computer-initiated modes), but *adaptive* dialogue styles are also becoming more common.

At their simplest, adaptive dialogue systems adjust the level of assistance by monitoring, for example, the delay in the user inputting a command or parameter: when a prespecified limit is exceeded, additional assistance on options available is displayed. Alternatively, when parameters are omitted from a command line, they can be prompted for by the system. In either case, a user-initiated dialogue is partially transformed to a computer-initiated style. Conversely, a computer-initiated menu selection system can be adapted to a user-initiated mode by allowing selections from subsequent menus to be given without waiting for the intervening menu(s) to be displayed (see Section 4.12 for an example of this). More complex techniques, for example the use of knowledge-based systems to predict users' capabilities by monitoring the content of their interactions (adaptive intelligent dialogues—see Chapter 7) remain a research problem at present.

Finally, we can distinguish *mixed-initiative* dialogues as being common in natural-language communication with computers: here, the free format of both input and output to the system allows the possibility of either the computer or the user leading the dialogue at different times.

4.2.2 Flexibility

A flexible system is one in which a particular objective can be achieved in a variety of different ways. This is not simply a matter of providing a very large command repertoire in the hope of covering every possibility, but should follow from an analysis of users' models of the activity. The objective is then to map the system onto representative users' models, rather than to force the users to work within a framework defined by the designer.

One of the less frequently recognized reasons for the success of the Apple Macintosh personal computer is that a great deal of attention has been paid in the design of its interface to this concept. Most functions can be accomplished in several different ways, corresponding to different models which the user may have of his or her activity (e.g., see Figure 4.2). Generally, users are unaware of this characteristic, since there is little incentive to investigate alternative methods of accomplishing a function once success has been achieved, but they may notice a higher success rate in trying out new functions than is common with other machines (which itself will tend to generate a positive response to the system).

Flexibility can also be conferred by providing opportunities for the user to *customize* and extend the interface to meet their own personal requirements. This capability is most commonly observed in the provision of programmable function keys on microcomputers, or programmable control code alternatives (*power keys*) to pull-down or pop-up menu selection options on WIMP interfaces.

The price paid for flexibility is in the complexity and efficiency of the

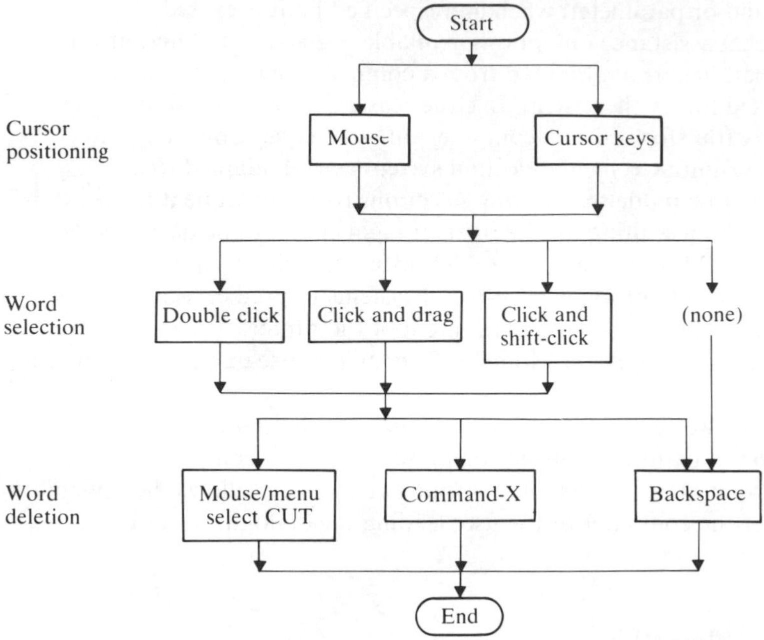

Figure 4.2 Word deletion strategies under Apple™ Macintosh MacWrite

interface software: clearly there is an overhead in providing additional functionality over and above the minimum required to perform the task. This overhead can however by minimized by careful organization of the command structure to eliminate duplication (see Section 4.2.6 below).

4.2.3 Complexity

In general, there is no benefit in making an interface more complex than necessary. Often, an apparently complex interface is in fact a symptom of a failure to analyse the structure of the interaction and organize the commands accordingly. Logical grouping is important in reinforcing the user's model of the system, and is commonly achieved by the use of *hierarchy* or *orthogonality* or both.

Hierarchy

This is the structuring of commands according to related characteristics and their relative importance. Rather than having a flat command structure requiring memorization of a large number of individual unrelated commands, the commands are grouped into a hierarchical tree, where related commands are associated in different branches of the

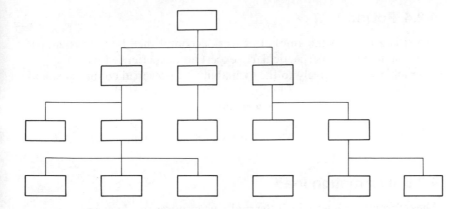

Figure 4.3 Tree structure of commands

tree (Figure 4.3). This maximizes the chance of memorizing the commands by recoding groups of commands as individual 'chunks', while at the same time simplifying decision making by offering a restricted set of options according to the current position in the tree.

Orthogonality

This is the structuring of commands according to independent characteristics (Figure 4.4). For example, specifying three independent command characteristics A, B and C, each of which is chosen from a set of 10 options, provides the capability to represent up to 1000 distinct commands, while requiring only 30 independent items (A1 ... A10, B1 ... B10, C1 ... C10) to be memorized. This technique is most commonly exploited in specifying command parameters.

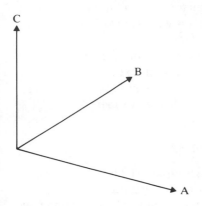

Figure 4.4 Orthogonality in command structures

4.2.4 Power

Power is defined as the amount of work accomplished by the system per user command. Users (particularly expert and experienced users) generally react positively to the availability of powerful commands, and conversely can be irritated by the pedantry of a system that requires excessive user input to achieve a specific function. Note that a requirement for powerful commands may conflict with the need for flexibility, and may affect the complexity of the system.

4.2.5 Information load

The information load which the dialogue imposes on the user in terms of both memory and decision making should be appropriate to the level of user. If too high a load is incurred, this leads to anxiety on the part of the user, which has a negative effect both on cognitive processing capability and attitude towards the system. If there is too low a load, this leads to resentment since the user sees the system as inhibiting his or her performance. Matching the information load to the user presents particular difficulties, since different loads are optimal for different categories of users, but any user who uses a system regularly will become more proficient and hence change categories over a period of time. Variable initiative dialogues provide one possible way of coping with this problem.

4.2.6 Consistency

Consistency is an important attribute in helping the user to develop his mental model of any computer system. A consistent system will encourage this by helping the user to extrapolate successfully from his or her current knowledge to explore new commands and command options. Once the user has used a particular command in one context, it is reasonable for him or her to expect that it will also work in any other context which he or she perceives as similar.

Consistency should apply to all aspects of user interface design. Commands should have a standardized syntax and parameter ordering; displays should have a consistent layout; the data entry format should be compatible and consistent with the data display format.

4.2.7 Feedback

Immediate feedback is needed for any user input. The feedback should unambiguously indicate the type of activity taking place, for example text input, mode selection, command input, pointing. It is amazing how many widely used systems fail to observe this fundamental requirement!

4.2.8 Observability

An observable system is one in which the system function is apparent and clear at a surface level, even if the underlying processing is complex. This can sometimes be difficult to achieve, particularly where a simple model of a complex underlying activity is presented to the user. Difficulties arise where the user exceeds the bounds of the model (for example due to errors) and the system is no longer able to present responses which the user can understand in terms of the model.

4.2.9 Controllability

Controllability is the converse of observability, and implies that the user is always in control of the system. For this to be true, the interface must provide means by which the user can determine:

- where he has been;
- where he is now;
- where he can go from here.

4.2.10 Efficiency

Efficiency in a closely coupled human–computer system is defined in terms of the throughput achieved by the person and the computer working together. Thus, although the efficiency of the engineering and software aspects of the system may be important if they affect the response time or display rate of the system, often the designer can afford to buy his way out of trouble (by specifying a more powerful computer if necessary), knowing that developments in technology will minimize the cost of this decision in due course. In contrast, the cost of skilled staff is increasing all the time, emphasizing the importance of using their time as effectively as possible, even at the expense of devoting a large proportion of the total available processing power to the user interface. The development and exploitation of workstations and computer-aided engineering vividly illustrate this point.

4.2.11 Balance

A basic design strategy for any human–computer system should be to subdivide the tasks in an optimum way between the person and the computer. Table 4.1 illustrates some of the relative capabilities of each. Essentially these differences reflect the complementary strengths and weaknesses of humans and computers: humans cope best with changing circumstances, uncertainty and incomplete knowledge, while computers are better suited to dealing with repetitive and routine activity, reliable

Table 4.1 Relative aptitudes of humans and computers (adapted from Shneiderman, 1987)

Human aptitudes	Computer aptitudes
Estimation	Accurate calculation
Intuition	Logical deduction
Creativity	Repetitive activity
Adaptation	Consistency
Subconscious concurrency	Multitasking
Abnormal/exceptional processing	Routine processing
Associative memory	Data storage and retrieval
Non-deterministic decision making	Deterministic decision making
Pattern recognition	Data processing
World knowledge	Domain knowledge
Error proneness	Freedom from error

storage and retrieval of data, and accurate computation of both numerical and logical functions.

At the interface between the human and the computer, the complementary aptitudes must be brought together in an appropriate way, otherwise the overall efficiency of the human–computer system will be degraded. Interface design therefore involves choices which affect not only the hardware configuration, but also the way in which the tasks are divided, and the structure of the dialogue between the person and the machine.

4.3 Human characteristics

Human characteristics, as they affect the design of systems and their user interfaces, can in some senses be viewed as an onion-like structure. At the centre is the system itself, and around this in concentric layers are the various human characteristics (Figure 4.5). Human cognition should be taken into account in designing the dialogue organization, whereas perception and motor control should respectively influence the graphical structure of the interface and the design of input devices. The dialogue style should be chosen with reference to the experience and expertise of the user. The influence on interface design of each of these characteristics is briefly reviewed below.

4.3.1 Ergonomics

The basic physical characteristics of humans provide initial criteria for judging the efficacy of human–computer interfaces, and indeed for

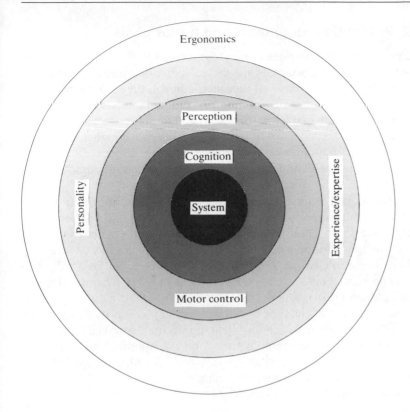

Figure 4.5 Onion-skin structure of human–computer interaction

specifying the surrounding environment (lighting, seating, table height, keyboard and screen angles, etc.). Anthropometric data concerning human dimensions and their statistical ranges and distribution are widely available (e.g., see Bailey, 1982, Chapter 5 for a review and sample tables). Although statistical averages can be calculated for any parameter, Bailey illustrates the fallacy of designing for the 'average' person by demonstrating that among a sample of 4063 men measured in a survey (Daniels and Churchill, 1952), no two were average in all 10 dimensions commonly used in clothing design. ('Average' was considered to be the middle 30 per cent of the measured range for each dimension.) A more satisfactory strategy is therefore to design for a particular percentile range, for example 5–95 per cent. In many cases (e.g., keyboards) a single design can meet this requirement, but where the range of human variation is large (e.g., seat height) then user control can be provided to allow optimization.

4.3.2 Perception, cognition and motor skills

In human–computer interface design, dynamic as well as static physical characteristics are important. Since these depend not only on human physical dimensions but also on muscular control, they are often categorized under the heading of *motor control* parameters (see Chapter 2). Parameters concerned with arm, hand and finger movement speeds are generally of most concern to interface designers, though voice control is also of fundamental importance to those in the speech-processing field, and has led to the development of complex and detailed models of the vocal tract (e.g., see Holmes, 1988).

If motor control represents the output of the human information processor, then *perception* provides the inputs. Vision and hearing are by far the most important perceptual faculties from the point of view of interface design, and the more important characteristics of each are briefly reviewed in Chapter 2. Further detail can be found in Card, Moran and Newell (1983), Chapter 2; in Bailey (1982), Chapters 4 and 7; and in Monk (1984), Chapter 1.

Cognitive models of the type developed in Chapter 2 provide the most specifically useful information and insight into user interface design. Short-term memory, long-term memory and the communication channel between them are used extensively in interactions with a computer; in closely-coupled activity between the human and computer, decision making and problem solving form the major human contribution to the dialogue.

4.3.3 Personality factors

Though less readily measured than more basic physical, perceptual, cognitive and motor characteristics, *personality* and *motivation* should also be considered in human–computer dialogue design. Characteristics such as extroversion and introversion, not to mention different behaviour patterns between sexes, can have a major impact on dialogues. Similarly, *tolerance*, *harassment*, *mood* and *fatigue* can all make the difference between ready acceptance and total rejection of a computer system. Unfortunately, these factors tend to introduce an element of instability in human–computer dialogues: for example, anxiety increases the difficulty in learning about a new computer system, which in turn reduces performance, which increases anxiety, and so on.

4.3.4 Experience and expertise

Background knowledge concerning the experience and expertise of the expected user population is important in designing the interface. *Experience* relates to the general understanding which the user has of the problem, and of computer technology in general; *expertise* implies the more specific detailed knowledge which the designer may expect the user to have in carrying out the task using the system. Clearly, neither of these factors is likely to remain static unless the system is used very infrequently; nevertheless, this situation can arise in the case of, for example, computer-based public information systems.

However, the concept of an 'expert' as someone with extensive knowledge of the system has been shown to be simplistic, at least in large systems with open learning (Draper, 1984). In a survey of use of the UNIX operating system and its screen editor, *vi*, by 94 users over 8 months, it was shown that there were no 'experts' using the system in the sense of people who used all the commands. Only 69 per cent of the total available UNIX commands were used at all over the period of the survey, and the highest individual vocabulary was 60 per cent of these. Users' expertise was idiosyncratic: 18 individuals used one or more commands not used by any other users. Thus schemes for classifying users, such as that proposed in the next section, should ideally take account of the context in which the user is working—an argument in favour of adaptive interface styles.

The same survey also showed that 'experts' were by far the heaviest users of the UNIX manuals, whereas the reverse might be expected to be the case. A possible inference from this is that expertise is not so much based on innate knowledge about the system, but is more a case of understanding how to use the system and its documentation to tackle and solve new problems. This is analogous to the skill of a librarian, whose expertise in navigating through the library's cross-referencing systems is often called upon by library users to help solve their own specialized problems. Thus expertise may be more associated with the acquisition of techniques and strategies for problem solving rather than any defined static body of knowledge.

4.3.5 Common user classifications

The characteristics described in the previous section can be represented as three orthogonal axes on a graph (Figure 4.6). Although any combination of characteristics can occur in principle (the axes are continuous), there are nevertheless a few frequently encountered user types which characterize many human–computer interface scenarios.

Casual users

These are not very knowledgeable about the task or knowledge domain which they wish to interact with, and are also unfamiliar with the system they will be using. Frequency of access may be low, and hence there is little motivation to study manuals or other training aids. Use of the system and its logical structure must be self-evident. Examples of systems intended for casual users include databases such as Prestel and

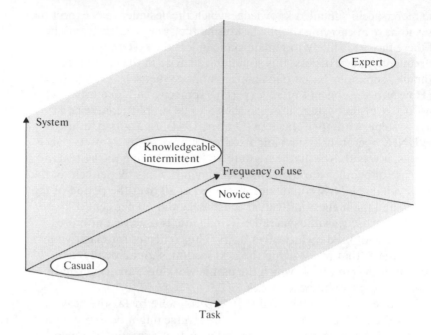

Figure 4.6   Dimensions of human capability in human–computer interaction

Teletext, computerized library search facilities, and computer-based banking facilities accessible to the general public. Most computer messaging systems ought to be designed for casual users, but are not!

Novice users

Although these may start out with the same characteristics as casual users, they are distinguished by being much more frequent users. There is therefore much more motivation for them to read manuals and other off-line training aids, and thus less need for on-line support. As experience and use increase, they may eventually become expert users. This category covers many white-collar workers who use office and data-processing systems regularly.

Knowledgeable intermittent users

Typically, these are professional staff who use a wide range of different types of computer support equipment. They generally have a clear idea of the task they wish to accomplish, and a good general understanding of the capabilities of computer technology, but only a limited amount of familiarity with the specific systems they need to use. Motivation to use the system is high in the general sense that they are aware of the 'power' improvements which the use of computers can bring, but tolerance is limited since they cannot afford to expend too much time learning the syntax of a system which will be used infrequently.

Expert users

Sometimes known as *power users*, these are fully conversant with both the task and the system they are using. Their main objective is to exploit to the maximum the capabilities the system provides for improving their performance. Excessive feedback and support is generally an irritant for these users, who are more interested in exploring ways of increasing the power of their interaction.

4.4 Task characteristics

Task characteristics are the complementary component of background knowledge which is required alongside knowledge of the characteristics of the human users before dialogue design can begin. Determination of task characteristics is accomplished using task analysis, which is analogous to the use of systems analysis to define requirements in other engineering fields. Task analysis can be thought of as comprising two major components, *task taxonomy* and *developing the user model*. Although determination of these components is best achieved using the formal techniques described in Chapter 5, in many cases a less formal approach can still yield valuable insights. Simply being aware of the need to envisage the task from the user's point of view, and taking steps to involve users in the early stages of design and prototyping are major positive steps.

4.4.1 Task taxonomy

Task taxonomy describes the somewhat mechanistic process of determining the set of tasks the system will be required to perform. The taxonomy will typically be represented as some kind of tree structure, with major tasks at its root and subtasks of each major task as the branches. The full structure may require several levels to map down from the primary functions to the basic atomic actions. The objective of the process is to develop a clear and logical hierarchy of functionality around which the dialogue can be built. In addition, producing the taxonomy will *per se* give the designer insights into how the system should be organized, both for clarity to the user and efficient engineering, by suggesting logical groupings of functions, and highlighting incompatibilities. Many methods of generating task and dialogue taxonomies have been proposed, for example command language grammar (CLG) (Moran 1981), task, action, language (TAL)

(Reisner, 1981, 1982) and goals, operators, methods and selection rules (GOMS) (Card *et al.*, 1983). Some of these have been discussed in more depth in Chapter 3.

4.4.2 User's task models

The task taxonomy is produced primarily according to the *designer's* perception of the required structure of system functionality, but this may differ markedly from the user's view. Many of the formal methods of task analysis (see Chapter 5) are intended to elicit an explicit *user's* task model by questioning users about their knowledge of a particular task, both in terms of the structure of the task and the objects and actions on those objects which constitute carrying out the task. By questioning a variety of users, and establishing the representativeness and commonality of particular structures, objects and actions, an objective view of the task is obtained.

This process is not the same as design-by-committee, which produced little more than a list of 'wants' with no inherent structure or association of value with function. An example of this latter strategy is embodied in the widely used UNIX *vi* editor, which provides an enormous number of functions, most of which are very rarely or never used by most programmers (Draper, 1984). Two principle reasons for this can be suggested. First, the command structure is flat: commands are not grouped in any logical way to encourage users to explore a variety of different methods of accomplishing a task. As a result, users tend to learn a minimum functional set of commands and add new ones to their repertoire only rarely. Second, the naming conventions for commands are haphazard: it is apparent that *vi* was designed and developed incrementally over a period of time. Had the full design been specified at the outset, a much more logical command set could have been chosen.

4.4.3 Creative system design

If human–computer system design consisted merely of mechanizing existing methods of performing a task, the opportunities for creative engineering design would be very limited. The opportunity for creativity is provided where the designer attempts to reconcile the information which emanates from the procedures of Sections 4.4.1 and 4.4.2 in a coherent way. The designer should not necessarily be bound to 'use the user's model' (Gaines, 1981), even though this is almost always better than using the designer's model! More important is that, whatever the model used, it should be readily discernible, predictable and consistent to the user.

Thimbleby points out the fallacy in always basing new designs upon their functional predecessor, using the car and horseless carriage as his example (Monk, 1984, Chapter 10). The problem is that organizing a system and its interface in a way which is inherently familiar to the user may expose technological limitations which substantially constrain the overall system performance. The job of the designer is to balance these purely technical constraints against the needs of the user to produce a compromise solution which provides optimum performance from the user and system in partnership.

4.5 Dialogue style classification

Sections 4.6–4.10 discuss dialogue styles under five headings: menus, form-filling, command languages, natural language and direct manipulation. These headings represent a reasonable classification of styles, but of course the boundaries are indistinct and some specific examples are not readily categorizable under any particular heading. For example, where does the boundary lie between a command language and a natural language dialogue? Early 'adventure' games used a form of so-called 'natural language' where the user could input any statement she or he wished, but the system only parsed the first four letters of each of the first two words. Undoubtedly the dictionary of valid words was larger than the typical command language, but was this really natural language, even if it appeared so to the user?

Another problem of classification is that several different dialogue styles may well be exploited for different purposes within a single system. For example, the Apple Macintosh variously uses direct manipulation (e.g., for file copying and transfer operations as part of its desktop metaphor), menus (e.g., pull-down menus for selecting options from the basic command list in the top status line), and form-filling (e.g. for specifying file names). In addition it provides other mechanisms such as dialogue boxes (for presenting system messages) and a variety of buttons for activating functions.

Martin (1973) defined over 20 styles of dialogue for alphanumeric display terminals alone, but Kidd (1982) noted that these could all be classified within the general categories of *menus, form-filling, command languages* and *natural language*. Her review was however written before the widespread introduction of graphics-based workstations and the WIMP style of interface, and thus largely ignored the concept of *direct manipulation* (Shneiderman, 1983). In view of the current prevalence of window system front-ends in computer workstations, together with the widespread use of graphically based displays in other areas such as industrial process control, air traffic systems and defence, it now seems reasonable to treat direct manipulation graphic systems as another distinctive dialogue style.

Sections 4.6–4.10 therefore review the distinctive characteristics of the five basic dialogue styles: Section 4.11 then presents various principles and guidelines which are relevant to all types of dialogue. Finally, Section 4.12 presents a case study of dialogue design based on a commercial teletext subtitle origination system.

4.6 Menus

4.6.1 Structures

The primary design problem in organizing a menu-based dialogue results from the fact that most realistic tasks require more commands than can conveniently be represented on a single menu. One possible solution is a linear (or circular) series of menus where the last option of each menu is 'other options'. This can work well for a limited number of menus where options are ordered according to their frequency of use, but is obviously impractical for large menu systems.

The most widely used technique is the hierarchical tree (Figure 4.3), which allows selection from a large number of choices with a relatively small number of options in each menu and few levels of the hierarchy. For example, a tree with 3 levels and 8 choices at each level can choose between 512 options. The structure need not be purely hierarchical. Additional paths allowing particular nodes to be reached by more than

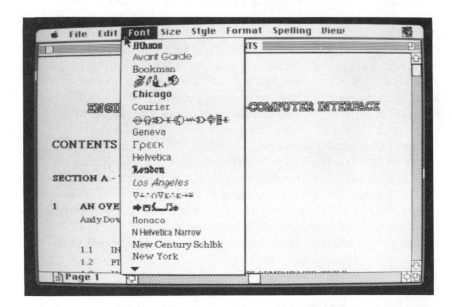

Figure 4.7 Example scrollable pull-down menu. (© 1989 Claris Corporation. All rights reserved. Claris and MacWrite are trademarks of Claris Corporation. Macintosh is a trademark of Apple Computer Inc.)

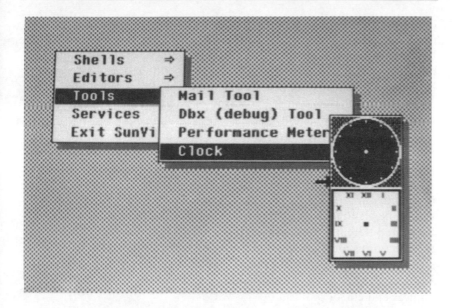

Figure 4.8   Example of pop-up menus with submenus. (Sun workstation)

one route can often be useful in representing alternative navigation strategies, and return paths offering shortcuts back up the hierarchy can be valuable where multiple selections must be made.

The hierarchy may be represented as a series of sequentially presented menus, but other formats are also possible. *Pull-down* menus (as on the Apple Macintosh, Figure 4.7), Microsoft Windows and other window systems) are principally a two-level hierarchy, while *pop-up* menus (e.g., on Sun workstations (Figure 4.8)) may allow submenus to be selected by dragging the mouse to the right from one of the initial selections, potentially to a depth of several levels (a similar capability has been added to Macintosh pull-down menus in recent software releases). Where a large number of menu options are required (for example to show alternative fonts in a word processor) a *scrollable* menu may be used, which shows only a subset of the available options initially.

4.6.2 Breadth versus depth: number of menu options

A binary decision such as:

```
Do you need help (y/n) ?
```

represents a minimal menu, but the desirable maximum number of choices on a single screen is less clear (and in any case depends to some extent on character size and screen resolution). A considerable amount of research has been carried out on the menu depth-versus-breadth issue, but results are generally equivocal. There seems some consensus that menus should not contain more than about 12 items per frame to minimize search time and maintain a clear uncluttered display; equally it is generally agreed (and has been demonstrated experimentally) that providing less than 4 choices per frame slows down navigation in large hierarchical menu selection systems.

It is not necessary for every menu to contain the same number of options; a more important criterion is that groups of options contained within a single menu should be logically compatible and consistent. Appropriate groupings should normally be defined by the task taxonomy (Section 4.4.1). However, where menu length varies care should be taken to ensure that style, layout and structure are consistent between different menus. For example, menu selection methods (see next section) should not change from one menu to the next, list structure should be consistent (e.g., alphabetic, or most frequently used items first), and screen layout should remain consistent so that the choices and cursor position do not vary.

4.6.3 Selection mechanisms

Three methods of selection are commonly used for menus. The first and most obvious is to list the options numerically and choose between them by typing the number of the required selection, as for example in the Prestel system (Figure 4.9). An alternative is to select the item by typing its name, or more commonly, an abbreviation of this name (see Section 4.12 for an example). This can have advantages in being able to construct memorable acronyms by concatenating command abbreviations at several successive levels of the menu hierarchy, such as IOT—'Input Offline Titles' (from the example in Section 4.12).

Finally, the menu choice can be made by pointing to the item, using cursor keys, a mouse, a joystick, a touch screen or any of the pointing devices discussed in Chaper 8. Typically, feedback will be provided to indicate the currently selected choice by the use of reverse video or a different colour (see Figure 4.8); the choice is then confirmed by clicking the mouse button or carrying out some other confirmatory act.

4.6.4 Organization

Menu organization and screen design (see Sections 4.11.2 and 4.11.3) are seldom given the attention they deserve by design engineers whose training and experience is usually more technically oriented. Aesthetic appeal and the ability to visualize the system from the user's point of view are vitally important; unfortunately, these skills vary widely among

Figure 4.9 Numerical menu choice on the British Prestel system

engineers and computer scientists and are seldom formally developed or evaluated as part of training. In the same way as possession of a personal computer and desk-top publishing software does not guarantee any ability to construct appealing printed material, dialogue design tools do not automatically produce the most effective and attractive interface design.

The organization of menus in a multiple-menu system is the single factor which most affects the user's perception of the interface, since the underlying dialogue and model of the system are defined by this organization. There is strong experimental evidence that both error rates and access time are reduced when menus are structured meaningfully rather than randomly. The semantic organization should normally be in accordance with the user's model of the task, rather than some other unrelated structure such as alphabetic ordering; hence the need to establish task characteristics before proceeding to interface design.

Prototyping tools for menu-based systems are widely available (Chapter 7), and can be used to simulate the user interface of systems not yet built, allowing early evaluation and thus providing feedback to the designer, either confirming the validity of the interface model or highlighting inconsistencies.

4.6.5 Advantages and disadvantages

The advantages and disadvantages of menu selection as a dialogue technique are summarized in Table 4.2. Compared with other methods, *minimal typing* is required (none if a mouse or other pointing device is used), hence there is less opportunity for keying errors, a particular advantage for infrequent keyboard users. Similarly, the *low memory load* and frequent closure encountered in a menu selection task, and the *well-defined structure*, help to simplify decision making for inexperienced users, who are always presented with a fixed, limited set of options to select from. These same advantages also mean that menu selection systems can be used effectively even in interruptive surroundings where attention has to be divided between the system and other activities.

Software design for menu-based systems is generally straightforward, though care must be taken with data validation, display layout and error handling. Methods for navigating backwards as well as forwards through the menus should be provided, by means of *abort*, *backtrack*, and/or *undo* mechanisms. The design of hierarchical menu structures is inherently compatible with structured software design but in addition, dialogue design CAD tools are now becoming available for many menu-based systems, allowing rapid prototyping and permitting aesthetic characteristics such as screen layout to be designed by specialists in graphic design who may not have the requisite software design skills.

The main disadvantages of menu mode result from the requirement to display a large amount of auxiliary data to assist in menu selection. Depending upon display rate, this may result in irritatingly *slow response* (more commonly perceived as a problem by experienced and expert users than by infrequent users), and also requires substantial *display space*, which may constrain the choice of display type, or restrict the amount of other material which can be simultaneously displayed.

However, type-ahead or bypass mechanisms can allow the user to input the next selection without waiting for all menu options to be displayed (as, for example, on Prestel), and provide an elegant method for novices and experts to be accommodated compatibly on the same

Table 4.2 Advantages and disadvantages of menu-mode dialogues

Advantages	Disadvantages
Minimal typing	Sometimes slow
Low memory load	Consumes screen space
Well-defined structure	Not suited to data entry
Straightforward software design	Not suited to user-initiated dialogues
CAD tools available	Not suited to mixed initiative dialogues

system. An alternative approach is simply to provide a
high-performance display system with sufficiently rapid response,
powerful commands and aesthetic appeal to satisfy the 'power' user as
well as the novice or intermittent user, as exemplified in window system
menu-based command mechanisms.

A more fundamental problem concerns the type of interaction
required. Menu selection is very suitable for *decision-making* tasks, but
unsatisfactory for *data entry*, where large amounts of text need to be
keyed into the system. If, for example, a number of parameters to a
command must be specified, and these cannot readily be encoded with a
menu (for example in an airline reservation where source and
destination airports, departure and arrival times, flight number, and the
name of the passenger must be specified), then a form-filling mode of
dialogue will be much more suitable.

4.6.6 Conclusions

Menu-based dialogues are very suitable for casual, intermittent and
novice users, all of whom can benefit from the explicit structure and
simple interaction inherent in menu selection. For expert users, menu
systems may be acceptable if system response and display rate are fast
enough to avoid annoying delays.

4.7 Form-filling

4.7.1 Structures and organization

Form-filling is a useful metaphor in human–computer dialogues because
humans are inherently familiar with the concept of filling in forms, and
because computers are widely used to manipulate and process databases
of information, which are stored as records containing different fields of
related information. These records are generally most conveniently
visualized as forms. Familiar examples include airline bookings, library
records, address lists, parts lists, personnel records, etc. (Figure 4.10).

The key benefit of form-filling cited by Shneiderman (1987, p. 122) is
that all information in the record is simultaneously visible, giving the
user a feeling of control over the dialogue. This implies that, whereas it
is possible to implement a menu selection dialogue on any alphanumeric
display device including a printing terminal, form-filling dialogues
require a terminal which supports cursor control, so that the full screen
of form information can be displayed and the cursor then moved
around to each of the required data entry fields.

Although most users are familiar with the *task* of form-filling, the
implementation of this task via the *system* may be less obvious. Unlike
menu selection, the user usually has a significant degree of control over
the process of data entry, and various application-specific syntactic rules

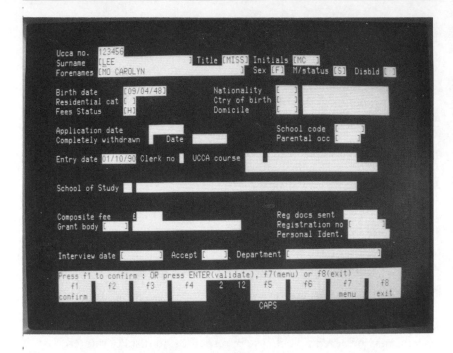

Figure 4.10   Example form-filling dialogue (from a university admissions database)

must therefore be learnt before proficiency is attained. Typical syntactic variables might include the following:

- *Display protection*—some areas of the display (generally all except the data entry fields) may not be accessible to the user.
- *Display field constraints*—data fields may be of fixed or variable length; user data entries may be constrained or free format.
- *Field content*—the user generally has to have some idea of permissible field contents: guidance may or may not be included as part of the form display.
- *Optional fields*—some fields may be optional; is this indicated textually or by some other display convention such as lower intensity level, different display colour, etc.?
- *Defaults*—are default entries possible? If so, are they indicated in the protected display area or in the data entry area?
- *Help*—additional help concerning filling in different fields may be available but concealed from the basic form display; if so, how is this additional information accessed?
- *Field termination*—data entry to a field may be terminated by the ENTER key, the RETURN key, or by filling the last available character space, or by moving to another field.

- *Navigation*—the cursor may be moved around the form using the TAB key in a fixed sequence, or using cursor control keys or another pointing device in any desired order.
- *Error correction*—the user may be able to correct errors by backspacing, by overwriting, by clearing and re-entering the field content, etc.
- *Completion*—how is completion of the whole form indicated?

As with menu systems, dialogue design tools for defining form-filling dialogues are readily available. In this case however, since there is a widespread need for tailored databases to support a variety of different database manipulation tasks, the dialogue design tools are often integrated with database application generator programs (for example Aston-Tate's dBASE and Microsoft's Excel).

4.7.2 Advantages and disadvantages

The advantages and disadvantages of form-filling as a dialogue technique are summarized in Table 4.3. The most significant advantage of this method is the basic familiarity with the *concept* of form-filling which any user has—all users can thus be classified as knowledgeable intermittent users, even though they may in fact be casual or novice users. Like menu mode, form-filling is a *structured dialogue* with *low memory load* for the user because it is computer-initiated. Data entry is simplified, but not as restricted as for menu mode, hence some *training* is required so that the user is aware of what constitutes a 'reasonable' response for each field. This may be viewed as an advantage compared with the flexibility of command and natural languages (see below), but a disadvantage compared with the minimal dialogue requirements of menu mode.

Software design is again relatively straightforward owing to the constrained nature of the dialogue, but more care is required in parsing and validating data entries than for menu mode. Many form-filling *dialogue design tools* are available as part of standard database

Table 4.3 Advantages and disadvantages of form-filling dialogues

Advantages	Disadvantages
Form-filling metaphor familiar	Sometimes slow
Simplified data entry	Consumes screen space
Limited training required	Not ideal for command selection
Low memory load	Requires display cursor control
Well-defined structure	Navigation mechanism not explicit
Straightforward software design	Some training needed
Dialogue design tools widely used	

application generators, but these may not be useful (except for interface simulation purposes) if the form-filling dialogue is intended to be part of a larger embedded system whose scope extends beyond the capabilities of the standard database package.

The basic disadvantages of form-filling mode are similar to menu mode: potentially *slow response* and the need for a large amount of *screen space*. In some ways, form-filling is complementary to menu mode in that the two dialogue styles are optimized for different dialogue types: form-filling is better for parameter entry, but less suited to command selection. Other disadvantages result from the need for users to have some familiarity with the *syntax* of the required dialogue, and the need for the display to be *cursor-addressable*—a possible hardware constraint.

4.7.2 Conclusions

Form-filling dialogues can be made suitable for all types of users, since all users are familiar with the basic concept of their use. Casual users may not have the specific system knowledge to complete the form unless any system-specific syntax is explicitly indicated as part of the on-screen data. Form-filling is better suited to parameter entry than command selection, and thus can often be used to advantage as a complementary dialogue technique where both styles of interaction are required.

To a large extent, the quality of form-filling dialogue depends upon the organization, presentation and content of the information provided in the form. Parameter fields need to be presented in a logical sequence while textual content needs to be succinct yet informative and unambiguous, form layout should be clear and uncluttered, and straightforward error recovery procedures are needed. Guidance on these requirements is presented in Section 4.11.

4.8 Command languages

4.8.1 Structures and organization

Command language dialogues are user-initiated and generally consist of the user typing a command or command string of syntactically correct words without prompting or help from the system. The most frequently encountered example of a command language for most computer users is the operating system language for their computer system. Other common examples of command languages include languages for text editors such as *vi* on UNIX systems. The distinctive feature of any command language dialogue is that no explicit support is provided to the user to show him the allowable set of commands: instead the user is expected to know (or learn) these commands. One implication of this is that the choice of command names is of particular importance in command language dialogues because these names must be memorized.

As with the menu dialogue mode, several command structures are possible. The simplest is a command list, as for example with the command set for the *vi* editor, which uses nearly every character of the ASCII character set (including control characters) to define some command (see Table 4.4 for a small example)! A disadvantage of this approach is the flat structure which results, making it difficult to remember the full command set, particularly since command names are not generally related in any logical or consistent way to their function. In consequence, this approach is advised only where the set of discrete commands required is fairly small. (It is generally a mistake to provide too much functionality in a system, just as it is to provide too little. Task analysis should reveal common strategies for achieving an objective; implementing additional '1-per-cent' functionality simply increases the amount of code and documentation, and thus may both reduce execution speed and slow user familiarization.)

Hierarchical command lists are also possible with command languages, and exactly parallel menu hierarchies, except that no explicit

Table 4.4 Sample cursor control commands for the Unix *vi* screen editor

Command	Function
(space)	right one character
$\wedge$ B	back one page
$\wedge$ D	scroll down half a page
$\wedge$ F	forward one page
$\wedge$ H	left one character
$\wedge$ N	down one character
$\wedge$ P	up one character
$\wedge$ U	scroll up half a page
+	start of next line
−	start of previous line
/ <string>	scan forwards for <string>
? <string>	scan backwards for <string>
B	back one word, ignoring punctuation
G <line no.>	go to line <line number>
H	start of top line
M	start of middle line
L	start of bottom line
W	forward one word, ignoring punctuation
b	back one word
e	end of current word
w	forward one word

prompting of allowable commands is provided in the command language. It is common to use subsequent words after the initial command word as qualifiers or parameters which specify the action of the command in more detail. The meaning of the subsequent words (or fields) of the command may be specific to each particular command (in which case it is accurate to view the command string as representing a hierarchy), or it may be possible for each of the words to identify a particular orthogonal characteristic of the command string, in which case the language may be viewed as an orthogonal structure. (Figure 4.4).

A practical problem in attempting to construct an orthogonal command language is that, in most cases, the required functionality cannot easily be accommodated by this structure. For example, the generic three-dimensional structure for an operating system command language might be of the form:

```
operation parameter filename
```

While this might fit some commands well (e.g., `edit`, `delete`, `compile`), others would not map easily onto the template (e.g., `copy` (requires both source and destination filenames), `directory` (no filename required)). In consequence, many command languages exhibit characteristics both of hierarchy and of orthogonality: typically the initial word specifies the basic command, with subsequent words adding command parameters (hierarchy), but at the same time there is some effort to generalize parameter structure across all commands (orthogonality).

4.8.2 Command syntax

Given this typical mixture of command language hierarchy and orthogonality, three command syntax styles have emerged, as follows:

Positional syntax

A positional syntax interprets the command words strictly according to their position within the command string. This type of syntax has been widely used in simple microcomputer operating systems such as CP/M and MSDOS. For example,

```
COPY TEMP FILE1
```

in a CP/M system might be assumed to have the meaning 'copy the file temp to filename file1'. In fact, the command copies in the reverse direction, succinctly illustrating one of the greatest dangers in using a positional syntax, namely, errors due to incorrect sequencing of the parameters. In this case, the 'logical' sequence of parameters is incorrect indicating an obvious error in the command structure, but in many cases the appropriate sequence for parameters in unclear, both to the designer and to the user. Where several parameters can follow the command, scope for error is increased: for 2 parameters only 1 incorrect sequence is possible, but for 3, five are possible and for 4, twenty-three.

Keyword syntax

Keyword syntax identifies each command parameter by an immediately preceding keyword. The actual sequence of parameters is then unimportant. Thus the previous example might be expressed validly by either of the following expressions using a keyword syntax:

```
COPY FROM FILE1 TO TEMP
COPY TO TEMP FROM FILE1
```

The delimiter between the keyword and its associated parameter is part of the syntax of the particular command language; space, equals (=) and hyphen (-) symbols are all commonly used. This method eliminates the possibility of sequencing errors, but at the expense of including additional redundant characters in the command line.

Mixed syntax

Mixed syntax simply combines the features of keyword and positional syntaxes to increase the allowable options, as for example in the UNIX command:

```
cc -o outfile cfile.c
```

where the parameter '-o' is used as a keyword to indicate that the next field specifies an output filename, and the field 'cfile.c' specifies a source file using positional notation. Although widely used and apparently more flexible than the use of keyword or positional syntax alone, mixed syntax can introduce confusion as to the required command string format where positional and keyword syntax rules conflict.

4.8.3 Advantages and disadvantages

Table 4.5 summarizes the advantages and disadvantages of command language dialogues. The advantages quoted are all only true for expert users: command languages have no real advantages for other types of users and many disadvantages.

The disadvantages highlight the reasons why command languages are suited to expert users. The need for substantial *training* and *regular use* to maintain proficiency define an expert user, and are likely to discourage any except the highly motivated. The reliance on the user's knowledge of allowable commands imposes a *high memory load*, but eliminates the need for extensive displays of menu options or other

Table 4.5 Advantages and disadvantages of command language dialogues

Advantages	Disadvantages
Fast	Long training
Efficient	Needs regular use
Precise	High memory load
Concise	Poor error handling
Flexible	
User-initiated	
Appealing	

support, leading to *concise* and compact use of the display. Providing meaningful *error messages* is much more difficult for command languages because the input is much less constrained, and the variety of possible errors is much larger than for menus or form-filling.

4.8.4 Conclusions

In summary, the command language dialogue style has several attractive advantages for frequent and experienced users, but is usually very discouraging for any other type of user. Where command languages are a legitimate choice, care is still needed to minimize training requirements and errors. Kidd (1982) gives the following succinct advice to minimize memory load and typing errors:

- choose memorable, non-confusable command words;
- use consistent command formats;
- keep command strings short;
- provide an explanatory backup online 'Help' facility;
- use the 'natural' ordering sequence for command parameters where possible;
- place optional and/or least used items at the end of the command list;
- use defaults to reduce typing where appropriate;
- provide clear and explicit messages;

and, if frequent errors persist,

- revert to a computer-initiated style!

4.9 Natural language

4.9.1 Justification

Science fiction has for many years propagated the idea of natural-language dialogue between humans and computers, but this superficial view is not supported by practical experience in the HCI field. The basis of the view may be an extrapolation from the fact that humans converse successfully with each other using 'natural language', but the flaw here lies in equating the computer with one of the humans involved in the dialogue.

As indicated in Table 4.1, human and computer aptitudes are complementary rather than equivalent, hence an optimal dialogue should aim to exploit the strengths of each partner. For example, natural-language dialogue between two humans normally assumes a symmetric communication channel: speech input and recognition speed in one direction is matched by speech output speed in the other. But human dialogue with computers generally uses asymmetric channels: the computer can output text to the screen very much faster than the human can type it in. Furthermore, the computer may have the capability to provide graphical or pictorial output as well as text. With these constraints on communication speed, it makes good sense to minimize typed input by the user (for example by use of menu selection), whereas extensive textual output can be supported.

Another aspect of the symmetry problem is the comparison between the style of input and output. In human–human communication each participant uses natural language, but the analogy fails when one human is replaced by a computer. On the one hand, if the computer uses natural language to 'speak' to the user, the underlying structure of the system being used immediately becomes more opaque and less readily determined; on the other, if the structure is made clearer, for example by means of forms or menus of options, then what is the point of requiring a (largely redundant) natural language input? (One class of system where the opacity of natural language is actually exploited is the ubiquitous adventure game: not only can the player attribute reassuringly 'human' capabilities to the computer, but also determining the underlying 'game model' represents the major intellectual function of the interaction.)

To add to these conceptual problems, natural-language dialogue is substantially more complex to program than any other dialogue style discussed. Natural-language recognition still represents a major linguistic research problem, and current natural-language processing systems are generally constrained to operate within limited knowledge domains using constrained syntax and restricted vocabularies.

An exception to this generally negative view of the potential of natural-language dialogues may exist in the case of natural-language speech communication with computers. Where data input is required to be by means of speech (in hands-off command and control operations, for example, or in speech input to computers via a telephone line—see Chapter 14), alternative dialogue modes such as single-word discrete input may require significant user training, ruling them out for casual and intermittent users. Acceptance of natural-language input for speech-controlled systems eliminates the need for the user to acquire specific syntactic knowledge about the interaction style.

4.9.2 Advantages and disadvantages

The advantages and disadvantages of natural-language dialogue are summarized in Table 4.6. The main advantage of natural language is the fact that *no special syntax* is needed. Natural language is also potentially *flexible* and *powerful*, though in practice these advantages depend to a large extent on how restrictive the specific dialogue implementation is. A further advantage is the potential for supporting mixed initiative dialogues, in contrast to the other dialogue styles discussed.

The major disadvantages of natural-language dialogues are those of natural language itself: by comparison with any purpose-designed artificial language, natural language is *ambiguous, imprecise* and *verbose*. In addition, in speech input applications, spoken natural language is significantly less well structured, accurate and syntactically correct than written language. From the designer's viewpoint, the software required to support a reasonably flexible natural-language dialogue is substantial: as a result natural-language input to computers is seldom as efficient, either in dialogue content or interface programming, as other dialogue styles.

A final problem with natural languages concerns the underlying perception of the system which a natural-language dialogue promulgates. Users can easily be misled by this style of dialogue into attributing much more intelligence to the system than is justified. This is due partly to the realistic and apparently thoughtful style of natural language response which such systems are programmed to generate (even when the system has in fact 'understood' very little of its natural language input), and partly to the fact that the difficulty in following the underlying logic of the computer's deductions from its input data readily persuades the user that these processes must be profound.

This point is amply illustrated by ELIZA (Weizenbaum, 1966; Weil,

Table 4.6 Advantages and disadvantages of natural-language dialogues

Advantages	Disadvantages
No special syntax	Ambiguous
Flexible and powerful	Imprecise
Natural	Verbose
Mixed initiative	Opaque
	Complex software design
	Inefficient

1965), a computer program written over twenty years ago to study
natural-language dialogue between humans and machines. Its mode of
operation was simply to identify key words within a specific knowledge
domain from the input (Weil discusses examples where the system was
programmed to respond as though it were a psychiatrist), and perform
simple transformations to generate its response. For example, by
converting first-person pronouns to second person and repeating the
input sentence with a question mark at the end, an apparently plausible
response is generated, with an implied request for elaboration:

```
Input:    My boyfriend made me come here
Response: Your boyfriend made you come here?
```

By means of a variety of tricks of this type, ELIZA was able to conduct
convincing conversations with a variety of users, some of whom
believed that they were communicating with a human rather than a
computer, yet the underlying basis on which responses were generated
was straightforward, and certainly involved no deep analysis of the
meaning of the input.

4.9.3 Conclusions

In general, it appears that natural language does not have much to offer
as a basis for dialogue design in most applications, being both complex
to program and inefficient for most dialogue situations. The main
exception to this may be where a speech-based dialogue is required,
particularly if both input and output use the speech modality. In this
case, the ephemeral nature of speech output, and the difficulty of
generating speech input with strict syntactic constraints may justify the
use of what otherwise is a verbose, vague and ambiguous method of
communication.

4.10 Direct manipulation

4.10.1 Styles and metaphors

Most computer users are by now familiar with the WIMP (Window,
Icon, Menus, Pointer) style of dialogue popularized by such machines as
the Apple Macintosh, but the desktop metaphor used by this machine is
only one example of a direct-manipulation dialogue. The essential
characteristic of such dialogues is that some kind of *direct representation*
of the task is presented to the user by the system, with the result that the
desired operation or command is achieved by *directly manipulating* the
virtual reality embodied in the display. The primary advantage of using
a *metaphor* to represent the actual function is that operations and
commands can be readily suggested by analogy between the computer
representation and its real life equivalent.

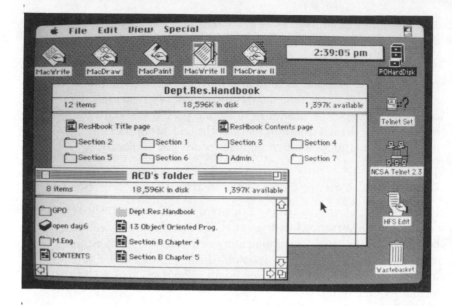

Figure 4.11 Macintosh desktop screen showing icons, folders and windows

Thus in the case of the Macintosh desktop (Figure 4.11), by using the metaphor of a folder to present a disk directory, the user may be expected to deduce that he can open the folder and see what is inside (list the directory in a new window), and then manipulate files within the folder (extract, insert, duplicate, discard into the wastebasket, etc.). The concept of hierarchical directories is readily conveyed by inserting a folder into an existing open folder (window). Open folders become documents (windows) on the desktop (screen) and documents can overlap, be placed on top of each other, and moved around at will. Icons with graphical images suggestive of their function are used to represent application programs such as word processors, graphics and communication packages. Supporting desktop operations requires significant processing power, but the biggest problem faced by the desktop metaphor is the limited size and screen resolution attainable using CRT technology, compared with an actual desk! In addition, direct manipulation commonly assumes the availability of some variety of pointing device, such as a mouse, stylus or finger (for touch screens).

4.10.2 Objects and actions

Although these concepts seem simple and obvious with hindsight, the trick of designing an effective direct-manipulation system lies in choosing a simple and readily understood metaphor. Central to this metaphor is an orthogonal division between *objects* which are represented as physical images (such as icons) on the screen, and *actions*, which are conveyed dynamically by manipulating the objects. The choice of metaphor is thus constrained by the need on the one hand to choose objects which are recognizable and memorable, and on the other to produce a set of actions which can be readily represented graphically and are as consistent as possible across all objects (Rosenburg and Moran, 1984). Furthermore, it may be possible within the metaphor to code particular tasks either as objects or actions, for example, the Xerox Star workstation represents the printer as an icon or resource which can be selected, whereas the Apple Macintosh treats printing as an action chosen using a menu.

Graphic design plays a fundamental part in creating an illusion of manipulable objects. Design of direct-manipulation interfaces requires a new breed of graphical designer who is not only capable of mastering the aesthetics of presenting static images on a bit-mapped graphics display, but also can cope with the dynamic aspects of such displays. Animation may be used in a wide variety of ways: to indicate selection of an object (e.g., inverse video), to indicate different modes (e.g., different cursor types), to indicate progress of a time-consuming operation (e.g., the watch or hourglass icon), to provide a visual focus on the object which is being manipulated. The example above might suggest that using animated graphics is a key to success: as the examples in the next section show, however, not all direct-manipulation interfaces require such complexities.

4.10.3 Examples

Process control

Process control systems in industries such as chemical engineering and power systems generation and distribution have for many years used visual representations of their systems as the interface between the human system controller and the computer-based control system. In most cases this is relatively easily achieved technically since the system being represented is static and so the basic display model can consist mainly of a symbolic pictorial representation of the system on a board. Fixed controls (switches, potentiometers, etc.) are used to adjust parameters of the system, and basic status information is supplied by means of illumination intensity, colour and other simple displays at appropriate points on the board.

Air traffic control and weapons guidance

Radar systems have always relied to a large extent upon the remarkable pattern recognition capabilities of the human to isolate the radar return corresponding to a plane from surrounding clutter. In essence, the three-dimensional world in which the plane flies is translated into a readily interpreted two-dimensional plan. Similarly, weapons guidance systems provide a simplified visual representation of the world with the target and method of controlling the weapon so as to hit the target emphasized.

Simulators and video games

Simulators are widely used in fields such as flight training and power station control to provide cheaper tuition than could be achieved by using the system itself, and to explore aspects of control which would be dangerous or impossible on a real system. Aircraft simulators may be so realistic as to appear almost identical to the actual aircraft visually and perceptually, but even with very much simplified display information, users can learn a great deal about the principles of flight, if the model accurately simulates flight dynamics. One class of video games simulates flight, car racing, and other sports with varying degrees of realism and accuracy, but in all cases the model represents a metaphor of the actual activity. Other video games may be more abstract in nature; nevertheless, there is usually an element of familiarity in the basic theme of the game which encourages analogy and experimentation on the part of the user.

Screen editors

Screen editors, where the computer screen represents a window in a text file and text is identified by moving a cursor on the screen using a mouse or cursor keys or both, are now the norm in most computer systems. The WYSIWYG concept (what you see is what you get) is central to modern word processors. However, in earlier interactive systems line-based editors were common, representing a command language approach to text editing (e.g., see the UNIX editor *ed*). While some gurus still welcome the power of line editors, the vast majority of computer users much prefer the visual clarity of a screen editor.

Graphics

Graphics generation of any sort on computer systems might seem to require graphics displays, pointing devices and digitizers, as embodied in a wide variety of microcomputer drawing, painting and business

Table 4.7 Advantages and disadvantages of direct-manipulation dialogues

Advantages	Disadvantages
Task analogy	May require complex or large software
Reduced familiarization/ learning	May require high-performance graphics display
Readily retained	May require auxiliary input devices (e.g., mouse)
Encourages exploration	Skilled graphics design required
Visually appealing	
Powerful	
Concise	
Design tools available	

graphics packages. Nevertheless, a wide variety of command language, driven software tools were produced in the past for use on minicomputers with character-orientated displays.

Computer-aided design

Similarly, first-generation CAD systems were based upon textual input of commands, for example, circuit analysis programs such as SPICE and HILO require component values to be specified in relation to numbered or labelled circuit nodes. Current systems, by contrast, attempt to provide a more direct representation of the simulation, for example direct schematic capture in the case of circuit analysis, or 2- and 3-dimensional models for finite-element modelling.

4.10.4 Advantages and disadvantages

Table 4.7 shows the advantages and disadvantages of direct-manipulation dialogues. The primary advantage is the direct *analogy* between the task and the system, which gives the user a sense of understanding and control from the start, and encourages *exploration*. In addition, it reduces the time required for the user to become *familiar* with the system, since many aspects should map directly onto his or her existing knowledge of the task, and *learning* is reduced since knowledge of the task is also knowledge of the system, and no independent set of commands is needed. With careful graphic design, direct manipulation can be *visually appealing* and satisfying, and can also be made powerful and concise, thus appealing specifically to expert users. (For example, a double click of the mouse button on a Macintosh application icon is equivalent to typing the command name in a conventional operating system.)

The major disadvantages of direct-manipulation dialogues are that they may require *complex and expensive hardware* to support a suitable graphics display, and *substantial software development* to implement the chosen metaphor realistically.

A variety of *design tools* are available for prototyping graphical direct-manipulation interfaces. Applications such as MacPaint and its equivalent on other workstations have been successfully used for simulating static graphics displays, while Hypercard and derivatives provide some capability to represent dynamic interaction as well. Most windowing systems provide development tools allowing rapid development of pop-up and/or pull-down menus, dialogue boxes, and icon and fount editors (see Section 10.8). The major disadvantages of all these tools is the restriction they place upon the designer, who must conform to the particular 'style' embodied in the tool (e.g., the card metaphor in Hypercard, the specific window and menu format and actions for a window system). The inclusion of first-class graphic design skills in the design team is also an essential requirement for direct-manipulation interfaces: this presents particular problems since the graphic designer's ideas may have to be mediated by a software engineer in order to produce a physical representation if adequate design tools are not available.

4.10.5 Conclusions

The technological disadvantages of direct-manipulation dialogues which have inhibited their development in the past are gradually disappearing with the availability of high-performance, cheap microprocessors and improvements in display technology. At the same time there is an increasing need for larger numbers of users to become familiar with more and more different computer systems. As a result there is a widespread trend towards direct-manipulation interfaces as representing an effective way to provide a system which is appealing to novices and experts alike, and which is easy to learn, encourages experimentation, and is readily retained once learnt.

However, direct manipulation dialogues are not a panacea; in many applications their technical complexity is not justified or may be impracticable or the target user population may be better served by some other dialogue style. Even where direct manipulation is appropriate, other dialogue modes may also need to be introduced to achieve functions which cannot readily be represented metaphorically.

4.11 Design principles and guidelines

Sections 4.6–4.10 have presented specific features of the five major different dialogue styles. In this section, more general design issues are considered which are relevant to all dialogue styles.

4.11.1 Design sequence

Dialogue design, like any other aspect of system design, should be carried out in a top-down fashion. Hebditch (1979) specifies the process of stepwise refinement as follows:

1 Choose dialogue style

The basic dialogue style must be selected from among the five styles discussed previously. The choice between these styles will be affected by the characteristics of the user population (expert or naive users, etc.), the type of dialogue required, and by the constraints of the available technology and application area. This will result in an individual style or combination of styles being chosen for the dialogue.

2 Design dialogue structure

The second stage is to undertake task analysis and determine the user's model of the task on which the dialogue structure should be based. Having proposed a dialogue structure, every effort should be made to obtain user feedback by means of informal discussion or more formal simulation of the interface.

3 Design message formats

Once a satisfactory dialogue structure has been achieved, more detailed attention must be paid to the display layout and textual content. Similarly, detailed user input requirements should be considered with the objective of maximizing efficiency, for example by avoiding unnecessary keying. These issues are considered in the following sections.

4 Design error handling

Having designed how the system will work when sensible data is input, consideration must be given to the ways in which user errors can be made. These include: *input data validation*, where checks must be made that sensible responses or values are given by the user; *user protection*, where the user must be protected from the consequences of his or her own errors (e.g., deleting important files); *error recovery*, that is, the provision of mechanisms for backtracking, undoing or retrying commands which were executed in error; and *meaningful error messages*. Again, these issues are considered in more detail below.

5 Design data structures

Once all aspects of the user interface have been specified, consideration can be given to the internal structure of the system, such as choice of data structures to support the required functionality. These structures should map directly onto the user's model of the system, though their complexity may vary considerably between different applications. For example, the graphics data structures required to support a WIMP interface are quite complex, whereas those required to support a text editor might be much simpler. In either case however, the structures should be derived from the interface specification (which in the case of the editor is, in effect, the user manual), so as to avoid conceptual mismatches between the user's and system's models of the system.

4.11.2 Screen design—text

Stewart (1976) has proposed six major factors which contribute to high quality textual screen layout: these are summarized below.

1 Logical sequencing

Information should be presented to the user in a sequence which logically reflects the user's task, even if this conflicts with the optimum system presentation sequence. If this is not possible, then the rationale for using an alternative sequence should be made explicit to the user.

2 Spaciousness

Clutter on a display greatly increases visual search time: the use of spacing and blanks is important in structuring the display and emphasizing those aspects to which the user's attention should be directed.

3 Grouping

Related items of data should be grouped together to provide higher-level structure to the screen as a whole. This reinforces the concept of 'chunking' and speeds up search times by allowing related items to be treated as a group. Even on character-based displays, auxiliary characters such as line segments may be able to be exploited to emphasize grouping.

4 Relevance

There is a natural desire on the part of the designer to include all which may be relevant to a display. However, displaying the maximum

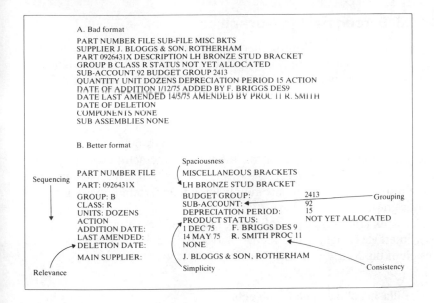

Figure 4.12 Screen textual layout guidelines (reproduced from Stewart, 1976)

amount on the screen is not the same as maximizing the information transfer rate, and it is this latter principle which is of primary importance.

5 Consistency

In frame-based systems where the user views a number of sequential screens full of information, it is important to be consistent in the use of display space, so that the user learns where different types of information are to be found.

6 Simplicity

The overriding consideration in screen design should be to present the appropriate quantity and level of information in the simplest way possible.

Figure 4.12 illustrates these points, and emphasizes the importance of aesthetic appeal in the design of the user interface: the interface is the 'shop window' on the product, and as such is the major factor influencing the user for or against the product.

4.11.3 Screen design—graphics

Graphic design is a well-developed and established area in printing and publishing, but its importance in human–computer interface design is only now becoming established as computer systems are more widely used, and more flexible and controllable display formats become feasible. To a significant extent, screen design is constrained by technological considerations: the response time, display rate, display bandwidth and display type (character- or graphics-oriented) of an interface all impose restrictions on the style of interaction which can be accommodated. For example, the display style will inevitably be much more restricted on a monochrome alphanumeric terminal than on a colour graphics workstation.

Verplank (1988) cites the following five principles of graphical user-interface design, which are primarily derived from experience in the design of the Xerox Star user interface and its predecessors:

1 The illusion of manipulable objects

Effective graphic design involves three distinct components. First, a set of objects appropriate to the intended application must be invented. This involves (hopefully) identifying generic stereotypes of the required objects on which icon design can be based. Next, the skills of graphic design must be used to represent these objects in a convincing way. Finally, consistent graphic mechanisms must be provided for indicating actions on the object such as selection.

2 Visual order and user focus

Graphical interfaces provide the opportunity to exploit very powerful visual stimuli, and features such as flashing, inverse video, strong colours and animation can lead to an overpowering and visually cluttered interface if they are used to excess. One important point is to ensure that the user can readily identify the part of the screen on which attention should be focused: hence, the most powerful attention-getting devices should be used sparingly for this function (e.g., use of flashing to identify the cursor, or use of inverse video on an icon or window title to indicate that it is selected).

3 Revealed structure

Parallels are commonly drawn between direct manipulation and the WYSIWYG concept, in that both are intended to minimize the difference between the observed screen and its effect. A particular problem of this approach however is that it fails to convey the underlying structure of the activity. For example, in textual documents,

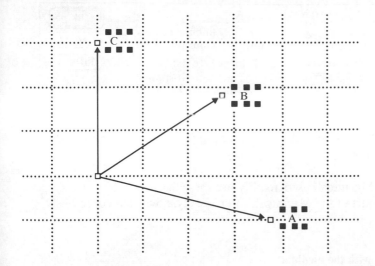

Figure 4.13   Revealed structure of Figure 4.4 showing handles and alignment grid

the layout is typically controlled by non-displayed control characters: although these are irrelevant on the final printout, they may be very important in defining the effect or scope of an action during editing. Typically, this need is dealt with by providing a display mode in which the structure is revealed (for example by showing rulers, e.g. MacWrite or control codes, e.g. Word). Similarly, graphical editors such as MacDraw require a mechanism for explicitly showing the diagram structure, and providing methods of selecting and manipulating elements of it (Figure 4.13). These 'handles' and other hidden elements such as alignment grids form a key element in the design of the graphical user interface, since they convey important information to the user concerning the structure and dynamic manipulation of the screen which is essential for effective interactive use.

4 Consistent and appropriate graphic vocabulary

As with text, it is important for graphic symbology to be used consistently throughout an interface design. There is evidence (Mayes *et al.*, 1988) that interaction with a computer involves a process of 'information flow' where local display information is picked up, used and discarded as necessary to meet functional needs: although the detail of the symbology may only be identified at a subconscious level, inconsistency will inhibit interaction and familiarization with the interface. Figure 4.14 shows some of the graphics conventions used in a MacWrite dialogue box (activation buttons; radio buttons (mutually exclusive set); check boxes (inclusive set); text entry windows). Note

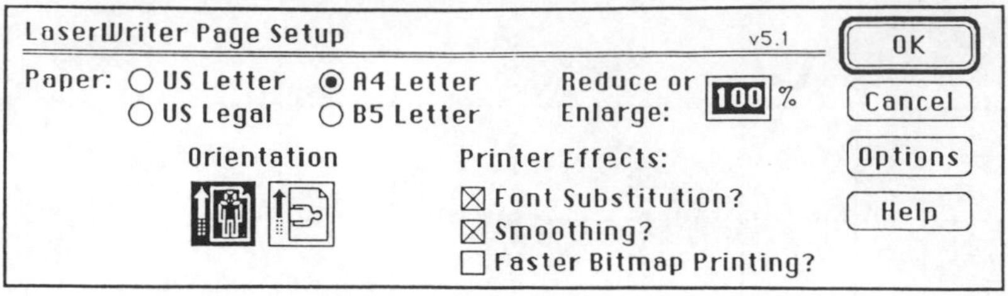

Figure 4.14   Example Macintosh dialogue box illustrating standard graphic symbology

that many Macintosh users readily use these features, which are a consistent part of the Macintosh interface style, without consciously being aware of their underlying definition.

5 A match with the medium

The specific characteristics of the display medium substantially influence the aesthetic appeal of different graphic constructs, and considerable time is required for graphic designers to become proficient in exploiting the capabilities of any particular display style. In the past, screen designers worked within the constraints of alphanumeric character-based displays; currently, many systems are based upon bit-mapped (1 bit per pixel) raster graphics displays; in the future, it is probable that much greater use will be made of grey-scale and colour graphics displays. The experience gained in current bit-mapped displays does not necessarily translate directly into appealing aesthetic design for colour or grey-scale displays, and we can therefore expect a delay of several years before the full potential of these displays is realized.

4.11.4 Response time

It is clear that slow response from a system can have an adverse impact upon the user interface, but the exact response speed required for satisfactory interaction depends to a large extent on the nature of the interaction taking place. Furthermore, *variability* in system response speed also appears to disrupt user performance. Martin (1973) suggests a broad division of response times into 5 categories, derived primarily from Miller's (1968) analysis of 17 situations in which maximum acceptable response times varied widely:

1 > 15 seconds

Response times of this order generally rule out interactive use of the system. The user's attention is likely to be diverted to other activities and only return to the screen on completion of these.

2 > 4 seconds

Response delays of this order are poor for short-term memory retention, and thus should be avoided in the middle of a sequence of related operations. They may be acceptable on completion of a major cognitive process when intermediate short-term data can be discarded ('closure'), for example dispatching a job to the computer.

3 > 2 seconds

Response delays of more than 2 seconds during interactive dialogues requiring a high level of concentration can be surprisingly disruptive.

4 < 2 seconds

A response time of this order is generally considered acceptable for interactive work, for command input, menu selection, form-filling, etc.

5 Almost instantaneous

Almost instantaneous response is required for very tightly coupled activities between the user and system, such as character-by-character response to keyboard input or tracking a mouse or cursor movement on a screen.

4.11.5 Error handling

It is human nature for the designer of a system to concentrate most of his design effort on the way he intends the system to work, rather than recovery from user errors. However, any system will inevitably be used at some time by inexpert users, and thus user input errors will occur and must be handled effectively by the system. Error handling can be subdivided into several distinct requirements, as follows:

System and user protection

Primary requirements are to protect the system from the user, and the user from the consequences of other users' actions (in a multiuser system). In multitasking systems these requirements are generally supported by hardware memory-managements systems and privileged modes. In simpler single-user systems there may be less protection and considerable effort must be devoted to testing all conceivable user interaction to avoid 'crashes': the 'infinite-number-of-monkeys' test. A secondary need is to protect the user from the system: this involves engineering the user interface so that irreversible actions (such as deleting a file) are not committed accidentally or without careful thought.

Pseudo-errors

Many systems are unreasonably pedantic about the syntax of user input. Programmers' experience of rigid syntax in programming languages gives them an insight into dialogue structures which is denied to other users. Such users will judge the dialogue on the basis of what is 'reasonable' (i.e., readily comprehensible and not ambiguous) for another human, rather than on the basis of some rigid and arbitrary syntax required by the system. For example, the dates

$$4/1/53 \quad 04/01/53 \quad 04/01/1953 \quad 4.1.53 \quad \ldots$$

are all readily interpreted as 4 January 1953 (unless you are American, in which case they represent 1 April 1953!), yet many computer systems are much more restrictive in the date format they will accept. These *pseudo-errors* result from lack of foresight on the part of the programmer: very little extra programming effort can make the interface appear much more friendly.

Error messages

Most computer users will have experienced error messages similar to the following:

```
FATAL ERROR - PROGRAM ABORTED
**SYNTAX ERROR**
WHAT?
INVALID DATA
ERROR OE7 IN DEVICE 080
```

Error messages should be *clear, concise, specific, constructive* and *positive*. The above examples achieve only the second of these requirements. *Clarity* and *specificity* are achieved by providing exact information about the conditions under which the error occurred and exactly what the error was, so that the user has some starting point for diagnosing the reasons for the error. *Constructiveness* implies that, wherever possible, the system will suggest ways of recovering from the error, or correcting it. Finally, error messages should adopt a *positive* and conciliatory tone, and not condemn the user's mistake: as in other commercial areas, the consumer is always right.

4.11.6 Documentation

Documentation includes both offline and online material provided to support the dialogue, and would require a separate chapter to do justice to the subject. In many engineering projects it fails to get the attention it deserves. High-quality documentation of a project at several different levels appropriate to designers, maintenance staff, training staff and users is a key requirement for any interactive system. An interesting recent trend has been the establishment of documentation companies, to whom software houses subcontract the preparation of documentation for their systems. This approach has two particular advantages: first, the documentation is handled by expert writers, rather than software engineers; second, the documenters are independent from the software development team, and are thus much better able to view the product from the user's viewpoint.

Excellent overviews and guidelines on documentation are provided in Bailey (1982), Chapter 19, and in Shneiderman (1987), Chapter 9.

4.12 Case study: *NEWFOR* teletext subtitle generation system

4.12.1 Introduction

The provision of television subtitles for the hearing-impaired via teletext has been growing since the introduction of teletext in the mid-1970s. Subtitle preparation is a complex and time-consuming task which typically required 30–45 hours per captioned programme hour using first-generation teletext origination equipment. The NEWFOR subtitle generation system was developed following research into the display requirements for captions for the hearing-impaired, and analysis of the operational requirements of the caption preparation process. The system is now available commercially, has been sold to a number of broadcasting organizations throughout the world, and is used for all subtitling carried out by ORACLE Teletext for Independent Television in the UK. A full description of the development of the system described below will be found in Downton *et al.* (1985).

4.12.2 Specification of subtitle requirements

Experience gained from foreign-language film captioning is not directly relevant to captioning for the hearing-impaired, since foreign-language viewers can be assumed to have normal literacy skills, and to be able to use their hearing to identify speakers, mood, sound effects and other subsidiary audible information. The objective of the initial phase of this project was therefore to determine the most effective techniques for conveying soundtrack information to the deaf and hearing-impaired.

A wide range of television programmes were therefore subtitled onto videotape and demonstrated at deaf and hard-of-hearing clubs throughout Britain. Viewers were shown a variety of contrasting subtitle

We've a lot in common.
A lot to give each other.

Figure 4.15 A sample teletext subtitle (courtesy ORACLE Teletext Ltd)

display formats and techniques and asked to express preferences and to comment on and discuss the captions. Over a period of time a consensus set of display guidelines were derived (Baker, 1981), and these guidelines provided a specification for the required display formats and styles of the subtitle preparation system. The guidelines specified format and amount of text per subtitle, subtitle positioning, display options (flashing, foreground/background colour, etc.) and text presentation rate. For example, it was found that subtitles should normally be presented in white, double-height mixed-case characters, left-justified within a black box, as shown in Figure 4.15.

4.12.3 Task characteristics

Subtitles are generally prepared in advance of programme transmission and stored on floppy disk. Figure 4.16 shows the block diagram of a workstation used for this task, and Figure 4.17 illustrates the typical task sequence involved in subtitle preparation (derived from observation of work on first-generation teletext preparation systems and interviews with subtitlers).

4.12.4 Dialogue design

The basic design strategy was to share the tasks of subtitle preparation in an optimum way. In captioning, the skills of the human operator lie

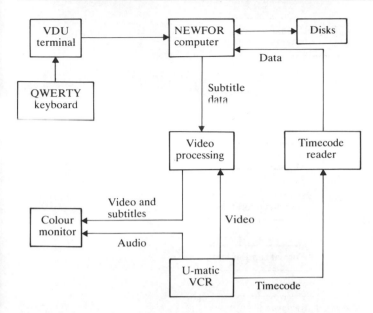

Figure 4.16   Block diagram of NEWFOR subtitling workstation

in linguistic intuition and creativity, understanding of the television programme, and the ability to control the captioning process and assess the results. The captioner may have no detailed knowledge of the technical aspects of teletext. The computer system is suited to handling routine tasks such as text and display format manipulation, data logging and storage and input/output control. Table 4.8 shows the final division of tasks between NEWFOR and the operator: in first-generation systems all of these tasks were explicitly carried out under operator control.

First-generation teletext origination systems mostly used a direct command input mode together with qualifying parameters as a method of control. To reduce the memory and training requirements, a hierarchical menu structure of commands, invoked by typing the first letter of the command, formed the basis of the dialogue with the NEWFOR system. The user's model of the captioning process was reinforced by grouping tasks into operating modes within the hierarchy which corresponded to the preparation strategies adopted by the captioners, as shown in Figure 4.18.

The menu acted as a prompt to the user initially, but as familiarity was gained, particular commands could be remembered by acronyms such as IOT (input offline titles), and the menu could then be bypassed. For novice users, a 'Help' option was available at every command level which gave further details of all commands available at that level.

A standard terminal display style was used throughout all NEWFOR

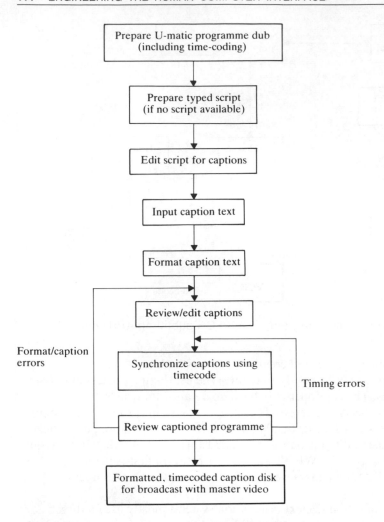

Figure 4.17 Example task sequence in caption preparation

modes, as shown in Figure 4.19. The upper 70 per cent of the screen provided a workspace for displaying current caption input or help information, while the remaining blocked-off display area provided various status displays. Subdivisions within the status block indicate current menu options, operational mode and non-textual characteristics of the current subtitle, such as time code, display time, foreground and background colour, and caption position.

4.12.5 System performance

Performance was assessed using two criteria: training time and productivity. In each case direct comparison could be made with

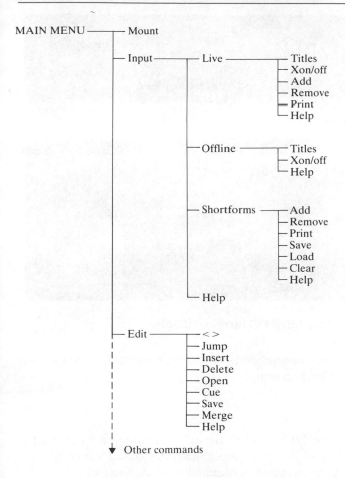

Figure 4.18   Part of hierarchical NEWFOR command menu

Table 4.8 Task division for NEWFOR subtitling system

Captioner	Computer
Text input	Text format (using geometric and linguistic criteria)
Position selection	Positioning of formatted text
Colour selection	Calculation of boxing outline
	Insertion of colour and boxing control characters
Synchronization	Calculation of on-air display time
	Storage of result

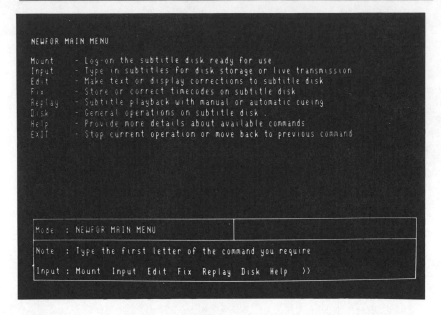

Figure 4.19 Sample NEWFOR terminal display

competing first-generation teletext origination systems used for the same process of subtitle preparation.

Training

Initial training to use NEWFOR in the offline input mode was a matter of only a few minutes, since little more than copy typing was required. By comparison, previous systems required an explicit knowledge of teletext display characteristics, including control characters, plus the capability to edit and position subtitle texts. Typically at least one week's training was required to achieve proficiency. A second, more extensive training period was required to achieve full working knowledge of all aspects of the system. This required about one month for NEWFOR, whereas competing systems typically required 2–3 months.

Productivity

The introduction of NEWFOR at ORACLE Teletext Ltd improved productivity from around 25–40 hours per captioned hour of programme material in 1984 to 10–15 hours per captioned hour in 1986. In addition to providing this substantial productivity gain, the offloading of many of the more mundane aspects of caption preparation meant that NEWFOR could also be used for pseudo-live captioning, which would have been quite impossible with first generation systems.

In fact, early versions of NEWFOR were used to subtitle a variety of important live events during its development phase, for example the royal wedding (1981), the papal visit (1982), the state opening of Parliament (1983) and the opening of the Thames Barrier (1984). A modified version of the system linked to a chord keyboard is currently used for live subtitling of the early-evening ITV and Channel 4 News.

References

Bailey, R. W. (1982) *Human Performance Engineering: A Guide for System Designers*, Prentice-Hall, Englewood Cliffs, NJ.

Baker, R. G. (1981) *Guidelines for Subtitling Television Programmes*, IBA/ITCA/Southampton University.

Card, S.K., T. P. Moran and A. Newell (1983) *The Psychology of Human–Computer Interaction*, Lawrence Erlbaum Associates, Hillsdale, NJ.

Daniels, G. S. and E. Churchill (1952) *The 'average man'?* WCRD-TN-53-7, Aero Medical Lab., Wright Air Development Center, Wright-Patterson AFB, Ohio.

Downton, A. C., A. D. Lambourne, R. W. King, R. G. Baker and A. F. Newell (1985) 'Optimal design of broadcast teletext caption preparation systems', *IEEE Transactions on Broadcasting*, **BC-31**, 3, 41–50.

Draper, S. W. (1984) 'The nature of expertise in Unix', in *Human Computer Interaction—INTERACT '84*, B. Shackel (ed.), 465–471.

Gaines, B. R. (1981) 'The technology of interaction—dialogue programming rules', *International Journal of Man–Machine Studies*, **14**, 133–150.

Hebditch, D. (1979) 'Design of dialogues for interactive commercial applications', in *Infotech State of the Art Report: Man/Computer Communication*, **2**, 173–192.

Holmes, J. N. (1988) *Speech Synthesis and Recognition*, Van Nostrand Reinhold, London.

Kidd, A. L. (1982) *Man-machine Dialogue Design*, Research study v.1, No.1, Martlesham Consultancy Services, British Telecom Research Laboratories, Ipswich.

Martin, J. (1973) *Design of Man-Computer Dialogues*, Section II, 87–131, Prentice-Hall, Englewood Cliffs, NJ.

Mayes, J. T., S. W. Draper, A. M. McGregor and K. Oatley (1988) 'Information flow in a user interface: the effect of experience and context on the recall of MacWrite screens', in *People and Computers IV: Proceedings of HCI'88*, 275–289.

Miller, R. B. (1968), 'Response times in man-computer conversational transactions', *Proceedings of the Spring Joint Computer Conference*, **46**, AFIPS Press, Montvale, NJ, 409–421.

Monk, A. (ed.) (1984) *Fundamentals of Human–Computer Interaction*, Academic Press, London.

Moran, T. P. (1981) 'The command language grammar, a representation for the user interface of interactive computer systems', *International Journal of Man–Machine Studies*, **15**, 3–50.

Reisner, P. (1981) 'Formal grammar and human factors design of an interactive graphics system', *IEEE Trans. on Software Engineering*, SE-7, 229–240.

Reisner, P. (1982) 'Further developments towards using formal grammar as a design tool', in *Proceedings of Human Factors in Computer Systems*, ACM, New York, 304–308.

Rosenburg, J. K. and T. P. Moran (1984) 'Generic commands', *Proceedings,*

INTERACT '84, 1st IFIP Conference on Human–Computer Interaction, 245–249.

Shneiderman, B. (1983) 'Direct manipulation: a step beyond programming language', *IEEE Computer*, August 1983, 57–69.

Shneiderman, B. (1987) *Designing the User Interface: Strategies for Effective Human–Computer Interaction*, Addison-Wesley, Reading, Mass.

Stewart, T. F. M. (1976) 'Display and software interface', *Applied Ergonomics*, **7**, 137–147.

Verplank, W. (1988) 'Tutorial notes', *HCI '88 4th Conference of the British Computer Society HCI Specialist Group*, Manchester, 5–9 September 1988.

Weil, A. T. (1965) 'Conversations with a mechanical psychiatrist', *Harvard Review*, **3**, 68–74.

Weizenbaum, J. (1966) 'ELIZA—a computer program for the study of natural language communications between man and machine', *Communications of the ACM*, **36**, January 1966.

5 Knowledge analysis of tasks: task analysis and specification for human–computer systems

PETER JOHNSON and HILARY JOHNSON

5.1 Introduction

Task analysis has emerged as an important aid to early design in human-computer interaction (HCI). It provides an information source from which design decisions can be made, and a basis for evaluating designed systems. Task analysis is an empirical method which can produce a complete and explicit model of tasks in the domain, and of how people carry out those tasks. It focuses design on users' tasks and goals, and the methods for achieving those goals, resulting in improved, more usable system designs.

Although task analysis is the investigation of what people do when they carry out tasks, a method of task analysis concerns more than simply observing how people perform tasks. An approach to task analysis involves a number of aspects:

- a theory of tasks;
- techniques of data collection;
- a method of analysing tasks;
- a representational framework for constructing task models.

In this chapter we describe a theory of task knowledge and then consider techniques of data collection, methods of analysing and generalizing from those data, and a framework for task modelling. The data collection, analysis/generification method, and framework for task modelling put forward are part of our approach to the knowledge analysis of tasks (KAT). This approach has been developed from earlier work on task analysis for knowledge descriptions (TAKD) (Johnson *et al.*, 1984; Diaper and Johnson, 1989). KAT has been described in Johnson, Johnson and Russell (1988) and is concerned with analysing and modelling the knowledge people possess and utilize in carrying out tasks. It is to be contrasted with task analysis techniques *not* concerned with knowledge, such as ability profiling (Fleishman and Quaintance, 1984), hierarchical task analysis (Annett & Duncan, 1967), and other techniques which have an evaluative role in assessing the complexity of task performance but have no explicit method of task analysis.

The work of Kieras and Polson (1985), Payne and Green (1986) and Card, Moran and Newell (1983) are good examples of current evaluative approaches in HCI which incorporate methods of predicting the difficulty of using an interactive computer system and assume some form of task model. Each of these approaches is capable, in varying degrees, of making recommendations about how proposed system designs can be used in terms of the ease with which users could perform given tasks. There are two important features to these approaches: first, they are not directly concerned with design generation and therefore assume both that decisions about what tasks the system should support have been made elsewhere and that one or more design solutions have already been proposed. Second, they focus on the evaluation and prediction of user performance and do not detail any particular method of task analysis. In contrast, TAKD and particularly KAT identify the knowledge requirements of tasks and are aimed at assisting in the generation of design solutions. KAT may, with further development, also form part of an evaluation methodology.

A similar intention underpins Olson's (1987) approach to a cognitive analysis of people's use of software. However, she does not attempt to identify the knowledge recruited or required by those tasks. Rather, she attaches a view of the cognitive demands of different types of tasks to a form of office system analysis. The cognitive demands considered by Olson are rather simplistic; tasks are described as requiring one or more of the following processes:

- transportation;
- transformation;
- algorithmic decision making;
- judgement-based decision making;
- information correlation;
- information analysis;
- communication;
- information creation.

She assumes that transportation, transformation, simple forms of correlating information, and algorithmic decision making are all suitable for computer support or automation since 'they require actions that are tedious for the human'. In contrast, judgemental decision making, more complex correlations of information, analysis of information, communication, and creation of information are 'to be allocated to human processing because they capitalize on human strengths.'

One interesting aspect of Olson's approach is her attempt to make explicit some of the criteria by which design decisions can be made from a task analysis which has been undertaken. This attempt is converse to the present and prevalent practice where design is not based on any rigorous task analysis and where decisions about allocation of function are made either from intuition or past, not always successful, design experience. By having explicit criteria (compare the design guidelines contained in Chapter 4 of this book) it is possible to check and evaluate the decisions against those criteria. With only intuition to guide the designer, it is often a matter of 'hoping for the best'.

Rather than leaving design for usability to luck and intuition, we want to identify methods of task analysis which can be used to inform the designer about those factors concerning users' tasks which can influence usability in advance of the designers making inappropriate design decisions. This chapter addresses this issue by describing the method of KAT and its underlying theoretical rationale, and makes recommendations as to how KAT could be used in the design process. The range and complexity of tasks with which we are concerned are not confined to simple keyboard tasks, and are not restricted to physical tasks. We are concerned with tasks as complex and rich as designing the room layout of houses, producing graphs, tables and multimedia documents, producing group documents, running meetings, controlling sophisticated building surveillance equipment, and fashion design. These are just some examples of the complex real-world tasks used as case studies during the development of the KAT methodology.

5.1.1 Theoretical basis for KAT

Before considering the methods for identifying knowledge in tasks, the theoretical underpinnings for three important aspects of KAT are discussed. These relate to the *representation of tasks as concepts, task structure*, and *action and object representativeness and centrality*.

Tasks as concepts

It is assumed that tasks are represented as concepts or general knowledge structures in long-term memory. This is akin to the theoretical position taken by Schank (1982) in assuming that knowledge of frequently occurring events is structured into meaningful units in memory. We have named these conceptual memory structures *task knowledge structures (TKS)*. Empirical support for our assumption can be found in the work of Galambos (1986). Galambos conducted a series of experiments which show that people recognize and use structures of events, such as the order, the sequence and the importance of activities within the event sequence to understand, explain and make predictions about these events. Further support for our view that task knowledge is represented in memory comes from the work of Graesser and Clark (1985), in which general knowledge structures, goals to causal and enabling states, plans for achieving goals, intermediate states and alternative solutions or paths are all assumed to be represented in a conceptual knowledge structure which is used to interpret events.

A TKS is a summary representation of the different types of knowledge which are recruited and activated in association with task performance. A TKS is related to other TKSs by a number of possible relations; among them *within-* and *between-role* relations. Within-role relations are one form of relation between TKSs in association with a given role. Those tasks which are related because they are performed by the same role will have the within-role relation property associating their respective TKSs. A second form of relation between TKSs is in terms of the similarity between tasks across roles. Each task may be performed differently in one or other respect in the context of a given role. However, a person assuming many roles would have a knowledge structure for each task within a role and also knowledge, not necessarily explicit, of the relations between these tasks across or between different roles.

Task knowledge structures contain *goal-oriented* and *taxonomic* substructures. Goal-oriented substructures represent the goals, plans and procedures for carrying out the task. The taxonomic substructure contains the action–object pairings, their respective properties or features and their role relation links. Further details, and an example of task knowledge structures, are provided later in Section 5.4 on task modelling.

Structure in tasks

Tasks would be unstructured if within a domain all possible components of tasks could co-occur with equal probability combined with all other possible components of tasks. This is obviously not the case; task components or behaviours do not occur independently of one another. Some pairs or even n-tuples of task components are quite probable, whereas others are improbable; some groupings of components while being logically possible may never occur in reality. Furthermore, within tasks some task components are naturally carried out together, precede, follow on from, or prime one another. Components of tasks are generally carried out according to some feasible temporal ordering, designated by a plan. For example, a builder who is building a house cannot begin to build until the bricks have arrived. An architect designing the layout of a house cannot design the upstairs layout until she or he knows how many bedrooms are required. The same architect might have to simultaneously consider certain related task components. For instance, in designing a bathroom layout, the respective position of the bath is considered at the same time as the positions of the wash-hand basin and w.c.

We assume that for the purposes of carrying out tasks a person's knowledge is structured in a similar manner to the structure of tasks reflected in task performance. We represent this structure in terms of task knowledge structures (TKS).

Representativeness and centrality

People's task knowledge includes information about objects, both physical and informational, and their associated actions. Objects and actions differ in how central and representative (or typical) they are. Representativeness (or typicality) refers to how representative an object is to a class of objects. For example, a particular chair may be a good representative instance of 'chairs'. One way to think of representativeness is as a 'good/bad example'. Thus, any particular chair may be a good or bad example of the general class of 'chairs'. Centrality refers to the centralness or importance of the object to the task. This argument is similar to that put forward by Rosch (1985) and colleagues (Rosch et al., 1976) to describe the relations between objects and their categorical representation in memory. Empirical psychological evidence for the centrality of the procedures and action/object representativeness in task behaviour has been obtained by Leddo and Abelson (1986), who found that for tasks such as borrowing a book from a library there were particular task segments which were more central to, and more representative of, going to the library than other segments.

Procedures, subgoals and plans differ in representativeness and centrality to the task by virtue of the typicality or centrality of the actions and objects of which they are composed. For instance, in a similar way to arguing that a 'robin' is a representative instance of the essence of the 'bird' category, so the procedure 'drawing house sketches' might be held to be more representative of an architectural task than 'painting country scenes', since 'drawing' is a more representative action. Both procedures may in some instances be used in the course of achieving the goal of designing a house. In a similar way some procedures may be more central to the task than others. For example, in a tea-making task a vessel in which the water and tea can be combined is considered to be a central object to the task and the action of 'brewing' or 'combining' the tea and water is also central (without it tea cannot be made). However, it does not matter if this vessel is the most typical instance of its class in the task-domain, namely a teapot, or alternatively an atypical instance such as an empty paint can (as has sometimes been used under extreme circumstances). Consequently, a procedure such as 'brewing the tea in the teapot' is central since it contains a central action and a central object. The distinction between centrality and representativeness is thus that central task elements are considered to be necessary and enable the task goal to be achieved, while representative task elements are the instances from the class of the domain which people most readily or typically associate with a given task.

5.1.2 Identifying knowledge

Having discussed the theoretical assumptions contained in task knowledge structures, it is now possible to consider which aspects of task knowledge should be identified by a task analysis. Different tasks may require particular collections of knowledge, and within a single task a variety of types of knowledge will be required for successful task execution. Therefore, we assume that there are subsets of knowledge which make up a person's total task knowledge.

In identifying the knowledge people utilize in successful task completion, the analyst first needs to identify the person's *goals, subgoals* and *subtasks*; in other words, how the person conceptualizes the *goal structure* of the task. Second, it is necessary to consider the ordering in which the subtasks are carried out: this is determined by the *task plan*. Third, the different *task strategies* (a strategy is a particular set of procedures) must be identified along with the circumstances under which those strategies are employed. Fourth, it is necessary to identify the *procedures* which contain the objects involved in the task and the actions which are associated with them: these are the *action/object groupings*. Finally, the *task objects and task actions* are categorically structured and this structure is a further important aspect of task knowledge which must be identified.

This introductory section has provided a brief summary of the theoretical assumptions from which our approach to task analysis has been derived. The next section describes a methodology for identifying the task knowledge components important for task analysis.

5.2 Knowledge analysis of tasks: KAT methodology (part 1)

This section presents in detail the methods of analysis associated with KAT. There are three parts to the KAT method. First, there are techniques for identifying and collecting data about the knowledge people utilize in performing tasks. Second, there are techniques for identifying the representativeness of a particular task knowledge component and establishing generic task knowledge. This can then be used in the third part of the task analysis method, namely the task knowledge structure (TKS) modelling process. The methodology does not address the issue of definition of the task domain or how to select sample tasks within a chosen domain. However, in Section 5.7 KAT is related to current practices in system design where the selection of tasks from task domains is considered.

5.2.1 Data collection: applying knowledge-gathering techniques to task analysis

This section is divided into two parts: the first part is concerned with general guidelines for task analysis, and the second provides guidelines for using the various techniques. The next section is concerned with guidelines for identifying task knowledge elements in KAT.

General guidelines for task analysis

Task analysis essentially involves *obtaining different types of information about a task or tasks from different sources using appropriate methods*. Task analysis is an iterative process where the analyst is constantly seeking to identify new information, confirm existing information and reject false information. These general rules of thumb are further qualified by four general guidelines:

1   identify the purpose of the analysis;

2   check the analysis with the task performer(s);

3   analyse more than one person and one task; and

4   make use of more than one technique for gathering knowledge.

Knowledge-gathering techniques

1   *Structured interviews and questionnaires*   Interviews and questionnaries are suitable for extracting rules, general principles behind task execution, background information covering low-probability events and the reasons underlying behaviour. Interviews may take less time to carry out than other techniques but they rarely provide detailed knowledge descriptions, and should be supplemented with direct or indirect observation of the task performance of a number of individuals. Interviews are a useful technique for providing an initial view of the task or set of tasks in the domain.

2   *Observational techniques*   These are particularly appropriate for providing corroborating evidence and gathering more detailed knowledge, when knowledge is context-bound and when the task involves many individual steps. However, these techniques are

time-consuming, cannot be used in isolation and require inference on the part of the analyst to identify the structure of the task and certain types of objects and actions. *Direct observational techniques*, for example looking over the person's shoulder, are intrusive and may seriously influence the person's behaviour. *Indirect observation*, for example video recording, is less intrusive but requires time and effort in setting up and analysis.

3 *Concurrent and retrospective protocols*   Protocols are verbal reports given by the person performing the task: they can be either concurrent with the task performance, or retrospective. Protocols provide detailed information on many aspects of a task, including task goals, task plans, procedures, actions and objects. However, protocols require some inference on the part of the analyst, the responses must be carefully coded and the enterprise is time-consuming. Furthermore, it is not always wise to rely solely on verbal reports since people are not always able to give accurate, precise or reliable verbal reports about their own behaviour. In *concurrent protocols (CPs)* subjects report what they are doing while they are doing it. CPs are appropriate when there is insufficient time to carry out retrospective protocols and when the analyst is interested in what a subject is doing at a given time. It should be noted that CPs may interfere with normal task behaviour in a serious and not always obvious way. In *retrospective protocols (RPs)* the subject is required to generate a durable memory trace while completing the task, and then the contents of the trace are verbally reported after the task has been completed. A retrospective protocol could be given while the task performer observes his or her own task performance, for example, using a video recording. RP reports are appropriate when the analyst requires more reliable information than is available through CP and when the subject can be called back to go over the task recording. Additionally, RPs are appropriate when the analyst is concerned with the reasons for and explanations of any behaviour, cognitive aspects of tasks such as planning knowledge, and the feelings and emotions the person entertains about the task. Both concurrent and retrospective protocols are normally collected along with direct or indirect observations.

4 *Experimental techniques*   Below follows a summary of several experimental techniques which may be employed in identifying the similarity of task components, for example the actions and objects, and the features or attributes of those actions and objects. All the techniques described in this section normally require the analyst already to have obtained detailed background information through completed interviews or analysed protocols.
(a) *Kelly's repertory grid* (adapted from Kelly, 1955)   The task

analyst must have already identified many or all of the components of knowledge associated with a task or set of tasks. The technique involves, first, selecting a given set of objects (or other task components, e.g., procedures) and then presenting these to the subject in groups of three. The subject is then asked in what way(s) any two of them are alike and different from the third. This grouping and separating process is repeated until all the objects have been presented to the subject. The result is a grouping of similar objects or other components which are assumed to share common attributes. One problem with this technique is that the analyst has to be very careful in choosing which three components are presented at any one time since the contrasting set can have a strong influence on any comparison or grouping. There is also a possibility of forcing a classification outcome which is arbitary, an artefact of the selection procedure, and not representative of the actual relationships between knowledge components in the task domain.

(b) *Card sorting* (adapted from Rosch, 1978)   In this technique the analyst is concerned with the similarity of task components. The task components can be objects, actions, procedures, etc. The procedure of this technique is somewhat similar to that of Kelly's repertory grid (above). Task components are entered on cards, one card for each component, and the subject is instructed to group 'similar components', or 'components which are the same kind of thing'. Rosch (1978) and other researchers generally instruct subjects to 'put together the things that go together'. The result of this technique, as with Kelly's repertory grid, is a structuring of similar components which are assumed to share common attributes. Unlike Kelly's approach, card sorting is much less likely to be subjected to experimenter bias.

(c) *Rating scales*   Rating scales can be useful in identifying representativeness. For example, the name of each object, or other task component, is entered on a separate card and subjects are instructed to judge the given object for its representativeness and/or centrality to the task on an appropriate scale, for example with the highest number of the scale representing greater representativeness or centrality. An alternative to this procedure is to instruct the subjects to sort the cards into an order of relative representativeness and/or centrality to the task.

(d) *Frequency counts*   With frequency counts the analyst must note on how many occasions a task knowledge component is either used or referred to in a task or across tasks. The assumption is that a knowledge component which is more central and/or representative will have a higher frequency score than a component of lesser centrality or representativeness. Frequency counts provide an index which can be used to compare individual differences across different people performing the same task, and also across tasks. Such comparisons provide some indication of differences in task organization and task plans across individuals. One problem with this technique is that it is likely to be very time-consuming and exacting for the analyst. Furthermore, frequency is only one criterion of centrality, and some task knowledge components may be infrequently used or mentioned but central to task performance in certain contexts.

5 *Other useful techniques*   Other techniques which might be used in addition to, or incorporated into, the above are:
   (a) knowledge competitions;
   (b) group discussions;
   (c) multi-choice questions;
   (d) task carried out by the analyst with instruction;
   (e) observation with a knowledgeable person providing the commentary;
   (f) asking for sample outputs',
   (g) cooperating subjects (two or more subjects working in groups).

For further details on these techniques see Welbank (1983).

5.2.2 Identifying knowledge components in KAT

KAT is concerned with identifying a person's task knowledge in terms of actions and objects, and the structure of those objects, procedures, the task plan, task goals and subgoals. The techniques considered in Section 5.2.1 above are now classified according to which aspects of knowledge they elicit most effectively.

Identifying objects and actions

Objects (and their associated actions) used in carrying out the task can be identified from one or more of the following techniques:

1   Selecting objects and the actions associated with them from textbooks, a tutorial session, pilot study or by the analyst herself carrying out the task.

2   Questionning the task performer in a structured interview about the actions and objects, and then listing all the relevant nouns and verbs produced by the person in answering the questions.

3   Asking the task performer to list all the objects they can think of which are involved in the task, and the actions carried out on them.

4   Directly or indirectly observing the person carrying out the task, carefully noting what objects they manipulate and in what ways.

5   Noting all the objects and actions mentioned by the person in either concurrent or retrospective protocols.

Identifying planning and procedural knowledge

This section summarizes techniques for identifying a person's knowledge of the task plan, the sequence of carrying out routine procedures, and strategies used in the task.

1   *Asking specific questions in the structured interview*   This involves asking a person how she or he plans the task, if the same plan is used for any other task, and identifying any modifications required to the plan. It is useful to ask specific questions of the sort, 'What do you do if', for example, 'X goes wrong or fails?' The analyst should also ask whether any particular strategies or procedures exist for carrying out some part of the task, and if so how they are used, and why they are there. A further question to ask is what indicates the end of one part of the task, and what triggers the start of another procedure.

2   *Protocols and observation*   This involves initially having some knowledge of the task so that the ending of one phase or part of the task and the starting of another can be easily identified. A schema for recording and interpreting the data is required.

3   *Card sorting*   This technique identifies the sequence of carrying out routine procedures and involves putting known task procedures on individual cards, which the person then sorts into an appropriate order for task execution. The results are then verified with other task performers.

Identifying subgoals and subtasks

The identification of goals, subgoals and subtasks can be obtained by one, a selection of, or all the following four techniques:

1   Asking specific questions in an interview about what are the goals and subgoals of the task.

2   Using a textbook, instruction manual, or any other available written material, which decomposes the task into goals and subgoals.

3   Asking or aiding the person to construct a tree, flow or hierarchical diagram of connected goals and subgoals of the task, making a specific requirement that they label different parts of the task.

4   Identifying different phases of the task either from observations, concurrent or retrospective protocols. When using observations a phase or part of the task may be identified by pauses. In concurrent or retrospective protocols, it is important to make a note of such statements as, 'Now, I intend/want to . . .', etc. The analyst should be sure which referents belong to 'this', 'that', 'it', etc. The task goal

structure can and should be verified by checking it against the goal structure provided by another person.

In this section we have discussed various techniques for collecting task analysis data. Together these techniques form part of the KAT methodology. The next section is concerned with analysis and generalization of the collected data.

5.3 Identifying representative, central and generic properties of tasks: KAT methodology (part 2)

This section is concerned with identifying representative, central and generic properties of tasks within a given domain or across domains. Some task components are more representative/typical of a task than are others. Central task components are those necessary to successful task execution: without these central components the task goal will fail to be achieved.

Generic task components, on the other hand, are those common across a number of task performers. The term 'generic' in the context of KAT relates to general rather than specific elements of tasks identified by the analyst. The essential function of identifying generic task components is to reduce variation both across subjects, across the technology and across instances of similar tasks in the domain(s).

5.3.1 Representativeness and centrality

Identifying representativeness and centrality

Task knowledge components can be structured in terms of their representativeness and centrality to the task, using one or more of the following methods:

1 *Frequency*   Count the frequency of times a particular task component is referred to, in either interviews or protocols. The assumption here is that the more representative/typical components will be the most frequently referred to.

2 *Ratings*   The analyst may use rating scales where the name of each task knowledge component is presented on a separate card or other medium, and the person asked to judge the relative representativeness/typicality or centrality of each component on a scale of, for example, 1 to 5.

3 *Ordering*   Presenting task components on cards as in (2), the subject is required to sort the cards into an order of increasing representativeness or centrality of the task.

4 *Recall* The analyst instructs the person to recall from memory all the task components. The order in which they are listed may reflect the order of centrality of each component within the task. The resulting lists recalled (one from each person) can then be correlated to determine the degree of agreement of task component centrality across the sample population.

5.3.2 A method of generification

A method of generification must be capable of identifying generic actions, objects, plans and procedures. Generification is the process of abstracting from instances of tasks, people and technology and thereby reducing the variance in task performance.

Generic actions and objects

The first step in identifying generic actions and objects is for the analyst to construct two separate lists, one for the actions and one for the objects that have been manipulated, mentioned or referred to in some way by the task performer(s). These lists will contain disparate (and often repetitive) information from each task performer over one or a range of tasks.

For example, in the task analysis of an architectural task, namely 'designing the room layout of houses', lists containing all the actions and objects suggested by two different architects were obtained. In many cases the same actions and objects were manipulated or referred to on both lists. Examples of the objects were *plans, symbols, windows, pipes, appliances, doors, pens, rulers*; examples of the actions were *draw, rehang, check, reposition*, etc.

The second step is to reduce the lists generated above to comprehensive and non-repetitive lists with each action and object appearing once only. However, the original lists are also retained, as they provide a measure of frequency of the respective objects and actions in the task and hence may be of use in the identification of representative actions and objects.

The third step is to choose generic actions and objects and is achieved in one of two ways. The first method is to assume a critical value or threshold of frequency across subjects and tasks. The analyst must decide at what level the frequency threshold is to be set in order to judge if something is or is not generic. (Caution must be taken in setting this level as some or possibly all the objects and actions may already be generic by virtue of being identified.) For example, it may be decided to treat an item as generic if it is referred to by two or more task performers. If this yields an unmanageable (i.e., too large) list of generic actions and objects then the threshold may be raised. Setting the threshold relies to some extent on the analyst's intuition and experience;

however, the analyst can systematically experiment with different threshold values. Threshold setting is an iterative process. Essentially, the essence of the approach is to treat frequency across people and tasks as an indicator of generic terms.

Alternatively, the generic actions and objects can be selected by grouping like terms. The assumption here is that the comprehensive and non-repetitive lists contain all actions and objects involved in the task and that these are then grouped. Grouping all like terms involves the following:

1　The analyst(s) relying on intuition and using an iterative procedure to associate a particular term with other similar terms. Similarity is determined by attempting to re-express the original task description in terms of the alternative or target term. If the alternative term was 'adequate' then the two are said to be similar.

2　Grouping by independent judges. The analyst asks one or more judges to sort objects and actions into groups with the instruction to 'group together the actions (objects) which go together, or are the same kind of action (object)'. The results of each judge's sorting can then be correlated to identify the agreed, generic task components.

After the groupings have been produced, the next step is to identify a generic label or term which might cover all the individual elements in a particular set. These labels then represent the generic task elements.

In the architectural task 'designing the room layout of houses', we used the threshold level method to identify generic actions and objects. This procedure was used since there was a time constraint and generally it is quicker to use a threshold value than to group like terms. By using this method we identified many generic actions (such as 'draw') and objects (such as 'plans'). The 'grouping like terms' procedure has advantages over the threshold method since it provides an opportunity for the task performer to judge whether the generic actions and objects identified are indeed generic. If the threshold method is used then some checking of generic elements can be achieved by involving the task performers in a validation process.

The fourth step is the validation of the generic elements. To validate the generic elements, all the actions and objects are listed separately from the generic labels. The task performers are then instructed to identify to which generic group each action or object belongs. If the action or object is not adequately covered by a generic title then the task performer is free to supply an alternative group title.

Generic procedures, plans and goal structure

Procedures, plans, goals and subgoals are considered together here. One obvious way in which procedures, plans, goals and subgoals differ from generic actions and generic objects is in terms of the number of alternative choices available to the person. For example, there may be a large number of objects and actions which have to be manipulated in performing a task. However, there are likely to be a smaller number of alternative plans involved in carrying out a task depending on circumstantial constraints and very few alternative task goals and subgoals. Task plans have generic features which are always present in carrying out a particular task, but there will also be specific features which make the plan and the ordering of procedures flexible and which depend on differing circumstances and contexts. The procedure for identifying generic procedures, plans, goals and subgoals is different from that of the identification of generic actions and objects, and consists of the following four stages:

1   List all the components and sequence-related details of plans, procedures, goals and subgoals which result from carrying out the identification procedures in Section 5.2.2 ('identifying planning and procedural knowledge', and 'identifying subgoals and subtasks') above.

2   Verify these details with a number of task performers by asking if the procedures are appropriate and if they are in the correct sequential order, or alternatively by having activities written individually on cards that task performers must sort into an appropriate order for carrying out the task.

3   Include in the generic description all generic procedures, provided by a chosen number of task performers and instances of the same tasks.

4   Verify this generic description with a sample of task performers by asking if this is how the task is usually carried out and by noting under which circumstances exceptions are appropriate.

5.4 Task modelling: KAT methodology (part 3)

5.4.1 Constructing task models

A task model is a model of the user's knowledge of a task. The aim of task analysis is to identify the functional attributes of a person's task knowledge (see Johnson *et al.*, 1988). In this section we provide a methodology to aid the analyst in constructing task models.

We demonstrate the task-modelling method here by constructing a model in the domain of the architectural task referred to previously. Four stages have been identified in the construction of a task model. These are as follows:

- construction of a summary task knowledge structure (TKS);

- construction of goal-oriented substructure;

- task procedures;

- construction of a taxonomic substructure from the generic task actions and objects.

Construction of a summary task knowledge structure (TKS)

In this, the first stage in task modelling, we assume that the analyst has identified the task(s) to be analysed, and then collected the appropriate data using the procedures outlined earlier in Section 5.1. These data should then have been subjected to a generification analysis by which common task knowledge components were identified (see section 5.2). These common task knowledge components then make up a subpart of the TKS.

A TKS includes a summary of all the knowledge a person possesses about a task and gives the task analyst the opportunity to label the identified knowledge. One significant advantage of modelling knowledge in this way is that links to knowledge required by similar tasks can be made. Through making such links commonalities between task knowledge may be identified, either by within-role relations or alternatively by identifying common task elements, for example objects, actions and/or plans. For example, a computer system and its user interface might be required to support several types of tasks both within and between roles. The summary TKS identifies what the common properties of knowledge across a variety of tasks are, and thus what the common requirements of the system might be.

Within a summary TKS there are goal-oriented and taxonomic substructures and procedures. The next section describes the construction and properties of goal-oriented substructures. Figure 5.1 is a summary TKS for the architectural task 'design the room layout of a house'.

Construction of a goal-oriented substructure

Planning activity involves satisfying a set of goals and subgoals by a prespecified sequence of procedures of actions upon objects. Therefore, plans are inherent in goal-oriented substructures. A goal-oriented substructure can be represented by a network of structured goal nodes which direct sequences of events which unfold over time, and eventually satisfy subgoal nodes. Goal nodes can vary in hierarchical level. An assumption made here is that goals and subgoals can be represented by nodes with links between them. Nodes can be treated as conditions, as states or as desired states (subgoals). Subgoals can also be hetirarchically and concurrently related to each other.

The goal-oriented substructure 'calls up' appropriate knowledge from

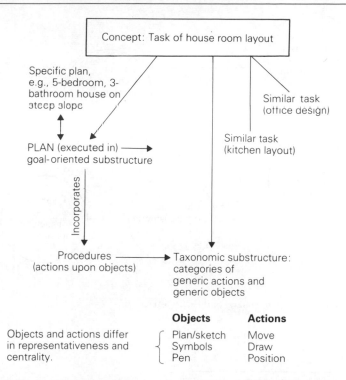

Figure 5.1 Task knowledge structure for the 'design the house room layout' task

the taxonomic substructure by the use of procedures. Associated with subtasks are sets of procedures which have to be executed in order to achieve subgoals directly or indirectly. It should be noted that any subgoal may give rise to further planning activity and subsequent subgoals and thus be indirectly related to a procedure set. Figure 5.2 is a subpart of a goal-oriented substructure for the room layout task.

Task procedures

Task procedures define the ordering of action object combinations in the execution of a given subgoal. The procedure contains sequence, iteration, and other control information which affects the execution of a subgoal. Task procedures are collected together in a procedure set (rather like a macro procedure). Task procedures are executable behaviours. The procedures can be modelled by production rules, by psuedocode or alternatively by frame-based representations as in Johnson *et al.* (1988) and Keane and Johnson (1987). Each task plan ultimately requires an appropriate procedure set before it can be realized in actual behaviour. Task procedures are the process by which the taxonomic substructure is activated.

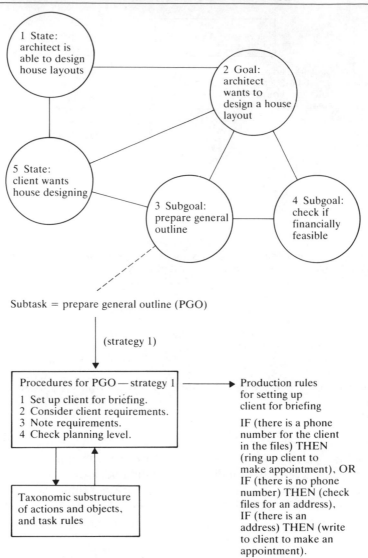

Figure 5:2 Subpart of a goal-oriented substructure of the architectural task

Not only may the task be decomposed in different ways; there may also be a choice between a number of different strategies which are context-dependent competing sets of procedures. One set of procedures may be more appropriate than other sets. Strategy appropriateness will be affected by contextual information and the circumstances under which the task is to be executed. Single procedures in a given strategy may differ in how central they are to the task as a whole. Some procedures will be so central to the task that a failure to execute will result in the task being unsuccessful.

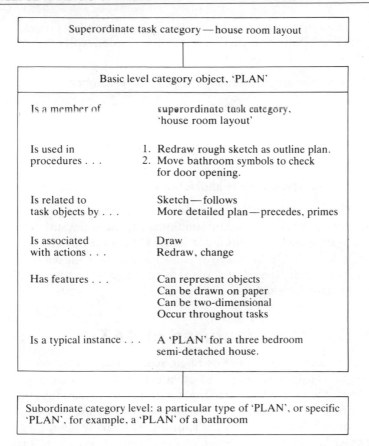

Figure 5.3 Taxonomic substructure for the architectural task illustrating the basic-level object 'PLAN', and its relations to the superordinate category levels

Construction of a taxonomic substructure

The taxonomic substructure contains knowledge about generic actions and objects and the relationships between them. The taxonomic substructure has three levels of abstraction (see Rosch *et al.*, 1976) but is not a static hierarchy.

The top level of the taxonomic substructure is the superordinate task category. In Figure 5.3 the superordinate category for the architectural example is 'house room layout'. The basic level of the taxonomic substructure contains the objects and their associated actions which constitute the superordinate task category. The basic level task category represents knowledge including the following:

- in which task procedures a category member is used;
- which other task objects a category member is related to, and what

that relationship is (i.e., whether the category member primes, precedes, follows or is carried out in conjunction with other task objects);

● which actions are associated with a category member;

● what features or properties a category member possesses;

● the usual circumstances under which a particular category member occurs (for example, whereabouts in the task the category member is manipulated);

● central and typical objects and actions.

Other features of knowledge may also be included at the basic level.

The bottom level of the taxonomic substructure is the subordinate task category which contains a particular type of the object represented at the basic level. The hierarchy is shown in Figure 5.3 using the example of a 'plan' (i.e., sketch plan) as the basic level category object from the architectural domain task.

5.5 Summary features of KAT

The KAT methodology presented here relies on category theory, general knowledge structures and other aspects of cognitive psychology to provide the rationale for making design recommendations and improving design usability. We believe that existing user knowledge will be maximized, leading to quicker learning, potentially fewer errors and easier task execution if the design of the system represents the task components which have been argued as forming a part of a TKS model. If representation of all task components is not possible then the most representative and central actions and objects which have been identified should be represented. A prediction here is that the usability of the system will decrease proportionally to the number of representative and/or central objects or actions not represented to the user at the interface.

Moreover, the user interface design should support the usual sequence for carrying out the task(s) as a default while allowing sequential flexibility by supporting the different, previously identified strategies, which are employed by task performers in usual circumstances of task execution.

5.6 Making design recommendations from KAT and TKSs

The TKS model contains useful information which can be used to influence the design of a computer system. Consider the design of a computer-based messaging system to support the common task of 'arranging a meeting'. This is a task common to architects, managers, secretaries and other job-roles. The manner in which the TKS model may influence design relies upon the overriding assumption that a computer system will be easier to use if the users are able to transfer some of their existing task knowledge to the newly created environment. This assumption underpins the use of metaphors such as 'desktops' or 'forms', in which the system design attempts to retain some identifiable links with a user's assumed extant knowledge about real desktops and paper-based forms.

However, it is clear that a metaphor is only one mechanism by which transfer of extant knowledge might be facilitated; furthermore, the way in which a metaphor might function is itself the subject of some debate. Moreover, not all aspects of a person's extant knowledge will be relevant or transferable to the new environment. For example, the knowledge of how to dial and use a telephone may have little relevance in supporting communication by a textual computer-based messaging system. Nevertheless, the knowledge a person utilizes in asking questions, making requests, or providing answers would be applicable to both the old and new environments for communication and could (should) be supported in the new environment.

5.6.1 The TKS design support hierarchy

The TKS model identifies the conceptual knowledge structures which a person is assumed to access when carrying out any task. Having constructed a TKS model the analyst has identified a number of important properties of user's task knowledge of benefit to the system designer. At the highest level the TKS shows the relations between tasks and roles. This information provides the designer with a view as to the different kinds of tasks the system will support by virtue of common task/role properties, and also how different roles might expect to have access to the same task functions and to those task functions specific to particular roles. Task role information is also of use to designers who may be concerned with configuring a system to suit the needs of a particular organization, since it shows the task/role match of the organization.

The next level of the TKS represents an overall summary of the plan, the procedures, and the objects and actions people associate with a particular task. This information may be of interest to the designer in so much as it provides an overview of particular contexts in which specific procedures might be used. It could also be used to provide the user with a summary representation of how the designer expects a task to be carried out.

At the next level of representation the TKS model identifies a person's knowledge about the identified goal of the task and the plans they construct for achieving the goal and subsequent subgoals. The procedures represented at this level of the TKS provide a description of the rules task performers would expect to follow, and the alternative procedures they would follow under particular conditions. A task performer's plan at this level of representation is related to our notion of task structuring where certain task components precede, prime or follow one another. Task structuring determines the sequence or ordering of procedures necessary for successful task execution. This information provides the system designer with a view as to how people structure their tasks under certain circumstances: it also allows the system designer to decide how the user will expect to make use of the objects and actions (functions) and identifies the most frequent or preferred procedure for achieving a subgoal. This information can be used to set up default modes of operation in the program design.

Finally, at the object and action level, the taxonomic substructure identifies the representative actions and objects within the domain and the features of those task elements. The work on concept and object knowledge of Rosch and her colleagues (Rosch *et al.*, 1976) leads to the suggestion that if the designer chooses to support this task and provide a visible representation of the objects and the actions that can be carried out on those objects, then the taxonomic substructure provides an informative and detailed description of the features a person will expect to associate with those objects. Additionally, the degree of representativeness of task objects and/or actions, and the centrality of the procedures containing those components (actions and objects), provides the designer with an indication of which are deemed to be typical and necessary for successful task completion. The consequences of overlooking both central and representative task components in system and user-interface design are likely to have severe consequences for the ultimate usability of the system.

5.6.2 Empirical support for TKSs

Empirical evidence for the improvement in usability afforded by modelling TKSs is provided by Davis (1988) in a pilot study of graph and table drawing. The first part of the study identified representative objects and actions, central procedures and sequencing of task procedures for the above 2 tasks across a population of 12 subjects. An experiment was then carried out in which 3 further groups of subjects were required to undertake graph and table drawing tasks using 1 of 3 different interfaces with the same underlying functions.

One interface was structured so that it positively supported representative and central task components, and task sequencing identified by the TKS modelling stage. The second interface was unstructured; representative and central task components were supported but representative objects were not identified with their associated actions and the sequencing of task procedures was not supported. A further control group had an interface which contained neither central nor representative task components, and which had no explicit task structure.

The results of the pilot study showed that subjects found the structured interface easier to use, and also this interface had a higher preference value from subjects. Additionally, the structured interface resulted in quicker task execution, and the resulting graph and table drawings were better quality in that they were more complete. Also, the unstructured but central and representative interface design produced better performance than the control group interface, but less than the structured interface group. The findings thus support the theoretical view that TKSs provide important information about users which can be used to design improved user interfaces.

5.7 Relating KAT to design practices

Software systems design occurs in many different ways, resulting in a certain reluctance on the part of academics and industrialists alike to speak of an ideal design process. However, it is becoming increasingly clear that task analysis has a part to play in current and future design practices.

In this section, the contribution KAT might make to current design practices is briefly considered. It is not, however, the intention to argue for the use of KAT in specific design methodologies, structured or otherwise, since KAT is potentially appropriate to many current design methodologies and practices.

The traditional system development life cycle described in Chapter 1 typically involves the following stages. First, a feasibility study is carried out to establish whether it would be possible to build a system to support users' tasks, and if there is a market for such a product. After the feasibility study has been completed, a requirements specification would be prepared, followed by the design of the system. The system design, determined by the nature and the content of the requirements set out in the requirements definition, is then implemented, the implementation is tested and the system subsequently released. After a period of time in use by the customer the system is updated and maintained.

We can envisage a scenario where task knowledge requirements identified by KAT could augment existing user requirements in the software (and/or hardware) design life cycle. First, we would expect user requirements to be taken into account in any feasibility study. This would involve a small-scale task analysis. Using KAT at this stage identifies commonalities across tasks through within-role relations and also by the identification of generic task elements. At the requirements definition stage a full-scale task analysis using the KAT methodology would be carried out to establish and document user task requirements in terms of users' plans, goals, subgoals, strategies, procedures and representative and central actions and objects.

The results of a TKS model can be easily decomposed into general, specific and interface design models, as shown by Johnson *et al.*, (1988), where the KAT methodology was used to produce frame-based representations of a messaging system, the virtual interface to that system and the dialogue structure.

KAT may also play a role in usability and learnability evaluation, before and/or after the construction of a prototype or full implementation. The use of KAT in evaluation relates to whether aspects of a person's task knowledge, identified by KAT, have been carried over into the designed, prototyped or fully implemented system. This specifically involves finding out whether all appropriate tasks have been supported; whether generic task elements have been taken into account; whether representative and central task actions and objects have been represented; whether sequencing of task procedures have been supported rather than violated; and finally, whether defaults have been correctly specified and supported.

If these factors are taken into account the user will be expected to be in a position to transfer appropriate extant knowledge to the newly created environment and as a result the system designed will be easier to use and learn. Furthermore, predictions can be made as to where this transfer will be unsupported, whether interference is likely to occur, and in which areas training might be necessary.

5.8 Conclusions

In this chapter we have described a theory and method of modelling the knowledge people possess about tasks and roles in a given domain, known as knowledge analysis of tasks (KAT). The information contained within the task models constructed within the KAT methodology is very rich and can be used as an information source to which designers can be given access; it prevents the designer having to rely on his or her own intuitions about peoples' task knowledge. Empirical evidence suggests that the TKS models identify important features of knowledge that can influence the usability of systems when the design recommendations arising from a TKS are followed. Finally, the contribution made by KAT and TKS models to current design practices is considered.

Acknowledgement

The research described in this chapter was developed as part of an ICL-funded University Research Contract research project on 'The development of task analysis as a design tool'.

References

Annett, J. and K. D. Duncan (1967) 'Task analysis and training design', *Journal of Occupational Psychology*, **41**, 211–221.

Card, S. K., T. P. Moran and A. Newell (1983) '*The Psychology of Human Computer Interaction*', Lawrence Erlbaum Associates, Hillsdale, New Jersey.

Davis, S. (1988) 'Knowledge structures in the human computer interface'. Unpublished manuscript, Queen Mary College, University of London.

Diaper, D. and P. Johnson (1989) 'Task analysis for knowledge descriptions: theory and application in training', in *Cognitive Ergonomics*, J. B. Long and A. Whitefield (eds), Cambridge University Press, Cambridge.

Fleishman E. A. and M. K. Quaintance (1984). *Taxonomies of Human Performance*, Academic Press, New York.

Galambos, J. A. (1986) 'Knowledge structures for common activities', in *Knowledge Structures*, J. A. Galambos, R. P. Abelson and J. B. Black (eds), Lawrence Erlbaum Associates, Hillsdale, NJ.

Graesser, A. C. and L. F. Clark (1985) *Structures and Procedures of Implicit Knowledge*, Ablex Publishing, Norwood, NJ.

Johnson, P. (1985) 'Towards a task model of messaging', in *People and Computers; Designing the User Interface*, P. Johnson and S. Cook (eds.), Cambridge University Press, Cambridge.

Johnson, P., D. Diaper and J. Long (1984) 'Tasks, skill and knowledge; task analysis for knowledge based descriptions', in *Human–Computer Interaction—INTERACT '84*, B. Shackel (ed.) North-Holland, London.

Johnson, P., H. Johnson and F. Russell (1988) 'Collecting and generalizing knowledge descriptions from task analysis data', *ICL Technical Journal*, **6**, 137–155.

Johnson, P., J. Johnson, R. Waddington and A. Shouls (1988) 'Task related knowledge structures: analysis, modelling and application', in *People and Computers: from Research to Implementation*, D. M. Jones and R. Winder (eds), Cambridge University Press, Cambridge.

Keane, M. and Johnson, P. (1987) 'Preliminary analysis for design' in *People and Computers*, D. Diaper and R. Winder (eds), Cambridge University Press, Cambridge.

Kieras, D. and P. Polson (1985) 'An approach to the formal analysis of user complexity', *International Journal of Man-Machine Studies*, **22**, 365–394.

Kelly, G. A. (1955) *The Psychology of Personal Constructs*, Norton, New York.

Leddo, J. and R. P. Abelson (1986) 'The nature of explanations', in *Knowledge Structures*, J. A. Galambos, R. P. Abelson and J. B. Black (eds), Lawrence Erlbaum Associates, Hillsdale, NJ.

Olson, J. R. (1987) 'Cognitive analysis of people's use of software', in *Interfacing Thought: Cognitive Aspects of HCI*, J. M. Carroll (ed.), MIT Press; Cambridge Mass.

Payne, S. J. and T. R. G. Green (1986) 'Task-action grammars: a model of the mental representation of task languages', *Human Computer Interaction*, **2**, 93–133.

Rosch, E. (1978) 'Principles of categorization', *Cognition and Categorization*, E. Rosch and B. Lloyd (eds), Lawrence Erlbaum Associates, Hillsdale, NJ.

Rosch, E. (1985) 'Prototype classification and logical classification: the two systems', in *New Trends in Conceptual Representation: Challenges to Piaget's Theory?*, E. K. Scholnick (ed.), Lawrence Erlbaum Associates, Hillsdale, NJ.

Rosch, E., C. Mervis, W. Gray, D. Johnson and P. Boyes-Braem (1976) 'Basic objects in natural categories', *Cognitive Psychology*, **8**, 382–439.

Schank, R. C. (1982) *Dynamic memory: A Theory of Reminding and Learning in Computers and People*, Cambridge University Press, New York.

Welbank, M. (1983) *A Review of Knowledge Acquisition Techniques for Expert Systems*, Martlesham Consultancy Services, British Telecom Research Laboratories, Ipswich.

6 Dialogue specification

PETER JONES

6.1 Introduction

Even a simple program requires some means of obtaining its input and presenting its results. For example, consider a typical introductory programming problem of converting a decimal number to its binary representation. Much of the design effort usually goes into the conversion algorithm with little attention being given to the problem of the user interface. If the exercise were to take into account the quality of the user interface then many other questions would require an answer. How would the user be prompted for input? How would the results be displayed? What should be done with erroneous input? Should on-line help be provided? Most programming environments provide only for simple, line-oriented input and output, and thus only a limited solution to these questions can be readily implemented. Even more problems would arise if the code were to be offered as a library routine for embedding in a larger system. How would the routine's input/output requirements be combined with other parts of the system? Again little support for solving such problems is provided with current programming languages.

If a modular approach to system design is adopted, some of these problems can be tackled by separating the interface software from the functionality of the application on the one hand, and from the device dependency of the actual hardware interface devices on the other. It is then possible to specify the dialogue using a device- and application-independent specification language. The dialogue specification language becomes a general tool that can be used in any dialogue design, and may also support evaluation and prototyping of the interface. For example, the language may be able to support at run-time several of the dialogue styles discussed in Chapter 4 (Kuo and Karimi, 1988). However, not all possible specification languages are equally useful. For example, an early form of dialogue specification relied on screen layout definitions giving position and format information for a screen. This notation fails to provide any notion of the dynamics of the interaction. What is needed of a notation is the provision of a precise representation that adequately describes all relevant aspects of the human–computer dialogue.

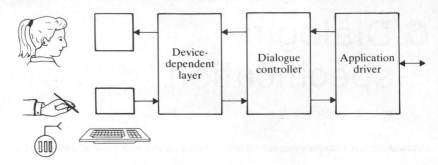

Figure 6.1 User interface explicitly defined

Before discussing specification techniques, an abstract model for a dialogue system is described. Systems that allow the implementation of the model are often referred to as *user interface management systems* or *UIMS* (Pfaff, 1985). Figure 6.1 shows a diagram of a possible model for the separation of the user interface from the application, the rightmost arrow showing a two-way communication with the application.

This modular model contrasts with many existing systems where the code for the user interface is distributed throughout the application as in Figure 6.2. Making changes to such a system to cope with a different interaction style would obviously be much more difficult in the latter case. Interactive systems can thus be divided into two parts, one for the algorithms and data constituting the functionality of the application, and the other representing the dialogue for the input of commands and output of results to the user. It is problematic where this division should be made (Cockton, 1986). Currently, the algorithmic part is often designed using formal methods before the implementation is begun, but the dialogue design is carried out in an *ad hoc* fashion during implementation. Ideally, the dialogue software should be separate from the algorithm software, its design should be implemented using its own dialogue implementation language, the dialogue component should

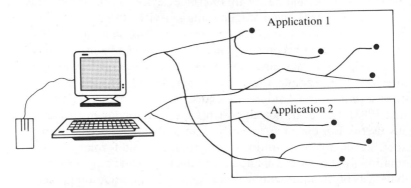

Figure 6.2 An unstructured system

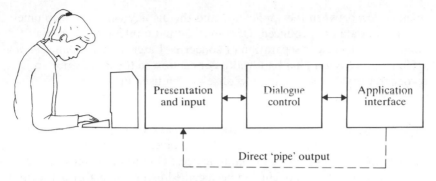

Figure 6.3 Abstract model of a UIMS

itself be subdivided as in Figure 6.1 to allow application and device independence, and it should be just as rigorously designed, evaluated and tested as the functionality. The advantages of such an approach are that the algorithmic component is relieved of dialogue details, both parts can separately be changed, specialists for the different parts can create the best possible design for each part, and the dialogue system is available for interfacing to other applications.

It is possible to argue against the splitting off of the interaction component for systems that have a great deal of semantic feedback, such as direct manipulation interfaces to spreadsheet programs. Here the interface and application functionality are so closely interwoven that the overheads imposed by the interfaces between the various components shown in Figure 6.1 might present undue communication demands. However, as mentioned in the next section, bypass mechanisms can be used to overcome this problem.

6.2 Abstract model of a UIMS

Several models have been proposed for user interface management systems and all attempt to separate the user interface from the application itself. The model proposed here is based on that developed at the 1983 workshop on user interface management systems at Seeheim, West Germany (Pfaff, 1985; Green, 1986). The goal of a UIMS is to cover all aspects of the production and implementation of user interfaces.

The abstract model introduced at this workshop, shown in Figure 6.3, indicates the components required logically to implement the different functions of the run-time part of a UIMS: a device independent presentation and input component; a component for the control of the dialogue and finally a component that is the interface to the application. This reinforces the separation of concerns for the user and those of the application programs. It is also proposed that there be a direct 'pipe' connection between the application and the display when large volumes of output data are produced. Of course, actual implementations may well have a less clear separation of concerns. Later models (Dance *et al.*, 1987) allow for a higher bandwidth connection to the application in order to provide the semantic feedback often used in direct-manipulation interfaces.

The presentation and input component is responsible for direct interaction with the user on the one hand and communication with the dialogue component on the other. This involves the creation of the display and the sensing of the input devices. Communication with the dialogue control component can be specified using some abstract form of input and output language: the presentation and input component is then responsible for transforming physical input commands into this abstract language and interpreting abstract display operations in terms of the physical display capabilities. Some examples of the application of device-dependent and device-independent display representations are given in Chapter 10 on windowing systems.

The dialogue control component defines the structure of the dialogue between the user and the application. The inputs from the user are the tokens produced by the input component, which then drives the dialogue to produce information to be sent to the application. Similarly, the dialogue controller receives information back from the application which may modify its state and then be sent to the presentation component.

The application interface is the component that takes requests from the dialogue controller. It may pass these on in some transformed manner to the application or directly respond where the request is not syntactically valid. Output from the application is received at the application interface, where it may be transformed before being passed on to the dialogue controller. Information held in the application interface may include such items as the names of application routines, their parameters and results, and side effects resulting from their invocation.

As an example, the Adaptive Intelligent Dialogues (AID) Project described in Chapter 11 adopted this model for its phase 1 exemplar. This was an adaptive interface to the electronic mail application Telecom Gold (Totterdell and Cooper, 1986). Figure 6.4 gives the overall architecture of the system and the tools used for the implementation of the various components. The communication with Telecom Gold was over the public switched telephone network, so the application and user interface were well and truly separate!

Although the software ran on a Sun workstation and experimenters were able to use the full functionality provided by the Sun windowing system, the end user interacted with a character-based terminal driven by the Sun. The presentation and input component were provided by the Rapid/USE (Wasserman *et al.*, 1986) system. This in turn used the

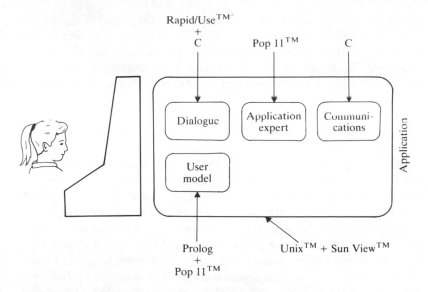

Figure 6.4 Architecture of the AID phase 1 exemplar

terminal capability database provided with the UNIX system in order to be independent of the physical capabilities of the terminal.

The dialogue control was provided by the state transition model of Rapid/USE with individual dialogue fragments chosen on the basis of recommendations from the user model component. This latter component was added in order to provide for some of the adaptiveness of the system. The application expert component was the interface to the application, accessed through the communications component. The application expert checked that requests were valid, added some extra functionality (another of the adaptation dimensions) and handled error recovery over the communications network.

6.3 Models of dialogue control

Before proceeding to a detailed discussion, it will be helpful briefly to review the three main dialogue control notations, namely *transition networks, context-free grammars* and *event-based dialogues*.

By far the most common notation for user interfaces is based on transition networks, also known as *state diagrams* or *state tables* depending on their representations. These can be traced back to an early interactive graphical system (Newman, 1968) and work on user interfaces (Parnas, 1969; Denert 1977) and speech understanding (Woods 1970). The transition network model views the user interface as a collection of states. User actions, time and application output cause state-to-state transitions. The notations are usually enhanced to include additional memory elements and the ability to modularize the net into subnetworks (Wasserman, 1985). Subnetworks facilitate the design and understandability of larger systems and allow reuse of common dialogue fragments. With recursion, transition nets can handle more complex dialogues. The Rapid/USE system, discussed in Sections 6.5 and 7.5.1, also includes a graphically based editor for the transition network, which makes the notation more explicit, and an interpreter for rapid simulation.

The grammar-based notations are equal in power to the augmented recursive transition networks (Hopcroft and Ullman, 1960). They view the dialogue between the user and the application as a language describable by a grammar. This work arose out of the study of the syntax of natural languages in the mid-1950s (Chomsky, 1957) and was subsequently adopted as a means of describing the programming language Algol-60 (Backus, 1960). The form of notation developed is referred to as Backus–Naur Form (BNF), and is now widely used for the formal specification of the syntax of programming languages. Its application to user interface design has been less widespread (Reisner, 1981; Edmonds and Guest, 1984). The notation is usually enhanced so that actions can be embedded in the production rules of the grammar. When a rule is used, the action, usually a call to a function written in a conventional programming language, can be carried out—for example prompting a user for the second point of a graphic line. Grammar-based notations have not proved as popular with designers as the transition network approach (Guest, 1982).

A more recent approach is the event-based notation. This views the user interface as a collection of events and event handlers. User actions give rise to events which are then passed to those handlers that have indicated they will handle them. Similarly, pseudoevents can be inserted into the system either by the handlers or as the result of information from the application. Event-based models have been extensively used as the design basis of windowing systems and are discussed in more detail in Chapter 10.

Production rule-based systems and Petri nets have also been proposed as bases for dialogue specification and control (Anderson and Gillogly, 1976; Peterson, 1977; Pilote, 1983).

6.4 Dialogue specification techniques

Jacob (1983) has proposed a number of desiderata for dialogue specification techniques. Any technique should:

- be easy to understand;
- reduce specification effort;
- be precise;
- be specific;
- be checkable for consistency;

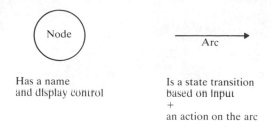

Has a name
and display control

Is a state transition
based on input
+
an action on the arc

Figure 6.5 Notation for transition networks

- be powerful;
- be able to implement non-trivial systems;
- separate function (what) from implementation (how);
- be able to provide rapid prototyping; and
- be able to match the cognitive concepts of the user.

Sections 6.5–6.7 describe a number of dialogue specification techniques that attempt to meet some of these needs.

6.5 State transition networks

State transition networks show, often in a graphical manner, the dynamics of a dialogue. The dialogue is shown as being in a particular state awaiting the next interaction with the user. It will then move to the next state as the result of this interaction. Other reasons for changes of state are also possible, for example an unconditional change or the completion of a time-out. The networks consist of *nodes* that correspond to a state and *directed arcs* that connect nodes. At a node there can be *actions* to control what is displayed, and then accept user input for matching to an exit label on an arc. As well as labels conditioning which arc is chosen, the arcs may also have actions, which themselves may return values to affect the path chosen.

A large system may have too many nodes to be readily understood, and furthermore some parts of the dialogue may be repeated, for example asking for confirmation of an action. In order to manage this complexity, the concept of *subnetworks* is introduced. The top-level design will then be made up of calls to the subnetworks, and common sequences at any level replaced with calls on a subnetwork.

It is usual to represent networks diagrammatically as in Figure 6.5.

Transition nets have several advantages. For example, the help and error texts can be placed where relevant in the net; similarly, the net can be searched to answer user's questions. The questions might take the form *how to do X*, *what can be done next*, or *how to get to Y*. Use of subnetworks allows the designer to break up lengthy dialogues, allows reuse of common interactions, isolates decisions so that changes need be made in only one place and matches natural hierarchies.

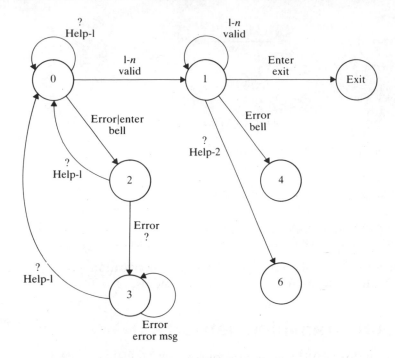

Figure 6.6 A partial diagram of the state transition network

The disadvantages are that transition nets are not very flexible in their parsing, context switching may be difficult, it is difficult to backtrack, and generation of the nets can be cumbersome without graphical tools.

6.5.1 State transition networks: example

Consider a menu selection system. The choices are to be numbered from 1 to n. A valid selection is made by keying in one of the digits in the range $1 \ldots n$. This selection is then highlighted. Further selections may be made, in which case the previous highlight (if any) is undone and the new selection highlighted. The user, having made a valid selection, can then activate it by pressing the ENTER key.

When handling errors, the first error will sound a bell. A second consecutive error will cause a '?' output to indicate the error. A third consecutive error will cause an error message to be shown. The user can press the ?-key to get help. A general help message will be given if there is no valid selection; otherwise a help message specific to the selection will be output.

The design is begun by drawing out a diagram, the initial part of which is shown on Figure 6.6. This diagram can be readily transcribed into a conventional programming language. For example, in the language C such a fragment is:

```
static struct state_table [ ] =
{/*            Events                                        */
/*State      VALID       ERROR      ?            ENTER      */
/*  0  */{  1,valid,   2,bell    0,help1    2,bell    },
/*  1  */{  1,valid,   4,bell,   6,help2,  -1,exit  },
/*  2  */{  1,valid,   3,quest,  0,help1,   3,quest  },
/*  3  */{  1,valid,   3,error,  0,help1,   3,help1  },
/*  4  */{  1,valid,   5,quest,  6,help1,  -1,exit  },
/*  5  */{  1,valid,   1,error,  6,help2,  -1,exit  },
/*  6  */{  1,valid,   4,bell,   1,help1,  -1,exit  }
};
```

where there are routines named valid, bell, help1, help2, quest, error
and exit. (Note that the table corresponds to a completed version of the
partial transition diagram in Figure 6.6.)

The initial state will be defined by a variable containing a zero
subscript to the first row of the state table. The routine to get the next
event will be called and this will return a subscript for the column. The
values held at the structure located by this row and column subscript
will indicate what is to be the next state (shown as an integer) and what
action (i.e., which C routine to call) to perform on the transition. Once
the appropriate table is set up and the routines written, it is
comparatively easy to understand the system, and to modify it if user
requirements change.

6.6 Context-free grammars

Human interaction with a computer needs a language. A formal
grammar is a tool that allows the structure of the interaction to be
described and analysed as a language. The formal grammar is specified
as a collection of rules that can be used for description and analysis.
The specification is normally based on Backus–Naur Form (BNF)
notation, but pure BNF needs to be modified so that an action is
associated with each rewriting rule if it is to be used for specifying and
describing human–computer dialogues (Lawson *et al.*, 1978; Reisner,
1981; Shneiderman, 1981).

There are problems with using BNF for the design of user interfaces. It
has proved harder to use than transition nets (Guest, 1982), and has
difficulty in providing control of interaction (Jacob, 1984). Although
these two approaches are identical in power, designers seem to prefer
state transition networks. State transition networks have the disadvantage
of becoming awkward when large, but Alty (1984) has proposed the use
of graph theoretic analysis techniques to overcome this problem.

6.6.1 Grammars for languages

The grammar is a set of rules from which it is possible to construct
sentences of the language. It can also be used to make an acceptor; that

is, given a sentence it can state if the sentence is legal. BNF is usually used as the underlying formal notation, or meta-language, but it is also possible to write the rules in the form of *syntax diagrams*, first used to describe the syntax of the programming language Pascal.

Formal language theory

Formal language theory developed from the work of Noam Chomsky in 1956 on syntactic structures for natural languages. Its components are *symbols* and *rules*. The symbols are either terminal symbols, which correspond to the basic words or tokens of the input, or non-terminal symbols, which are names of rules for structuring the dialogue. It is usual for the tokens to be recognized by a low-level routine that uses a regular and simple grammar for describing and recognizing their internal structure. One of the non-terminals is specially named as the starting symbol, for example 'sentence' or 'program' from the domains of natural language and computer languages respectively.

The following restricted grammar for simple English sentences illustrates how grammar rules can be applied to parse sentences:

< sentence >	→	< subject > < verb > < object >
< subject >	→	< article > < noun >
< verb >	→	hit | likes
< object >	→	< article > < noun >
< article >	→	a | the | The
< noun >	→	hammer | nail

In this set of rules, sharp brackets surround meta-symbols used for naming non-terminals, '→' means 'is replaced by', '|' means 'or', adjacency implies sequence and literals stand for themselves. The grammar can then be used to analyse the structure of sentences, for example 'The hammer hit the nail,' which results in the parse tree shown in Figure 6.7.

Since the grammar above specifies only the allowed syntax of a sentence, a nonsense sentence such as 'The bottle caressed the onion' can still be correctly parsed. Higher-level semantic analysis is thus needed to determine fully the legitimacy of a sentence (or dialogue component). Other problems also exist; for example, there may be more than one legitimate parse for a sentence. In the sentence 'They are flying planes' it is not clear in isolation whether the word 'flying' is being used as a verb (in which case the sentence is about pilots) or if it is being used as an adjective (in which case the sentence is about the planes themselves). Even when the language is severely restricted (for example a programming language), ambiguities can arise. For example, some programming languages have an ambiguity in matching the 'else' in an if-statement: this is usually resolved by a rule such as 'It matches the nearest preceding unmatched if.'

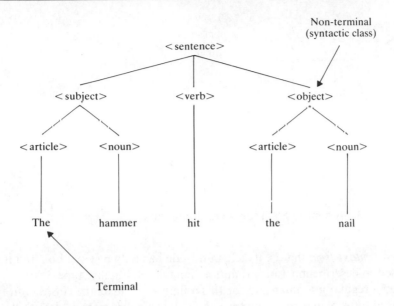

Figure 6.7 A parse tree for a sentence

Another example is a simple command language for an operating system. The MSDOS-style command,

```
C> erase a: menu_opt.c
```

can be analysed with the following BNF grammar, extended to show repetition with subscripts and superscripts:

< erase cmd >	→	erase < path name >
< path name >	→	< drive > : < file name > | < file name >
< drive >	→	a | b | c | d
< file name >	→	< name > . < ext > | < name >
< name >	→	< alpha > < alphanumeric > $_0^8$
< ext >	→	< alphanumeric > $_1^3$

6.6.2 Types of grammars

Grammars have rules of the form:

non-terminal → replacement string

Increasingly stringent restrictions can be placed on the left- and right-hand sides of these rules (or *productions* as they are sometimes called). The grammars can then be classified according to these restrictions. Type-0 has no restrictions. Type-1 allows context sensitivity, that is, it allows any combination of symbols on the left-hand side with the right-hand side being the same as the left side with one symbol expanded, e.g., ABC → AbC (where upper-case letters stand for non-terminals and lower-case letters for terminals). Type-2 is

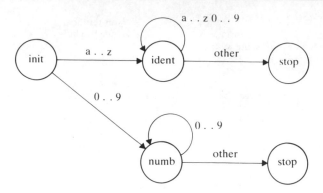

Figure 6.8 A simple FSM for lexical analysis

called *context-free*, that is, its left-hand side has only one symbol, and it is used to describe most programming languages. Finally, type-3 is called a regular grammar and for this a finite-state machine (FSM) can be used to recognize regular expressions. Its rules are restricted so that the right side is either a single terminal symbol or a terminal symbol followed by a single non-terminal symbol, e.g., D → a|aD. Typical uses are to form tokens from individual characters, for example a number or a name.

Lexical analysis

A finite-state machine (FSM) can be used to recognize type-3 sentences, for example the names and integer constants for a programming language. The following grammar would achieve this (using a..z and 0..9 to denote all the characters from a to z and all the numbers from 0 to 9 respectively):

< name >	→	a..z | a..z < alphanumeric >
< alphanumeric >	→	a..z | 0..9 | a..z < alphanumeric >
		| 0..9 < alphanumeric >
< number >	→	0..9 | 0..9 < number >

This grammar can be implemented using either a simple state transition network (Figure 6.8) and corresponding state table, or it can be transcribed into a program as follows (in pseudocode):

```
switch ( c )
{
    case 'a..z':   read_ident(); break;
    case '0..9':   read_numb(); break;
    . . .
}
```

6.7 Tools to support dialogue design

In the design of a user interface there are several phases of development that need to be supported. Most tools focus on the phases of design, implementation and evaluation. A *dialogue editor* can be used to enter and make changes to the specification of the dialogue design. A *dialogue verifier* can then be used to look for loops, unreachable nodes, consistency, style, etc. During the early stages a *dialogue simulator* can be used to allow rapid prototyping of the interface, for example experimenting with screen layouts. For evaluation, where empirical data needs to be collected during trial interactions, a *dialogue monitor* can be used to capture either time-stamped raw user input or perhaps some higher-level protocols, for example the names of nodes visited and what the user input was.

A full user interface management system (UIMS) design suite will provide an interface specification language, screen layout generators, specialized graphical editors for icons, menus and other graphic objects, and text editors for textual items such as prompts, system responses, error and help messages. There will be a dialogue generator and possibly an interpreter to support rapid prototyping of the interface, and finally run-time support for the dialogue will be provided.

An alternative approach is a restricted UIMS design suite that supports the implementation phase only, leaving out the earlier phases of user requirements analysis, design and the important area of evaluation.

Often no UIMS design tools are available at all: a more restricted approach is then to produce lexical analysers and parsers from high-level descriptions. This approach has been successfully used in several commercially available systems for the rapid production of user interfaces. For example, if the system is a drawing package then the grammar could specify a command such as 'draw line' together with its parameters. The lexical analyser could be used to hide details of how the command and parameters would be input; for example, the command might come from an iconic menu while the parameters for the start and end of the line would be specified by the pointing device. The parser would then receive this preprocessed input and check for syntactic and semantic correctness.

Tools exist to help automate the production of these analysers and parsers. For example, within the UNIX environment, *yacc* (Johnson, 1975) is a general tool for generating a parser from a specification that describes the syntactic structures of the user input, together with some program fragments which are invoked when non-terminals are recognized. A companion tool, *lex* (Lesk, 1975), can be used to create the lexical analyser required to process the raw user input into lexical items (or tokens) required by the parser.

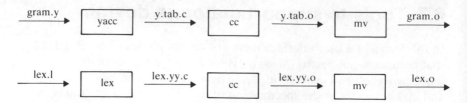

Figure 6.9 Generating parsers and lexical analysers

6.7.1 yacc

yacc takes the grammatical specification of an input language together with code to be invoked as each item is recognized. The steps in the process are as follows:

1 Write a grammar, i.e., specify the syntax of the language.

2 Augment each rule with an action, i.e., define what needs to be done when an instance of that form is parsed. This action is written in C.

3 Write the lexical analyser either in C or using lex (see the next subsection).

6.7.2 lex

lex takes a specification of the lexical rules, and defines actions in C syntax to be executed when a matching string is recognized. Like the line editors *ed* or *ex* found with UNIX, it uses *regular expressions* to specify the strings to be recognized.

6.7.3 Using lex and yacc

The process of using lex and yacc is illustrated diagrammatically in Figure 6.9. The grammar is specified within the file 'gram.y', which is processed by the tool *yacc*. The specification for the tokens is in the file 'lex.l', which is processed by the tool *lex*. Each of these tools produces output files in C source format, and these are compiled to produce object files 'gram.o' and 'lex.o' respectively. The object file gram.o will then be linked together with any further routines to form the executable parser *yyparse*. This expects to be able to call the function *yylex* which is the executable lexical analyser generated by lex.

6.8 Summary

Research in recent years has identified a number of ways in which the processes of dialogue specification and design can be formalized. An important initial consideration is to separate the user interface both from the application functionality and from the device dependency of the actual hardware. This leads to the development of a three-component user interface management system comprising a device-dependent presentation and input component, a dialogue controller, and an application interface. The dialogue controller may, depending on complexity, be further subdivided into logically separate functions, as for example in the Adaptive Intelligent Dialogues project.

Given a dialogue controller that is independent of both the physical input/output devices and the application, its functionality can be specified using one of several formalisms. The three most common formalisms are transition networks, context-free grammars, and event-based notations. Transition networks have proved to be the most popular dialogue specification method, and a number of dialogue specification and implementation tools based upon transition networks have been developed, some with graphical input capabilities. Dialogue specification and implementation based upon context-free grammars have also been extensively investigated, and event-based notations have been exploited in window managers.

Some UIMS design tools support purely the implementation phase of the UIMS, but ideally they should also support requirements analysis and specification prior to the design, and post-design evaluation. In the case where no formal UIMS design tools are available at all, general-purpose compiler design tools such as lex and yacc have proved valuable in implementing UIMSs.

References

Alty, J. L. (1984) 'The application of path algebras to interactive dialogue design', *Behaviour and Information Technology*, **3** (2), 119–132.

Anderson, R. H. and J. J. Gillogly (1976) *Rand Intelligent Terminal Agent (RITA): Design Philosophy*, Rand Corporation, Santa Monica, Calif.

Backus, J. W. (ed.) (1960) 'Report on the algorithmic language Algo160', *Communications of the ACM*, **3**, 229–314.

Chomsky, N. (1957) *Syntactic Structures*, Mouton, The Hague.

Cockton, G. (1986) 'Where do we draw the line?', *People and Computers: Designing for Usability, Proceedings of the Second BCS HCI Conference, Sept. 1986*, Cambridge University Press, Cambridge, 417–432.

Dance, J. R., T. E. Granor, R. D. Hill, S. E. Hudson, J. Meads, B. A. Myers and A. Schulert (1987) 'Report on the run-time structure of UIMS-supported applications', *Computer Graphics*, **21** (2), 97–101.

Denert, E. (1977) 'Specification and design of dialogue systems with state diagrams', *International Computing Symposium*, North-Holland, Amsterdam, 417–424.

Edmonds, E. A. and S. P. Guest (1984) 'The SYNICS2 user interface manager', *Interact—1st IFIP Conference on HCI*, 53–56.

Green, M. (1986) 'A survey of three dialogue models', *ACM Transactions on Office Information Systems*, **5** (3), 244–276.

Guest, S. P. (1982) 'The use of software tools for dialogue design', *International Journal of Man–Machine Studies*, **16**, 263–285.

Hopcroft, J. E. and J. D. Ullman (1960) *Formal Languages and Their Relationship to Automata*, Addison-Wesley, Reading, Mass.

Jacob, R. J. K. (1983) 'Using formal specifications in the design of a human–computer interface', *Communications of the ACM*, **26**, 259–264.

Jacob, R. J. K. (1984) 'An executable specification technique for describing human–computer interaction', *Advances in Human–Computer Interaction*, H. R. Hartson (ed.), Ablex, NJ.

Johnson, S. (1975) 'Yacc: yet another compiler compiler', *Computing Science Technical Report* No. 32, Bell Laboratories, Murray Hill, NJ.

Kuo, F-Y. and I. Karimi (1988) 'User interface design from a real time perspective', *Communications of the ACM*, **31**, 1456–1466.

Lawson, H. W., M. Bertran and I. Sanagustin (1978) 'The formal definition of human–machine communications', *Software—Practice and Experience*, **8** (1), 51–58.

Lesk, M. E. (1975) *Lex: a Lexical Analyzer Generator*, Computing Science Technical Report No. 39, Bell Laboratories, Murray Hill, NJ. (Also in section 20, vol. 2B, of the *Unix Programmer's Manual*.)

Newman, W. M. (1968) 'A system for interactive graphical programming', *AFIPS SJCC*, **32**, 47–54.

Parnas, D. L. (1969) 'On the use of transition diagrams in the design of a user interface for an interactive computer system', *Proceedings of the 24th National ACM Conference*, 379–385.

Peterson, J. L. (1977) 'Petri nets', *ACM Computing Surveys*, **9**, 223–252 (Sept.).

Pfaff, G. E. (1985) *User Interface Management Systems*, Springer, Berlin. (Reports on the 1983 Seeheim Workshop.)

Pilote, M. (1983) 'A programming language framework for designing user interfaces', *ACM SIGPLAN Notices*, **18** (6), 118–136.

Reisner, P. (1981) 'Formal grammar and human factors design of an interactive graphics system', *IEEE Transactions on Software Engineering*, **SE-7** (2), 229–240.

Shneiderman, B. (1981) 'Multi-party grammars and related features for defining interactive systems', *IEEE Transactions on Systems, Man and Cybernetics*, **SMC-12** (2), 148–154.

Totterdell, P. A. and P. Cooper (1986) 'Design and evaluation of the AID adaptive front end to Telecom Sold', *Proceedings of the BCS Conference on HCI*, M. J. Harrison and A. F. Monk (eds), Cambridge University Press, Cambridge, 281–295.

Wasserman, A. I. (1985) 'Extending state transition diagrams for the specification of human–computer interaction', *IEEE Transactions on Software Engineering*, **SE-11** (8), 699–713.

Wasserman, A. I., P. A. Pircher, D. T. Shewmake and M. L. Kersten (1986) 'Developing interactive information systems with the user software engineering methodology', *IEEE Transactions on Software Engineering*, **SE-12** (2), 326–345.

Woods, W. A. (1970) 'Transition network grammars for natural language analysis', *Communications of the ACM*, **13** (10), 591–606.

Further reading

Alexander, H. (1987) 'Formally-based techniques for dialogue design', in *People and Computers III: Proceedings of the Third BCS HCI Conference, Sept. 1987*, Cambridge University Press, Cambridge, 201–213.

Anstey, P. (1988) 'How much is enough? A study of user command repertoires', in *People and Computers IV: Proceedings of the Fourth BCS HCI*

Conference, *Sept. 1988*, Cambridge University Press, Cambridge, 491–507.

Beech, D. (ed.) (1960) *Concepts in User Interfaces: a Reference Model for Command and Response languages*, Springer, Berlin.

Callahan, J., D. Hopkins, M. Weiser and B. Shneiderman (1988) 'An empirical comparison of pie vs. linear menus', *Proceedings, CHI '88 (Washington, May 15–19)*, Soloway, Frye, and Sheppard (eds), Addison-Wesley, 95–100.

Carroll, J. M. and S. A. Mazur (1986) 'Lisa learning', *IEEE Computer*, **19** (Nov.), 35–49.

Cockton, G. (1988) 'Generative transition networks: a new communication control abstraction', *People and Computers IV: Proceedings of the Fourth BCS HCI Conference, Sept. 1988*, Cambridge University Press, Cambridge, 509–527.

Embley, D. W., S. E. Engel and R. E. Granda (1975) *Guidelines for Man/Display Interfaces*, TR 00.2720, IBM Poughkeepsie Lab., Poughkeepsie, NY, 197–216.

England, D. (1988) 'Graphical prototyping of graphical tools', *People and Computers IV: Proceedings of the Fourth BCS HCI Conference, Sept. 1988*, Cambridge University Press, Cambridge, 407–417.

Foley, J., C. Gibbs, W. C. Kin and S. Kovacevic (1988) 'A knowledge-based user interface management system', in *Proceedings, CHI '88 (Washington, May 15–19)*, Soloway, Frye and Sheppard (eds), Addison-Wesley, Wokingham, 67–72.

Foltz, P. W., S. E. Davie and P. G. Polson (1988) 'Transfer between menu systems', in *Proceedings, CHI '88 (Washington, May 15–19)*, Soloway, Frye, and Sheppard (eds), Addison-Wesley, Wokingham, 107–112.

Gaines, B. R. and M. L. G. Shaw (1986) 'Foundations of dialogue engineering: the development of human–computer interaction, Part 2', *International Journal of Man–Machine Studies*, **24**, 101–125.

Grzegroczyk, A. (1953) 'Some classes of recursive functions', *Rozprawy Matematczyne Warsaw*, **4**, 1–45.

Helander, M. (ed.) (1988) *Handbook of Human–Computer Interaction*, North-Holland, Amsterdam.

Henskes, D. T. and J. C. Tolmie (1987) 'Rapid prototyping of man–machine interfaces for telecommunications equipment using interactive animated computer graphics', *Human–Computer Interaction—INTERACT '87, Proceedings of the 2nd IFIP Conference, Sept. 1987*, North-Holland, Amsterdam, 1053–1058.

Jacob, R. J. K. (1985) 'A state transition diagram language for visual programming', *IEEE Computer*, **18**, 51–59 (Aug. 1985).

Jacob, R. J. K. (1986) 'A specification language for direct-manipulation user interfaces', *ACM Transactions on Office Information Systems*, **5**, (4), 283–317.

Johnson, S. C. (1980) 'Language development tools on the Unix system', *IEEE Computer*, **13**, 16–21.

Kohl, A. and W. Rupietta (1987) 'The natural language metaphor: an approach to avoid misleading expectations', *Human–Computer Interaction—INTERACT '87, Proceedings of the 2nd IFIP Conference, Sept. 1987*, North-Holland, Amsterdam, 555–560.

McDonald, J. E., M. E. Molander and R. W. Noel (1988) 'Color-coding categories in menus', in *Proceedings, CHI '88 (Washington, May 15–19)*, Soloway, Frye and Sheppard (eds), Addison-Wesley, Wokingham, 101–106.

Reisner, P. (1981) 'Further developments toward using formal grammar as a design tool', *Proceedings, Human Factors in Computer Systems (March 1981)*, Gaithersburg, Maryland, 304–308.

Scott, M. L. and Yap, S-K. (1988) 'A grammar-based approach to the automatic generation of user-interface dialogues', in *Proceedings CHI '88 (Washington, May 15–19)*, Soloway, Frye and Sheppard (eds), Addison-Wesley, Wokingham, 73–78.

Shneiderman, B. (1983) 'Direct manipulation: a step beyond programming languages', *IEEE Computer*, **16**, (8), 57–69.

Shneiderman, B. (1987) *Designing the User Interface: Strategies for Effective Human–Computer Interaction*, Addison-Wesley, Reading, Mass.

Totterdell, P. A., M. A. Norman and D. P. Browne (1987) Levels of adaptivity in interface design, *Human–Computer Interaction—INTERACT '87, Proceedings of the 2nd IFIP Conference, Sept. 1987*, North-Holland, Amsterdam, 715–722.

Walker, N. and J. R. Olson (1988) 'Designing keybindings to be easy to learn and resistant to forgetting even when the set of commands is large', *Proceedings CHI '88 (Washington, May 15–19)*, Soloway, Frye and Sheppard (eds), Addison-Wesley, Wokingham, 201–206.

7 Dialogue delivery systems: example research systems

PETER JONES

7.1 Introduction to dialogue delivery systems

In Chapter 4, part of the discussion was based on the idea of classifying dialogue styles. The main styles identified were *command language*, *menu selection*, *form-filling*, *natural language* and *direct manipulation*. In Chapter 6, an abstract model for a dialogue system was developed. Systems that implement the model are referred to as *user interface management systems* (*UIMS*). This chapter examines several dialogue delivery systems chosen to illustrate important aspects of these styles, which in reality may overlap.

In addition to being exemplars of the styles, the systems were also chosen to demonstrate a variety of approaches to the specification of the dialogue component of interaction. Command language is covered only briefly as it is assumed that most readers will be familiar with such interfaces. However, some recent work on extending command language interfaces is described. Next the *ZOG* menu- and frame-based system is described; then a form-filling metaphor is illustrated with *COUSIN*. The use of transition networks to specify a dialogue is shown in *Rapid/USE* and *CONNECT*. Natural language is introduced through some early work by Weizenbaum on the application of natural language to man–machine communication. Then its use both in medical interviewing and the *Mycin* expert system is described, leading on to the natural-language help system used in the *UNIX Consultant*.

The systems, which come mainly from the research environment, have been chosen to illustrate how actual implementations differ from the abstract model presented in Chapter 6. In general, the discussion is not detailed, but instead concentrates on bringing out what is seen as the important ideas embodied in the implementation. However, further details can be found in the references.

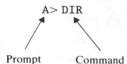

Figure 7.1   A CP/M prompt with a command

7.2 Command languages

Command languages are exemplified by the user interface to most operating systems (Beech, 1986). In the early days of computing, designers of such systems knew that the users were likely to be highly motivated experts and therefore concentrated on delivering the maximum functionality. Many early operating systems operated purely in batch mode, where the user presented a complete task with commands and data. Any feedback to the user was provided much later in the form of a hard-copy listing showing the progress of the commands, the data used and the output produced. Later operating systems allowed for more interaction with the user in order to control and monitor what was going on.

7.2.1 Digital Research CP/M

With the advent of the minicomputer in the mid-1960s and the microcomputer in the 1970s, more users began using computers interactively. From the user's point of view, the CP/M operating system from Digital Research was of great importance as the first general-purpose operating system to be widely used on microcomputers, and hence by the novice user. Its technical success stemmed from the fact that it was designed to be largely independent of the particular hardware on which it ran, and thus it established a large base of users and application software. Nevertheless, it had many awkward features (in common with many other command language systems): the prompts were rather cryptic, error messages were barely intelligible, there was an almost complete lack of help, and a crude command syntax with position-dependent arguments were used. For example, the prompt merely shows the currently selected disk drive, (Figure 7.1), while on switching to a subsystem, for example a text editor, the prompt changes, but with very little other feedback to the user (Figure 7.2).

```
A> ED HCI.TXT
  :*
```

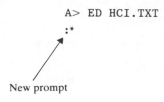

New prompt

Figure 7.2 Change of prompt in the editor

This style of interface was very poorly suited to the new and inexperienced computer users who were attracted to microcomputer systems by their low cost compared with previous generations of mini- and mainframe computers. Fortunately, the support provided for CP/M application programmers in the form of system calls and access to the file system made it possible for applications to provide their own, completely independent, support for common operating system functions. Thus successful end-user CP/M applications such as *Wordstar* (Figure 7.3) entirely replaced the basic CP/M command language with menu-based command selection and a form-filling mechanism for specifying filenames.

7.2.2 Dialogue Development System (DDS)

More recently, other approaches have been taken to increase flexibility in command language dialogues. At the University of Bradford, UK, a multilevel adaptable system, *Dialogue Development System* (*DDS*), was proposed for use with Ada (Robinson and Burns, 1985). As well as

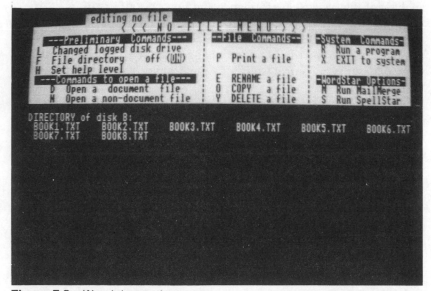

Figure 7.3 Wordstar main menu

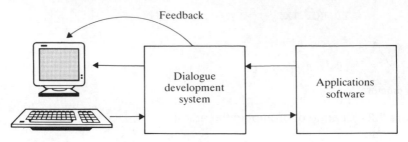

Figure 7.4   Proposed DDS system

emphasizing the adaptiveness required, this provided a separate high-level specification of the interface in order to relieve the application programmer's task of dealing with the interaction. A *user interface specification language* (UISL) was proposed to encourage this separation. Another key objective was to automate aspects of providing user feedback: for example, the type of an object could automatically provide for user feedback on erroneous input.

DDS is a range of tools that includes a *dialogue manager* (DM), which interprets the UISL, provides feedback, and controls the adaptation. A *terminal database* provides a virtual terminal that is device- and machine-independent. A *validator* is interposed between the application software and the DM to check the interface. As can be seen from Figure 7.4, the user interface system is run as a separate Ada task communicating with the other tasks forming the application. A *screen formatter* is provided to allow the construction of non-textual dialogues such as menus. Finally, a *system monitor* is used to provide a constant analysis of the system's performance and how this affects users.

Although a command-style interface is used, DDS provides for a mixed initiative interaction, for example prompting when arguments are missing. An example would be the issuing of a 'file copy' command when the user is in control (shown by the prompt of ' > > '):-

```
>> COPY
```

DDS then realizes that the arguments are missing and takes control to ask for them,

```
from file> FRED
```

and then,

```
to file> JOHN
```

with the prompt of ' > ' to show that control is now with DDS.

```
file copied.
>>
```

and control is returned to the user.

7.3 Menu selection: ZOG

Menu systems are straightforward to implement. All that is needed is to list the options available and then to ask the user to choose from among them. For example, several commercially available communication packages for connecting personal computers have a scripting language that can readily be used to generate menu systems without the need for any expertise in programming. It is more interesting, however, to investigate systems that provide a generalized notation for the specification of menu systems.

ZOG (Robertson *et al.*, 1981) is a rapid-response, large-network, menu selection system. Work on ZOG began originally in 1972 and restarted in 1975 at Carnegie-Mellon University, Pittsburgh, USA. The later work was inspired by the interface style used in the PROMIS (Walton *et al.*, 1979) medical information system at the University of Vermont. The name ZOG was chosen as a short arbitrary name and is not an acronym.

In the period 1975–80 ZOG was developed on Digital Equipment Corporation's PDP-10s and Vaxes. Subsequent development moved ZOG to a personal workstation, a PERQ, with high-resolution graphics and a pointing device. In the early 1980s the PERQ version was used as a computer-assisted management system on the aircraft carrier USS *Carl Vinson* (Akscyn and McCracken, 1984). Most recently, development has resulted in a distributed hypermedia system called *knowledge management systems* (*KMS*) (Akscyn *et al.*, 1988b), which is a commercial version of ZOG available on Sun and Apollo workstations.

ZOG has been used as an interface for a command language system, a database retrieval system, a CAI system, a guidance system, an interrogation system and a question-answering system. It is based on a hierarchy of subnets. Each subnet is a tree of frames in the form of a database. The system displays the frames to the user; a self-descriptive version is shown in Figure 7.5.

The frame has a title and a unique number. Then comes some context information, which could, for example, indicate how the user came to

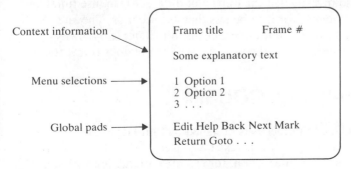

Figure 7.5   An outline of a ZOG frame

this particular frame. Below that can be several lines of descriptive text followed by columns of menu selections, shown as options in Figure 7.5. At the bottom is a line of global pads, or menu choices, that appear on all frames. For example the user could choose *goto* and proceed directly to a known frame.

The user traverses these frames by making selections. Additionally, a selection can evoke an action to accomplish a task. The selection can be made either by using touch-sensitive pads overlaying the selection or by entering a single character from the keyboard. The user therefore navigates through a structured set of subnetworks of interconnected frames, gathering information on the way. As an aid to navigation the user can see a list of frames visited, or a list of frames marked (i.e., anchor points) and can search for a particular frame.

The frames are built using a frame editor, ZED. This can be used at any time by the developer, including when using the system. A user might also use the editor for a limited amount of personalization.

The internal structure of a frame contains not only the visible information as seen by the user but also additional features. For example, there is a maintenance field that contains, among other items, the name of the owner of the frame and access privileges indicating whether it may be modified or viewed by others. The frame builder has the responsibility of providing guidance, on-line documentation and help.

Selections and frames may include action text. This text is sent to the communications multiplexer, which arranges for it to be sent to the correct destination. The frames also have an external format. This supports portability to other ZOG implementations as well as allowing for external maintenance manipulation.

ZOG is really a hierarchical menu system together with a generalized mechanism for the display of information and triggering of actions. As with any menu hierarchy, users can get lost, but are provided with some significant features that aid navigation. The limited display area places a heavy load on short-term memory; even so, evaluation revealed evidence that users failed to read the information in frames. The researchers also investigated the impact of different response times and provide some evidence for it to be less than 0.5 seconds. The later KMS system overcomes many of these problems, for example by always showing two frames so that the user can see the previous frame too.

7.4 Form-filling: COUSIN

COoperative USer INterface was designed by Phil Hayes at Carnegie-Mellon University (Hayes and Szekely, 1982). It is aimed at typical command-level interaction, for example interacting with an operating system, and not the more fine-grained interactions within, say,

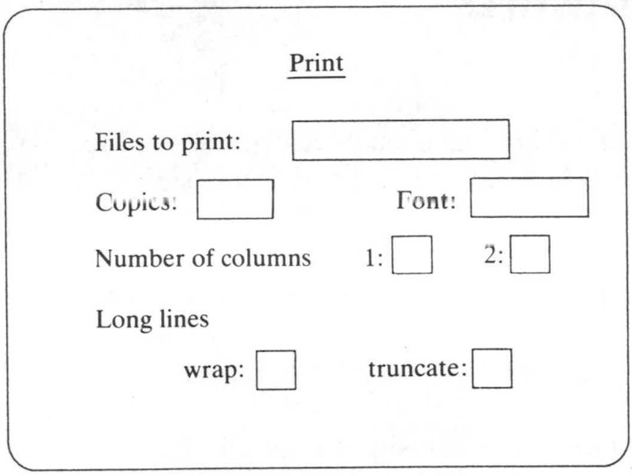

Figure 7.6   A COUSIN form

an editor. COUSIN aimed to present a consistent interface for all applications and to provide the benefit of reduced implementation time.

COUSIN uses a form-filling metaphor. This provides a single interface to several applications. The form-filling has intelligent support, mainly from the type information held in each field.

The (simplified) example in Figure 7.6 shows a command (print) and a set of arguments which must be supplied. Fields for the arguments can have default values that may be overtyped by the user. Each field has a data type and an attribute indicating whether the field is optional.

Three modes of operation are supported. A *non-interactive mode* is used for batch applications: COUSIN ensures correct command arguments are supplied before calling the application. In the *interactive mode* the application is started and can then prompt the user, when needed, for further information. Finally, in the *command loop mode* the user is in control and can issue commands with arguments and observe the feedback from the system.

Several variants of COUSIN were produced, but the main application reported is an interface to the UNIX operating system. In this application, the user typed a command, then COUSIN loaded an appropriate form and assisted the user in filling it in. Once completed, the command and arguments were parsed with COUSIN helping the user to remove errors. The user could save the form for later use, for example, the form could be partly filled in with the user's particular default settings.

The form-filling approach makes good use of bit-map displays, allows arguments to be filled in out of order and permits fields to have defaults. However, applications need modifying before they can be used with COUSIN. Although providing COUSIN as a front-end interface halved the speed of UNIX, this did not seem to be a problem with the experimental users.

7.5 Transition networks

7.5.1 Rapid/USE

Rapid/USE (Wasserman *et al.*, 1986) has been developed at the Medical Information Science Centre at the University of California since 1975. It is based on graphical specification of the required dialogue using families of state-transition nets and subnets and can rapidly produce either a menu or a form-filling dialogue. Diagrams are created using a graphical *Transition Diagram Editor* (TDE) on Sun workstations, or textually by using a special language entered with an ordinary text editor.

The diagram is a representation of a transition network. Each diagram is given a *name*, a *start node* and an *exit node* together with a network of *interior nodes* and *arcs*. A *node definition* is a description of what to do with the screen, for example screen control, display of text and contents of variables. An *arc definition* describes the structure of the diagram. It is labelled with the transition conditions and can have actions, including links to a relational database (TROLL).

Input can be a single key or a fixed-length reply, and can include a default to handle errors. Additionally a time-out can be included. The actions can be routines written in C, FORTRAN or Pascal or can be commands to operate on the relational database. A simple method for calling a single procedure with an integer parameter is also provided. Figure 7.7 shows a typical transition diagram created using the TDE.

A text file such as that shown can then be compiled from the transition diagram, or alternatively the text file can be created directly using a conventional text editor.

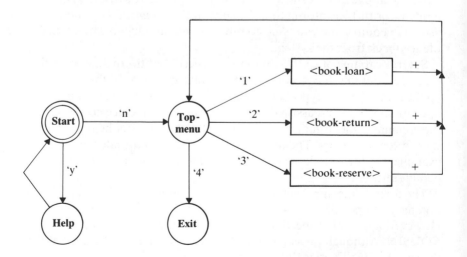

Figure 7.7   A Rapid/USE transition diagram

```
diagram library entry Start exit Exit

node Start
  cs,r1,c_ 'University Library System'
  r+2,c10 'Do you need help (y/n)?'
...
arc Start
  on 'n' to Topmenu
  on 'y' to Help
...
arc Topmenu
  on '1' to <book-loan>
  on '2' to <book-return>
...
arc <book-loan> skip to Topmenu
```

A *transition diagram interpreter* (TDI) can be used immediately on this text file in order to demonstrate and evaluate the menu system. As an aid to evaluation, Rapid/USE can also record two logs of the raw input and the transitions occuring within the system (time, diagram, node, action, input).

7.5.2 The CONNECT system

The CONNECT system (Alty, 1984a) was developed at the University of Strathclyde from 1983 onwards. It is a front-end to the CP/M and MS-DOS operating systems and is based on transition networks together with a production rule system. This latter feature enables the network connectivity to be altered to provide an adaptable interface.

At any time the network is dealing with one node. It then determines which node to move to in response to input from the user. A node can be either a *connector* to communicate with the user, a *task* to invoke a task, a *subnet* for structuring or an *assistor* to help routing as well as playing a role in adaptivity.

Transitions along arcs are determined by parsing the user's input, and can occur on detection of identical text, text somewhere in input, or numerically equal. Actions that are possible when the transition is chosen are *null*, *do a task*, *show screen*, *assign to a global*, *call a subnet*, or *prompt the user*. Display updates work on parts of the screen in the form of non-overlapping panes. Global variables are used to provide communication between the application and the user.

Production rule system

For every network the designer can provide a production rule system as a set of statements of the form:

```
if ... then <action-rules>
```

Each time a node is reached the production rule system is invoked. The *if* parts of the rules access a database and the actions can then modify global variables. Exit arcs from nodes that are labelled with these variables can then have their action modified in the light of the production rules. This provides a level of adaptability, which allows different interfaces to be presented according to the different network paths traversed. The designer or the user (by using function keys) can adapt the dialogue according to user characteristics.

CONNECT comes with a family of tools to help build the system:

- BUILDNET, an interactive network constructor;
- BUILDSCR, to construct screens;
- VIEWNET, to examine nets and screens;
- EXECNET, to execute the net;
- BUILDTSK, to construct tasks;
- TESTSCR, to test a single screen;
- PERFNET, to examine net statistics.

A support system based on Path Algebras (Alty, 1984b) has also been developed. This allows the designer to analyze the net for consistency and to examine the net behaviour. Using this system, it would, for example, be possible to determine what would be on the screen at any particular point in the dialogue.

7.6 Grammar-based systems: SYNICS

Grammar-based notations such as Backus–Naur Form (BNF) are also often referred to as 'production rule' systems in that the application of the rules can be viewed as 'producing sentences (programs) in the language'. For use as a notation for a dialogue system the grammar defines the input language and sometimes the output too (Shneiderman, 1981). The terminals of the grammar correspond to the user's input tokens (mouse clicks, keyboard characters) and the non-terminals are related to the higher-level structure of the dialogue.

The user interface is thus (as far as input is concerned) a parser for this grammar. In order to act on the user input, actions are attached to rules of the grammar. These actions may be calls to procedures within the application or prompts to the user. This is the approach taken in the design of the *yacc* compiler–compiler available under UNIX. The main advantage of using context-free grammars is that a wealth of related work exists from their use in programming languages. However, they have proved awkward to use, particularly in controlling when actions are performed. Additionally, they are only well suited to parsing linear textual input and not to more graphically based interactions.

An example of the form of the notation is shown below in a command from a screen-based editor. The designer defines non-terminal

symbols (shown with < and >) as a series of rules defined (shown as
:: =) in terms of a series of terminal symbols (shown as UPPER-CASE
or as single-quoted characters) and other non-terminal symbols. Choices
are separated with a vertical bar and repetition indicated with an
asterisk. Terminal symbols must be matched with user input, while
non terminal symbols are for structuring purposes.

```
<locate> ::= <get line> <move to line>
<get line> ::= <find command> | <scroll>*
<move to line> ::= <cursor movement>*
<find command> ::= '/' <search string> CR
<scroll> ::= '^D' | '^U'
<cursor movement> ::= '⇐' | '⇑' | '⇒' | '⇓'
```

SYNICS (Edmonds, 1981) was developed in 1978 at Leicester
Polytechnic and also described by Guest (1982). The name SYNICS is
taken from SYN tax and semantICS. The initial idea was to use BNF to
specify the dialogue. The system produced a table-driven, top-down
recognizer that accepts strings of text from the user.

Subsequently this was augmented with a transition network front end
(dialogue definition language, DDL). In adding the transition net
front-end the BNF is now associated with arc conditions and therefore
combines the expressive power of the string matching of BNF with the
more attractive features of transition networks.

Later work has produced SYNICS2 (Edmonds and Guest, 1984).
This uses *dialogue events*, which contain GKS output and control, then
take input from the application or user and are followed by any
required application action and setting of variables. For example:

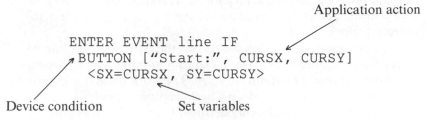

Thus the device condition is tested for whether the button is pressed,
and, if so, the variables are set to the (x, y) coordinates of the pointer
locations and the event is sent to the application, indicating that this is
the start of a line with parameters set from the variables containing the
(x, y) coordinates.

7.7 Natural language

Natural-language communication has long been viewed as a Holy Grail
in human interaction with computers (Rich, 1984). Among other

objectives, this is one of the aims within the man–machine communications component of the Japanese Fifth Generation Project (Simons, 1983). However, the use of natural language has its dangers as was shown by early work on natural language communication at MIT (Weizenbaum, 1966). Weizenbaum developed a pseudonatural language program named ELIZA (after Eliza Doolittle in Shaw's play *Pygmalion*), which used keyword and template matching and would then trigger off output that was some simple transformation of the input. A variety of other stratagems such as standard stock phrases were also used, and in addition ELIZA could refer back to earlier inputs when there were lulls in the user response. That it was so successful at creating the illusion of being able to carry on a conversation, and yet had virtually no understanding, is a warning that the use of natural language may cause users to imbue the interface or application with more intelligence than is the case.

In subsequent research into natural language dialogues it has generally been found that the more successful applications have either limited its use to output only, or have operated within a narrow knowledge domain.

At the UK National Physical Laboratory (NPL), Dr Chris Evans developed a medical interviewing system (Bevan and Pobgee, 1981) that showed a successful use of natural language for textual output. The output of Evans's system consisted of questions for the patient to answer, and also reassuring phrases. The user input was confined to selecting one of three possible answers using buttons labelled 'yes', 'no' and 'don't know'. The system also split the logic of controlling the dialogue from the interview text itself, thus modularizing the system so that non-programmers could prepare the interview text. The NPL work always made it clear that the computer was simply repeating text and collecting simple replies.

Work on expert systems has shown that the NPL approach can be successfully extended to provide full language output with a terse input of a restricted form of natural language. The work on Mycin (Shortliffe, 1976), for example, developed a medical diagnosis expert system for infections. An abbreviated example from Mycin is shown below:

```
[5] What is the infection?
**  PRIMARY-BATEREMIA
[6] Please give the date and time where...
**  MAY 5, 1975
...
```

Eventually the Mycin system offers a diagnosis and a suggested therapy.

With less constrained natural language input, a more restricted domain is generally required. Work at MIT by Dr Terry Winograd on his SHRDLU (Winograd, 1972) project demonstrated quite impressive understanding in the constrained world of model blocks. However, it is not clear how this could be extended to larger domains.

7.7.1 UNIX Consultant (UC)

UNIX Consultant (Wilensky *et al.*, 1984) was developed at the University of California, Berkeley in 1984 and acts as an advisor to a user of the UNIX operating system. It is a natural language interface that comprises an input analyzer, an output generator, a context and memory model, a common-sense planner, extensible knowledge bases for UNIX and English and a goal analysis system for acquiring new knowledge. Users can query UC on actions to be performed, ask about command names and formats, receive on-line definitions and get debugging help. If this fails to help, then the user is at least still able to proceed, as UC sits to one side of the user interacting with UNIX.

An example interaction (taken from the Wilensky *et al.*, 1984 paper) is as follows:

```
User: How do I delete a file?
UC:   Typing 'rm filename' will remove the
file with filename from your current
directory.
User: A directory?
UC:   Typing 'rm -r directoryname' will
recursively delete the directoryname and all
the files and directories contained in the
directory.
User: How do I print a file on the
lineprinter?
UC:   To print a file on the lineprinter type
'lpr filename'
...
  some intervening interactions
...
User: Has the file foo been printed yet?
UC:   The file foo is in the lineprinter
queue.
User: How can I cancel it?
UC:   To remove files from the line printer
queue, type 'lprm username'
```

Some problems can arise if the form of help, while being correct, results in the user making an error. For example, the following, imaginary, conversation would result in the user removing all his or her files!

```
User:   How do I get more disk space?
Naive: Use the command 'rm *' to get more
disk space.
```

It is reported that in experimental use the response times were very slow—up to 15 seconds on a VAX 11/780.

In summary, as indicated above, there are problems with users forming incorrect conclusions from the use of natural language interfaces. Natural language is also ambiguous (Hill, 1983) and requires large programs even for narrow domains. Typing complete sentences as natural language input is far from an ideal interaction style, and even speech recognition, where natural language input would seem most appropriate, may not be the answer given the current state of the art.

7.8 Adaptive dialogues

We understand human behaviour much less than we understand computers. With the interface as a separate module the design can be modified in the light of user experience. It must therefore be easy to change. The aim is to minimize the cognitive load and to compensate for the weaknesses of the human. Hence the first need is to identify the weaknesses and strengths of particular users.

7.8.1 Agents for adaptation

Adaptive interfaces are concerned with ways in which interfaces can be built so that *while in use* they can be adapted. Edmonds (1981) suggested a variety of possible adaptation mechanisms: adaptation by the system automatically; adaptation by the system in cooperation with the user; adaptation by exploiting an expert intermediary; and adaptation by the end-user himself or herself.

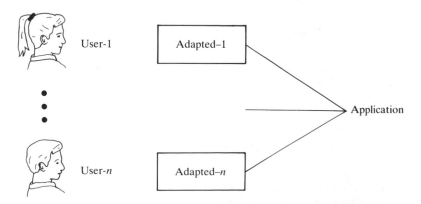

Figure 7.8 One application with several users' adapted interfaces

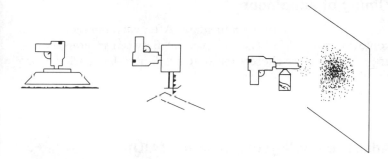

Figure 7.9   A common tool adapted to different tasks

In traditional linear system development (see Chapter 1), the system as a whole often fails because system interface needs cannot be anticipated and met. Of course, users are themselves adaptable, but in many situations they may not want to adapt to an inflexible system. In any case, users' needs are diverse and constantly changing. As shown in Figure 7.8, the application need have only one user interface if that could be adapted to the needs of different users and can have differently adapted parts of the system for an individual user over time.

7.8.2 Forms of adaptation

Some possible forms of adaptation are:

- dialogue style,
    e.g., yes/no, menus, forms, command language, natural language;
- current task context,
    e.g., contents of a directory or mail box,
    macros for frequent commands,
    context-sensitive help and error measages;
- the task,
    e.g., setting an appropriate environment for this task.

Figure 7.9 illustrates the concept of the tool being adapted to different tasks yet presenting the same interface to the user. If this approach is compared with the alternative of having a separate sanding machine, jigsaw and paint-spray, the interfaces may well be quite different. In human–computer interaction, the two alternatives are readily illustrated by comparing the Macintosh 'universal' interface style with the wide range of interfaces presented by different application packages for the IBM PC. A further consideration is how well the two approaches allow the user to complete a task, for example in using the saw to create a hole in wood or metal.

7.8.3 Timing of adaptation

Choices must also be made of *when* to adapt. After each interaction? After a context change? After task completion? Between sessions? Whatever time quanta are chosen, the system will need feedback, i.e., *an evaluation of the user's performance with the current adaptation*. This is problematical, since both the user and the system are adapting simultaneously.

7.8.4 Adaptive intelligent dialogues (AID)

The phase 1 exemplar of the AID project was an adaptive interface to the electronic mail system Telecom Gold. Its principal adaptation dimensions were the level of guidance, the use of context, recognizing commands from analogous systems, allowing user tailoring, and informing the user about additional unused functionality. Under guidance from the user model, the system could vary the level of prompting, the amount of feedback and the help level.

Though superficially appealing, the design of a complete adaptive dialogue system proved to be problematical, and the two later phases of the AID project therefore attempted to break down the issues involved in adaptation into more tractable components (see Chapter 13).

The most important conclusion from the project was that adaptation is not a single idea but a family of techniques that can be applied from the earliest stages in design through to run-time. Although the AID project did not achieve any specific major breakthrough which delivered outstanding user benefits, it contributed enormously to the understanding of the mechanisms of adaptation, both within humans and machines. In particular, it established constraints which had not previously been realized on the circumstances in which adaptation could be used effectively in interface design.

7.9 Summary

This chapter has discussed a variety of dialogue delivery systems. In general, a modular system structure is adopted, with the objective of making the range of dialogues and applications supported as wide as possible. Each system provides some form of *specification language* for the user input, but most are weak on describing the output side of the interactions.

Different systems provide different levels of support for *dialogue design and development*. Some systems are simply *toolkits* for building interfaces of a particular type; others also provide support for subsequent *simulation* and *evaluation*. Where post-design support is provided, it may be either independent of, or integrated with, the application software. However, there are as yet no aids to check whether the designer is adhering to HCI guidelines. Similar approaches are taken in the design of direct manipulation dialogue systems: in view of their importance and widespread exploitation, these are discussed under the general heading of *windowing systems* as Chapter 10 of this book.

References

Akscyn, R. M. and D. L. McCracken (1984) 'ZOG and the USS Carl-Vinson: lessons in systems development', *Interact '84, Proceedings of 1st IFIP Conference on Human Computer Interaction*, **1**, 303–308.

Akscyn, R. M., E. Yoder and D. McCracken (1988a) 'The data model is the heart of interface design', *CHI '88, Conference Proceedings on Human Factors in Computing Systems (Washington, May 15–19)*, Soloway, Frye and Sheppard (eds), Addison-Wesley, Wokingham, 115–120.

Akscyn, R. M., D. I. McCracken and E. A. Yoder (1988b) 'KMS: A distributed hypermedia system for managing knowledge in organizations', *Communications of the ACM*, **31** (7), 820–835.

Alty, J. L. (1984a) *The Conversational Node Executor: CONNECT*, University of Strathclyde MMI Group, Glasgow.

Alty, J. L. (1984b) 'The application of path algebras to interactive dialogue design', *Behaviour and Information Technology*, **3** (2), 119–132.

Beech, D. (ed.) (1986) *Concepts in User Interfaces: A Reference Model for Command and Response Languages*, Springer, Berlin.

Bevan, N. and P. Pobgee (1981) 'MICKIE—a microcomputer for medical interviewing', *International Journal of Man–Machine Studies*, **14**, 39–47.

Edmonds, E. A. (1981) 'Adaptive man–computer interfaces', in *Computing Skills and the User Interface*, M. J. Coombs and J. L. Alty (eds), Academic Press, Orlando, Fla., 389–426.

Edmonds, E. A. and S. P. Guest (1984) 'The SYNICS2 user interface manager', *Interact '84, Proceedings, 1st IFIP Conference on Human Computer Interaction*, vol. 1, 53–56.

Guest, S. P. (1982) 'The use of software tools for dialogue design', *International Journal of Man–Machine Studies*, **16**, 263–285.

Hayes, P. J. and P. A. Szekely (1982) 'Graceful interaction through the COUSIN command interface', *International Journal of Man–Machine Studies*, **19** (3), 285–305.

Hill, I. D. (1983) 'Natural language versus computer language', in *Designing for Human–Computer Communication*, M. S. Sime and M. J. Coombs (eds), Academic Press, Orlando, Fla., 55–72.

Rich, E. (1984) 'Natural language interfaces', *IEEE Computer*, **17** (9), 39–47.

Robertson, G., D. McCracken and A. Newell (1981) The ZOG approach to man–machine communication, *International Journal of Man–Machine Studies*, **14**, 461–488.

Robinson, J. and A. Burns (1985) 'A dialogue development system for the design and implementation of user interfaces in Ada', *Computer Journal*, **28** (1), 22–28.

Shneiderman, B. (1981) 'Multi-party grammars and related features for defining interactive systems', *IEEE Transactions on Systems, Man and Cybernetics*, **SMC-12** (2), 148–154.

Shortliffe, E. H. (1976) *Computer-based Medical Consultations Mycin* (North-Holland), Elsevier, New York.

Simons, G. L. (1983) *Towards Fifth-generation Computers*, NCC Publications, Manchester.

Walton, P. L., R. R. Holland and L. I. Wolf (1979) Medical guidance and PROMIS, *IEEE Computer*, **12** (11), 19–27.

Wasserman, A. I., P. A. Pircher, D. T. Shewmake and M. L. Kersten (1986) 'Developing interactive information systems with the user software engineering methodology', *IEEE Transactions on Software Engineering*, **SE-12** (2), 326–345. Also in Baecker and Buxton (see under 'General').

Weizenbaum, J. (1966) 'Eliza—A computer program for the study of natural language communications between man and machine', *Communications of the ACM*, **9** (1), 36–45. Reprinted in *Communications of the ACM 25th Anniversary Issue, Jan. 1985*, **26** (1), 23–27.

Wilensky, R., Y. Arens and D. Chin (1984) 'Talking to Unix in English: an overview of UC', *Communications of the ACM*, **27** (6), 574–593.

Winograd, T. (1972) *Understanding Natural Language*, Academic Press, Orlando, Fla.

Further reading

General

Baecker, R. M. and W. A. Buxton (eds) (1987) *Readings in Human–Computer Interaction*, Morgan Kaufmann, (Afterhurst), Hove, E. Sussex. (The editors have selected about 60 papers from major researchers in the HCI field.)

Pfaff, G. E. (ed.) (1985) *User Interface Management Systems*, Springer, Berlin. (Reports on the 1983 Seeheim workshop.)

Introduction

Alexander, H. (1987) *Formally Based Tools and Techniques for Human–Computer Dialogues* Ellis Horwood, Chichester.

Anderson, R. H. and J. J. Gillogly (1976) *Rand Intelligent Terminal Agent (RITA): Design Philosophy*, Rand Corporation, Santa Monica, Calif.

Backus, J. W. (ed.) (1960) 'Report on the algorithmic language Algol60', *Communications of the ACM*, **3**, 229–314.

Chomsky, N. (1957) *Syntactic Structures*, Mouton, The Hague.

Cockton, G. (1986) 'Where do we draw the line?—derivation and evaluation of user interface software separation rules', in *People and Computers, Proceedings of the Second BCS Conference on HCI*, M. J. Harrison and A. F. Monk (eds), Cambridge University Press, Cambridge, 417–431.

Dance, J. R., T. E. Granor, R. D. Hill, S. E. Hudson, J. Meads, B. A. Myers and A. Schulert (1987) 'Report on the run-time structure of UIMS-supported applications', *Computer Graphics*, **21** (2), 97–101.

Green, M. (1986) 'A survey of three dialogue models', *ACM Transactions on Graphics*, **5** (3), 244–275. Also available in *User Interface Management Systems*, G. Pfaff (ed.), Springer, Berlin, 1985.

Guest, S. P. (1982) 'The use of software tools for dialogue design', *International Journal of Man–Machine Studies*, **16**, 263–285.

Newman, W. M. (1968) *A System for Interactive Graphical Programming*, *AFIPS SJCC*, **32**, 47–54.

Rosson, M. B., M. Susanne and W. A. Kellog (1988) 'The designer as user: building requirements for design tools from design practice', *Communications of the ACM*, **31** (11), 1288–1298.

Totterdell, P. A. and P. Cooper (1986) 'Design and evaluation of the AID adaptive front end to Telecom Gold', in *Proceedings of the BCS Conference on HCI*, M. J. Harrison and A. F. Monk (eds), Cambridge University Press, Cambridge, 281–295.
Wasserman, A. I. (1985) 'Extending state transition diagrams for the specification of human–computer interaction', *IEEE Transactions on Software Engineering*, **11** (8), 699–713. Also in Baecker and Buxton (see under 'General').

COUSIN

Hayes, P. J., P. A. Szekely and R. A. Lerner (1985) 'Design alternatives for user interface management systems based on experience with COUSIN', *CHI '85, Conference Proceedings on Human Factors in Computing Systems*, Addison-Wesley, Wokingham, 169–175.

Transition networks

Cockton, G. (1985) 'Three transition network dialogue management systems', *People and Computers, Proceedings of the First BCS Conference on HCI*, Johnson and Cook (eds), Cambridge University Press, Cambridge, 138–147.
Denert, E. (1977) 'Specification and design of dialogue systems with state diagrams', *International Computing Symposium*, North-Holland, Amsterdam, 417–424.
Parnas, D. L. (1969) 'On the use of transition diagrams in the design of a user interface for an interactive computer system', *Proceedings of the 24th National ACM Conference*, 379–385.
Wasserman, A. I. (1985) 'Extending state transition diagrams for the specification of human–computer interaction', *IEEE Transactions on Software Engineering*, **11** (8), 699–713. Also in Baecker and Buxton (see under 'General').
Woods, W. A. (1970) 'Transition network grammars for natural language analysis', *Communications of the ACM*, **13** (10), 591–606.

CONNECT

Alty, J. L. and A. Brooks (1985) 'Microtechnology and user friendly systems, the CONNECT dialogue executor', *Journal of Microcomputer Applications*, **8**, 333–346.
Brooks, A. and C. Thorburn (1988) 'User driven adaptive behaviour, a comparative evaluation and an inductive analysis', *People and Computers IV, Proceedings of the Fourth BCS Conference on HCI*, D. M. Jones and R. Winder (eds), Cambridge University Press, Cambridge, 237–255.

Grammar-based systems

Fountain, A. J. and M. A. Norman (1985) 'Modelling user behaviour with formal grammar', *People and Computers, Proceedings of the First BCS Conference on HCI*, Johnson and Cook (eds), Cambridge University Press, Cambridge, 3–12.
Hopcroft, J. E. and J. D. Ullman (1960) *Formal Languages and Their Relationship to Automata*, Addison-Wesley, Reading, Mass.

Reisner, P. (1981) 'Formal grammar and human factors design of an interactive graphics system', *IEEE Transactions on Software Engineering*, **SE-7** (2), 229–240.

Scott, M. L. and S.-K. Yap (1988) 'A grammar-based approach to the automatic generation of user-interface dialogues', *CHI '88, Conference Proceedings on Human Factors in Computing Systems (Washington, May 15–19)*, Soloway, Frye and Sheppard (eds), Addison-Wesley, Wokingham, 73–78.

Natural language

Weizenbaum, J. (1976) *Computer Power and Human Reason: from Judgment to Calculation*, W. H. Freeman, New York.

Adaptive dialogues

Browne, D. P., R. Trevellyan, P. Totterdell and M. Norman (1987) 'Metrics for the building, evaluation and comprehension of self-regulating adaptive systems', *Interact 87, Proceedings of 2nd Conference on HCI*, H. J. Bullinger and B. Shackel (eds), North-Holland, Amsterdam, 1081–1087.

Cockton, G. (1987) 'Some critical remarks on abstractions for adaptable dialogue managers', *People and Computers, Proceedings of the Third BCS Conference on HCI*, D. Diaper and R. Winder (eds), Cambridge University Press, Cambridge, 325–343.

Fowler, C. J. H., L. A. Macaulay and S. Siripoksup (1987) 'An evaluation of the effectiveness of the adaptive interface module (AIM) in matching dialogues to users', *People and Computers, Proceedings of the Third BCS Conference on HCI*, D. Diaper and R. Winder (eds), Cambridge University Press, Cambridge, 345–359.

Gargan, R. A., J. W. Sullivan and S. W. Tyler (1988) 'Multimodal response planning: an adaptive rule based approach', *CHI '88, Conference Proceedings on Human Factors in Computing Systems (Washington, May 15–19)*, Soloway, Frye and Sheppard (eds), Addison-Wesley, Wokingham, 229–234.

Hoppe, H. U. (1988) 'Task-oriented parsing—a diagnostic method to be used by adaptive systems', *CHI '88, Conference Proceedings on Human Factors in Computing Systems (Washington, May 15–19)*, Soloway, Frye and Sheppard, Addison-Wesley, Wokingham, 241–247.

Totterdell, P. A. and P. Cooper (1986) 'Design and evaluation of the AID adaptive front end to Telecom Gold', *Proceedings of the BCS HCI Conference on HCI*, M. J. Harrison and J. F. Monk (eds), Cambridge University Press, Cambridge, 281–295.

Totterdell, P. A., M. A. Norman and D. P. Browne (1987) 'Levels of adaptivity in interface design', *Interact '87, Proceedings of 2nd Conference on HCI*, H. J. Bullinger and B. Shackel (eds), North-Holland, Amsterdam, 715–722.

Tyler, S. W. (1988) 'SAUCI: a knowledge-based interface architecture', *CHI '88, Conference Proceedings on Human Factors in Computing Systems (Washington, May 15–19)*, Soloway, Frye and Sheppard (eds), Addison–Wesley, Wokingham, 235–240.

Direct manipulation

Bewley, W. L., T. L. Roberts, D. Schwit and W. L. Verplank (1983) 'Human factors testing in the design of Xerox's 8010 "Star" office workstation',

Proceedings of CHI '83, Conference on Human Factors in Computing Systems, ACM, 72–77. Also in Baecker and Buxton (see under 'General').

Carroll, J. M. and S. A. Mazur (1986) 'Lisa learning', *IEEE Computer*, **19** (10), 35–49.

Jacob, R. J. K. (1985) 'A state transition diagram language for visual programming', *IEEE Computer*, **18** (7), 51–59.

Jacob, R. J. K. (1986) 'A specification language for direct-manipulation user interfaces', *ACM Transactions on Office Information Systems*, **5** (4), 283–317.

Shneiderman, B. (1983) 'Direct manipulation: a step beyond programming languages', *IEEE Computer*, **16** (8), 57–69. Also excerpted in Baecker and Buxton (see under 'General').

Smith, D. C., C. Irby, R. Kimball, B. Verplank and E. Harslem (1982) 'Design of the Star user interface', *Byte*, **7** (4), 242–282. Also in Baecker and Buxton (see under 'General').

PART III

Interface hardware and software

8 Input/output hardware

GRAHAM LEEDHAM

8.1 Introduction

In Chapter 2 a model of the human–computer interface was introduced
which illustrated the human input/output requirements which have to
be met by computer input/output devices. These input/output
devices can be divided into three main groups: textual input devices,
pointing and picking devices and displays. In this chapter a review of
input/output hardware is given and the advantages and disadvantages
of each device discussed.

8.2 Sequential keyboards for text input

8.2.1 The QWERTY keyboard

The QWERTY keyboard layout (see Figure 8.1) was invented in 1878
by Scholes, Glidden and Soulé and was used in the first commercial
typewriter (Adler, 1973). It is by far the most widely used layout for
typewriter and computer input terminals. It was standardized on
commercial typewriters in 1905 but the justification for the layout is not
clear. Possibly it was designed to separate frequently used keys and so
avoid key bar clashes in the early typewriters, or perhaps it was based
on the letter order used in the printing industry. Whatever its origin, its
popularity has been maintained by its prevalence, its early

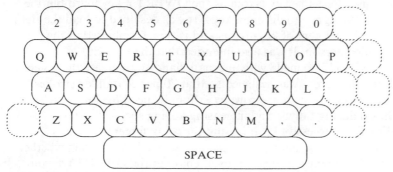

Figure 8.1 The QWERTY keyboard layout

standardization, and the large numbers of users which have built up over the decades.

The maximum speed typists can achieve using a QWERTY keyboard is typically between 80 and 90 words per minute. If 7 or 8 keys are pressed for each word (an average of 6 to 7 letters, plus the space character (Kucera and Francis, 1967)) this corresponds to over 600 keystrokes per minute. From observations made in Chapter 2, this approaches the physical limits of human capability. Speeds higher than 90 words per minute are only achieved by exceptional individuals, as is apparent from the typing rates reported in the Guinness Book of Records (1986).

Although the QWERTY keyboard is widely used it has a number of inefficiencies (Noyes, 1983; Cooper, 1983; Bailey, 1982). For example, 48 per cent of the movements between consecutive keys are one-handed, whereas two-handed operations are usually faster. Only 32 per cent of keystrokes are on the home row and therefore long reaches are frequently needed to locate subsequent keys on different rows. The left hand is overloaded with 56 per cent of keystrokes which, for the right-handed user, is the wrong way around. In addition there are a large number of awkward one-handed fingerings, as in the words 'tipple', 'was' and 'were'. Finally, the load on each finger is not well allocated to relieve strain. The little finger of each hand, which is the weakest, has a considerable number of keystrokes assigned to it.

Even with these inefficiencies it is apparent from the speeds achieved that there is little scope for speed improvement for one-key-at-a-time keyboards and the QWERTY keyboard has thus proved adequate in most computer applications. There have, however, been a number of alternative layouts proposed which alleviate some of its inefficiencies. Some of these alternatives are described below.

8.2.2 The Dvorak or simplified keyboard

The Dvorak keyboard layout (Figure 8.2) was designed in 1932 to reduce some of the inefficiencies of the QWERTY keyboard (Cooper, 1983). It uses the same key layout as the QWERTY keyboard but the letters are reassigned to different keys. It was designed to load the right hand with 56 per cent of keystrokes and is therefore biased to the right-handed person. It was also intended that the majority of keystrokes would be made with alternate hands to increase the potential speed. In addition, it was designed so that 70 per cent of keystrokes would be made on the home row, avoiding the need for long reaches and thus reducing fatigue and increasing keying speed. The layout also aimed to avoid excessive keying using the weak fingers.

A number of experiments have been performed to ascertain whether the Dvorak keyboard is any improvement over the QWERTY layout (Cooper, 1983). These experiments indicated that there is a marginal

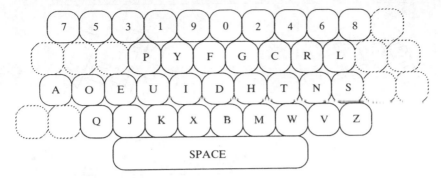

Figure 8.2 The Dvorak keyboard layout

speed improvement of between 10 and 15 per cent. This is much as expected owing to the physical keying limitations identified in Chapter 2. The main advantage of the Dvorak keyboard layout is the reduction in user fatigue due to ergonomic improvements. In spite of these documented advantages, the Dvorak keyboard has never achieved any commercial success and is unlikely to do so given the established base of the QWERTY keyboard. However, it is occasionally offered as an alternative layout on word-processing systems where the key allocation is software-defined.

8.2.3 The alphabetic keyboard

An alternative key assignment to the QWERTY and Dvorak design is the alphabetic ordering shown in Figure 8.3. This layout has been used in some specific applications and can be observed in many toy typewriters which are, presumably, intended as an aid to learning the alphabet. A two-row version of an alphabetic keyboard layout was used in the first typewriter in the mid-nineteenth century. The reason frequently given for choosing an alphabetic rather than the QWERTY layout is that it is thought to be more familiar and therefore more

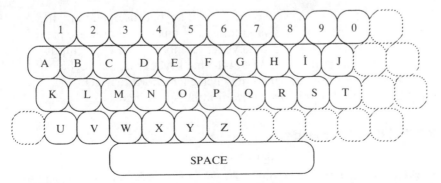

Figure 8.3 The Alphabetic keyboard layout

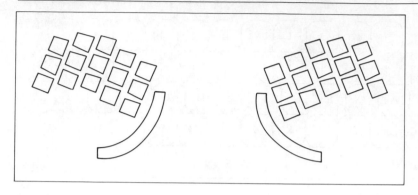

Figure 8.4   The key layout of the Klockenberg keyboard

efficient for non-typists. However, tests have shown that in this situation an alphabetic layout produces no noticeable improvement over the QWERTY keyboard layout (Cooper, 1983). In fact most of the tests show that the alphabetic layout is slower!

8.2.4 The Klockenberg keyboard

This keyboard differs from the QWERTY and Dvorak layouts in that it employs a separate set of keys for each hand rather than a row-by-row arrangement. It was first suggested by Klockenberg in 1926 and implemented by Kroemer (Bailey, 1982) (see Figure 8.4). The separated keygroups are intended to relieve the stress on the arms and shoulders. The key layout may also give some slight increase in speed, but experiments are inconclusive. As with the Dvorak layout the most significant advantage is the reduction in stress and fatigue. More recently the Maltron keyboard, designed in 1977, has used a similar key layout.

8.3 Chord keyboards for text input

Unlike one-key-at-a-time keyboards, chord keyboards operate by the depression of groups of keys simultaneously much as chords are played on a piano. Where the group of keys represents a single letter, input speed will be slower than one-key-at-a-time keyboards, but keyboard systems have also been designed in which each chord represents a syllable or word, leading to significant input speed increases.

8.3.1 The Microwriter

The Microwriter was developed in the late 1970s and was heavily marketed at the time. Its layout is shown in Figure 8.5 and consists of a small, handheld device with 6 buttons on it which are positioned so that

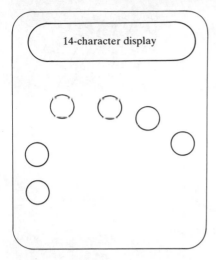

Figure 8.5   The Microwriter key layout

they fall naturally under the hand. In addition it has a small, 14-character display at the top. It operates by assigning a chord or group of keys to represent one letter. Some examples of these chords are shown in Figure 8.6. It is estimated that the maximum speed of this device is somewhere between 50 and 60 words per minute, or approximately 60 per cent of the speed of the QWERTY keyboard layout. This limitation in speed is due to the human hand's limited ability to press chord combinations repetitively. The main advantage of the Microwriter is that it is portable, one-handed and can be used in many situations where two-handed keyboards are impractical.

8.3.2 Palantype—the British machine shorthand system

In this shorthand system, words are recorded phonetically rather than orthographically. A group or chord of keys represents the phonetic

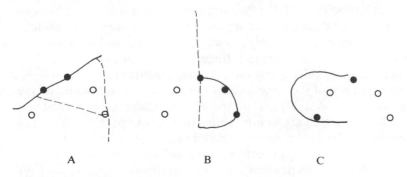

A   B   C

Figure 8.6   Example of Microwriter chord patterns

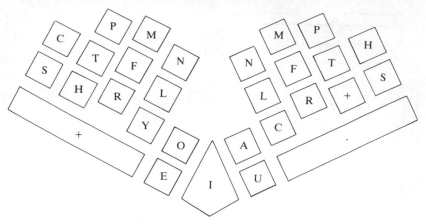

Figure 8.7 The Palantype keyboard layout

structure of each syllable. For example the words 'cat' and 'sip' are recorded as single chords in each case. The layout of the Palantype keyboard is shown in Figure 8.7, and consists of three groups of keys. On the left-hand side is a group of consonant keys which define the initial consonant sound of the syllable. In the middle is a group of 5 vowel keys to define the intermediate vowel sound, and on the right-hand side there is a further group of consonant keys which define the last consonant sound in the syllable. Consonant and vowel sounds which are not explicitly provided on the keyboard are represented by key combinations, for example T+ represents the sound 'D' and OU represents the sound 'OO'

The Palantype system can be used to record speech at more than 180 words per minute and is capable of recording verbatim speech. It has been used extensively in court reporting but seldom in the office environment. Currently there are only a few hundred proficient users. With the recent introduction of computer-aided transcription using the Palantype keyboard the number of users is increasing and a new training scheme has been initiated.

The main problem with the Palantype system as a means of text input to computer is that correct spelling cannot be guaranteed. For example, homophones such as 'bite', 'bight' and 'byte' are encoded using the same chord and are therefore indistinguishable although there are keying techniques which allow the keyboard operator to distinguish different spellings of the same word. Furthermore, word boundaries are not explicitly encoded (there is no space key) and are reconstructed using a longest-match algorithm applied to a Palantype–English dictionary. As a result, computer-aided transcription (CAT) systems cannot guarantee to output perfect orthographic English, and generally can only achieve 95–98 per cent correct transcription. Commercial CAT systems (one is shown in Figure 8.8) therefore also include an optimized

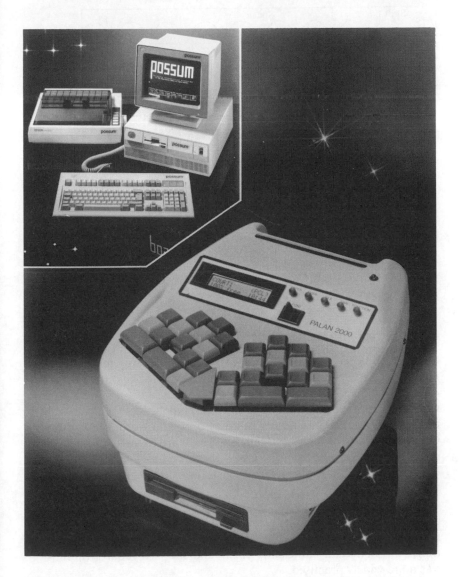

Figure 8.8 A commercial system for verbatim reporting which uses the Palantype keyboard. This device incorporates a printer and floppy disk for recording keystrokes. The data is transcribed into English using a transcription computer (inset) (photograph courtesy of Possum Controls Ltd, and Words and Pictures, Slough)

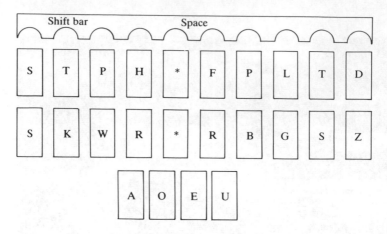

Figure 8.9 The Stenotype keyboard

Palantype–English editor for proofing transcripts (Downton and Brooks, 1984).

8.3.3 Other machine shorthand systems

Other machine shorthand systems work in a similar way to the Palantype system but use slightly different keyboard layouts. For example the Stenotype system uses the layout shown in Figure 8.9. The speed of this machine is similar to the Palantype's. It is widely used in the USA for verbatim reporting of court proceedings, and Stenotype CAT systems are also well established. There are estimated to be well over 100 000 stenotypists in the USA. Machine shorthand systems optimized for other languages also exist, for example, the French system Grandjean.

These chord keyboards are mostly used in specialized areas such as court reporting but could be used extensively in the office as a replacement for written shorthand or tape dictation if computer-aided transcription became sufficiently cheap and chord keyboard training was more widely practised.

8.4 Special-purpose keyboards

8.4.1 Numeric keypads

These keyboards are used to enter numeric data into computer systems. The standard layout found on one-key-at-a-time keyboards and adding machines is shown in Figure 8.10(a). Note that this system differs radically from the push-button telephone keyboard layout shown in Figure 8.10(b).

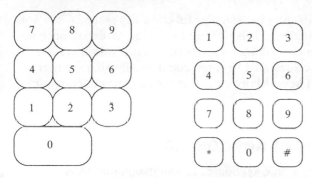

Figure 8.10 Numeric keypads **(a)** The standard calculator keypad
(b) The standard pushbutton telephone keypad

8.4.2 Function keys

Function keys provide the capability for functions of the (computer)
system to be invoked directly via a single keypress rather than by
naming the function using a group of alphanumeric keys.
Unfortunately, since the functions to be supported depend upon the
functionality of the system there is no standardization of key function
and little standardization of key placement. The advantages claimed for
function keys are:

- reduced memory load;
- greater ease of learning;
- greater speed (because there are less keystrokes);
- reduced error rate (by reducing keystrokes and options).

Function keys have a number of problems of their own. One particular
problem is the need for a large number of keys if there are a large
number of options. A large keyboard is expensive and causes slow key
location, slower learning and increased error rates. One solution to this
problem is to have soft function keys as found in cash dispensers at
many high street banks. This may be achieved by positioning each key
immediately below a corresponding explanatory display on the display
screen or by providing a liquid-crystal display on each key. The
alternative is to have more than one function for each key as is often
specified on calculators (and is also provided on the QWERTY
keyboard in the form of the shift and control keys). This has been
shown to increase the error rate but saves space and is a cheaper
solution.

Function keys are useful if the number of options is small (30 or less).
The objective is to design a function key layout which minimizes the
learning time, the operational effort and the number of errors
introduced into the system. General rules to achieve this are, firstly, to
group related keys together, and secondly, to group commonly used

keys together. The difficulty in designing function key systems is in not allowing for all eventualities. It is difficult to change hardware once the keyboard has been built, making it expensive to adapt and therefore inflexible. This can be alleviated to some extent by allowing the user to define the function of keys. Many current computer terminals support this requirement.

8.5 Overview of keyboards

Generally, one-key-at-a-time keyboards have a maximum operational speed of between 90 and 100 words per minute owing to the physical limitations of the human fingers' ability to press keys sequentially. The most significant advantage of alternative keyboard layouts over the standard QWERTY layout is the reduction in fatigue. This saving alone has not proved sufficient for any of these alternative keyboards to break the virtual monopoly of the QWERTY layout. The only way other keyboard layouts can encroach on the domain of the QWERTY keyboard is to achieve a significantly higher speed while retaining good ergonomic design. To achieve greater speeds radically different keyboard styles need to be considered.

Figure 8.11 summarizes the keyboards described above for text input to computer. From plotting the number of proficient users against the

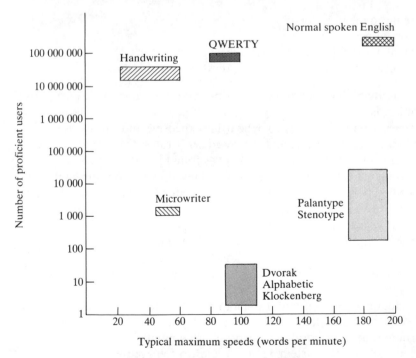

Figure 8.11 Comparison of text input to computer

typical maximum speed in words per minute for each keyboard it is clear that no keyboard approaches normal spoken English in popularity. The most popular keyboard system by far is the QWERTY system which has, it is estimated, around 100 million proficient users. Because it is used so extensively and can achieve reasonable speeds (approximately half the speed of normal spoken English) it is difficult to foresee the widespread introduction of any other keyboard into the office environment. The other sequential layouts (Dvorak, alphabetic and Klockenberg) have only a slight speed advantage over QWERTY, but may reduce operator fatigue. The only real advantages the Microwriter has over one-key-at-a-time systems is that it is one-handed and portable. Chord keyboard machine shorthand systems (such as Stenotype and Palantype) are capable of transcribing speech at normal spoken speeds but require lengthy periods of training. To date their use has therefore been confined to specialized applications such as verbatim reporting.

Ergonomic factors also need to be considered when specifying or designing a keyboard, and must be chosen to match the intended environment and users of the system. The most important factors are key size and shape, the angle of the keyboard to the user, the pressure required to operate a key, the key's distance of travel, the type style wording or icon indicating the key's function, and the relative key positions. Tactile feedback when the key is pressed is also an important factor. A number of keyboards can be found in the marketplace which do not provide any tactile indication that the key has been pressed, and many people find these keyboards quite disconcerting to use.

8.6 Cursor control and picking devices

These devices are generally used for selecting an item, specifying a position, rotating an object, drawing a line, specifying a value or quantity, or entering text. These six interactive tasks are specified as *select, position, orient, path, quantify* and *text* respectively by Foley *et al.* (1984), who also state the requirements of a cursor control device as follows:

A positioning technique that provides dynamic continuous feedback and allows movement in arbitary directions must be supported by a continuous motion input device such as a tablet or light pen or touch sensitive panel; furthermore the display device must be able to update a cursor position 20 to 30 times per second.

That is, in controlling a cursor there must be virtually instantaneous feedback of the effect of the movement on the screen. This leads to the definition of a ratio known as the C/D (control/display) ratio, defined as follows:-

$$C/D = \frac{\text{Movement of the hand or other responder}}{\text{movement of the cursor}}$$

This factor is particularly important in dealing with perception and fatigue. It is, of course, dependent upon screen size and distance from the operator.

The preceding sections on keyboards considered suitable devices for text entry operations. The following sections consider devices suitable for select, position, orient, path and quantify operations.

8.6.1 The touch-sensitive panel

These devices are referred to as touch panels because they detect the presence of a finger or stylus directly on the screen. They operate by interrupting a matrix of light beams (outside the visible spectrum) or by detecting capacitance changes or even ultrasonic reflections. Because their operation involves touching the screen they are direct pointing devices therefore have a C/D ratio of unity. Touch panels are fast and efficient and do not need any special pointing device (a finger is typically used). A feature of touch panels is that the number of touch-sensitive points on the screen can be varied and several points can be selected simultaneously. This is particularly useful for menu selection.

A number of problems are associated with the touch panel. When placed over conventional vertical displays they are tiring to use for long periods, and the preferred viewing distance for the display is not always the same as the preferred pointing distance. In addition, using the finger to point on a display will usually create a dirty screen. The light beams must be raised above the CRT display to allow for its convexity, which causes parallax problems particularly at the edges. It is therefore necessary to view the screen perpendicularly and this causes additional problems because fingers are fairly wide and blunt pointing devices, and so create difficulties when trying to select small areas of the screen. The finger and hand also tend to obscure the screen, making it difficult to select areas directly beneath the finger. Operations such as line drawing are very erratic, due to the width of the fingertip.

The touch panel is most useful as a pointing device for menu selection. It is particularly suited to some forms of hostile environment (such as public places or shop floors) where mechanical equipment such as a keyboard would be unsatisfactory because of the dirty environment or potential vandalism. Touch panels are not well suited to text editing or drafting operations. Generally they have become unpopular over the last few years and are not widely used, except in specialized environments (Olson, 1987).

8.6.2 The light pen

The light pen is usually attached by a coiled spring cable to a cathode
ray tube and operates by detecting a burst of light from the display
screen phosphor during the raster scan (Foley and van Dam, 1982;
Salmon and Slater, 1987). It is a direct-pointing device and has a C/D
ratio of unity. Since it is a relatively accurate pointing device, it can
address single pixels on the screen, and can thus be used for text editing,
menu selection and drawing purposes.

However, the light pen has a number of deficiencies. As with the
touch panel (and indeed any direct pointing device) the preferred
viewing distance often differs from the preferred pointing distance. The
pen is often bulky and awkward to use and may obscure what is being
pointed at. The pen is also fragile and easily broken when dropped, and
can be lost when put down on an untidy desk. Holders are usually
provided for the pen but in practice they are rarely used. A common
complaint from users is that the pen is tiring to use on conventional
upright displays. Since the light pen has no significant advantages
compared with indirect pointing devices such as the mouse, and several
disadvantages, it has become unpopular in recent years and is no longer
widely used.

8.6.3 The digitizing tablet

The main features of the digitizing tablet are that it is an indirect
pointing device and produces a series of (x, y) coordinates defining a
puck or pen movement on the tablet surface. Tablets are available in
different sizes and based upon several different principles of operation.
Two typical ones are shown in Figure 8.12. The *resistive* tablet works on
the principle of detecting point contact between two separated resistive
sheets (e.g., the Micropad tablet; Figure 8.12(a)). The advantage of the
resistive tablet is that it does not require a special stylus and can be
operated with an ordinary pen or even the user's finger. Another very
popular form of digitizing tablet is based on magnetism. Current pulses
are detected in a magnetic field by means of a small loop coil housed in
a pen stylus. The original BitPad marketed by the Summagraphics
organization, and compatibles marketed by a number of other
companies, are popular examples of this type of tablet. There are also
other tablet technologies, such as capacitive, electrostatic and sonic
digitizers. The sonic digitizer has the particular advantage that it does
not need any special writing surface. An ultrasonic pulse emitted by the
pen is detected by two or more microphones, usually positioned within
1 metre of the pen. Three-dimensional digitizers, which use three
microphones to detect (x, y, z) coordinates, are also available based on
this principle.

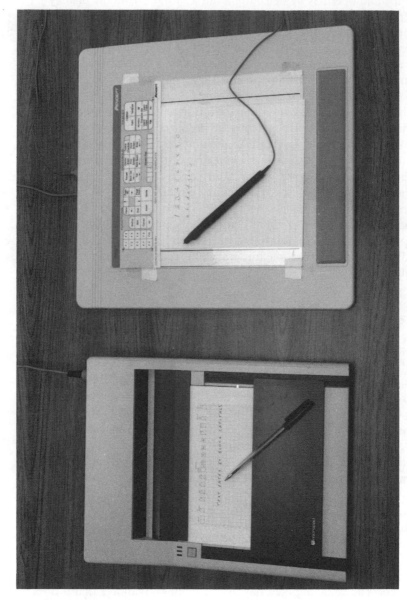

Figure 8.12 Examples of typical digitizing tablets **(a)** Micropad **(b)** Penpad

The majority of digitizing tablets have a very high resolution (0.001 in static resolution is typical). They are available in different writing sizes from A5 up to 60 in × 60 in for full-sized drafting tablets. The sampling rate, which determines the dynamic resolution, is usually between 50 and 200 samples per second. For example, a pen moving at 100 mm per second on the surface of a tablet with a sampling rate of 100 samples per second would only have a dynamic resolution of 1 mm even if the static resolution was considerably higher. The C/D ratio of tablets is specified by software scaling, but varies typically from 0.3 to 1.0. Values of the C/D ratio outside this range usually lead to some perceptual distortion and make the tablet difficult to use in path and orient operations.

An advantage of digitizing tablets is that they can be used to control a cursor in absolute or relative mode. Absolute mode provides a one-to-one mapping from tablet to display, while relative mode only moves the cursor when there is motion on the tablet. The latter mode is very similar to the mouse, which is described below in Section 8.6.6. Unfortunately, digitizing tablets are not perfect and they can introduce imperfections into the series of (x, y) coordinates (see Section 9.5.1).

Writing tablets are easy to use and not especially tiring, but they are expensive in comparison to the mouse. They are most suited to drafting applications but have also been used extensively for direct and indirect menu selection and for cursor positioning. Unlike any of the other devices in this section, if supported by suitable character recognition software, they can be used for text input as well as pointing and picking functions. Their main problem is that the tablet requires a considerable amount of desk space and is not easily moved to the preferred working position.

8.6.4 The joystick

The joystick (see Figure 8.13(a)) is an indirect pointing device. Cursor movement is controlled by movement (the absolute joystick) or by pressure on the stick (the isometric or velocity controlled joystick). Buttons are usually provided for selection or are associated with a keyboard. The joystick takes up very little desk space and the C/D ratio is variable. For an absolute joystick the C/D ratio is defined as:

$$C/D = \frac{\text{fraction of circle movement} \times \text{circumference of circle}}{\text{cursor movement}}$$

It is not possible to define the C/D ratio for the isometric joystick because no proportional movement takes place; velocity rather than position is proportional to pressure on the stick.

Because it is remote from the display screen the joystick has the advantage that it does not obscure the screen: it is also usually quite inexpensive. Joysticks are therefore frequently used in the lower-priced end of the computer market, particularly for games, and have also proved very useful for more general orientation, positioning and picking operations. They are often built into the keyboard or computer console and therefore are difficult to move to the preferred working position.

8.6.5 The tracker ball

The tracker ball (see Figure 8.13(b)) is a mechanical rolling ball or sphere set into a surface with buttons associated near it for selection purposes. The direction and speed of rotation govern the direction and speed of the cursor on the screen. The tracker ball is a fairly accurate positioning device and an indirect pointing device. The C/D ratio is difficult to calculate owing to the flywheel effect, but if this is ignored the calculation is very similar to that used for the absolute joystick. The tracker ball is an inexpensive device and fairly easy to use and is also not particularly tiring. However, picking needs additional selection switches adjacent to the tracker ball.

8.6.6 The mouse

The mouse is a small, hand-held box usually about 8 cm × 5 cm which is moved about on a flat surface with motion detected by one of several techniques. The most popular form of mouse uses a rolling ball to transmit motion to two orthogonal potentiometers or optical sensors within the mouse housing (Figure 8.14(a) and (b)), and thus is equivalent to an inverted tracker ball. Mice of this sort are widely used on personal computers such as the Apple Macintosh and the IBM PC and compatibles. Another form of mouse uses a pair of orthogonal wheels to detect vertical and horizontal motion directly. Other mice detect the horizontal and vertical movement by optical means. The optical mouse is widely used on Sun workstations in the form of the Summagraphics mouse (see Figure 8.14(c)). The disadvantage of the optical mouse is that it needs a correctly oriented special surface with optically detectable lines in the vertical and horizontal directions to determine the movement, but it has the advantage of being less susceptible to contamination by dust and dirt. There are also a number of foot-operated mice but their performance is unassessed at the moment.

The mouse typically has one, two or three buttons on its top for making selections. Most types of mouse (with the exclusion of the optical mouse) can be used on any preferred working surface and are reasonably pleasant and easy to use. The preferred range of C/D ratio is 0.3 to 1.0, as with the writing tablet. The mouse has proved particularly good at picking from menus or positioning a cursor and also even for drafting. It is quite inexpensive, as it is easy to manufacture and at the moment is by far the most popular cursor control device. Nevertheless, there are still some problems associated with it. The trailing lead is

(a)

(b)

Figure 8.13 Examples of a typical joystick and a tracker ball device **(a)** Joystick **(b)** Tracker ball

203

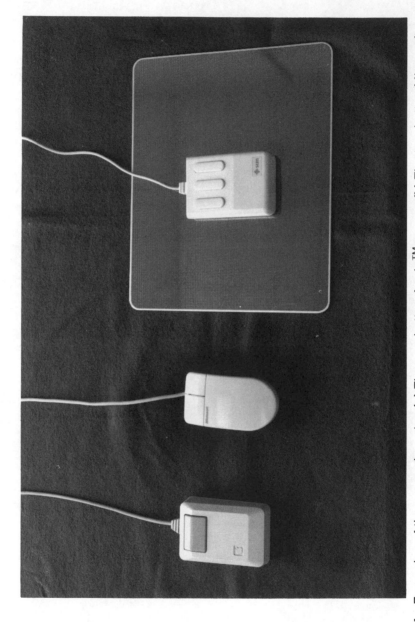

Figure 8.14 Examples of three popular mice **(a)** The one-button Apple™ mouse **(b)** The two-button Microsoft mouse **(c)** The three-button Summagraphics mouse

awkward and the need for a flat surface near the work area on which to operate the mouse can be a disadvantage, particularly for a portable personal computer.

8.6.7 Cursor control keys

Four keys (left, right, up and down) are normally provided on current computer keyboards to control the movement of the cursor on the screen. There are several possible arrangements of these four keys (e.g., in a line, a square, or a diamond), but no standardized configuration. Their main advantage is price: they are the cheapest form of cursor control device. Cursor location or positioning is very slow even with auto repeat keys when the movement is large. Nevertheless, in limited-text editing operations, where the movement is small, they have an acceptable performance. Relative performances of cursor keys, joysticks and mouse have been fully investigated for text-processing operations, and it has been shown that here the mouse has significant performance advantages: it is the fastest and also has the lowest error rates, while cursor keys are the slowest, with a positioning time proportional to the number of keystrokes (Card *et al.*, 1978).

8.6.8 Thumb wheels

These are two orthogonal dials which are used for horizontal and vertical movement of a cross-hair cursor on a graphics display screen. They have a fixed position on the display terminal and are relatively inexpensive. However, they are fairly slow for cursor positioning and have mostly been superseded by the tracker ball, joystick or mouse. They were extensively used on Tektronix graphics terminals in the early 1970s.

8.7 Overview of pointing and picking devices

Pointing and picking devices can be split into two distinct groups: direct pointing devices, where the user points directly onto the screen, and indirect pointing devices, where the user's movement elsewhere controls the cursor movement on a screen. The two main direct pointing devices, the touch panel and the light pen, are tiring to use on conventional displays, while the indirect pointing devices, such as the joystick tracker ball, cursor control keys and thumb wheel, are relatively easy to use but have disadvantages in particular circumstances (Buxton, 1988). The most typical operations carried out by cursor control devices are (as defined by Foley *et al.*, (1984) *select, position, orient, path* and *quantify*. The most popular indirect pointing devices which compromise between

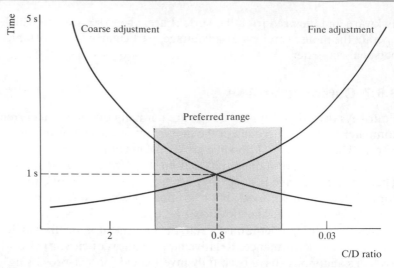

Figure 8.15 Speed/accuracy trade-off for indirect pointing devices (numbers are for a typical graphic display and desk and chair situation; based on a diagram from Foley *et al.*, 1984)

these five basic requirements are the mouse and the digitizing tablet. This may change in the near future with the development of high-resolution flat-screen technologies (see Section 8.8 below) when a direct pointing device in a similar form to the light pen may become more popular again.

Selecting a pointing device for a particular display technology or application is not always straightforward. For indirect pointing devices there is a trade-off between the C/D ratio and the time to make a selection. As shown in Figure 8.15, the time to make the movement for a selection decreases rapidly as the C/D ratio decreases, but at the same time, the time to make fine adjustment increases very rapidly. The preferred range of C/D ratio optimizes the overall performance over both these tasks. Typically this corresponds to a C/D ratio of about 0.8 and a selection time of around one second. In addition, it is necessary to consider the types of interaction which are needed from the interface: menu selection, cursor positioning, object orientation, path definition or quantity specification.

Picking and pointing devices are currently going through the same evolutionary development cycle of diversity followed by rationalization which occurred with keyboards in the late nineteenth century, spurred by the widespread introduction over the last decade of bit-mapped computer displays and supporting software packages. It is therefore possible to predict that a degree of standardization in picking and pointing devices may ultimately emerge, with the mouse looking most likely to be adopted as the 'standard' device at present. It is unlikely that a 'universal' device will emerge, however, as the variety of

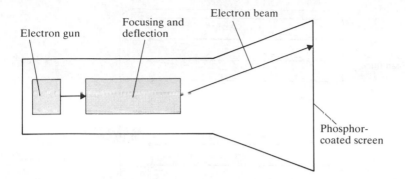

Figure 8.16   The CRT principle

applications and environments in which pointing devices are used is too diverse for any one device to be optimum under all circumstances (for example, the mouse is unsatisfactory in portable applications, where a flat surface may not be available (Milner, 1988).

8.8 Visual displays

8.8.1 The cathode ray tube (CRT)

The cathode ray tube has been the dominant technology for many years and many millions of CRT's are in current use. The principle of operation is illustrated in Figure 8.16. A stream of electrons is emitted from an electron gun and focused and deflected by an electric field onto a phosphor-coated screen which glows at the point of contact with the electrons (Foley and van Dam, 1982). There are three main types of cathode ray tube in common use: raster scan, random scan and the direct-view storage tube. The operation of these three types of the device is described below. The reader wishing to obtain a fuller description of the characteristics and operation of CRTs is directed to the works of Hearn and Baker (1986), Salmon and Slater (1987), Foley and van Dam (1982) and Sims (1969)

The raster scan CRT

The raster scan system is the most commonly used form of CRT and is the type found in television sets. The beam of electrons is directed sequentially from left to right across the screen working down the screen one line at a time until the bottom of the screen is reached, when the whole process starts again from the top. This raster scanning is illustrated in Figure 8.17. Varying the intensity of the electron beam produces different shades of grey on a black and white CRT. The frame rate, or rate at which a whole screen is updated, is usually 30 Hz or

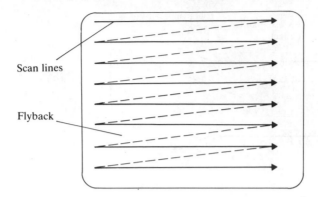

Figure 8.17 Raster scanning

higher to minimize the flicker effect. *Interlacing*, which is the process of scanning odd lines first through the whole screen and then scanning the even lines, is also used to reduce flicker. Another method of reducing the flicker is to use a high-persistence phosphor on the screen, but this tends to cause smearing of the image if there is a significant amount of animation. Using a standard monochrome television CRT, approximately 512 × 512 pixel resolution graphics or up to 24 lines × 40 characters per line of alphanumeric text can be displayed but the text has poor legibility. Higher resolution is possible at a higher price, and typical current workstations have resolutions up to about 1600 × 1200 pixels.

In the colour CRT tube three electron guns are used, each of which produces a different colour by illuminating different-coloured phosphor dots on the screen. These phosphor dots are red, green and blue and are focused by the *shadow mask*. It is because of this shadow mask that colour CRT systems have lower resolution than monochrome CRTs. An alternative method producing colour is by what is known as the *beam penetration* method. The principle is that the type of phosphor used will glow a different colour, depending on the intensity of the electron beam. The beam penetration method is used less frequently than the three-beam system.

The main disadvantage of the CRT tube is that it is bulky owing to the electron gun and focusing circuitry directly behind the screen. Also, diagonal lines tend to look jagged because of the raster scan process. This problem can be reduced either by using a high-resolution CRT tube or a technique known as *anti-aliasing*, which softens sharp edges of line segments. Eye strain and fatigue caused by flicker, poor legibility and the low contrast of the CRT display have also been identified as ergonomic problems. The main advantages of CRTs (and the reason for their extensive use) are that they are inexpensive for low to medium resolution, they are fast enough to display rapid animation, and they

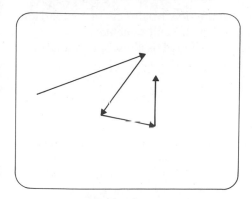

Figure 8.18   Random scanning

have a very high colour capability. The price increases rapidly as the ˙
resolution increases.

The random scan CRT or directed-beam refresh or vector display

Whereas the raster scan CRT updates the whole screen sequentially from
top to bottom, the random scan CRT draws the lines which are to be
displayed directly in sequence. This is illustrated in Figure 8.18. As with
the raster scan CRT, the random scan CRT updates the screen display at
30 Hz or more to reduce the effect of flicker. Because the lines are
produced by direct-beam manipulation, higher resolution is possible
than in a raster scan system, up to 4096 × 4096 pixels. In addition,
slanted or diagonal lines do not appear jagged. The main disadvantages
of using a random scan CRT are that only four colours are possible
because the beam penetration technique is used, and the colours
produced are also generally of a poorer quality than those achieved on
the raster scan CRT. The raster scan CRT, like the random scan CRT, is
bulky owing to the electron gun and focusing mechanism and eye strain
and fatigue are again frequently reported due to the flicker. Random
scan CRTs are also more expensive than equivalent raster scan CRTs.

The direct-view storage tube (DVST)

The principle of operation of the DVST is very similar to that of the
random scan CRT except that the image is maintained within the tube
using flood guns rather than being repetitively updated by rescanning.
The advantage of this is that there is no flicker on the screen. It is
possible to add selectively to the display but selective erasure of parts of
the screen is not possible. To achieve this function it is necessary to
erase the whole screen and redraw the image excluding the deleted
components. As with random scan CRTs, it is possible to produce
DVSTs with very high resolution, typically 4096 × 3120 pixels. DVSTs

have the disadvantage of low contrast and low brightness in comparison to other CRT displays, and colour is very difficult to achieve. The DVST is quite widely used on analogue storage oscilloscopes and also on older-style graphic display systems.

Other CRT displays

It is possible to produce three-dimensional and stereoscopic displays using CRTs, but these are very expensive and are necessary only for specialized applications (see Ikedo, 1984, and Roese and McCleary, 1979).

Health hazards

There are health worries with regard to prolonged use of CRT equipment owing to the emission of low levels of potentially harmful radiation. This radiation hazard is not fully understood although it is believed that it is not a major health risk (Ong *et al.*, 1988; Smith, 1984; Myers, 1984; Murray, 1984).

CRTs emit *X-ray radiation* but this is largely absorbed by the glass screen, and since all CRT screens manufactured since 1970 have to meet stringent international standards this is not thought to be a cause for concern. CRTs also emit *ultraviolet* and *infrared radiation* from the phosphor coating on the inside of the screens. However, the level is insignificant. They also emit *radio-frequency radiation*, and *ultrasound* (at around 16 kHz) is generated.

The high voltages used in CRTs create an *electrostatic field*, which 'leaks out' through the tube to the user. The stength of this field is dependent upon the screen, the distance from the screen and the voltage level. The strength of the field also depends on such factors as humidity; if the humidity is greater than 45 per cent then the field is minimal. It has been shown that in a low-humidity environment this field can cause rashes in some people, but this can be avoided by raising the humidity and using antistatic carpets.

Electromagnetic fields are also generated around CRTs in the frequency range 50 Hz to 0.5 MHz. The main source comes from the coils on the CRT which deflect the electron beam. These magnetic fields create induction currents in conductive materials including the human body. Two types of effects are generally attributed by VDU operators to this radiation. The first is an effect on the visual system leading to concern about the incidence of cataracts among VDU operators. Secondly, there is concern about the reproductive disorders such as miscarriages and birth defects among VDU operators.

VDU operators who wear glasses report more visual problems than those who do not. In surveys (Ong *et al.*, 1988) it has been reported that 75 per cent of full-time VDU operators developed some form of symptom or stress associated with their eyes during their shift period. These symptoms usually disappeared rapidly after the end of the shift. Various explanations have been proposed for these occurrences including display brightness, flicker, contrast and lengthy periods spent at the screen. No study has shown conclusively that there is any oculometer change attributable to VDU work.

8.8.2 Flat-panel displays

The major advantage of flat-panel displays is that they are smaller than the CRT and do not suffer from radiation problems. They are also matrix-addressable and therefore do not need any special memory for a frame store as is needed in bit-mapped CRT systems. A number of different flat-panel display technologies exist (Hobbs, 1981). The main ones are plasma panels, liquid-crystal displays and electroluminescence. The basic principle of these displays are described below but further information can be obtained in Salmon and Slater (1987), Hearn and Baker (1986) and Pleshko (1989). Other flat-display technologies are also under investigation. These include electrochromic, electrophoric, magnetic optic and the flat CRT tube where the electron gun and focusing beam are at right angles to the display tube.

The plasma panel

The plasma display has the highest resolution of all commercially available flat panel displays, with resolutions up to 1280×1729 pixels. Its principle of operation is shown in Figure 8.19. Two glass panels are separated by a small gap which contains neon gas (orange glowing). The

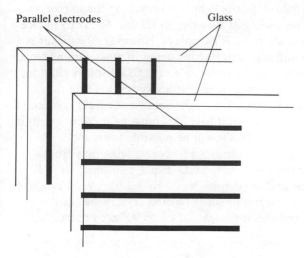

Figure 8.19   A.C. plasma panel

two panels of glass are covered by orthogonal parallel electrodes and a 50 Hz, 250 V ac signal maintains glow when applied to these electrodes. A superimposed 100 V timed pulse on this 250 V ac signal is used to turn the glow on or off. On most of these displays it takes several microseconds to write each pixel. Turning on individual pixels produces a discrete point of light which produces images which appear to have a higher resolution than similar points of light on a CRT tube. This is because the axial light distribution of a plasma panel pixel is more like a rectangular pulse than the Gaussian distribution of a CRT tube pixel. It is possible to produce different colours and even grey scales using a plasma panel, but such devices are only at the research stage and are not available commercially at present. One of the advantages of the plasma panel is that due to its glass construction it is transparent and can thus be superimposed on other displays. There is limited demand for these displays at the moment and they are consequently expensive (around ten times the price of a comparable CRT display). The power consumption is high, making them unsuitable for use in battery-powered equipment. This high power consumption also causes them to emit an appreciable amount of heat when a large number of pixels are illuminated.

The liquid-crystal display (LCD)

The principle of operation of the LCD is that a thin layer of liquid crystal is placed between two conducting plates. One plate is transparent and the other, the lower one, is a mirror or transparent surface. External light normally passes through both the top transparent plate and the liquid crystal and is reflected back from the mirror to the eye. When a voltage is applied across the plates it changes the crystal polarization and therefore stops the light from reaching the mirror. LCD displays require refreshing at between 30 Hz and 60 Hz to reduce the flicker, as with conventional CRT displays. However, the flicker is usually not noticeable and they can be considered in most circumstances to be flicker-free displays. Colour is possible on LCD displays (Patton, 1989). Their main advantage over other display systems is that they are less tiring to use and produce less eye strain because the light is reflected and not emitted. If the display is not backlit it must be used in a well-lit environment. High-resolution LCDs will be possible soon and 640 × 400 pixel displays (EGA compatible) are available now from a number of manufacturers. Most early LCD displays suffered from a restricted viewing angle and the display was only legible over a range of a few degrees. However, the use of super-twisted crystals has now reduced this problem and viewing angles of up to 90° are observed (Pleshko, 1989).

Electroluminescent displays

The principle of operation of the electroluminescent display is that a thin layer of phosphor similar to that used on CRT displays is trapped between two conducting plates. The plates are arranged as parallel rows and columns and a voltage is applied across them, causing the phosphor to glow. This type of display has to be refreshed to reduce flicker and this is usually performed at around 60 Hz. It is not possible to produce colour using these displays but grey-scale versions have been constructed (Tannas, 1986).

8.9 Overview of visual display devices

Generally, flat-panel displays are becoming more and more attractive as alternatives to the CRT but their prices are still very high as their manufacturing process is much less developed and on a smaller scale than that of the CRT (Product Focus, 1987; Zuckerman, 1984). Nevertheless, the CRT display has already been replaced by flat panels in laptop computers and undoubtedly will be replaced in other application areas in the future. The widespread introduction of portable LCD television sets also indicates the beginning of this trend. The main limitations of flat-panel displays compared with CRTs are their poor colour and grey-scale capability. Liquid-crystal displays seem to have the most promising colour capability and plasma panels are the most promising on physical size and resolution. The electroluminescent displays also seems to be a rapidly increasing contender in this development race. Most of the other technologies do not show any great promise of success at the moment (Smarte and Baran, 1988).

A generally accepted advantage of flat-panel over CRT displays is that they are more rugged and are capable of withstanding higher shock loads. With the exception of the liquid-crystal display their most serious disadvantage is that they have fairly high power requirements and are therefore not always useful in portable or handheld applications.

8.10 Reading from visual displays

Reading text from a display device is by far the most frequent requirement in any standard computer application. With books and printed articles the average reading speed is between 250 and 300 words per minute. While reading, the eyes do not scan smoothly over the text; instead they progress in a series of jerks and fixations. The jerks between the fixations usually last approximately 20 milliseconds and the fixations about 150–300 milliseconds, (Monk, 1985). In addition, the sequence of fixations and jerks is not always from left to right across the page. Some fixations can be from right to left (this is called a regression) and the number and size of regressions depends largely upon the capability of the reader. It can also depend upon the quality of the text being read.

8.10.1 Factors affecting legibility

It is widely accepted that there is a difference between reading text from a display screen and reading text from conventional paper. There have been a number of studies carried out to quantify this difference (Matthews, 1987; Jin Kang and Muter, 1989; Van Nes, 1986; Creed *et al.* 1987; Wagner, 1988).

Experiments were carried out by Wilkinson and Robinshaw (1987) to compare the effects of document proof-reading using hard copy and visually displayed text in terms of the accuracy and speed of checking for errors and the decline in vigilance during the proof-reading session. Their experiments used a CRT display with light-green letters on a dark-green background and had a format of 80 characters by 25 lines. Their conclusions were at some variance with those obtained by other researchers. Creed *et al.* (1987) also carried out proof-reading tests with paper, VDUs and photographs of the VDU screen; they also reviewed the work of others. The general conclusions in all studies was that reading from VDUs was up to 30 per cent slower than from paper and was also less accurate and caused more fatigue.

Possible reasons suggested for the poorer performance reported in these reading experiments are the following:

- lack of familiarity with VDUs;
- the novelty factor causing lack of concentration on the reading task;
- the reduced amount of text on the VDU in comparison with paper (approximately 70 per cent of each page visible on each VDU screen);
- the number of characters and words per line;
- the reading position is constrained by the VDU, whereas a book or piece of paper can be oriented as the reader wishes;
- the screen update rate;
- the type fount used;
- the colour and contrast of the screen;
- the ratios between line spacing and letter spacing;
- the line length.

Many VDU operators prefer coloured characters, though they cannot give a rational argument for this. Some VDUs use yellow or green characters which are in the middle of the visible spectrum where the eye is most sensitive. Van Nes (1986) studied the effect of different means of text display on VDUs (in particular teletext displays) and gives a set of practical guidelines relating to use of space, colour and typography. The essence of these guidelines is given below.

The *case* of the letters is an important factor in legibility. Mixed-case

CAPITAL   capital

CABINET   cabinet

Figure 8.20   Illustration of word shape

letters are more legible than upper case as they maintain the shape of the word (Figure 8.20). When printed in upper case, the words 'capital' and 'cabinet' have very similar word shapes and are not easily distinguished. When they are written in lower case the ascenders and decenders maintain the shape of each word particularly around the 'p' in 'capital' and the 'b' in 'cabinet', making the two more easily distinguished. Experiments have shown that upper-case characters are read about 20 per cent slower than lower-case ones.

The *type style* used in the script is also an important factor in its legibility. In Figure 8.21 a number of different typestyles are shown. Although it is difficult to determine any legibility measures from such short passages, experiments have shown that plain non-stylish text with clear ascenders and decenders is more legible than the more ornate scripts.

The *size of the script* is also a factor which affects the legibility. For the average person the size of the text should be such that it creates a visual angle of greater than 20 minutes of an arc.

In addition, the *line*, *letter* and *word spacing* all combine to affect the legibility to a considerable extent. A page filled with text is hard to read and the emptier a page the easier it is to search it. For example, the text in Figure 8.22 illustrates that in general the proportion of character spacing to word and line spacing should be such that letter spacing is approximately 10 per cent that of word spacing. Line spacing should give not less than 50 per cent of character height between top and bottom of adjacent lines.

To improve the legibility, *positive contrast* is recommended (i.e., normal black text on white paper). For visual display screens the

Which of these is the most legible?

Which of these is the most legible?

Which of these is the most legible?

Which of these is the most legible?

𝕎hich of these is the most legible?

Figure 8.21   Different type styles

In general the proportion of character

width to word and line spacing should

be such that letter spacing is approximately

10% that of word spacing and letter
spacing should   be   approximately
10%   -   20%
of character width. Line spacing
should be such that

there is not less than 50% character height

between top and bottom of adjacent lines.

Figure 8.22 Example of poor text spacing

previous standard was to produce white on black or green on black. The current trend among modern workstations is to use black pixels on a white background.

With high-resolution display screens it is possible to produce text containing a very large number of words on each line. The *number of words on each line* also affects the legibility of script; experiments have shown that between 8 and 15 words per line produces the optimum legibility. In addition text should be divided into paragraphs of 3 to 5 lines.

No more than three colours should be used on one page for sizeable quantities of text but if colour is used it must be used consistently.

Another factor is the *number of displayed lines* on the screen. With conventional visual display units the maximum number of lines which could be displayed was 25 but with modern, high-resolution workstations up to 100 lines can be displayed. The ideal is to try to simulate the appearance of paper. Simulating an A4-size sheet of paper at the 300 pixels/inch resolution currently provided by laser printers would require a display with 3000×2400 pixel resolution.

A major limitation of visual display screens is the inability to browse. With conventional books the reader can flick through glancing at parts of pages very quickly. This is very difficult to achieve on visual display screens. The use of windows may help but is less than ideal, as screen refreshing and updating are too slow.

The resolution of a *dot matrix representation* of a character is also a factor which affects the legibility. A typical dot matrix character is produced from a 7×5 matrix. The legibility of this script is very poor. Helander and Rupp (1984) overviewed and discussed current standards and guidelines concerned with VDUs. Among other things they noted that the more a dot-generated character resembled a stroke generated character the greater was its legibility. However, they also observed that a resolution of more than 9 by 11 dots produced only marginal improvements in legibility. The shape of the dots is also important and square or rectangular pixels are preferred to round pixels. In general,

for good legibility, sufficient resolution is needed to hide the dot
structure at normal viewing distances.

8.10.2 Hard-copy display devices

These are not truly interactive but are mentioned here for completeness
and because they are sometimes used for interactive communication,
albeit at a very slow rate. There are three main categories of hard-copy
devices: impact and non-impact printers and pen plotters. The impact
printers include daisy wheel and dot matrix devices and line printers.
The non-impact devices include ink jet printers, laser printers, and
thermal and electrostatic printers. The pen devices are pen plotters and
chart recorders.

Dot matrix printers have good graphics capabilities and can also
provide high-resolution characters in a variety of founts, depending
upon the matrix resolution. Early devices used 7- and 9-pin heads, but
12- and 24-pin heads are now common. Daisy wheel printers have
excellent character capability but only very limited graphic capability.
In fact even changing the fount of a daisy wheel printer is awkward.

As with soft-copy display devices we can classify hard-copy display
devices to be either raster scan or random scan types. An example of a
raster scan device is the dot matrix printer where each line is scanned
from left to right, down the paper. The pen plotter on the other hand is
a random scan device which draws one line at a time in any direction on
the paper.

In general, hard-copy output is still of much higher quality than can
be produced on display screens. Until the capability exists of displaying
an image without any loss in resolution or detail on a display device
with physical characteristics as ergonomically and aesthetically
acceptable as conventional paper, compromises will continue to be
necessary and a range of different display devices will be needed.

8.11 Selection of an interactive display device

When selecting an interactive display device a number of factors should
be considered (Haber and Wilkinson, 1982; Swezey and Davis, 1983).
What symbols are to be displayed: text only, pictures or both? Is a
dynamic presentation required and, if so, how fast must the screen be
updated? How much information must be displayed at once? What
effect will ambient lighting have on the display? The display device must
also have the required colour capability, the necessary display size and
resolution, and the necessary luminance capability. Display ergonomics
and health hazards should also be considered.

With conventional displays the choice is between a raster- or vector-scanned cathode ray tube. Raster scan tubes have the greatest colour capability and also are by far the cheapest. The vector CRT displays have poor colour capability and are more expensive but can achieve higher resolution. The liquid crystal display is the only flat panel display which can provide full colour capability, whereas the electroluminescent display is the most robust and plasma displays have the highest resolution.

References

Adler, M. H. (1973) *The Writing Machine: a History of the Typewriter*, George, Allen and Unwin, London.

Bailey, R. W. (1982) *Human Performance Engineering: a Guide for System Designers*, Prentice-Hall, Englewood Cliffs, NJ.

Buxton, W. (1988) 'Input: thinking about the first two letters in interaction', tutorial notes from HCI '88, UMIST, Manchester, 5 September 1988.

Card, S. K., W. K. English and B. J. Burr (1978) 'Evaluation of mouse, rate-controlled isometric joystick, step keys and text keys for text selection on a CRT', *Ergonomics*, **21**, 601–613.

Cooper, W. E. (1983) *Cognitive Aspects of Skilled Typewriting*, Springer, Berlin.

Creed, A., I. Dennis and S. Newstead (1987) 'Proof-reading on VDUs', *Behaviour and Information Technology*, **6**(1), 3–13.

Downton, A. C. and C. P. Brooks (1984) 'Automated machine shorthand transcription in commercial applications', *Proceedings, Interact '84, IFIP Conference on Human–Computer Interaction, September 1984*, 2.80–2.85.

Foley, J. D. and A. van Dam (1982) *Fundamentals of Interactive Computer Graphics*, Addison-Wesley, Reading, Mass.

Foley, J. D., V. L. Wallace and P. Chan (1984), 'The human factors of graphics interaction techniques', *IEEE Transactions on Computer Graphics and Applications*, **4**, 13–48.

Guinness Book of Records (1986) Guinness Superlatives, London.

Haber, R. N. and L. Wilkinson (1982) 'Perceptual Components of Computer Displays', *IEEE Transactions on Computer Graphics and Image Processing*, **2**(3), 23–35.

Hearn, D. and M. P. Baker (1986) *Computer Graphics*, Prentice-Hall, Englewood Cliffs, NJ, Chapter 2.

Helander, M. G. and B. A. Rupp (1984) 'An overview of standards and guidelines for visual display terminals', *Applied Ergonomics*, Sept. 185–195.

Hobbs, L. C. (1981) 'Computer Graphics Display Hardware', *IEEE Transactions on Computer Graphics and Image Processing*, **1**(1) 25–39.

Ikedo, T. (1984) 'High Speed Techniques for a 3-D colour graphics terminal', *IEEE Computer Graphics and Applications*, **4**(5), 46–58.

Jin Kang, T. and P. Muter (1989) 'Reading Dynamically Displayed Text', *Behaviour and Information Technology*, **8**(1) 32–42.

Kucera, H. and W. N. Francis (1967) *Computational Analysis of Present Day American English*, Brown University Press, Hanover, NH.

Matthews, M. L. (1987) 'The influence of colour on CRT reading performance and subjective comfort under operational conditions', *Applied Ergonomics*, Dec. 323–328.

Milner, N. P. (1988) 'A review of human performance and preferences with different input devices to computer systems', *People and Computers*, D. M. Jones and R. Winder (eds.), Cambridge University Press, Cambridge, 341–362.

Monk, A. (1985) *Fundamentals of Human–Computer Interaction*, Academic Press, London.

Murray, W. E. (1984) 'Video display terminals: radiation issues', *Computer Graphics and Applications,* April, 41–44 (gives three references for further reading).

Myers, W. (1984) 'The ergonomics of video display terminals', *Computer Graphics and Applications,* Jan., 7–15 (gives 23 references for further reading.)

Noyes, J. (1983) 'The QWERTY keyboard: a review', *International Journal of Man–Machine Studies*, **18**, 265–281.

Olson, J. B. (1987) 'Case study: the first automotive-display touch panel', *Information Display*, Jan. 12–16.

Ong, C. N., D. Koh and W. O. Phoon (1988) 'Review and Reappraisal of Health Hazards of Display Terminals', *Displays*, Jan., 23–26.

Patton, T. (1989) 'Market analysis: colour TFL-LCDs', *Information Display*, **10**, 4–7.

Pleshko, P. (1989) 'Flat Panel displays for laptop computers', *Information Display*, **3**, 12–16.

'Product focus: display devices', *Electronic Engineering*, Jan. 1987, 50–69.

Roese, J. A., and L. E. McCleary (1979) 'Steroscopic Computer Graphics for Simulation and Modelling', SIGGRAPH '79 proceedings, *Computer Graphics*, **13**(2), 41–47.

Salmon, R. and Slater, M. (1987) *Computer Graphics: Systems and Concepts*, Addison-Wesley, Wokingham.

Sims, H. V. (1969) *Principles of PAL Colour Television and Related Systems*, Butterworths, London.

Smarte G. and Baran, M. (1988) 'Face to Face, Display Technologies', *Byte*, Sept. 243–252.

Smith, M. J. (1984) 'The physical, mental and emotional stress effects of VDT terminals', *Computer Graphics and Applications*, Ap., 23–27 (gives 16 references for further reading.)

Swezey, R. W. and E. G. Davis (1983) 'A case study of human factors guidelines in computer graphics', *Computer Graphics and Applications*, Nov. 21–30.

Tannas, L. E. (1986) 'Electroluminescence catches the public eye', *IEEE Spectrum*, Oct. 37–42.

Thomas, C. and S. Milan (1987) 'Input devices for tasks using interactive video', *NPL Report DITC 87/87*, Apr.

Van Nes, F. L. (1986) 'Space colour and typography on visual display terminals', *Behaviour and Information Technology*, **5** (2), 99–118.

Wagner, E. (1988) *The Computer Designer's Handbook*, Chartwell-Bratt, Lund, Sweden.

Wilkinson, R. T. and H. M. Robinshaw (1987) 'Proof-reading: VDU and paper text compared for speed, accuracy and fatigue', *Behaviour and Information Technology*, **6**, (2) 125–133.

Zuckerman, M. M. (1984) 'Innovative display technologies—why a flat panel when you can have a CRT?', *IEEE Transaction on Computer Graphics and Image Processing*, Apr. 9–15.

9 Speech and handwriting

GRAHAM LEEDHAM

9.1 Introduction

Speech and handwriting are forms of human communication which have evolved over many generations and are used by the vast majority of the world's population. The typical rate of normally spoken speech is 180 words per minute, but speeds can exceed 400 words per minute for short periods of time. Handwriting is slower than speech, and, depending whether the words are printed as separate characters or joined together in cursive script, typical rates are between 20 and 50 words per minute. Handwritten shorthand (which requires fewer pen strokes than cursive or printed handwriting) is faster than handwriting, with typical recording rates of between 120 and 140 words per minute. The majority of people can read handwritten script far faster than they can write it and reading speeds of between 150 and 400 words per minute are typical (Bailey, 1982).

The main distinction between speech and handwriting as communication media is that speech is most commonly used for fast real-time interactive communication while handwriting is generally used for slower, non-interactive communication. There are, of course, exceptions to this rule; for example, the use of telephone answering machines makes speech communication an alternative to a written message, and telex and FAX machines enable semi-interactive communication using handwriting. Telewriting systems which allow real-time communication over telephone lines using handwriting are also available (Singleton, 1988).

It is apparent from Figure 8.11 that cursive and printed handwriting are by far the most popular forms of textual communication. Handwriting is approximately half the speed of the QWERTY keyboard, which in turn is about half the speed of normal spoken English. At first glance this would appear to suggest that the QWERTY keyboard is inferior to speech and that the text input problem would be solved if direct speech input to computers was feasible. In contrast, the slow speed of handwriting would appear to rule out its use in favour of keyboard entry. There are, however, good reasons why all three text input methods should be considered, as each offers its own particular advantages in specific applications. The major advantage and reason for studying the automatic recognition of handwriting and speech is that both are natural forms of communication as opposed to forms based on the requirements of some mechanical tool (excluding pens and pencils). They therefore have advantages in office or industrial environments where the need to learn typing skills is unpopular or unlikely to be cost effective.

In this chapter, speech and handwriting input and output systems are considered for interactive communication in the office environment. Section 9.2 reviews the structure of speech signals generally, while Sections 9.3 and 9.4 consider speech synthesis and speech recognition respectively. Section 9.4 looks at handwriting and hand-generated gesture input for interactive applications.

9.2 The structure of speech

To appreciate the problems associated with synthesizing and recognizing speech and their impact on the design of speech-based human–computer interfaces, some understanding of the nature of speech is needed. In this section the structure of speech is first discussed before considering the implications of using synthetic speech or speech recognition in an interactive human–computer environment.

9.2.1 Speech sounds and signals

Depending upon the accent analysed, the English language can be considered to be composed of approximately 40 distinct speech sounds or *phonemes*, comprising 24 consonant sounds and 16 vowel or diphthong sounds (Figure 9.1). These basic speech sounds can, in theory, be concatenated together to form any word in the English language. The spectral components of speech vary from approximately 80 Hz to 8 kHz with the most significant proportion of the spectrum, for intelligibility purposes, being below 4 kHz (O'Shaughnessy, 1987; Holmes, 1988).

Although a description of speech in terms of its spectral components or basic speech segments is a valid exercise, it does not illustrate the nuances of speech, which combine to convey a large amount of the information in the speech signal. Speech is not a blank monotone; all voices vary in quality and tone owing to health, physical features, the emphasis and stress of a word (including silent pauses) and many other causes. This variation is termed *prosody* and conveys meaning and emotion. For example, in the word 'extract' (the noun for an extract from a book and the verb 'to remove') different stress is usually sufficient for a listener to determine the intended usage without the aid of context within the sentence. Prosodic information provides the naturalness of speech and improves its intelligibility. If the stress within

24 consonants		16 vowels/diphthongs	
/P/	-ape	/A/	-bag
/B/	-oboe	/I/	-if
/K/	-oak	/AH/	-car
/G/	-go	/E/	-bet
/T/	-out	/AY/	-pay
/D/	-day	/EE/	-please
/F/	-face	/O/	-top
/V/	-vote	/AW/	-jaw
/TH/	-moth	/U/	-up
/DH/	-they	/OW/	-oboe
/S/	-sew	/OÓ/	-book
/Z/	-zero	/OO/	-blue
/SH/	-show	/IY/	-by
/ZH/	-usual	/OI/	-boy
/CH/	-chum	/OU/	-out
/J/	-age	/UU/	-duty
/N/	-no		
/NG/	-thing		
/M/	-may		
/L/	-load		
/W/	-way		
/R/	-ray		
/Y/	-yes		
/H/	-hot		

Figure 9.1 Phonemes of the English language

a sentence is changed, this may change the meaning of the sentence
quite considerably. For example, consider the sentence shown in Figure
9.2. By changing the stress to place the emphasis on each of the four
different words in turn, four subtly different meanings of the sentence
can be conveyed to the listener. Changing the pitch pattern of the
sentence provides additional cues, for example a rising pitch as the
sentence progresses produces a question.

Different stress

Where has he gone?

Where has he gone?

Where has he gone?

Where has he gone?

Different pitch

Where has he gone?

Figure 9.2 Stress and pitch variation changing the meaning of a
sentence

It is easy to forget that speech is our natural language and underestimate the difficulties that exist in creating synthetic speech by computer or mimicking human speech recognition. We are lulled into a false sense of technology by science fiction films in which computers or robots communicate using speech as correctly and naturally as if speaking to an articulate human. This level of speech synthesis and understanding is far beyond the current capability of speech technology. The reality is that current speech synthesizers are not articulate and few make any attempt to add prosodic information.

It might be inferred from Figure 9.1 that since the English language can be defined as 40 distinct phonemes, unrestricted synthetic speech can be generated simply by concatenating the phonemes together to form words and sentences. However, the speech quality produced by this method is unnatural and has poor intelligibility. Not all of the loss of intelligibility is due to the lack of prosodic information. Another feature of speech, known as *coarticulation*, causes the same basic phoneme sounds to vary slightly due to their preceding and following phonemes. This variation is due to the articulation of speech. When a word is spoken, the tongue, lips and jaw are placed in relation to each other to produce each particular sound. Their positions vary slightly for the same phoneme sound in different words owing to the inertia involved in moving the articulators between the preceding and following phoneme positions. For example the /IY/ sound, as in eye, guy, my, sigh, pie, etc., is in each case produced by slightly different articulatory positions because of the preceding or following sounds. Consequently, the resonances of the vocal tract are slightly different and have a discernible effect on the sound produced (see *formants* below).

This variation in phoneme sounds due to their contextual position in relation to neighbouring phonemes produces what are known as *allophones*. It is estimated that there are between 120 and 130 allophones in the English language. The exact number depends on what a particular speech analyst considers to be a significant enough difference between two versions of the same phoneme to require the specification of a new allophone, and what particular dialect of the English language is analysed.

In the production of speech, the vocal tract acts as a resonant tube, the dimensions of which vary with time owing to different positions of the tongue and mouth. This resonant tube is excited by periodic pulses generated by the vocal cords. These resonances (or *formants*) apply only to voiced sounds, however. (The fricative sounds, e.g., /F/ and /S/, are formed by air turbulence in the vocal tract. Nasal sounds, e.g., /M/ and /N/, are produced, as their name suggests, by closing the mouth and causing the sound to come out of the nose.)

If a spectrum analysis is made of speech it quickly becomes apparent that each sound segment has a particular pattern of formant frequencies. There has been a considerable amount of research into the

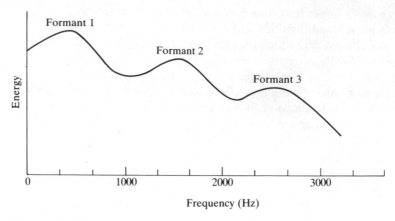

Figure 9.3 Formant frequencies

nature of formants and attempts have been made to produce synthetic speech by modelling the formant frequencies and their trajectories. There are usually approximately five formant frequencies in any one voiced speech sound, but the first three are the most critical and contain most of the naturalness of speech. For example, the /I/ sound in 'if' will typically have three formant frequencies centred at 360 Hz, 2060 Hz and 2220 Hz for a particular voice, while the /O/ sound in 'top' has three formant frequencies at 380 Hz, 940 Hz and 2300 Hz for the same voice. These formant frequencies relate to energy in the speech signal as illustrated in Figure 9.3.

9.2.2 Natural language

Whilst it is a valid exercise to analyse the speech signal and classify it into basic segments (phonemes, allophones, words, formant frequencies and their trajectories, etc.), such analysis does not consider the complex higher-level mechanisms by which humans use the speech communication channel to convey information from person to person. It has already been mentioned above how prosodic variation in stress, pitch and timing can be used to modify meaning in a spoken sentence, but the choice of the words in the sentence obviously conveys much of the meaning. Rules of grammar determine this aspect of the language.

Speech can be thought of as hierarchical levels of units and structures which are concatenated together according to a set of rules to form the language. At the lowest level, a small number of basic speech sounds (phonemes or allophones) are concatenated to form a large number of words or *morphemes* (a morpheme is the smallest unit of grammar which conveys meaning as part of a word or a complete word in its own right, e.g., the words 'copy-ing', 'copy-ist', 'cop-ier' and 'cop-ied' are all composed of two morphemes which have separate meaning.) At a higher level, syntax rules are required to concatenate words and morphemes into a virtually infinite number of phrases and sentences. Prosodic information is a still higher level which modifies the words and sentences to subtly change their meaning.

The grammar of a language is defined by rules which govern the concatenation of verbs, nouns, adverbs, articles, conjunctions, etc. (see Section 6.6). For example, the sentence 'Do you watch television?' is composed of (auxiliary verb + pronoun + verb + noun) and is a question enquiring whether the listener watches television. If the words are ordered differently as 'Watch television do you?' or 'You do watch television?' they still ask a question, but the meaning of each sentence is subtly different. They now also convey information about the prior knowledge of the questioner concerning the television viewing habits of the person being questioned, and consequently affect the subsequent reply to the question. It must also be noted that each language has its own grammar. For example, the question 'Do you watch television?' in French is 'Regardez-vous la télévision?', which literally translated is 'Watch you the television?'. While the grammar is correct in French it is incorrect in English.

This richness of language has implications on the future design of automatic speech synthesis and recognition systems. For example, a speech recognition system capable of dealing with natural language questions must be able to parse the question correctly, to understand the meaning implied by the grammar and prosody, and to formulate a syntactically correct response. The performance of current speech technology is far from achieving this level of communication and can generally operate only with unnatural low-level, highly restricted grammars. Up to now, much of the work on speech synthesis and recognition has concentrated on the low-level engineering problems associated with the production or location and recognition of phonemes and words. Combining state-of-the-art implementations of the low-level processing systems with knowledge-based systems which address the higher level issues of grammar and language is still largely the province of research.

There are nevertheless many applications where communication using speech with restricted grammars is useful and some of these are discussed later in this chapter. A specific case study of a system for an automatic voice-activated telephone enquiry service for train timetable information (VODIS) is described in Chapter 14.

9.3 Speech output—speech synthesis

Synthetic speech can be produced by various means, ranging from the simplest approach of playing back parts of recorded messages using a tape recorder, to the complexity of generating any combination of spoken words from a textual representation of the word or sentence.

9.3.1 Speech synthesis techniques

Direct waveform encoding

Direct waveform encoding involves digitizing real speech, storing it in some compressed form and replaying selected parts of it through a digital-to-analogue (D/A) converter and loudspeaker. The speech signal must be sampled at two or more times the maximum frequency of interest. For good-quality speech this typically requires a sampling rate of 16 kHz. To store any significant amount of speech a large storage capacity is therefore required. For example, if the speech signal is sampled at 16 kHz and each sample is 8 bits (giving 256 discrete sample values), data will be generated at the rate of 16 kbytes for each second of speech. To reduce the amount of storage some means of data compression is required. One method is to use *companding*, but the storage requirements are still high for good speech quality. Other techniques include *delta modulation* and a fringe technique called *Mozer encoding*. The Mozer technique can store intelligible speech using between 1 and 2 kbits of data for each second of speech (Sclater 1983). Detailed descriptions of companding and delta modulation of speech can be found in Rowden (1991) and O'Shaughnessy (1987, Chapter 7).

Linear predictive coding

One of the most popular data-reduction techniques is linear predictive coding (LPC), which can reduce the data rate for intelligible speech to as little as 1000 bits per second. The principle of LPC is that it is only necessary to store and update control parameters for a digital filter at around 25 ms intervals because the rate of change of spectral components in a speech signal is relatively slow owing to the physiological limitations of the human speech production system. Detailed discussions of LPC techniques can be found in O'Shaughnessy (1987), Rowden (1991), Cater (1983), Holmes (1988) and Witten (1986).

A block diagram of an LPC speech synthesizer is shown in Figure 9.4. The excitation source to the filter is provided by either a periodic signal (for voiced sounds) or a noise source (for unvoiced sounds), and a control parameter is provided to decide which should be applied to the filter. Gain control is provided to determine the amplitude of the signal, which is then fed into a recursive digital filter whose parameters are changed at 20–50 ms intervals using data stored in ROM. The output of the digital filter is passed through a D/A converter and from there to an amplifier and speaker.

Formant synthesis

Another speech synthesis technique is to model the formant frequencies of the speech signal. This is typically done by providing three bandpass

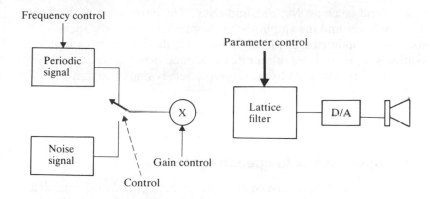

Figure 9.4 An LPC speech synthesizer

filters, one for each of the most significant formant frequencies. A schematic diagram of a formant synthesizer is shown in Figure 9.5. As with the LPC synthesizer, a noise source and a periodic source are provided for voiced and unvoiced sounds respectively; these are fed into a bank of three formant filters. In addition to the formant filters, two additional filters are provided. One is supplied from the noise source and is intended to produce the fricative sounds found in the /S/ and /F/ phonemes. The other is supplied from the periodic source and produces

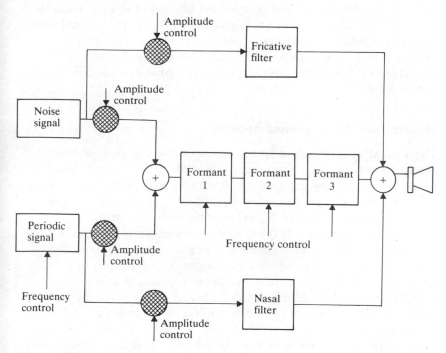

Figure 9.5 A formant speech synthesizer

nasal sounds such as /M/, /N/, and /NG/. The parameters of the three formant filters and the amplitude of the noise and periodic signal sources are updated typically at 10 ms intervals. This enables speech synthesis to be achieved at bit rates of around 600 bits per second. The speech quality produced by such synthesizers is similar to that achieved by LPC. Further information about formant synthesis can be found in O'Shaughnessy (1987), Rowden (1991), Holmes (1988), Morgan (1984), and Witten (1986).

9.3.2 Approaches to speech synthesis

The previous section described how speech can be modelled, encoded and compressed using linear predictive coding, formant synthesis, or direct waveform coding. Synthesis is then achieved by regenerating the speech using the stored components. The next issue to be addressed concerns the units to be used to represent speech: words, phonemes, allophones, or other speech segments.

Word-based synthesis

The simplest method is to store whole words and concatenate them together to form sentences. This is adequate for restricted-vocabulary applications and is usually based upon LPC techniques. The allowed vocabulary is entirely dependent upon the amount of storage available, as the storage required increases in proportion to the size of vocabulary. Typically, a maximum of 1000 to 2000 words is used. The speech produced by word concatenation is very disjointed and unnatural and is restricted to the stored vocabulary; however, individual words in isolation are reproduced with high quality.

Phoneme- and allophone-based synthesis

The alternative approach to speech synthesis is to concatenate basic speech segments such as phonemes or allophones to form individual words. This technique is essential in text-to-speech systems where an unlimited vocabulary is necessary. The difficulty arises when a set of rules are needed to convert the text automatically to a string of phonemes or allophones. If the number of speech units is limited (say 40 phonemes) then the rules are complex but manageable. The speech quality, however, is poor because coarticulation is not taken into account and the transition from one speech segment to another is not smooth and often creates unintentional buzzes and clicks in the audio output. When the number of speech segments is made larger to allow for allophonic variation, the rules for text-to-speech segment conversion become extremely complex and are the main factor restricting successful implementation.

Naturalness

The statement 'It's not what you say but how you say it' is never more
clearly exemplified than when listening to the output of speech
synthesizers. As described earlier, prosodic information can change the
meaning of a set of words quite considerably. Rhythm, pitch and stress
can be controlled to some extent in isolated words or short phrases in
limited vocabulary systems. However, in the general case machine
understanding of the speech is required if the prosodic information is to
sound natural. Generalized prosody rules can be applied in speech
synthesizers and work reasonably well in most situations but
considerable further research will be needed before an unlimited
vocabulary synthetic voice becomes indistinguishable from a human
speaker.

9.3.3 Human factors and application areas

Speech output from machine has a seemingly significant human-factors
advantage over other output modes because it is a natural
communication medium for humans. However, a number of problems
exist which the designer should consider before incorporating a speech
synthesizer into a system.

A problem with any speech output is that the information transfer
rate is less than that for vision. The ability to browse, which we use
frequently in visual analysis, is far more difficult in speech as it is a
transient serial stream which can not be searched randomly. The
problem can perhaps be compared to reading a printed document
through a small hole in a piece of paper placed immediately over it.

Human adaptability in recognizing speech causes particular problems
with synthetic speech. The apparent intelligibility of a speech
synthesizer increases with the listener's exposure to it, in exactly the
same way as with conventional speech spoken with a strong accent, or a
foreign language. It is often the case that a designer who incorporates
synthesized speech output into a system has listened to the synthesizer
for so long during development that he has no difficulty in
understanding it, and thus is inclined to misjudge its intelligibility to less
familiar users. It is therefore important for designers to assess user
reaction and acceptability of the synthesizer objectively before
expending a great deal of effort incorporating it into a system.

An important characteristic (and possible disadvantage) of speech
output in an interactive system is its obtrusive nature. Unlike visual
output, speech output from a system cannot be ignored. This can
produce an unacceptable working environment if a number of
workstations with speech output are sited together. The only solution in
such a situation is for each user to wear headphones and a
head-mounted directional microphone or for each workstation to be

placed in a separate sound-insulated enclosure. Both of these solutions impose environmental constraints which may be unacceptable.

Speech output is also perceived as giving a computer personality, whereas if text is presented on a display screen this personality is not so apparent. Newell (1986) suggested that the computer's apparent personality was the cause of most complaints from the users. The question also arises: should a male, female or child's voice be used? The fundamental problem is that synthetic speech attempts to mimic normal human communication, and people are very sensitive to all the nuances of human speech. Consequently, deficiencies in the synthetic speech are immediately detected and are not well tolerated by humans.

Despite the above disadvantages, a number of significant application areas for speech synthesizers can be identified. One of the most worthwhile is in aids for the blind such as the talking typewriter or the Kurzweil reading machine (Witten, 1986). The blind are much more tolerant than other users of the imperfections in current speech synthesizers because they are highly motivated. Even a poor-quality speech channel provides them with access to information which was previously unavailable. Other promising application areas include applications where speech is the only communication medium available (e.g., voice telephone enquiry services—see Chapter 14), and applications where there is a high visual concentration and the speech output provides an additional channel for warnings or short information bursts (e.g., aircraft and automotive applications).

In general, finding suitable applications for speech output is difficult. Unfortunately, a number of designers have added speech output to systems without considering the implications of doing so, producing gimmicky results which have been widely criticized. In many cases, simple visual communication methods (e.g., a flashing light) would have been cheaper, more straightforward to implement, and more effective. Therefore, in general, speech output for a system should be used with a great deal of caution, where there is a clear advantage in using an additional information channel, or where there is no alternative.

9.4 Speech input—speech recognition

Speech recognition is widely considered a more complex problem than speech synthesis. A simile used by Bristow (1986) is that speech synthesis is like squeezing toothpaste out of a tube and speech recognition is like trying to get it back in again. If we accept this simile then the limited success of most speech synthesizers gives some indication of the problems found in speech recognition.

9.4.1 The main problem areas

One of the main problems with speech recognition is that speech is
continuous. Normal speech seldom contains silent breaks between
words; conversely, breaks sometimes occur in the middle of words after
a stop consonant, as for example between the /P/ and /T/ sounds in
'captain'. Therefore, isolating the boundaries of individual words in
continuous speech is very difficult. Other problems include the
following:

- *background noise* such as from traffic or from other voices;
- *redundant utterances* such as coughs, grunts, stuttering, 'ums' and
  'ers';
- *variation between speakers*, including pitch, prosody, accent, dialect,
  stress and speech speed;
- *language*, i.e., the grammar and meaning of the spoken words.

Because speech is a natural form of communication, people are adept
at solving these problems. In fact their ability to solve them quite
unconsciously makes it very difficult to comprehend the problems
involved in trying to make a machine do the same sort of analysis.
Research into speech recognition was begun in the late 1950s, and at the
time it was predicted that unrestricted speech recognition would be
achieved within 30 years. Similar predictions are still made today!
Considerable progress has been made in speech research, but this
progress can largely be characterized as increasing our understanding of
the problems of speech recognition rather than solving them. While the
capabilities of speech recognizers are certainly improving, it will be
some considerable time before the automatic recognition of
unrestricted-vocabulary connected speech from any speaker will be
possible.

9.4.2 Levels of complexity

The term 'speech recognition' is normally taken to mean recognition of
conventional speech in everyday surroundings. Current recognizers
cannot cope accurately with this situation. However, the problems can
be simplified to some extent by defining constraints on the allowed
speech, on the speakers, and on the environment. The simplest speech
recognition systems are intended only to recognize a limited vocabulary
of isolated words spoken by one or a small number of trained speakers.
Constraining speakers to utter words in isolation means that word
boundaries are more easily located, and limiting the vocabulary size
improves recognition performance and reduces error rate. Obviously,
the type of speech input possible with such a system is both unnatural
and slow, and therefore such systems are restricted to applications
which only require simple item selection.

The following speech recognition problems are representative of successively higher levels of complexity:

- recognition of key words in connected speech;
- speaker identification from speech;
- recognition of restricted vocabulary connected speech;
- recognition of unlimited vocabulary connected speech.

The last example is the level at which humans operate and implies speech understanding of the domain of communication, and consequently a very high level of artificial intelligence.

All of these examples can be tackled in the presence of background noise or can be constrained by the use of a head-mounted directional microphone or a quiet environment. In addition, any system can be trained for a single user, a small group of users or any user. As might be expected, recognition systems trained to a single user have significantly higher performance than those which can be used by any user. Applications are limited by the tolerable error rate of the recognition system, which is seldom less than 1–2 per cent and may approach 10 per cent. Achieving graceful interaction under these circumstances requires careful choice of dialogue style, considerable attention to the dialogue structure and design, and flexible error-recovery procedures.

9.4.3 Approaches to the problem

For single isolated words or short phrases the easiest method of recognizing the speech pattern is to use template matching. The principle of this technique is that each word or separate speech utterance to be recognized is recorded and stored in a set of reference or template patterns for each word. New incoming utterances are then compared, in turn, with each of these template patterns using a distance metric (Holmes, 1988). If the best match is better than some predefined threshold the unknown utterance is considered to be the same as the template with the best match. Template matching is a standard technique in pattern recognition and is used widely for many different types of pattern-matching problems (Schwab and Nusbaum, 1986; Suen and deMori, 1982; Young and Fu, 1986). With speech recognition the difficulty is that no word is spoken the same twice, as the speaker will inevitably vary speed, amplitude or stress. The patterns to be compared will therefore not be identical but similar.

While template matching is adequate for a small number of isolated words or short phrases it is not successful in recognizing large vocabularies of words. Extensions of template matching have been used in more sophisticated recognition systems (Lea, 1980; Bristow, 1986). These systems attempt to recognize a number of words in a restricted vocabulary which could be connected together to form sensible sentences. The technique involves the compilation of knowledge of the restricted vocabulary which is to be used at two levels. At the semantic level a word network is formed to give all the acceptable sentences in the vocabulary. At the phonetic level all words are segmented and represented in all acceptable phonetic pronunciations, that is, to produce an acceptable phoneme network.

The recognition process involves the analysis of the speech waveform from beginning to end to match all likely phonemes to the template phonemes. The most likely phoneme matches are retained. By this means a recognition tree can be generated through the speech utterance which is consistent with the knowledge source and also consists of high match segments. Because of the overhead in generating the very large and sophisticated knowledge source of allowable sentences and allowable pronunciations for each word, only small vocabularies can be dealt with by this means.

The recognition of unlimited-vocabulary connected speech is a far more difficult problem which currently remains beyond the boundaries of research. Large-vocabulary recognizers are becoming available (Speech Technology, 1989) but their performance is vastly inferior to human recognition performance and they are still restricted to constrained application areas.

9.4.4 Human factors and application areas

Chapanis et al. (1977) carried out a number of experiments which concluded that two people working on a problem were able to reach a solution to the problem faster using speech communication than using manual means. However, the work assumed cooperative speakers and listeners, and thus cannot be reliably extrapolated to the situation where one of the parties is a machine. Current speech technology imposes substantial constraints on the human user such as restricted vocabulary, syntax and knowledge domain, and the need for user training and cooperation. The error rate is also likely to be high. In consequence, speech communication with a computer is anything but 'natural language', and very artificial and stilted dialogue styles are required.

The use of speech technology is strongly driven by economic pressures. Speech recognition is still a very expensive technology and this increases the difficulty of identifying cost-effective applications. Successful applications have nevertheless been found: for example parcel sorting, transport and military uses, and aids for the disabled; but the high price and limited performance of current recognizers is a disincentive to their widespread use.

The designer must also consider what tasks are to be performed and how speech input could help in an interactive computer interface. The environment must be considered: is the background noise too high or is the user wearing protective clothing which will make it difficult to use a microphone? Recognizer performance must also be considered, and may need to be evaluated under realistic conditions before issues such as dialogue design can be resolved. If the dialogue structure implicitly assumes a high-recognition performance level which is not achieved in practice then a very unsatisfactory system will result.

The fact is that, in many applications, speech input offers no significant advantage over other standard input devices such as keyboards and pointing devices (Welch, 1977; Poock, 1980; Brandetti *et al.*, 1988). Published results can be contradictory, depending upon the experimental task specified. However, in general, speech is useful when the hands or eyes are busy, where there is a need to be mobile, or when the user is remote from the system as when using a telephone. That is, speech input should be viewed as a channel additional to conventional input and output channels which is useful in high-workload environments, where it can reduce the mental and physical load and can produce faster interaction and increased efficiency. For example, studies by Mountfield and North (1980) showed that simulation of voice selection of radio channels by pilots (in comparison with keyboard selection) reduced channel selection errors and improved the pilot's ability to maintain simultaneous navigational tracking using a joystick.

One of the most often quoted applications or goals of speech recognition is that of the 'talk-writer' or speech dictation machine, in which unlimited vocabulary connected speech is simultaneously recognized and converted to printed text. The intention is that such a system would be used in the office environment and also in court reporting as an alternative to shorthand or tape transcription. A common mistake in considering such applications is to view the transcriber simplistically as someone who is transcribing what is said. Closer analysis reveals this to be far from the truth. For example, in an office dictation environment, the transcriber is performing a complex speech interpretation function, distinguishing between command (editing operations) and text input, expanding brief instructions to produce a full-length document, editing out spoken repetitions and non-textual utterances, and tidying up the overall English style, all in real time. Studies by Gould (1978), Gould *et al.* (1983), Newell *et al.* (1987), Newell (1987) and Dye *et al.* (1989) have investigated some of these issues by simulation using a QWERTY typist and a Palantypist respectively as the simulation of a high-performance speech recognizer.

Similarly, experiments with tape transcription for court reporting as an alternative to machine or handwritten shorthand have shown that this is inferior to verbatim reporting in terms of the quality of transcription and significantly more costly (HMSO, 1977; Osmond Committee, 1972; County of Los Angeles, 1972). The deficiencies identified in tape transcription would also apply to speech transcription by machine: the principal problem is the lack of a human within the speech acquisition system to ensure that all speakers are continuously audible and understandable.

The general conclusion is that current speech recognition technology is not competitive with keyed input for primary data entry, but speech recognition has many potentially useful applications in high-workload environments.

9.5 Handwriting

Handwriting, like speech, evolved naturally over several thousand years and is therefore a natural form of communication for people. Despite its apparent slowness in comparison with speech and the QWERTY keyboard, in some circumstances it has significant advantages for interaction with computers (Buxton, 1988; Paper versus screen, 1985). In particular the ability to position a cursor or draw a line from one point to another (abstract operations defined as *position* and *path* (Foley *et al.*, 1984) are not easily accomplished using speech or keyboards.

9.5.1 Current technology and possible application areas

For interactive computer dialogues involving handwritten text, sketches or pointing operations, online or real-time entry and processing of the pen's movement is required. Therefore, the handwriting must be digitized in some way and presented to the computer system as it is written. This can be achieved using digitizers (see Section 8.6.3) which produce a series of (x, y) coordinates of a pen's movement on their surface (Figure 9.6).

For offline systems, the handwriting is scanned by optical means some time after it was originally written. This produces a binary image of the handwriting which may require significant preprocessing to thin characters, to join separated segments and to generate a 'clean' representation of the original pen movements (Figure 9.7).

For online applications digitizers can be separate from the display, creating an indirect input mechanism, or combined with the display to form a more natural simulation of writing on paper in the form of a direct-input device. The concept of 'electronic paper' in the form of a direct-input device is shown in Figure 9.8. A flat-panel display has a

Figure 9.6 Examples of online script

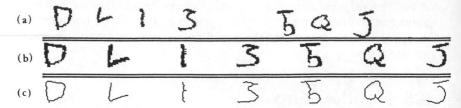

Figure 9.7 **(a)** Example of offline hand-printed characters **(b)** Normalized characters **(c)** Normalized and thinned characters

transparent digitizer placed on top of it and a pen stylus used on the digitizer causes a simultaneous display on the display screen beneath the pen tip as if writing on paper. A high-resolution (typically 0.01 mm) for both digitizer and display screen is required for accurate representation of the pen's movement. A number of digitizer and flat panel display technologies are available at the moment but none ideally suit the purposes of electronic paper. Previous investigations into electronic paper (Tappert *et al.*, 1986) and more recent work (Higgins *et al.*, 1990) produced simulations of electronic paper using a resistive digitizer superimposed on a flat panel display. Commercially available versions of electronic paper have recently appeared on the market (Scriptel, 1989; Linus, 1989). Such systems enable the possibilities of electronic paper to be demonstrated and its implications investigated, but current products and research developments are not ergonomically ideal for handwriting input, nor do they incorporate the sophisticated pattern recognition and processing algorithms necessary for full electronic paper.

The main problems with current versions of electronic paper are associated with the ergonomics of the pen and the tablet. Parallax caused by the pen tip and display point on the screen being physically separated by the thickness of the display and digitizer surfaces is one problem which causes a slightly confused perception between the observed handwriting in comparison with writing on real paper. In addition, the majority of digitizers are manufactured for

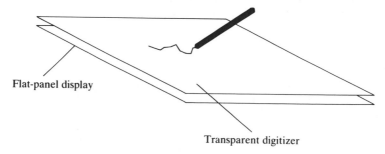

Flat-panel display

Transparent digitizer

Figure 9.8 The concept of electronic paper

computer-aided design applications which favour the use of a puck
cursor rather than a pen. Consequently, the pen stylus provided with
the systems is not well designed for handwriting applications. The pens
are often more bulky than conventional pens and have a thick,
cumbersome cable connecting them to the digitizer. There is also a
switch on the pen which is activated either by pressure of the pen tip on
the tablet surface or by a separate button near the pen tip which is
operated by the writer's forefinger. Such pens are adequate for pointing
and menu selection but are difficult to use for handwriting.

The preferred physical size of the electronic paper surface is also a
subject for discussion. For the office environment it may be that the
electronic paper needs to be virtually the size of a desktop. For a
portable application, as in a pocket or handheld digitizer, an A4 or A5
size may be most appropriate.

Digitizer tablets also introduce imperfections into the handwriting
(Ward and Phillips, 1987; Meeks and Kuklinski, 1990). These are
caused by limitations or calibration errors within the tablet technology.
These deficiencies can be static (that is, present when the pen is
stationary) or dynamic (dependent upon the pen's speed and direction
of movement). While they are usually relatively small they can and do
introduce errors into the digitization of the hand-generated pen strokes
which can adversely affect automatic processing and recognition.

Assuming that the technology is available to implement electronic
paper, the question arises of what type of interaction would be useful
using such a system. One form of input would be normal handwriting,
allowing a user to input text in their own handwriting without having to
resort to using a keyboard, thus simulating the usual operations
performed with real pen and paper. In addition, sketches and graphical
input may be required. It would also be useful to be able to handwrite
mathematical formulae using standard mathematical symbols directly
onto the electronic paper. In all of these text and data entry applications
it is also necessary to provide a means of editing and correcting the
handwritten input.

Once entered, the handwritten text, mathematical formulae and
sketches either can be stored and redisplayed purely as images of what
was entered, or can be automatically recognized and interpreted by the
system and displayed in a processed format. In the former case, the
electronic paper acts as an intelligent sketching or painting environment
operating on pixel data, while in the latter the system interprets the
pixels as symbolic data (e.g., letters or words), and can subsequently
perform symbolic processing on this data. This distinction is vital in
defining the type of editing and processing operations which can be
performed. For example, at the symbolic level, words or sentences can
be deleted and cut-and-paste operations can be used to move a word,
sentence or paragraph around within a document, while the document
can be reformatted with different margins, linespacings, etc. With pixel

data, the operations are confined to 'painting' operations on pixel blocks only. Suitable gesture-based symbolic editing operations, based upon typical handwritten annotations, have been defined and investigated (Gould and Alfaro, 1984; Gould and Salaun, 1987; Thomas, 1986; Welbourn and Whitrow, 1990). Examples of suggested editing symbols are shown in Figure 9.9.

Correcting a hand-edited document on a conventional keyboard-operated word processor is slow for the following reasons:

- People spend time visually searching between the original document and the screen.
- Decision making is required to determine how to locate the text in the word-processed document and make the revision.
- The edited document is reread to check that the correction has been carried out correctly.

Gould and Alfaro (1984) carried out a number of experiments in document editing using speech, handmarking and a keyboard-operated text editor. They simulated nearly ideal speech recognizers and handwriting recognizers. Their conclusion was that a well-designed writer recognition system or speech recognition system could form the basis of a potentially good editor for typists as well as senior management.

9.5.2 Forms of handwriting

One of the factors limiting the development of systems exhibiting the seemingly attractive interaction styles possible using handwriting is the wide variation of handwriting. Worldwide, many different writing styles have developed (e.g., Arabic and Kanji) but only the handwriting styles associated with the English language will be considered here.

As illustrated in Figure 9.10, handwriting styles used for recording the English language vary widely. For example, the writing can be composed of a mixture of individual separated characters and joined cursive characters; letters can be written in upper or mixed case; letters can be formed vertically or at a slant, the ascenders and descenders (in such letters as g, y, h and l) have different extents and may or may not contain loops; letters requiring closure (such as a, o and b) may not be completely closed. No two people have exactly the same handwriting and indeed the same person's handwriting will be affected from time to time by many factors including the type of pen, the quality of paper, the writer's state of health, the writer's posture, etc. (Kao *et al.*, 1986). This personal style variation applies to all forms of a person's handwriting, and also extends to other scripts such as shorthand.

It is this style variation which, like the variation in speech, makes automatic recognition and processing of handwritten gestures and symbols difficult.

Delete letter	In the final
Delete letters/word	Then the blue car
Delete paragraph	.. and is one of the main reasons for using pen and paper. Some people prefer to use ink pens in preference to ballpoint pens. This is mainly a matter of ..
Delete text	It is frequently necessary to (often it is also) carry an umbrella.
Move words	With all the effort people
Move paragraph	Aaaaa aa aaaaa aa aaaaaaa aa aaa aaaa aaaaaaa aa aa a. Bbbbb bb bbbb bbbbb bb bbbb b bbbbbb bbb bb bb bbbb. Ccccccc c ccccccc cc cccc cc ccc cccc cc ccc cc cc.

Move text	The main reason it is difficult to alter (of the chair) the position.is due ..
Insert	Once upon∧time
Transpose letters	It is teh typing speed
Change case	The method usED to lift
Join paragraph	Aaaaa aa aaaaa aa εaaaaaaa aa aaa aaaa aaaaaaaa εa aa a. B bbbb bb bbbb bbbbb bb bbbb b bbbbbb bbb bb bb bbbb.
Make paragraph	Aaaaa aa aaaaa aa εaaaaaaa aa aaa aaaa aaaaaaaa aεa aaa aa aa a. Bbbbb bb bbb bbbbb bb bbbb b bbbbbb bbb tb bb bbbb.

Figure 9.9 Examples of hand-generated editing symbols

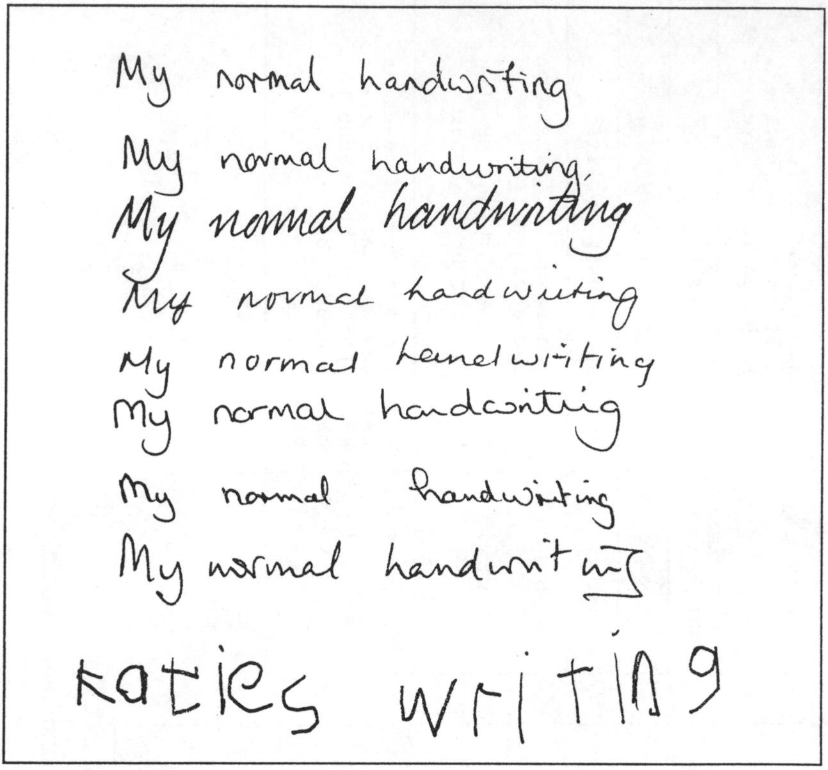

Figure 9.10 Examples of different handwriting styles

9.5.3 Automatic recognition of handwriting

The recognition problems associated with handwritten scripts are by no means trivial (as is apparent from the previous section) but are slightly simpler than those associated with speech recognition. While word separation is a problem in speech recognition systems, this problem is less significant in handwriting recognition because words are usually separated by clear gaps. The separation problems are mostly associated with separating letters within each word.

Handwritten words are written in several ways. They can (rarely) be composed of clearly spaced separate letters which are easily isolated by simple physical separation, or (more commonly) be composed of discrete letters which may occasionally touch or overlap. More typically, words are formed from a combination of separated and overlapping characters combined with some joined or cursive letters. The separation of letters in words which are joined or overlapping is far from trivial and has never been adequately solved (Friday and Leedham, 1989). Indeed, owing to the poor formation of characters within joined or cursive writing, it is unlikely that letter-by-letter recognition would be successful even if letter boundaries could be accurately located.

To simplify the separation of characters, constraints have often been imposed in character recognition systems which require the user to write each character within a clearly defined bounding rectangle. This constraint usually improves the recognition performance but makes character input less natural.

Currently, commercial on-line character recognition systems exist which can cope with reasonably unconstrained writing of separated individual characters from the same writer, but performance deteriorates rapidly if they are not retrained for each user (Tappert *et al.*, 1988).

Cursive script recognition systems are still subject to research and will remain so for the foreseeable future. Like continuous-speech recognition systems, they rely upon integrating higher-level syntactic and contextual knowledge to produce good overall word recognition performance, even where individual characters can not be successfully recognized. In this respect they are attempting to emulate the human reading process, which recognizes complete words and phrases rather than letters (Ford and Higgins, 1990).

9.6 Conclusions

In this chapter the use of speech and handwriting in interactive human–computer situations has been examined. Both speech and handwriting are more natural forms of communication than keyboards or other commonly used input devices and consequently would appear to offer significant human-factors advantages. While a number of possible scenarios exist where speech and handwriting could be used, they do not offer a panacea to human interface design. Instead each has its own particular advantages in specific applications. The range of applications for both speech and handwriting are restricted by the limited capability of the technology.

Speech synthesis can be achieved by a number of techniques but the quality of currently available speech synthesizers is generally poor and none sounds natural. The problems of producing natural-sounding, unlimited-vocabulary speech has not yet been resolved. Even if high-quality, unlimited-vocabulary speech becomes available, great care will have to be taken in defining suitable application areas because speech is a slow and transient information channel when compared with vision. Because speech synthesizers mimic human communication, the computer is perceived as having a personality as conveyed by the particular synthesized voice. This personality may be disliked by the users. Speech is also intrusive and can be annoying in working environments such as open-plan offices.

Speech recognition technology is not as advanced as speech synthesis and the current capabilities of commercial recognizers are limited to a small number of isolated words or short strings of connected words selected from an even smaller vocabulary. In addition, the recognizers have to be trained to the voice of each user and operated in a quiet environment or with a head-mounted directional microphone.

The automatic recognition of unlimited-vocabulary connected speech is not likely to be possible for many years. Therefore, designers will be restricted to expensive, limited-vocabulary devices which can only be used for simple command or selection applications with a constrained dialogue. Application of speech recognizers will be primarily driven by their cost effectiveness in particular market niches.

In general, speech synthesis and speech recognition are useful in environments where there is no clear alternative (e.g., aids for the disabled) or in high-workload environments where the user's eyes and hands are busy with some other primary task. Determination of suitable application areas is best achieved by case studies which simulate the specific interactive tasks and then evaluate them using real users.

Handwriting has significant advantages over speech in situations where the user needs to position a cursor or define the path of a line. This is required in such operations as handwriting, sketching and editing of documents and diagrams. The enabling technology behind this is the digitizer tablet. While tablets have been available for many years, few are designed specifically for handwritten input and they thus have many ergonomic deficiencies for handwriting input. A further recent advance is in the provision of 'electronic paper' which is the superposition of the digitizer tablet directly over a flat-panel display. Electronic paper offers a number of exciting possibilities in terms of direct natural manipulation of documents and images including handwritten input for text, mathematical expressions, sketches and editing.

The automatic recognition of handwriting is not simple. There is considerable variation in writing from one writer to another and the problems are not dissimilar to those encountered in speech recognition. Currently available systems can recognize reasonably unconstrained separate handprinted characters if the user has trained the system to his or her writing. The recognition of other handwritten information including normal cursive script, mathematical symbols and editing operations is still at a relatively early stage of research and commercial systems are not available.

Technological advances in speech synthesis, speech recognition and handwriting recognition are made each year and the possibilities for human–computer interfaces using these media will therefore continue to grow. They remain challenging areas for the system designer. Successful niche markets for speech or handwriting computer interaction have been identified where this type of interface is cost effective and improves the safety, utility, effectiveness, efficiency and usability of a system.

References

Bailey, R. W. (1982) *Human Performance Engineering: A Guide for System Designers*, Prentice-Hall, Englewood Cliffs, NJ.

Brandetti, M., P. D'Orta, M. Ferretti and S. Scarci (1988) 'Experiments on the usage of a voice activated text editor', *Proceedings of Speech '88, 7th FASE Symposium, Edinburgh*, 1305–1310.

Bristow, G. (1986) *Electronic Speech Recognition: Techniques, Technology and Applications*, Collins, London.

Buxton, W. (1988) 'INPUT: Thinking about the First Two Letters of Interaction', *Tutorial Notes from HCI '88 conference, 5th September 1988, Manchester*.

Cater, J. P. (1983) *Electronically Speaking: Computer Speech Generation*, Howard W. Sams and Co., Indianapolis, Ind.

Chapanis, A., R. N. Parrish, R. B. Ochsman and G. D. Weeks (1977) 'Studies in interactive communication: II. The effects of four communications modes on the linguistic performance of teams during cooperative problem solving', *Human Factors*, **19** (2), 101–126.

County of Los Angeles (1972) *Recording and Transcription of Los Angeles Superior Court Proceedings*, September.

Dye, R., J. L. Arnott, A. F. Newell, K. E. P. Carter and G. Cruikshank (1989) 'Assessing the Potential of Future Automatic Speech Recognition Technology in Text Composition Applications', *Proceedings, Conference on Simulation in the Development of User Interfaces, Brighton, 18–19 May*, 216–225.

Foley, J. D., V. L. Wallace and P. Chan (1984) 'The human factors of graphics interaction techniques', *IEEE Transactions on Computer Graphics and Applications*, **4**, 13–48.

Ford, D. M. and C. A. Higgins (1990) 'A dictionary-based tree search technique in comparison with N-gram letter graph reduction', in *Computer Processing of Handwriting*, R. Plamondon and C. G. Leedham (eds), World Scientific Press, Singapore, 291–312.

Friday, P. D. and C. G. Leedham (1989) 'A Pre-Segmenter for Separating Characters in Unconstrained Hand-Printed Text', *Proceedings, IEEE International Conference on Image Processing, Singapore*, 299–303.

Gould, J. D. (1978) 'How experts dictate', *Journal of Experimental Psychology: Human Perception and Performance*, **4**, 648–661.

Gould, J. D. and L. Alfaro (1984) 'Revising documents with text editors, handwriting recognition systems and speech recognition systems', *Human Factors (USA)*, **26** (4), 391–406.

Gould, J. D. and J. Salaun (1987) 'Behavioural Experiments on Handmarking', *ACM Transactions on Office Information Systems*, **5** (4), 358–377.

Gould, J. D., J. Conti and T. Hovanyecz (1983) 'Composing letters with a simulated listening typewriter', *Communications of the ACM*, **4** (4), 295–308.

Higgins, C. A. and R. J. Duckworth (1990) 'The PAD (Pen And Display)—a demonstrator for the electronic paper project', in *Computer Processing of Handwriting*, R. Plamondon and C. G. Leedham (eds), World Scientific Press, Singapore, 111–132.

HMSO (1977) *Third report from the Select Committee on the House of Commons (Services): The Recording of Select Committees, Session 1976–7, 1 March 1977*.

Holmes, J. N. (1988) *Speech Synthesis and Recognition*, Van Nostrand Reinhold, London.

Kao, H. S. R., G. P. van Galen, and R. Hoosain (eds) (1986) *Graphonomics: Contemporary Research in Handwriting*, North-Holland, Amsterdam.

Lea, W. A. (1980) *Trends in Speech Recognition*, Prentice-Hall, Englewood Cliffs, NJ.

Linus write-top (1989) Information obtainable from Linus Technologies Inc., 11130 Sunrise Valley Drive, Reston, VA 22091.

Meeks, M. L. and T. T. Kuklinski (1990) 'Measurement of dynamic digitiser performance', in *Computer Processing of Handwriting*, R. Plamondon and C. G. Leedham (eds), World Scientific Press, Singapore, 88–110.

Morgan, N. (1984) *Talking Chips*, McGraw-Hill, New York.

Mountfield, S. J. and R. A. North (1980) 'Voice entry for reducing pilot workload', *Proceedings of the Human Factors Society*, 185–189.

Newell, A. F. (1986) 'Speech communication technology—lessons from the disabled', *Electronics and Power*, Sept.

Newell, A. F. (1987) 'Speech simulation studies—performance and dialogue specification', *Unicom Seminar, London, 8th–10th December*.

Newell, A. F., J. L. Arnott and R. Dye (1987) 'A full speed speech simulation of speech recognition machines', *Proceedings, European Conference on Speech Technology, Edinburgh, 2nd–4th September*.

O'Shaughnessy, D. (1987) *Speech Communication: Human and Machine*, Addison–Wesley, Reading, Mass.

Osmond Committee [1972) *Report on Recording Court Proceedings*, Lord Chancellor's Office, London.

'Paper versus screen: the human factors issues' (1985) *IEE Colloquium Digest*, No. 1985/80.

Poock, G. K. (1980) *Experiments with Voice Input for Command and Control*, Naval Postgraduate School Report, NPS55–80–016, Monterey, Calif.

Rowden, C. G. (ed.) (1991) *Speech Processing*, McGraw-Hill, London.

Schwab, E. and H. C. Nusbaum (eds) (1986) *Pattern Recognition by Humans and Machines, Volume 1: Speech Perception*, Academic Press, Orlando, Fla.

Sclater, N. (1983) *Introduction to Electronic Speech Synthesis*, Howard W. Sams and Co., Indianapolis, Ind.

Scriptel PenWriter (1989) Information obtainable from Scriptel Corporation, 4145 Arlington Plaza, Columbus, Ohio, USA 43228.

Singleton, S. (1988) *Telespan's 1988 Buyers Guide to Teleconferencing and Business Television Products and Services*, USA.

Speech Technology (1989) *Man Machine Voice Communication*, Special issue on large vocabulary recognisers, **4** (4), April/May 1989.

Suen, C. Y. and R. deMori (1982) *Computer Analysis and Perception—Volume 1: Visual Signals*, CRC Press, Boca Raton, Fla.

Tappert, C. C., A. S. Fox, J. Kim, S. E. Levy and L. L. Zimmermann (1986) 'Handwriting Recognition on Transparent Tablet over Flat Display', *SID International Symposium Digest of Technical Papers*, 308–312.

Tappert, C. C., C. Y. Suen and T. Wakahara (1988) 'On-line handwriting recognition—a survey', *Proceedings, 9th International Conference on Pattern Recognition*, 1123–1132.

Thomas, C. M. (1986) 'A Pilot Evaluation of an Electronic Paper Text Editing System by Comparison with MacWrite', *National Physical Laboratory Technical Memorandum* DITC TM5/86.

Ward, J. R. and M. J. Phillips (1987) 'Digitiser technology: performance characteristics and the effects on the user interface', *IEEE Computer Graphics and Applications*, Apr., 31–44.

Welbourn, L. K. and R. J. Whitrow (1990) 'A gesture-based text and diagram editor', in *Computer Processing of Handwriting*, R. Plamondon and C. G. Leedham (eds), World Scientific Press, Singapore, 221–234.

Welch, J. R. (1977) 'Automated data entry analysis', *Rome Air Development Center Report*, RADC TR–77–306, Griffiss Air Force Base, NY.

Witten, I. H. (1986) *Making Computers Talk: an Introduction to Speech Synthesis*, Prentice-Hall, Englewood Cliffs, NJ.

Young, T. Y. and K. S. Fu (1986) *Handbook of Pattern Recognition and Image Processing*, Academic Press, Orlando, Fla.

10 Windowing systems: high- and low-level design issues

SIMON JONES and ANDY DOWNTON

10.1 Introduction

Windowing systems are an increasingly familiar part of personal computers and workstations, and have been popularized to a large extent by the commercial success of the Apple Macintosh. However, their origins lie in research work undertaken at Xerox Palo Alto Research Centre during the 1970s. Two essential prerequisites of any windowing system are a computer with sufficient power to allow real-time manipulation of a variety of graphic objects, and a pixel-mapped graphic display linked to the computer by means of a high-bandwidth communication channel. This type of configuration (now familiar on any personal computer) was first implemented in the Xerox *Alto* personal computer (Thacker *et al.*, 1982), which was never sold commercially, but acted as a research environment and testbed for many of the concepts embodied in direct-manipulation interfaces (desktops, icons, windows, WYSIWYG, etc.). Subsequently, these concepts were refined and repackaged as a coherent system within the Xerox *Star* workstation, which appeared in 1981 (Smith *et al.*, 1982). The origins of the Apple Macintosh and its predecessor, the Lisa, are said to lie in a visit to Xerox PARC made by Steve Jobs, Apple's founder, in 1979.

In this chapter a taxonomy of windowing systems is provided, with particular emphasis on emerging windowing system standards which may be observed in the (predominantly UNIX) workstation environment. Workstations exhibit a variety of high-level windowing system design issues which have not yet been observed in personal computers (multi-tasking, network transparency of windowing systems, distributed processing, display device and processor-independent windowing systems), and thus present the widest possible coverage of software engineering design issues, even though practical

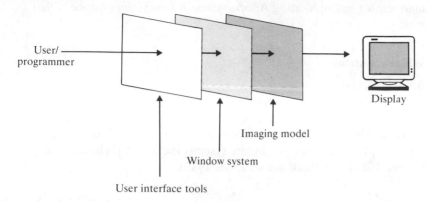

User/programmer

Display

Imaging model

Window system

User interface tools

Figure 10.1 Windowing systems classification

implementations in most cases do not yet provide the full direct-manipulation functionality, and consistency of, for example, the Macintosh.

The description of windowing systems is based upon a hierarchy which has at its base the *imaging model* used by the display system. Superimposed upon this is the *window system* itself, and superimposed on this in turn are a variety of *user interface tools*, which can be subdivided into those provided as tools for the user (the *window manager* and the *desktop*), and those which are programmer's tools (*interface toolkits* and *prototyping tools*).

10.2 Terminology and classification

The term 'windowing system' encompasses a wide range of software facilities which operate on a general class of raster-scanned, bit-mapped displays. To simplify their description the following bottom-up classification can be made, starting with the lowest layer, concerned with images, and building up to the highest layer, concerned with the user interaction. This layered structure is common among windowing systems and is reflected in the order of contents in this chapter. Unfortunately, author's descriptions of individual systems may use slightly different terminology from that employed here, owing to a lack of standardization in methods of description. However, the following classification is common to most systems (Figure 10.1).

Imaging models

The imaging model describes the basic graphic display structure in a static way. This could be in a device- or vendor-specific manner such as Sun Microsystem's *pixrect* (Sun, 1986a) or in a device-independent manner, for example using Adobe system's *PostScript* (Adobe, 1986) model.

Window systems

Window systems manage the dynamics of the window environment such as events, production and destruction of windows, and keyboard or mouse devices in a policy-independent manner, i.e., independently of decisions about what mouse buttons are associated with which actions, for example. Examples of window systems include *X* (Scheifler and Gettys, 1986) and *SunWindows* (Sun, 1985).

User interface tools

User interface tools fix policy which establishes a particular *look and feel* (*LAF*) to the application environment. These policy decisions can be as simple as defining the background window colour, or as complex as defining what a button looks like and how the button acts. Examples of user interface tool sets are the X window system widget set *Xaw* (Swick, 1988), *SunTools* (Sun, 1985), *XView* (Sun, 1988) and *Motif* (Oldenburg, 1989).

Windowing system

This is the collective term for an image system, a window system and a set of user interface tools which function together to form a complete application environment.

Two more general names for what we define as windowing systems are now appearing in the literature. The terms are *User Interface Management System* (*UIMS*), which is used to refer to the user's part of a windowing system, and *User Interface Design Environment* (*UIDE*), which refers to the programmer's part of a windowing system. The origin and formal definition of what constitutes a UIMS has already been covered in Section 6.2.

Not all systems allow the programmer access to every individual layer: some, such as the Macintosh toolkit constrain the programmer to the highest-layer user interface tools only and therefore fix the appearance of the system and its application. This constraint ensures that all applications have similar interfaces and that operations learnt by a user from one application will be appropriate to another, for example the cut-and-paste operations common to all Macintosh applications.

10.3 Imaging systems

The *imaging system* provides the lowest-level device-independent description of the capabilities of the image display. It consists of the hardware which actually implements the image display, combined with software which is analogous to the device drivers in an operating system. This software receives as its input *display commands* issued by higher-level software such as the window system, and transforms these commands into operations which actually implement the specified function on the physical display hardware. The set of allowable display commands and their syntax and structure are defined by the *imaging model*, which is normally specified in a device-and-display-resolution-independent manner. The *PostScript* imaging model is described below at the end of this section and the *X Windows* protocol model in Section 10.7.

10.3.1 Hardware structures for imaging systems

Although many different refreshable display devices are available (see Chapter 8), and there is an increasing trend towards flat-panel displays (particularly in portable personal computers), the overwhelming majority of windowing systems are currently based around the raster scan CRT display device. In the following sections therefore, this display device is assumed.

Raster scan frame buffer architecture

Figure 10.2 shows a general architecture of a frame buffer display system. Depending upon the display application and performance requirements, the display processor may be the same general-purpose processor as is used for all computation within the workstation, or a coprocessor or independent display processor may be used. The frame buffer memory may appear within the same address space as all other workstation memory, or there may be independent address and data bus connections from the display processor. An essential requirement of the frame buffer memory however is that it is *dual-ported* such that access to it is shared between the video display generator and the display processor.

The video display generator reads data from the frame-buffer memory according to the raster scan format. In the simplest case, a monochrome single bit per pixel display, words within the frame buffer generally represent consecutively displayed pixels and so are serialized and then converted directly into an analogue signal which switches on or off the scanning electron beam. In the more general case, where the display provides grey-scale or colour capabilities, p bits are used to specify the grey-scale or colour value of the pixel within the frame

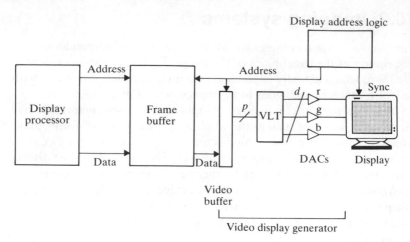

Figure 10.2 Raster scan frame buffer architecture

buffer. Each pixel value fetched is then used to index a *video lookup table* (VLT) which typically maps the 2^p possible grey or colour values specified in the frame buffer into a larger set of 2^d possible grey or colour display values. For example, if $p=8$ and $d=15$ (5 bits for each primary colour), a set of 256 displayable colours can be selected out of a colour palette of 32 768 possible colours. The VLT is itself normally connected to the processor address and data busses so that colour palette selection can be accomplished under program control (for clarity, this connection is omitted in Figure 10.2). In the case of grey-scale or colour displays of course, digital-to-analogue converter(s) are also required to convert the d bits of the specified grey level or colour into the corresponding analogue signals which control the intensity of the electron beam(s).

The frame buffer dual-port memory is designed to allow both the video display generator and the display processor to access it without interference. To achieve this, access from these two components is interleaved in some way. The video display generator obviously has to have highest priority, since failure to obtain access at the correct time in the raster scan would cause breakdown of the displayed image. If the raster scan rate is synchronized with the clock rate of the processor then the frame buffer design may allow interleaving such that, for example, alternate clock cycles are allocated to display generator and display processor access. If the display operates asynchronously with respect to the processor, a more restrictive access method may be required, for example access to the display processor only during horizontal and vertical flyback periods.

Recent frame buffer designs incorporate a number of innovations to speed up display processing. One of the most important has been the introduction of video RAMs (VRAMs) which include an internal shift register. This provides an additional path through which a row of bits can be parallel-loaded from the chip's row sense amplifiers in a single clock cycle. These bits can then be shifted out independently of normal access to the chip, increasing substantially the proportion of clock cycles which are available for display update. In effect, the shift register provides a second independent port dedicated to the raster display generator.

A further development has been to use the video generator circuitry to combine the output from several independent frame buffer memories, corresponding, for example, to independent windows. This provides support for a number of dynamic effects, and, if each frame buffer is supported by its own display processor, can also increase display bandwidth generally, since each display processor is responsible for maintaining only part of the screen.

Display processor architecture

Figure 10.3 shows a number of possible display processor architectures. The simplest option (Figure 10.3 (a)) is for the system's general-purpose processor to control the frame buffer directly. In this case, the frame buffer memory is accessed in the same way as any other system memory. A common alternative in workstations and personal computers is for the general-purpose processor to be augmented by a graphics coprocessor or *RasterOp processor* (Figure 10.3(b)). This device typically provides support for rapid execution of simple Boolean operations between specified source and destination pixel regions, allowing independent components of the display to be rapidly and flexibly combined, moved, cleared or overlaid (Bennett, 1985). At the same time, the general-purpose procesor retains full access to the frame buffer so that functions not supported on the coprocessor can be implemented directly.

If a full range of display processing capabilities can be provided independently of the general-purpose processor, the architecture of Figure 10.3(c) may be used, where the host processor communicates exclusively with the display processor, which in turn has exclusive access to the frame buffer. This architecture was originally developed for use in applications where the communication link between the host and the display processor was of limited bandwidth, for example in high-performance graphics displays for minicomputers. Though not widely used in host-based windowing systems, it is re-emerging as an important architecture in the design of network-based windowing systems, where network communication overheads preclude the transmission of low-level graphics primitives (see Section 10.4.3). Although the host is relieved of much of the computational requirement for updating the display, the disadvantage of this configuration is that the host and display memories are completely independent, so the

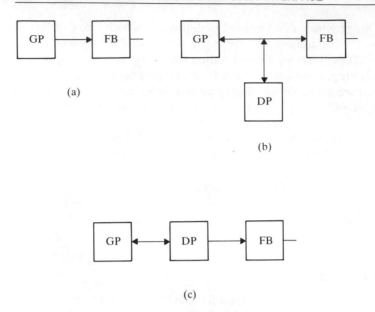

Figure 10.3 Alternative display processor architectures

display has no access to host data structures such as fount definitions or display lists corresponding to application data structures (see the next section).

A more complete review of raster scan image display architectures will be found in Sproull (1986).

10.3.2 Graphics data structures for windowing systems

The data structures used to represent the imagery of a windowing system obviously depend to some extent upon the imaging model, which in turn depends upon the hardware support for imaging provided by the display processor. Where the display processor is the system's general-purpose processor, all image data structures have to be defined explicitly in software. Where a display coprocessor or dedicated display processor are used then some of the display functionality is embedded in the additional hardware support which the special purpose processor provides. In a RasterOp processor, this support is limited to simple Boolean operations on display regions (Bennett, 1985). In a dedicated display processor, higher-level primitives may be supported, for example geometric objects such as polygons and lines, and characters (possibly with different founts and styles). The example data structures below assume a system with no display processor support, where all graphics structures are generated explicitly by the general-purpose processor.

General characteristics

Windowing systems are in general based around the Cartesian coordinate system: this maps readily onto bit-mapped pixel displays, and minimizes the complexity of arithmetic manipulation associated with image operations. With few exceptions, arithmetic is performed in integer format.

Data structures

The data structures used to generate images in window systems are characterized as being highly structured and hierarchical. Extensive use is made of pointers, linked lists, structure data types and dynamic memory allocation. Most current windowing systems have been implemented in C, a language which is efficient and well suited to the required operations.

   Typical data structures used to represent window systems constructs are reviewed below in a bottom-up fashion. Viewed in a top-down fashion, the full screen is represented as a window on a graphics metafile which contains a linked list of *segments*, each of which in turn contains a linked list of *nodes* containing primitive data types and their attributes. The segments define the image content, not the image display, and are displayed by calling a segment display function. This invokes mapping, clipping and scaling functions to determine which components of the segment currently appear within the displayed image.

Graphic primitives

Although a wide range of graphics primitives can be defined, most of the functionality of window systems can be achieved using a much more restricted set (Sobelman and Krekelberg, 1985). The most commonly required primitives are the *point*, the *rectangle*, the *multipoint line/polygon*, and *text primitives*. Each primitive has a data structure which defines its physical shape and position in terms of the Cartesian coordinate system, together with an associated set of C functions which create it, display it, and insert or delete it within a graphics segment.

   The simplest graphics primitive is the *point primitive*: its data structure consists solely of a Cartesian coordinate position definition:

```
struct point_prim {
    int x, y;
};
typedef struct point_prim point_type;
```

Points can then be created and initialized as data structures in memory (but not displayed) by executing a function call of the form

```
point_type *create_point (x,y)
```

which calls the standard C function `calloc` to allocate contiguous memory for the primitive and returns a pointer to the point structure.

Rectangles are extensively used in window systems: they are needed for drawing windows and their borders, and for defining 'bounding boxes' around arbitrary geometric shapes. 'Bounding box' descriptions are extensively used in clipping operations (see below), and so rectangle primitives are used to define the area within which any arbitrary shape or set of shapes (for example a segment) lie. The rectangle data structure is defined in terms of coordinates which specify the position of its top, bottom, and left and right edges.

```
struct rect_prim {
    int left, bottom, right, top;
};
typedef struct rect_prim rect_type;
```

Rectangles are then created by invoking the following function, which creates a rectangle structure with the specified coordinates, allocates memory for it, and returns a pointer to it:

```
rect_type *create_rect (left, bottom, right, top)
```

A variety of primitive operations are carried out on rectangles, many of them candidates for hardware support within a RasterOp display coprocessor. They include intersection and union operations between rectangles, move, resize and copy operations on individual rectangles, and Boolean functions which return a value specifying whether a point is within or outside a rectangle.

Multipoint lines and *polygons* are essentially identical as data structures and differ only as to whether an (implied) line is drawn to connect the last point defined back to the first. Since they can have an arbitrary number of line components, they are specified in terms of a linked list data structure, which consists of a head of list, followed by a list of nodes. Each node is itself a structure consisting of a `poly_point` (identical to the point primitive already defined above) and a pointer to the next defining point of the multipoint line/polygon. Thus the `poly_point` data structure is:

```
struct poly_point {
    point_type point;
    struct poly_point *next;
};
typedef struct poly_point ppoint_type;
```

This data structure can then be incorporated into the linked-list data structure which defines the multipoint line or polygon:

```
struct poly_prim {
    int num_points;
    rect_type *bbox;
    struct ppoint_type *point
};
typedef struct poly_prim poly_type;
```

Here, the header information for the linked list specifies the number of points in the multipoint line or polygon, and bbox is a pointer to the bounding box structure for the linked list as a whole. The multipoint line is created by a series of function calls which initially create the data structure and allocate memory for it, and then append additional nodes to the linked list, adding memory for each node as it is created and appended. Finally, a function call returns a pointer to the completed data structure.

```
/* declare line pointers */
line_t *myline, *end_line ();

begin_line();
con_point (x1,y1);
con_point (x2,y2);
...
con_point (xN,yN);
myline = end_line();
```

In many display systems, basic-character primitive shapes are stored in memory, and accessed via character codes. If this is not the case, they can be created in software using stroke or pixel primitives, but in either case this slows the display update rate. If the *text* primitive is viewed as a string of characters, then in addition to specifying the character string, for display purposes it is also necessary to know the position of the text on the screen, its bounding box, and other attributes such as fount size (points) and style. A variety of different founts may also be available. As in the previous examples, the text and attributes together are stored in a data structure, for example:

```
struct text_prim {
    point_type origin;
    rect_type *bbox;
        ...                    /*other attributes */
    char *text;
};
typedef struct text_prim text_type;
```

Attributes

Attributes specify modifications which can be made to the style of display of any graphic primitive. The current attribute state is specified using a Finite State Machine (FSM), and stays in force until a change of attribute is specified. Attributes are coded as arbitrary constants, and selected by case statements. Example attributes are given below.

Mode attributes specify the way in which the new display component is to be combined with existing components. This will typically be a simple Boolean function such as copy, OR, AND or XOR. *Colour* attributes specify a variety of selectable display colours where a colour display system is available. The *fill* attribute is applied to operations on polygons and rectangles, and specifies whether the polygon is to be displayed as a wire frame or filled. The *reset* attribute resets the FSM to an initial default state.

Geometrical transformations

A common requirement is to *clip* a graphic object so that only that part of the object which appears within the display window is drawn on the display. This is important in maintaining the illusion of independent windows upon the display, but is also essential to avoid more general aliasing problems where the pixel structure of the display would cause the unwanted part of the image to wrap around onto the opposite edge of the window or screen if it were not removed.

Clipping of graphical objects is a subject which is covered in depth in many standard textbooks on graphics, for example Newman and Sproull (1981) and Foley and van Dam (1983). For clipping purpose, the primitives described above can be split into three classes, points, lines and other primitives, and these classes dealt with separately (see Figure 10.4).

Clipping points is trivial. The point is either within or outside the window, and this can be determined by comparing the pixel address with the coordinates of the edges of the window, leading to a Boolean inside/outside result.

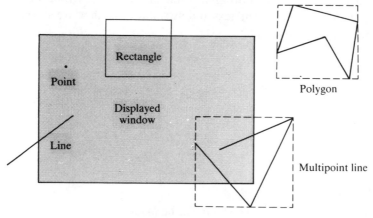

Figure 10.4 Clipping graphics primitives to a displayed window

Lines are clipped using the standard Cohen–Sutherland algorithm. This algorithm tests the two end points of the line against the boundaries of the window, and according to the results obtained assigns the line to one of three categories. If both points are within the window, the whole line should be displayed. If both points lie to the same side of the window, or both are above, or both are below, then none of the line is within the window, and it should be rejected. Otherwise the line intersects at least one edge of the window, and must be split into the part within the window and the one or two parts outside the window by calculating the intersection point(s). The particular beauty of the Cohen–Sutherland algorithm is that it allows detection of the first two cases above in a very simple and fast manner by binary code comparisons, thus minimizing the computational time required when clipping large graphical objects to a small window.

Other primitives and more complex objects comprising structures of primitives are clipped by first comparing the coordinates of their bounding box to the window coordinates. Again this leads to three possible results. If the bounding box lies completely within or outside the window, then the complete object is displayed or rejected respectively. If the bounding box overlaps the window, then the graphic object must be broken down into its constituent primitives, and each of these examined individually. Wire frame primitives can be broken down into their constituent lines, and each line examined separately using the Cohen–Sutherland alogorithm. Filled objects, such as polygons, are clipped using a polygon clipping algorithm such as the Sutherland–Hodgman algorithm (Sutherland and Hodgman, 1974), wherein the polygon is successively clipped against individual edges of the window.

Graphic operations

As stated previously, a complete graphic image consists of a list of *segments*, each of which contains a list of *nodes*. Each node contains a primitive or attribute type, data describing the primitive or attribute and a pointer to the next node. Thus segments are variable-length data structures, organized as a linked list of linked lists. Typically, each segment might represent one graphic entity (such as a window and its contents) on the complete image. The complete image is often described as a *graphics metafile* by analogy with disk files: like a text file, the content can be saved on disk. The graphics metafile defines the content of the image in the same way as a text file defines the content of a document: at any given time, however, the image display represents a window on the metafile, in the same way as a screen editor provides a window displaying part of a text file.

Operations on graphics segments are also analogous to operations on text files: initially a segment is created; then graphics primitives or structures of primitives are added to the segment to define its content; finally the segment is closed, returning a pointer to the segment. Using this data structure, the segment can be displayed by executing a segment display routine which takes as its entry parameter the pointer to the segment. The routine then traverses the segment linked lists displaying each component.

A typical segment data structure would be as follows:

```
struct segment {
    int num_inst, visible, locked;
    char *name;
    rect_type *bbox;
    key_type *data, *last;
    struct segment *next;
}
typedef struct segment seg_type;
```

The first three code lines of this structure represent the header information for the segment. To minimize storage requirements, only one copy of the segment is maintained in the metafile however many times it is used in the image. This means that the segment should not be deleted when a reference to it is deleted unless this was the only reference to it: this information is tracked using `num_inst`. The variable `visible` allows display of the segment to be turned on and off without it being deleted from the image. The variable `locked` is used to prevent a segment from being deleted from memory. The variables `name` and `bbox` are respectively pointers to a string defining the textual name of the segment and to the bounding box of the segment.

The last line of the segment structure defines a pointer to the next segment, implementing the linked list of segments. Finally, the line preceding this defines pointers to the beginning and end of the linked list of nodes which makes up the segment. Each of these nodes is itself defined as a data structure containing three components: a primitive or attribute type (represented simply using a table of integer variables); a union of all possible primitive structures; and finally, a pointer to the next node. These are illustrated below for the graphics primitives already defined:

```
struct node {
   int type;    /* primitive/attribute type */
   union {      /* of all primitives/attributes
       point_type *point;
       rect_type *rect;
       poly_type *poly;
       text_type *text;
```

```
    } node_key;
    struct node *next;
}
typedef struct node node_type
```

10.3.3 The PostScript imaging model

PostScript (Adobe, 1986) is a language for describing the appearance of
pages in documents. It specifies the page in terms of the character
positions and orientations and graphic objects the page contains, and
can also describe scanned images. The language design allows complex
digital graphics to be expressed in a device-independent manner; it also
includes features specifically for the high-level manipulation of
characters as graphic objects.

The PostScript language has three distinct features (Adobe, 1988): it
is *interpreted*, it is *stack-based*, and it uses a unique data structure called
a *dictionary*. If an object placed on the stack is not a data object it is
assumed to be an operation and executed from the dictionary. An
operation may remove data items from the stack, modify the displayed
image and/or return a result to the stack. New commands can simply be
placed on the stack and directly executed, or stored, with a unique
identifier, within the dictionary. When the operation is required again
only its unique identifier needs to be used.

PostScript *imaging model* provides standard operations for typesetting
and rendering graphics. The model can be stated as follows:
'Algorithmic paths are created to define an area or a series of lines, and
ink is applied to those paths through one of several methods, including
stroking, filling, halftoning, text rendering and clipping.' (Adobe 1988).
This can be summarized as *Path and Paint*: a *path* is specified over
which *paint* is applied. The path description is device-independent;
actual device characteristics only affect the final stage of the *painting*
process when the displayed image is created. The language example in
Figure 10.5 shows the specification of a path, its positioning in the
coordinate space and then its painting to the device.

The actual image created is controlled by the PostScript interpreter
by performing translations from the *user coordinate system* used by the
application program into the *device coordinates* used by the actual
output device. True device-independent graphic and text are created by
all applications, which work in terms of user space coordinates based on
points (72nds of an inch).

Although originally designed for the description of document pages
for laser printers, PostScript is equally suitable for the description of
displayed images. An extended version, Display PostScript, has been
standardized for use on interactive displays. Another set of extensions
to the original language specification form the basis of the Network
extensible Window System, NeWS, described in Section 10.4.4.

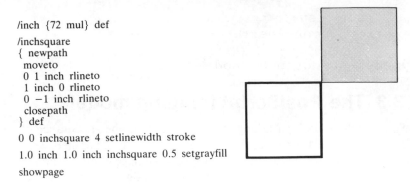

```
/inch {72 mul} def

/inchsquare
{ newpath
  moveto
  0 1 inch rlineto
  1 inch 0 rlineto
  0 −1 inch rlineto
  closepath
} def

0 0 inchsquare 4 setlinewidth stroke

1.0 inch 1.0 inch inchsquare 0.5 setgrayfill

showpage
```

Figure 10.5   PostScript language example

10.4 Window systems

The central component of most user interface systems is the *window*, which provides a mechanism through which the user can interact with a source of information. Typically a user will have a number of windows visible on the display at any one time, each providing the facility to view information from a source and to pass user input to the source (Figure 10.6).

The form of the information displayed is described by the underlying imaging model. For the system to be usable the windows and inputs must be controlled in a uniform manner; this is achieved by the display and event managers which together form the window system.

10.4.1 Display manager

The windows which can be described by the imaging model and realized by the window system have to be managed to form a usable system by means of a *display manager*. The display manager is responsible for the maintenance of the information required to form the display. This information consists of the static representation described by the imaging model and the dynamic or state information relating to the creation, interaction and manipulation of the windows. The image displayed to the user is created from a number of windows, each of which will be associated with an application or item of information. The order and position of these windows is controlled by the display manager.

As windowing systems have developed, the facilities offered by display managers have evolved from a simple emulation of a mechanical printer to the provision of multiple windows containing full-colour graphics. Systems can be classified according to the manner in which the display manager extends the virtual size of display beyond the basic physical capabilities of the display screen (Card *et al.*, 1985).

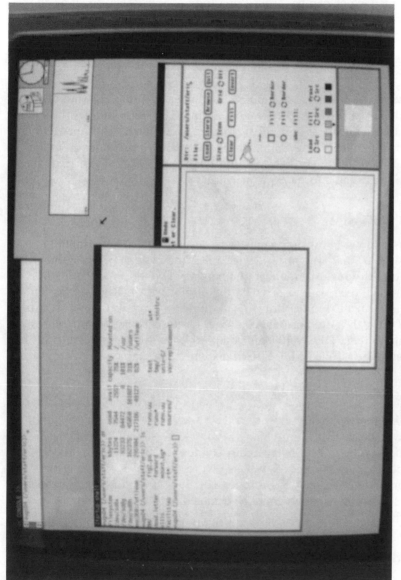

Figure 10.6 A typical workstation display

261

Scrollable windows

These are the simplest windows, and are common to all display terminals. The display presents a window on the information to be presented which can be scrolled up (and possibly down) to allow all the information to be viewed. Most commonly, such windows provide text-only displays, though scrollable graphics windows are also possible.

Frame-at-a-time

A frame-at-a time system supports a number of scrollable windows of which only one can be displayed at a time. The system allows the user to select which frame is currently displayed. The operation of these systems is equivalent to having a number of virtual character terminals to the same operating system. This interface can be run on basic terminals and provides a simple forms type interface.

Split windows

Split windows allow the display to be sectioned with horizontal divisions so that a number of scrollable windows can be simultaneously viewed. Although the number and heights of windows can be controlled, their width is fixed by the display width. This mechanism was implemented in the Bravo text-editing system developed at Xerox PARC for the Alto personal computer, and is also supported by many terminals (e.g., DEC vt100 and compatibles) since it enables part of the screen to be scrolled while a fixed display is maintained elsewhere.

Tiled windows

Tiled window systems allow the display screen to be both horizontally and vertically divided into many windows. To support this model fully requires the use of bit-mapped display devices, thus allowing the introduction of graphics as well as text to the display. This idea was originally used in the Cedar (Teitelman, 1984) system where the location and size of the windows could be changed but they could not be overlapped.

Overlapping windows

Overlapping windows can be resized and positioned independently and placed above or below each other. This allows a window to be brought to the top so that its contents can be viewed, thus simulating a desktop with overlapping documents placed upon it. With overlapping windows the position of the windows is largely controlled by the user. Most current windowing systems support overlapping windows.

Table 10.1   Display dimensions of window systems

Display Mode	Dimensions
Scrollable windows	1
Frame-at-a-time	1
Split windows	2
Tiled windows	2
Overlapping windows	2.5
Pop-up windows	2.5

Pop-up window

A pop-up window is just a special case of an overlapping window; a pop-up window is dynamically created and *pops up* in front of the window which initiated its creation. Pop-up windows are usually used for dynamic interaction with the user, for example in menu selection and dialogues.

Display manager modes

The display modes described above are summarized in terms of the number of dimensions over which the information is presented. A simple scrollable window presents information in a single vertical dimension. A tiled window presents information in two dimensions, both horizontally and vertically. Overlapping windows provide limited display capabilities beyond the two screen dimensions and thus give a two-and-a-half-dimension display. This is summarized in Table 10.1.

10.4.2 Event manager

From the user interface point of view, windowing systems are principally driven by asynchronous events generated by the user. These events are generated by the two basic input devices provided on most systems: the *mouse* (or alternative pointing device such as data tablet or joystick) and the *keyboard*. Additionally, there may be other background events which influence the display, for example timer events used to update a displayed clock. The exact definition of what constitutes an 'event' depends upon the set of user actions which it is required to detect and the window management philosophy of the system. For example, the set of events required to support region-based window management may differ somewhat from those required to support menu-based window management: in the region-based window manager, subclasses of events corresponding to user actions within border regions of a window may be needed which have no equivalent in the menu-based system (see Section 10.5.3).

In general, events are allocated to classes according to their source, the principle sources being mouse events, keyboard events, combined events and system events. At the hardware–software interface level, raw hardware actions will be detected by means of interrupts and inserted into a queue for event processing. Since the raw hardware actions may differ from what the system defines as 'events', preprocessing is required at this stage to combine the raw actions into compound events which are meaningful to the system. For example, a button click on the mouse comprises button-down and button-up operations, but the interpretation of these actions in terms of events recognized by the system depends also upon whether any mouse movement occurs between the two actions: if so, the action is interpreted as a 'drag' event rather than a 'click' event. Thus the preprocessing stage is used to combine raw events from a variety of sources into compound events capable of mapping user actions to functional execution within the windowing system.

In many systems, to achieve adequate response to the required events (particularly instantaneous cursor tracking of the mouse), much of the low-level event processing is offloaded to a dedicated I/O processor, which is then responsible for communicating an ordered and buffered queue of events to the main procesor. Each event is stored in the queue in a standard data structure, which might for example have the following format:

```
struct event_record {
    int event;    /*integer value defining type of event */
    char keystroke; /* character typed for event, if any */
    point_type where; /* cursor position during event ·*/
    int when; /* time in microseconds for sequence control */
};
typedef struct event_record event_type;
```

Mouse events

These include the detection of button-down and button-up events for mouse buttons and mouse motion. These basic actions may be combined together to define events such as click, double-click (which also requires reference to a system clock) and drag. Mouse movements are also important in defining events: not only must the screen cursor track the mouse instantaneously, but also knowledge of the current mouse position is often required in order to interpret what event should be associated with the current mouse action (e.g., in region-based window managers, as described above). Furthermore, specific classes of mouse movement may constitute events in their own right; for example, mouse movement across the boundary between one window and another in some systems causes a context switch of the active window.

Keyboard events

At the lowest level these correspond to key-up and key-down actions for each key. At a higher level these actions may be combined to generate a character input event.

Combined events

These are supported on many systems, where holding down the control or shift key in combination with a mouse action has the effect of modifying this action. Thus in this case the event is generated by a combination of low-level mouse and keyboard actions.

System events

Included among these would be events generated by devices such as real-time clocks.

The event loop

Since the user interface is event-driven, the basic software mechanism for handling events is an event loop or event handler. In fact, a hierarchy of event loops is used to keep track of the different contexts within which user interaction with the system may be taking place, and the occurrence of an appropriate event in the current event loop may pass control to a new event loop corresponding to new context. Thus, in the event of mouse movement across a window boundary as mentioned above, the event generated by this transition may be used to trigger a context switch. Similarly, double-clocking on an application icon in a Macintosh environment generates an event which results in the corresponding application being launched, and subsequent events being handled by the application's own event loop.

The event handler itself consists of a loop which fetches events in sequence from the event queue and then executes a switch statement based upon the type of event fetched. Prototypically, the event loop has the following structure:

```
for  ;;) { /* execute loop indefinitely */
    /* return pointer to next event on queue */
    evp = get_event ();
```

```
    /* what kind of event was it? */
    switch (evp->event) }
        /* example event types for a text editor */
        case KEY_EVENT :     /* keyboard input event */
            putchar(evp->keystroke);
            break;
        case CLICK_EVENT :   /* mouse click event */
            put_cursor(evp->where);
            break;
        case D_CLICK_EVENT : /* mouse double-click event */
            select_word(evp->where);
            break;
        case OUT_OF_WINDOW : /* mouse movement outside window*/
            context_switch(evp->where);
            break;
        /* etc, etc */
    }
}
```

Where the window system is running on a single-tasking operating system (for example a PC running MS-DOS or PC-DOS), the event loop can consist of a continuously polled loop as shown above since no other task is competing for the processor's resources. In a multitasking system, execution of the event loop is initiated by the occurrence and queuing of an event from an input device, and only continues until all events in the queue have been processed. The detail of actions taken, and indeed of events which are considered to be significant, will vary according to the context (i.e., according to the code included within the specific event loop).

10.4.3 Architectures for window systems

The architecture of a window system describes how the functions it provides are implemented and the manner in which its modules are interconnected. This affects how an application which has a window-based user interface interacts with the system supporting the window system. The manner in which the application is programmed is discussed in Section 10.6 below. The architectural concern is how the window library software linked into the application interacts with the window system software running on the system. Two different architectures have been used for windowing systems. A *host-based* system constrains the application and windowing system to run on the same host machine. In a *network-based* architecture, the application and the windowing system communicate by an interprocess communication mechanism, IPC, and are therefore not constrained to run on the same host machine. These architectures are distinguished in Figure 10.7 (Williams, 1986).

AAP Application   TK User interface toolkit

TTY Terminal emulator   WM Window manager

WS Window system   IPC Interprocess communication mechanism

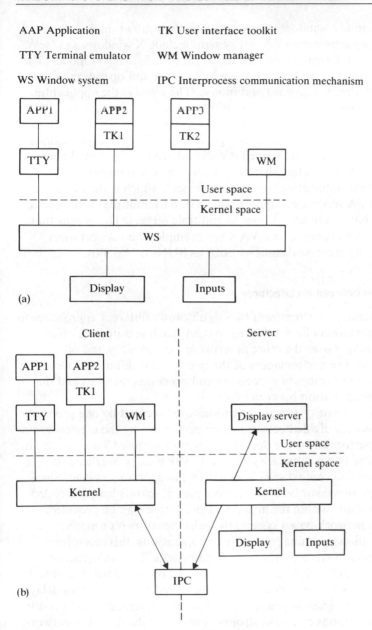

(a)

(b)

Figure 10.7   (a) Host-based window system architecture
(b) Network-based window system architecture

The Macintosh window system and Sun View are examples of host-based systems: network-based systems include X windows and NeWS.

The network-based systems are based on the *client-server* model. The *server* provides the facilities for the management and operation of the bit-mapped screen, keyboard and mouse. The *client* is the application programme, and communicates with the server using a graphics protocol. (Note that this represents a reversal of the usual connotation of the terms *client* and *server* in computer networks.) All input actions performed by the user are termed *events* and are managed by the server. The server determines the window in which the event occurred and sends an event notification to the client process which is the owner of the window. A server can support connection to multiple clients and a client may have connections open to multiple servers. This means that one application, running on a VAX for example, can support users working at different workstations, such as SUNs or Apollos.

Comparison between architectures

The two architectures represent two significantly different approaches to the implementation of a windowing system. Each architecture offers some advantages over the other in terms of functionality and of performance. The performances of the two systems differ because of the variation in the number of processors and processes involved and the cost of communication between them.

In the host-based system all operations are executed by one processor and the tasks are divided between those performed by the user program and those performed by the operating system's kernal. Communication between these two occurs via system calls which carry overheads due to data transfer and context switching within the operating system. Since only a single processor is involved, only pseudo-parallelism controlled by task switching within the host operating system can be provided.

Within a network-based system, the existence of two or more processors allows genuine parallelism of operations: this can offer improved performance over a host-based system. The performance penalty of the network-based system is the delay due to the interprocess communication between the client processes and the server. This delay is an order of magnitude greater than that for a system call. As a result the communications overhead strongly influences the design of network based systems. For example, any operation which requires the client to wait for an acknowledgment from the server will entail a minimum of a round-trip network delay, which can be several milliseconds. Obviously if every operation were acknowledged the performance would be unacceptably slow. In a network system the communication is therefore asynchronous with commands flowing from the client to the server and event information passing from the server to the client. Synchronization of action is performed only when explicitly required by the client.

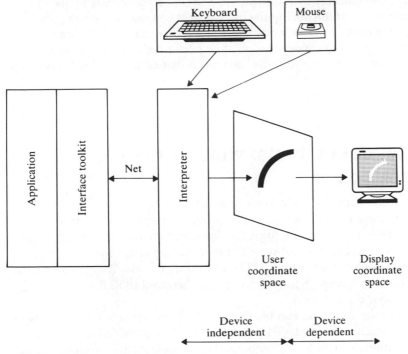

Figure 10.8   NeWS windowing system architecture

Functionally the two architectures differ in the provision of interfaces to network-based applications. These are implicitly supported by the network-based systems but are difficult to implement on a single host-based architecture.

10.4.4 The NeWS windowing system

A secondary problem of a network-based system is the volume of data that may need to be sent between the client and the server. This can significantly restrict performance, especially if the communication protocol only supports low-level graphic operations. To provide a system that supported all high-level operations would be impossible; however, it is possible to define a communication protocol that allows high-level operations to be defined at the server and then utilized with the same ease as low-level ones.

This principle is the basis of Sun's *Network extensible Window System*, NeWS (Figure 10.8), which uses a communication protocol based on the *PostScript* (Adobe, 1986) document description language with some extensions to provide garbage collection and lightweight processes (Gosling, 1986). The NeWS server is initialized with the basic set of PostScript operations required to manipulate the displayed image:

new commands are then downloaded to the server increasing its functionality and reducing the interprocess communication required. Unfortunately, a server's command storage capacity will be limited, so some dictionary management must be performed. This is commonly implemented by removing the least recently used user-defined command to free storage for a new definition. A recovery mechanism is required to handle any subsequent use of a removed command; this is achieved by a request back to the client program for the command to be redefined.

10.5 Users' tools: window managers and desktops

The combination of an image system and a window system provides the mechanisms to describe and realize window-based displays. It is usually possible to program directly at this level, but the facilities provided are low-level, and require substantial programming effort to realize even a simple window (Rosenthal, 1987). Obviously this is not desirable and all windowing systems therefore provide higher-level tools for programmers and users.

User interface tools can be divided into those provided to allow users to manipulate the displayed windows and those provided for programmers to build applications. Users' tools include *window managers* that allow control of the display and *desktops* that provide a visual representation of the system. Programmers' tools include *toolkits* that provide interface elements that are combined to build an interface and *prototyping tools* that allow interfaces to be described, modelled and built.

10.5.1 Users' tools: window manager

A window manager provides a user interface to the display and window management facilities to allow a user to control the windows presented on the display. Typically these facilities are concerned with the size, placement, order and display of new and existing windows.

Often, the user interface provided by a window manager is perceived, by a user, to be that of the whole windowing system. This is usually incorrect, as a particular window manager provides only one of the many possible user interfaces that could be implemented. The misconception arises because the window manager presents a particular *look and feel* for the system, which is of more practical interest to the users than the underlying mechanisms.

10.5.2 Window manager facilities

The facilities offered by window managers fall into the following categories:

Placement: move, iconify, initial placement.
Size: expand/contract edge, expand/contract corner.
Order: raise, lower, cycle.
Display: refresh, redraw, freeze, focus.

Placement operations

These allow the user to control the layout of windows on the display in a manner similar to moving papers about on a desk. Windows can be stowed into an iconic form when not in current use, the *icon* representing in text or graphical form the nature of the original window. When a new window is created some window managers allow interactive control of its initial placement; other systems automatically place the window in a default position.

Size operations

Using these, a user can manipulate the size of a window during its use. For this to be successful the underlying application must know how to respond to a change in window size; for example, if the application is a text editor it should be able to fill the new window size with text.

Order operations

These control how windows overlap. When a window system allows windows to overlap, a mechanism must exist to allow a window to be brought to the top or placed below others. The normal functions are to selectively raise or lower one window or to cycle the order of all windows bringing up each in turn to the top.

Display operations

With these, the user is able to request the redrawing of individual windows or the complete refreshing of the display. Most window systems attempt to do this automatically, but if client processes unexpectedly fail or connections die then user action may be required. Display operations include management of the keyboard input: typically, the input from the keyboard is directed to the window that contains the mouse. *Focus* operations allow keyboard input to be focused to one window and not follow the mouse; *unfocus* removes the facility

10.5.3 Window manager facility selection

The method of initiating window manager facilities varies between systems, but can, in general, be divided into two categories: *menu* or *region*. For *menu* operation the facility is usually initiated by a mouse action to generate a pop-up menu; the desired operation is then triggered by menu selection. For *region* operation a specific portion of a window's border is used to initiate each action.

The choice between region and menu operation is embedded within the implementation of the window manager; Table 10.2 lists options available on some common windowing systems. All the window managers support overlapping windows except *rtl*, which supports tiled windows.

Table 10.2   Operation initiation in window managers

Manager	System	Operation initiation
uwm	X window	Only menu-based selection
rtl	X window	Both region and menu selection (tiled)
Motif	X window	Both region and menu selection
Open Look	X window	Both region and menu selection
Suntools	Sun	Both region and menu selection
Oriel	Whitechapel	Only region-based selection
Macintosh	Macintosh	Region-based with menu support
wm	Apollo	Region-based with keyboard support
	Microsoft Windows	Region-based

From the table it can be seen that many different user interfaces can be provided for the X window system. This emphasizes the separation of policy and mechanism between the window manager and the window system inherent within the X window system. The table also highlights the differing approaches used by different window managers. This can lead to a problem when a user has to use different windowing systems and learn a new set of different, but often confusingly similar, operations.

Region-based window managers

In a region-based window manager, all windows currently visible on the display are bounded by a border that is divided into regions. Window manager operations are initiated by mouse actions occurring within the border regions. Figure 10.9 shows a window similar to that from the Whitechapel Oriel system.

Region-based systems are simple and fast to operate and require little learning time if the region identifiers are clear. The limitation of region-based systems is that only a limited number of operations can be successfully represented without cluttering the border. With the Whitechapel system, the identifiers for moving and sizing the window are clearly shown and are emphasized by distinctive pointer icons whenever the relevant region is entered; however, the other functions are not visible and can only be found by experimentation or reference to the manual.

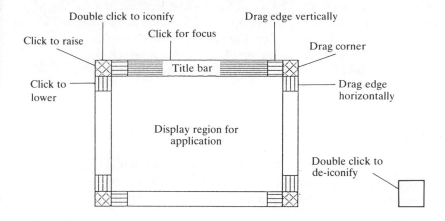

Figure 10.9   Region-based operations of the Whitechapel window manager

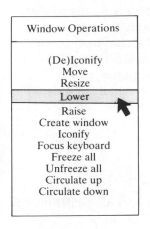

Figure 10.10   Typical window manager menu from the X window system

Menu-based window managers

With menu-based window managers all actions are initiated following a menu selection. The sequence of actions is as follows: the menu is popped-up (normally by means of a mouse button press in the root or background window), the desired action is selected from the menu, the window is identified and finally the action is performed. A typical menu from the *uwm* window manager, distributed with X windows, is shown in Figure 10.10.

Menu-based systems allow each operation to be clearly identified by its menu item, and each menu can offer many actions and subactions (with 'walking menus'). This simplifies implementation of a consistent user interface, and provides the capability for a virtually unlimited set of mouse-initiated actions. The disadvantage is the complex action sequence required for even the simplest operation, which slows interaction and distracts the user from his or her intentions.

Menu- and region-based window managers

Many window managers combine the facilities of both region- and menu-based operation selection. They aim to combine the benefits of fast direct action provided by region-based systems with the range of facilities available via menu selection. Often, as in the case of SunTools, the same operation can be initiated using either mechanism.

Window manager accelerators

A window-based user interface to a system offers many advantages over a simple text-based one; however, there are some cases where text-based interaction can be faster in use. This is particularly true for expert users who are familiar with the application and know command abbreviations etc. Some windowing systems therefore provide a similar mechanism that allows quick initiation of common operations: these are called *accelerators*. For example, many Macintosh applications provide keyboard accelerators to avoid complex menu interaction (see Figure 10.11). Other systems allow key combinations to be used with the mouse interaction to extend the set of operations accessible without menu interaction.

10.5.4 Users' tools: desktops

A desktop provides a stylized user interface to an operating environment. The principles of the metaphor are discussed in Section 6.10.

X Desktop (IXI)

The desktop metaphor can be implemented by most windowing systems and on many operating systems. The X Desktop (IXI, 1988) developed by IXI Limited implements a desktop that is portable between UNIX systems and can be used on any display running the X Windows server. This makes it portable and provides inherent networking.

The desktop implements a menu- and region-based window manager that provides the full range of window management functions. As X Desktop is implemented using standard X libraries applications do not have to be specially configured. When an application requests the X server to create a window, the desktop manager intercepts the request and attaches a *title bar* to the application's window. The title bar

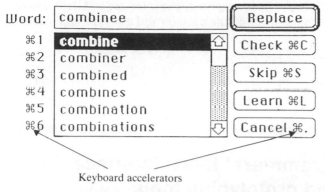

Keyboard accelerators

Figure 10.11 Macintosh keyboard accelerators (© Claris Corporation. All rights reserved. Claris and MacWrite are trademarks of Claris Corporation. Macintosh is a trademark of Apple Computer Inc.)

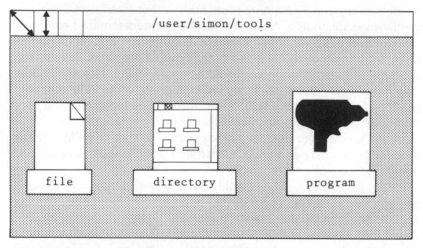

Figure 10.12 Example of X-Desktop window

consists of a number of subwindows that provide region-based operations or pop-up menus.

The interface to UNIX is provided by icons and windows, with an icon representing a file contained within a directory represented by a window (Figure 10.12). The image within the icon represents the type of file, and beneath the icon is the file or directory name. Each file has an associated icon rule set, which describes the characteristics of the icon and the actions associated with mouse events.

By programming the rules it is possible for most file actions to be initiated under mouse control, for example, for C language files:

- Double left click is 'vi < filename >'   Edit the file
- Double right click is 'cc < filename >'   C Compile the file

The system therefore provides a stylized user interface to UNIX plus a window manager for controlling the desktop and any X11 application.

Macintosh desktop

Macintosh computers provide a *desktop* as the standard (in fact the only) interface to their operating system. This combines a region-based window manager with icons representing applications and files. The operation of the Macintosh user interface is described in Section 4.10.

10.6 Programmers' tools: interface toolkits and prototyping tools

The term *toolkit* is an accurate analogy both to the purpose an interface toolkit provides and to the tools it contains. Much as an automobile mechanic's toolbox contains the tools to work with engines and would be useless for building a dining room table, a user interface toolkit contains specific tools to build interfaces for a predetermined or visualized set of applications. Thus the designers of the toolkit select the *objects* or *widgets* or *toolpieces* to fit the types of problems, or interfaces, which they imagine the toolkit would be used to solve. Hence it is clear that not all applications can be served by a given toolkit. The obvious corollary is that not all toolkits can be used to develop similar interfaces for a given application—just like a plumber's, or an automobile mechanic's, or an electrician's toolbox cannot be used to build a dining room table (at least not a table that would resemble what could be made using a cabinetmaker's toolbox).

Ideally toolkit technology should contribute to good user interface and application design. There should be no need to recompile an application when the user interface changes. If these problems can be solved then a person with expertise in human factors, graphic arts or related disciplines could design the interface. The ease of such a design process would encourage iterative design techniques and interface tuning. Design economics would encourage the provision of multiple interfaces to match the needs of both the advanced user and the novice (Teitelman, 1984).

Prototyping tools may provide very much the same interface component building blocks as toolkits, but are distinguished by providing explicit support for rapid development and prototyping of the window-based user interface. Thus, prototyping tools enable interactive evaluation of the user interface at a stage when the underlying application software may not be available.

Through the development of feature-rich prototypic tools, developers can develop and refine their designs for advanced user interfaces. More importantly, the tools provide an application development platform, which ensures a consistent *look and feel* (LAF) to all applications. With the advent of portable windowing systems such as *X* and *NeWS* and toolkits built on top of them such as the *Xt+*, *XView* and *The NeWS Toolkit* (TnT), it is now possible to develop software systems that provide a consistent LAF across a wide range of computer environments.

10.6.1 Look and feel style guides

The variety of window systems and toolkits for different platforms could potentially lead to a different look and feel for each system, which is obviously undesirable. This problem has been prevented by the production of look and feel *style guides*, which define how the system appears and operates independently of its realization, i.e., the look and feel is independent of the toolkit. The look and feel style guide describes how the user interface objects will appear on the screen and defines how the user interacts with them; this interface specification is then implemented by each toolkit.

A look and feel can therefore by supported by different toolkits for various platforms but still produce applications that provide the same interface look and feel to the user. However, toolkits may have different programming interfaces, e.g., language bindings, or support different window system protocols, e.g., X or PostScript.

Open Look

Open Look is a user interface look and feel that is rapidly becoming adopted as an industry standard. Open Look is window-system and toolkit independent, and is a written specification of a graphical user interface. Toolkits exist to support the development of applications with an Open Look look and feel for UNIX (Xt+ and XView, NeWS, TnT), and for the Macintosh and OS/2, (MCP).

OSF/Motif

Motif is a graphical user interface which has been developed by the Open Software Foundation (OSF) and is also becoming established as a vendor-independent interface for UNIX systems. The Motif look and feel is defined by a style guide which aims to define a consistent behaviour and appearance for the system. However, Motif is offered as more than just a style guide and a toolkit: in addition it provides a user interface language compiler and window manager.

10.6.2 Using software tools for user interface development

The discussion of user interface tools above has outlined the facilities the user interface programmer has at his or her disposal. How can these facilities best be applied to solving actual user interface problems? The

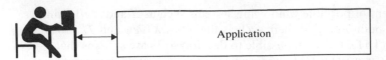

Figure 10.13 User's view of a window system

task of programming an interactive application using a windowing system is simplified if the following steps are performed:

- *Application partitioning*: abstracting the interface from the application.
- *Interface design*: designing the information presented to the user.
- *Prototyping*: prototyping the interface to investigate usage.
- *Constrution, testing and evaluation*: standard software development practice.

Application partitioning

All windowing systems present the user with a graphical representation of the interface to the application. This interface is normally abstracted from the application and hides the details of the application's internal operation from the user (Figure 10.13).

From the programmer's viewpoint the divisions within the application are important. For most windowing systems these can be generalized into application and interface code (Figure 10.14). The application code describes the specific operation of the application. The interface code describes the interface to the user and controls the operation of the interface devices, typically screen, keyboard and mouse.

The boundary between the application and interface codes varies between windowing systems. For example, in the X window system the division between interface and input/output device control code is explicitly made. The input/output devices are controlled by the display server process and the interface defined by library code linked into the application process.

In the application development process the programmer must make the distinction between interface operations and applications operations within his or her programming and define the interaction between the interface and the application. A fundamental design decision that has to be made at this stage is the source of control. Does the interface drive the application or does the application drive the interface? Traditionally applications drove the interface, that is, they had full control of the information presented to the user and prompted the user for input when required. In programming terms, the thread of control remained within the application. However, most user interface tools are designed to control the application, the interface making callbacks to the application code in response to users' actions. The interface tool treats

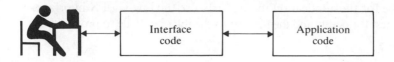

Figure 10.14   Programmer's view of a window

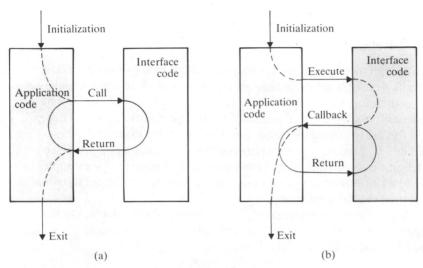

(a)   (b)

Figure 10.15   (a) Conventional application control flow **(b)** Control
flow for toolkit programming

the application as a library of functions. In programming terms, the
thread of control belongs to the interface and is passed to the
application, as a function call, to fulfil a user's operation request.

If the interface is to drive the application, the application should be
configured as a set of functional routines, with each routine being
activated in response to a user action. The application's state should be
updated by the routines before returning to the interface code. If the
application is to drive the interface, some mechanism must be provided
to pass control from the interface code into the application. This can be
achieved by an initial input from the user. Once the application has
control, the interface can be manipulated by changing the data
structures for the interface (which is the equivalent in the X toolkit to
mapping and unmapping widgets). Control is only passed back to the
interface when user interaction is required (Figure 10.15).

These rules cannot be enforced for all applications. For example, an
interactive printer queue monitor needs the application to update the
information displayed regularly, but simultaneously should allow user
input at any time. Solutions to this problem are not explicitly supported
in current UIDEs. With the X toolkit (Section 10.7), one approach

would be for the application to regularly use the low-level X interface, Xlib, to test for events and then return to the interface code to process them.

Interface design

The design of the user interface should reflect the required style of human–computer dialogue and the task model used by the application (Shneiderman, 1987) (see Part 2 of this book).

Prototyping

Although most user interface tools allow flexibility of design, the later in the development cycle changes are made the more expensive they are. It is therefore advisable to construct a prototype of the interface at the earliest possible stage. The ease of prototype construction will depend on the use interface tool used. Some systems, for example Open Dialogue, provide a prototyping facility which allows the interface definition to be realized and evaluated. Other systems, for example the X toolkit, require the programmer to provide stub routines to mimic the interface to the application.

A good prototype should allow all aspects of the interface to be realized to allow it to be fully evaluated. Interface evaluation techniques are covered in Part 4 of this book.

Construction, testing and evaluation

This is standard practice for the development of software systems and there is much published literature.

10.6.3 Toolkit performance

The performance of a toolkit may be viewed in two ways, the *ease of programming* the required interface and the *processing efficiency* of the implementation. The performance of an interface programmed with a high-level toolkit can be compared to that of one programmed using the low-level interface. The comparison is analogous to the choices between high level and assembly language programming.

Rosenthal (1987) reports a performance comparison between the X window system toolkit *Xt* and the low-level X library interface *Xlib*, in which he programmed a windowed version of the classic C language 'Hello World' program. The *Xlib* library version required 40 executable statements to program compared with 5 statements for the *Xt* toolkit. The performance of the toolkit version was better for some actions, such as resize, and resulted in the complete removal of some round-trip network communications and a reduction in the overall amount of data transferred. This was due primarily to a better resize strategy being programmed in the toolkit.

10.7 Example windowing system: the X window system

The X window system was developed at MIT and has become established as an industry standard for window-based applications in the UNIX workstation environment. The X window system provides a high-performance graphic system based on a set of hierarchical resizeable windows. The X window system does not provide a specific user interface style, but instead supports a rich set of tools to build user interfaces and can provide different styles and policies. One of the primary design goals of the project was to specify mechanism and not policy.

Another major design goal of the X window system was portability. Although the original developments were based on DEC VS100 displays and VAX hardware, X display servers are available for most UNIX-based graphic workstations, including SUN, Apollo, IBM, HP, and many more. These and other companies have supported the development of the X window system and their interest has helped establish the commercial acceptance of X.

X windows design goals

The principle design goals of the X-window system are listed below, and are described more fully by Scheifler and Gettys (1986).

- The system should be implementable on a variety of displays.
- Applications must be display device independent.
- The system must be network transparent.
- The system should be extensible.

Other design goals provide for facilities that have come to be expected of all windowing systems such as multiple windows, graphics, text founts and styles, etc. It is these goals that help to distinguish X from other windowing systems; for example, the Macintosh window system does not meet the first three of the above goals.

Functional separation

With the X window system the division between interface and input/output device control code is explicitly made. The input/output devices are controlled by the display server process and the interface defined by library code linked into the application process. This division into separate processes allows the server and application to execute on different machines and enables each to communicate with more than one other display server or application.

The communication between a server and its clients is described the *X protocol*, which can be used over any reliable, duplex, byte stream interprocess communication mechanism. If the server and client are on the same machine then local interprocess communication is used. If they are on different machines then an inter-machine connection is established, for example via TCP over an Ethernet. Therefore networking and multiprocessing applications are inherently built within the X window system.

X window system, version 11

The X window system has developed through a number of versions, the latest version being number 11. It is intended that this version will be stable and that no further changes will be made to the basic protocol, except bug fixes. This stability does not mean that the facilities of X are frozen, as the layered architecture and inherent extensibility mean that further development and enhancement is possible, and is in fact encouraged. It will however ensure that application developers can be sure of the stability and compatibility of X11 systems and hence of their applications.

System model

The structure of the X window system is based on the client–server model. Communication is via the X protocol which provides the structure to represent both graphics and control operations. The client program is not written to generate the raw protocol directly; instead, calls to the standard X library, *Xlib*, are made to perform actions at the server.

10.7.1 The X window system protocol

In the X window system the control of the displayed image is manipulated by a display server, which in turn is controlled by commands sent using the *X Protocol* (Scheifler, 1988). This is a graphics and operation description protocol that provides the functionality required to build a network-based windowing system. Communication occurs using one of four protocol formats:

Request format is the basic mechanism for operation initiation. Each request contains a major opcode that defines the protocol operation. A set of opcodes are reserved for protocol extension. Each opcode is followed by a length field and operation data. Every request on a connection is given an implicit sequence number that is used for replies, errors and events.

Reply format returns data relating to a specific request identified by the sequence number.

Error format provides for error reports. These contain an 8-bit error code, the opcode and the sequence number of the failed request.

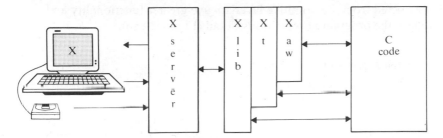

Figure 10.16   Programmer's view of X window software

Event format   provides for the server to report events to the client. These are principally mouse and keyboard actions. The format contains an 8-bit type code detailing the type of event and any supporting data. Also returned is the sequence number of the request that was currently being processed.

This protocol allows for communication between multiple clients and servers and can operate over any reliable byte-stream inter-process communication mechanism. The protocol is asynchronous; that is, requests are not normally acknowledged nor is there any implicit synchronization between a client request and server action. If synchronization is required by the application it must be explicitly programmed by making requests that return the required status information.

Inter-client communication

The X protocol describes all communication between a client application and a display server. Direct client-to-client communication is not supported under X as clients may be operating on different processors and communicating to the server via incompatible communication mechanisms, for example DECnet and TCP. A client-to-client communication has therefore to be made via the server, and the primary mechanism for information exchange (such as cutting and pasting text between windows) is made using the selection mechanism. To ensure correct communication between X clients an Inter-Client Communications Convention (ICCC) has been defined (Rosenthal, 1988).

Software structure of X window system development environment

The structure of the X software is easily extended, as new interface components can be programmed and added to the toolkit, and new facilities can be included in the server and accessed by the extension mechanism provided in the protocol. Each software layer is further abstracted from the primitive layer to give greater functionality and relieve the program of repetitious detail (Figure 10.16).

Xlib, the X protocol interface

Xlib is the programming language interface to the raw X protocol. Program calls at the Xlib level directly correspond to individual protocol elements sent to the server. This level of interface provides access to all the functionality of the display server but entails a high programming overhead and is used only to provide specific operations that are extensions or special cases from the higher-level libraries.

10.7.2 The X toolkit and the Athena widget set

Introduction

The X toolkit provides the base functionality necessary to build a variety of application environments. The X Toolkit is extensible and supportive of the independent development of new or extended components. . . .

The X toolkit is a library package layered on top of the X window system. This layer extends the basic abstractions provided by X and thus provides the next layer of functionality. . . .

(Swick, 1988)

The X toolkit consists of two libraries: *Xaw* (the Athena widget library) provides a set of user interface objects (*widgets*) for building application interfaces, and *Xt* (the tool library) provides the necessary support facilities to build, combine and operate the widgets. The widgets form the basic building blocks for interface design. The user interface is therefore defined as a tree of widgets. Hierarchical groups of widgets (*composite widgets*) form the nodes of the tree. The final child widgets (*primitive widgets*) determine the actual interface to the application and the display of application state.

Application interface

The links between the application code and the user interface code are defined when the widgets are created, by binding callbacks and data structures to them. A *callback* is an application routine that is called by a widget in response to an event such as a button click. The callback routine then initiates the application's response to the user's action, for example display more data, exit, etc. The *data structures* allow the displayed state of the interface to be controlled, for example change label, colour etc.

The structure of the interface can be changed by creating and deleting widgets during the operation of the application; for example, new

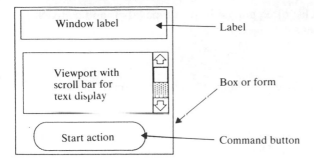

Figure 10.17   Example widgets from the X windows widget set

command widgets can be added to a menu. This facility allows the interface to change dynamically to reflect the status of the application and help the user in his or her task. The programming of the interface will depend on how the application is partitioned between user interface code and pure application code. This is discussed in Section 10.6.1 above.

The basic widgets

The widget set distributed with X version 11 release 3 contains a selection of widgets that can be grouped according to their functions (Swick and Weisman, 1988). Some examples are illustrated in Figure 10.17.

Display widgets

These provide for the display of information to the user, and include *label widgets*, which provide an uneditable text string that is displayed within a window, and *text widgets*, which provide a way for an application to display one or more lines of text.

Interaction widgets

These provide mechanisms for user interaction. The *command button widget* creates a rectangular window that contains a text label. When the pointer cursor is on the button, its border is highlighted to indicate that the button is available for selection. Then, when a pointer button is clicked, the button is selected, and the application's callback routine is invoked. The *scrollbar widget* is a rectangular box that contains a slide region and a thumb (slide bar). The *viewport widget* consists of a frame window, one or two scrollbars, and an inner window. The inner window is the full size of the data that is to be displayed and is clipped by the frame window. The *dialog widget* implements a commonly used interaction semantic to prompt for auxiliary input from a user. The *grip widget* provides a small region in which pointer events are handled. The *list widget* provides a list of command button type labels and callbacks but is managed as a single widget.

Management widgets

These are the tools required to manage the presentation of the other widgets on the screen, for operations such as creation, exposure, resize, etc. The *box widget* provides geometry management of arbitrary widgets in a box of a specified dimension. The *VPaned widget* manages children in a vertically tiled fashion. The *form widget* provides geometry management for its child widgets, based upon information provided when a child is added to the form.

Extending the widget set

The set of widgets that is included in the core of the third release of X11 may appear rather limited, but is extended by additional widgets that are included in the user contributed software. Nevertheless, complex interfaces can readily be built as the widgets available provide most of the fundamental interface components that are required.

The structure of the widget set has been designed so that it is simple to introduce new widgets providing different or extended functions. In most cases an interface requirement can be met by extending one of the existing widget classes. This is a moderate task for a competent programmer as the X window system distribution includes the source code for all of the system. New widgets are thus typically generated by examining the existing widgets to identify the one that most closely approximates the features required and then copying and extending its code to include the required new features.

The X window manager

The X window system is distributed with a number of alternative window managers, allowing users to select the facilities they require. The standard window manager, *uwm*, provides a set of functions and facilities that can be configured by the user to provide an individual system interface. *Uwm* uses the server's facilities to grab input and creation events from the server and prevent them from passing to the application. This allows a client process to provide window management facilities. *Uwm* is configured on initialization and informs the server of the events it desires to intercept and the context for these to occur in. The context, root window, window and icon, enable very flexible window management facilities to be provided. Whilst *uwm* is principally a menu-based manager, combining contexts and events allows accelerator actions to be created, for example a click in an icon could initiate the deiconify operation. An example *uwm* menu is shown in Figure 10.10 above.

Since *uwm* operates as a standard client process it is not constrained to run on the same processor as the X server. This allows X servers to be developed for single tasking systems, such as IBM PCs running PC-DOS, which can then become low-cost displays for applications running on other networked machines.

10.8   User interface development tools

This section describes two systems that provide more than just a user interface toolkit. Open Dialogue provides a user interface specification language and a previewer. Sun Microsystem's *devguide* provides an interactive prototyping tool for Open Look.

10.8.1   Open Dialogue

Open Dialogue (Apollo 1988a) is a user interface development environment that attempts to provide a rich set of user interface building blocks to allow an interface designer to rapidly prototype, modify and examine a user interface without affecting the code for the application. A user interacts with the Open Dialogue system via an interface consisting of object such as pop-ups, menus, icons and text display fields. Open Dialogue then passes information down to the application layer via an application interface. After processing the input, the application can return control, and any output to be presented to the user, back to Open Dialogue. For defining an interface, Open Dialogue provides mechanisms such as parsers and interface previewing tools.

Using the parser, a designer can define a source language version of the interface using the declarative *Interface Definition Language* of Open Dialogue. The parser then translates the source level version into a binary database. The database consists of a series of object definitions that specify the attributes for each object and the relationship of that object to the other objects in the interface.

The primary advantage of an interface definition language is the possibility of previewing and interacting with the interface, and thus obtaining valuable early feedback on its design. This can occur regardless of whether any of the application software has been written. In this manner the user interface to an application can be developed and evaluated in parallel with application development.

The object-oriented approach of Open Dialogue

Open Dialogue has an object-oriented design in which objects and classes are analogous to the variables and types defined and declared by conventional programming languages. Individual objects are instances of their respective classes. The programmer defines a class to establish a type of object and its associated properties, or methods. The interface, which uses many objects (or instances) belonging to the menu class, does not define the menu class again, but merely uses the defined menu class. Classes thus allow an object-oriented approach to be extensible.

In Open Dialogue, as in any object-oriented program, each object belongs to a specific class. The class describes not only the data, but also the operations that can be performed on the data. In object-oriented programming these operations might be called methods or properties. The data and associated operations are common, by default and the rules of inheritance, to all classes derived from a particular class.

For example, in Open Dialogue there is a graphic object class for all objects visible on the screen—menus, icons, text display fields, etc. These all share common features of their base class 'graphic object', such as outline shape and width, etc. The interface designer, using objects, creates instantiations of their classes, thus a specific icon is an object instantiation from the class 'icon'. Class 'icon' is a concrete class, meaning it is a class with associated objects, derived from the abstract class 'graphic object'. The abstract class identifies a class with no associated objects thus defining only common abstractions.

The interface definition process

Using the available objects and classes, the programmer defines an interface for a given application by producing an interface definition file (Apollo 1988b). The interface definition process for an example application called *ged* is shown in Figure 10.18.

This definition is then parsed using the *dlg* parser. The result of this parsing producing three output files. Two of the files are C program files. One contains the constants for passing values and communication between the Open Dialogue Interface and the application, and the other is a stub file to the application interface. The third file is the *Interface Object Space*, which is a heaped collection of the objects used during execution. The two C files are then compiled and linked with the rest of the application's binary files, yielding an executable application.

The run-time model

During run-time the user interacts with the Interface Object Space via X and the run-time library. The library may callback to the application or the library may be able to handle the action directly, for example by displaying a pop-up, depending on the interface definition in the Interface Object Space. The Open Dialogue run-time model for the example application *ged* is shown in Figure 10.19.

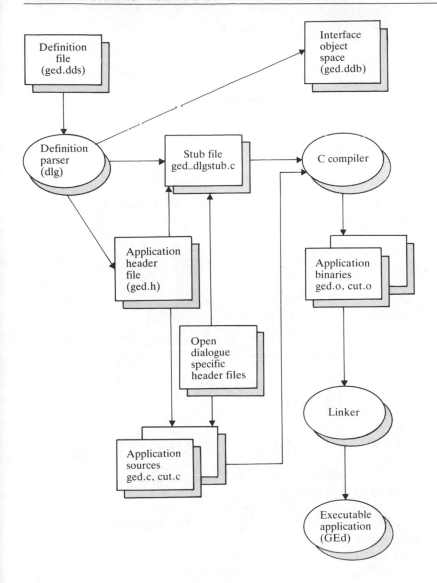

Figure 10.18   Example of Open Dialogue interface definition

10.8.2 Devguide

Sun Microsystem's devguide is a graphical user interface design tool
that allows the programmer to interactively draw the user interface for
an application. The designer draws the desired interfaces on the screen
and the tool then creates the necessary C or C++ language programs
to build the interface. The interface is automatically prototyped; what
the designer sees is the interface the application will have. When the

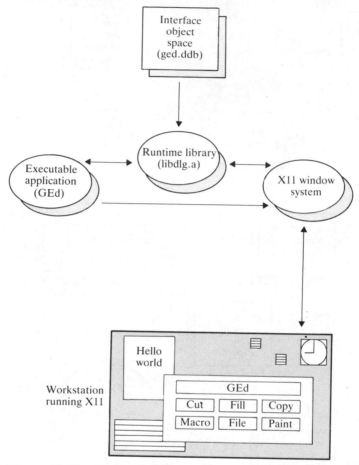

Figure 10.19 Open Dialogue run-time model

interface has been specified the programmer has only to implement the functionality of the application.

Devguide implements the Open Look look and feel for the application by generating program calls to the XView user interface toolkit. The generated code is well formatted and easily readable and can be edited or directly compiled.

10.9 Conclusions

This chapter has attempted to present a bottom-up layered overview of windowing systems. The presentation is complicated by the fact that such systems are not static, but are continuously being developed and refined. Early standards were based upon proprietary hardware architectures, host-based systems and single-tasking operating systems. Current developments are concerned with more general windowing system solutions, and so are addressing problems of display device independence, architectural independence, network transparency, extensibility and modularity. At the time of writing, the X windows system seems closest to meeting these design requirements.

For those concerned with user interface design, an important issue is the tools and support provided for rapid prototyping and development of window-based user interfaces. At the lowest level, support is provided through library functions, but programming at this level requires considerable knowledge of the underlying windowing software structure. More recently, support has been provided for software development at a higher level, either through a toolkit approach (as embodied in X windows), or through applying the principles of extensibility and reusability embodied in object-oriented design (as in Open Dialogue). In either case, software development can be considerably more rapid than with the earlier approach. Finally, in keeping with the iterative design and rapid prototyping philosophy developed for human-computer systems, evaluation of windowing systems is now beginning to be supported. In the case of Open Dialogue, this support not only allows the user interface to be fully simulated before any of the application software is written, but also provides some monitoring of user–system interaction for subsequent analysis.

References

Adobe (1986) *PostScript Language Manual*, Adobe Systems Inc, Palo Alto, Calif.

Adobe (1988) *PostScript Language Program Design*, Adobe Systems Inc, Palo Alto, Calif.

Apollo (1988a) *Open Dialogue Reference*, Apollo Computers Inc., Chelmsford, Mass.

Apollo (1988b) *Creating User Interfaces with Open Dialogue*, Apollo Computers Inc., Chelmsford, Mass.

Bennett, J. (1985) 'Raster operations', *Byte*, **10**(12), 187–203.

Card, S. K., M. Pavel and J. E. Farrell (1985) 'Window-based computer dialogues', *Human–Computer Interaction—INTERACT '84*, North-Holland, Amsterdam, IFIP 1985, 239–243.

Foley, J. D. and A. van Dam (1983) *Fundamentals of Interactive Computer Graphics*, Addison-Wesley, Reading, Mass.

Gosling, J. (1986) 'SunDew—a distributed and extensible window system', in *Methodology of Window Management*, F. R. A. Hopgood, D. A. Duce, E. V. C. Fielding, K. Robinson and A. S. Williams (eds), Springer, Berlin.

IXI (1988) *X.desktop*, IXI Limited, Cambridge.

Newman, W. M. and R. F. Sproull (1981) *Principles of Interactive Computer Graphics*, 2nd edn McGraw-Hill ISE., Singapore.

Oldenburg, H. (1989) OSF motif: the user interface standard, *IEE Colloquium on User Interface Management Systems, November 1989*, Digest No. 1989/135.

Rosenthal, D. S. H. (1987) *A Simple X11 Client Program or How Hard Can It Really Be to Write 'Hello World'?*, Sun Microsystems Inc., Mountain View, Calif.

Rosenthal, D. S. H. (1988) *X Window System, Version 11, Inter-Client Communication Conventions Manual*, MIT Project Athena, Draft 25/2/1988. Cambridge, Mass.

Scheifler, R. W. and J. Gettys (1986) 'The X Window System', *ACM Transactions on Graphics,* **5**(2), Apr., 79–109.

Scheifler, R. W. (1988) *X Window System Protocol Release 2*, MIT Project Athena, Cambridge, Mass.

Shneiderman, B. (1987) *Designing the User Interface: Strategies for Effective Human–Computer Interaction*, Addison-Wesley, Reading, Mass.

Smith, D. C., C. Irby, R. Kimball, B. Verplank and E. Harslem (1982) 'Design of the Star user interface', *Byte*, **7** (4), 242–282.

Sobelman, G. E. and D. E. Krekelberg (1985) *Advanced C: Techniques and Applications*, (Que Corporation), Indianapolis, Ind.

Spraill, R. F. (1986) 'Frame-buffer display architectures', *Ann. Rev. Comps. Sci.,* **1**, 19–46. Also in *Readings in Human–Computer Interaction: a Multidisciplinary Approach*, R. M. Baecker and W. A. S. Buxton (eds), Morgan Kauffman, 1987.

Sun (1985) *SunView 1 Programmer's Guide*, Sun Microsystems Inc., Mountain View, Calif.

Sun (1986) *Pixrect Reference Manual*, Sun Microsystems Inc., Mountain View, Calif.

Sun (1988) *X View Programmer's Guide*, Sun Microsystems Inc., Mountain View, Calif.

Sutherland, I. E. and G. W. Hodgman (1974) 'Reentrant polygon clipping', *Communications of the ACM*, **17**(1), 32, Jan.

Swick, R. R. (1988) *X Toolkit Intrinsics—C Language X Interface*, MIT Project Athena, Cambridge, Mass.

Swick, R. R. and Weisman, T. (1988) *X Toolkit Athena Widgets—C language X Interface*, MIT Project Athena, Cambridge, Mass.

Teitelman, W. (1984) 'The Cedar Programming Environment: A Midterm Report and Examination', *Tech. Report No. CSL-83-11*, Xerox Corp., PARC, Palo Alto, Calif.

Thacker, C. P., E. M. McCreight, B. W. Lampson, R. F. Spraill and D. R. Boggs (1982) 'Alto: a personal computer', in *Computer Structures: Principles and Examples*, D. Siewiorek, D. G. Bell and A. Newell (eds), McGraw-Hill

Williams, A. S. (1986) 'A Comparison of Some Window Managers', in *Methodology of Window Management*, F. R. A. Hopgood, D. A. Duce, E. V. C. Fielding, K. Robinson and A. S. Williams (eds), Springer, Berlin.

11 Object-oriented programming and interface construction*

BRUCE ANDERSON

11.1 Introduction

Computer-based systems depend on software, made up of both program code and some overlying organization including libraries, structures and standards. Object-oriented programming (OOP) is a new approach to programming which addresses these system issues, moving the focus from programs to software. It holds out the promise of systems that are easier to build and easier to understand, and of relating closely to powerful design ideas. In particular, it can help to make overt at several levels the architecture and structure of complex applications, and it is that characteristic that is of special relevance in designing human–computer interfaces.

OOP is widely used in research and development laboratories, but more and more reports are being published of its successful use in commercial applications of many kinds. Although it offers advantages for large and continuing software projects, the same facilities can be very useful on a much smaller scale. While any improvement in programming technology is to be welcomed for such a difficult area as HCI, OOP is particularly relevant to the HCI domain because it encourages a problem-solving, or system-designing, approach that fits well with the concerns of the interface engineer. This chapter briefly outlines a framework for looking at interfaces and shows how OOP is relevant to it before describing in more detail the principles of OOP and their use in software construction.

---

* This chapter is based on an article first published in *Microprocessors and Microsystems*, **12**, 433–442 (1988).

11.2 Interfaces and objects

11.2.1 Models in HCI

The starting point is the notion of *model*. This is taken, in a quite
informal sense, to mean a description of what is manipulated and how.
The model may be quite explicit, for example the application
programmer with a very clear idea of 'text-file', or it may be implicit, for
example a new user with a still-forming concept of 'selection'.

In examining the user interface, there are three models to be
considered, as follows:

User's conceptual model (UCM)

This is the model that informs and drives the user's thoughts and
actions in the interaction. Some of it will be explicit and easily expressed
('you just double-click on the word you want'), some quite implicit (for
example details of the filing system) and some of it on the boundary
('now you ask me, I can see that I think that Save As . . . is just
for saving files')

Interface model (IFM)

Somehow the interface must present a model for manipulation by the
user, for the user's purposes. Thus the Unix Bourne shell model
contains the notions of command, file and filename. The current
generation of WIMP interfaces provide very concrete models, for
example via (explicit) illusions of items that can be manipulated directly
(see Section 4.10).

Programmer's model (PM)

Within the application itself are software structures that describe and
support interaction with the hardware and operating system and with
the user interface, as well as those that implement the functionality of
the application. An example is a notion such as 'bytes required for
current window list'.

The notion of model is important because it provides a concrete focus
for many of the questions that arise in HCI design and implementation.
The very idea raises many issues, such as the descriptions of the models,
their content, and their relationship with each other, which are not
pursued here. OOP provides a framework for those descriptions and for
discussion of the issues.

11.2.2 OOP basics

Here the underlying notions of OOP are introduced; they will become clearer with the technical description given later in the chapter.

The fundamental concept is the *object*:

- An object is a conceptual entity from the domain (e.g., a paragraph of text).
- It includes both data and procedure (e.g., some sentences, an editing method).
- Objects communicate only via *messages*. These are requests (e.g., to insert a word at a position) and returned values.

In class-based systems every object belongs to a *class*:

- Classes may be seen as templates for the objects that are instances of them (e.g., class `Paragraph`).
- They have *methods*, which are the code describing the instance's response to a message.
- Classes are related by inheritance. A *subclass* of a class may define new data and new behaviour, which is added to that of the original class.

11.2.3 The OOP approach

OOP attempts to provide more than just a new way to package code and data structures, by suggesting that a good way to think about a problem is in terms of the objects involved in its solution. For example, a document editor may manipulate paragraphs; rather than thinking of commands or data formats, OOP encourages the designer to focus on the notion of paragraph, and to describe it in a class `Paragraph`. This class's messages provide an abstract interface, quite separate from the implementation details of the methods. This encapsulation allows a clear approach to the separation of concerns in interface design and building (see Section 7.2).

It is useful to think of models in an object-oriented way, i.e., in terms of objects and their messages, their classes and the class hierarchy. This helps in several ways:

- Objects provide natural units for both thinking and expressing—or, rather, designers can use objects directly to express the units of their thought and expression.
- The level of description is raised from the procedures or data to a structure that is more abstract and conceptual, yet still concrete in terms of implementation.

- The use of encapsulation allows and encourages a shift of focus to things and actions, to abstract properties, and away from details.
- The use of messages allows more consistency about actions across the model since they can operate on all objects, encouraging uniformity.
- Consistency is encouraged by the use of inheritance; designers and programmers can search out, or design, commonalities and related properties and express them directly.

11.2.4 OOP for the models in HCI

These ideas work for each model. The structure of the UCM can be expressed with features such as tasks, actions, attributes and constraints. At the level of the interface model, OOP is already in wide use in window managers such as MIT's X (see Section 10.7), interface kits such as Apollo's Open Dialogue (see Section 10.8) and generic applications. The software engineering of the programmer's model can be enhanced using class libraries and reusable components.

The greatest power to be derived from OOP is that the *same* objects can be used in *all three* models, i.e., at all three conceptual levels. Thus, for example, the notion of paragraph in the PM (files, character arrays, font descriptors) can be related to that in the IFM (screen coordinates, bitmaps) and made an appropriate object for the UCM. The implementation details so vital to the actual execution of the model can be hidden, allowing work at all levels with the appropriate abstract idea. OOP supports an approach that has a consistent vocabulary across all models and allows users, interface designers and application programmers to work together. All the advantages of OOP catalogued above are brought to bear.

The appropriateness of the OOP model should not be surprising, since one of its roots is in languages for writing simulations that describe and animate models of the real world.

11.2.5 Working practice with OOP

OOP is not only an enabling technology for a consistent view of HCI, but is also suggestive of the process to be used in design and construction. The designer should focus on the objects in the domain that the application manipulates; should choose the classes of which they are instances; and should relate the classes in an inheritance hierarchy. This keeps the focus off the interface, and also off the commands that might be provided, and on the abstract objects that the application is about. The following questions can then be asked:

- Do these concepts at least allow a reasonable UCM to be formed?
- How can these concepts be presented in the interface?

- How can these objects be implemented in the application?

These questions must be asked again of the interface: What are the interface notions (window, icon) and how are these related in a class hierarchy? This is not a design method, but it does provide a framework for such methods. There are many other aspects of the task, for example to provide fluent access to these objects and to make sure that users can navigate in the space provided.

11.3 Architecture for object-oriented programming

OOP provides four architectural features for structuring software systems:

- *Encapsulation* This is the ability to wrap up a structure so that it is accessed in terms of its properties rather than its implementation, and accessed in a way that is carefully controlled and defined. The more implementation details are hidden, the better the chance of writing truly modular software (Parnas, 1972).
- *Dynamic binding* OOP allows a single variable to refer to different kinds of things, and provides support for leaving until run-time the decision as to which piece of code is appropriate to implement an operation on that variable. This dynamic binding greatly simplifies code that deals uniformly with many different structures.
- *Inheritance* Typically, in programming a need is found to provide some functionality that is very like something that has been written already, but is an extension or modification of it. Inheritance allows the reuse of code while knowing only its properties and without altering it.
- *Storage management* Modern styles of programming encourage the creation of internal structures corresponding to things in the problem domain. Object-oriented languages provide features for the structured allocation and release of memory to do this safely and efficiently.

Each of these features has been present in languages in the past, but only recently have they been combined effectively in practical systems.

11.4 Mechanisms of object-oriented languages

OOP is based on powerful ideas, some of which can be used in traditional languages such as LISP and FORTRAN. However, the ideas are best expressed in a language specifically designed to support OOP.

Most examples in this chapter are given in the languages SMALLTALK-80 (Goldberg and Robson, 1983) and C++ (Stroustrup, 1986), which are widely available and offer practical opportunities to appreciate and try out object-oriented ideas. Really getting to grips with OOP, rather than just its mechanisms, is quite difficult, and the unusual syntax of SMALLTALK-80 is used initially to emphasize that. (Generally the syntax is suggestive rather than accurate, but upper and lower case letters are used carefully in names.)

The architectural features of OOP are provided in different languages by different constructs and to differing degrees. There is, however, a common terminology, referring to a common conceptual framework, derived mainly from SMALLTALK. The key concepts, which were introduced above, are *object*, *message*, *method*, *class* and *subclass*. These ideas are presented here through SMALLTALK, and then in C++; the contrast may aid understanding.

11.4.1 Objects in SMALLTALK

An object represents something, often from the application domain, e.g., a car, an IC or a window. The variable

```
aBox
```

could be used to refer to a `Box` object with height, width and depth. Objects correspond to data structures such as numbers, arrays and records in conventional languages. In SMALLTALK everything is an object, and objects have type but variables do not, so that any variable may refer to any object. Names of objects have lower-case initial letters.

11.4.2 Messages

A message is a request to an object, for example to access or update it, and there is always a return value. If `height` is a message to obtain the height of a box then

```
aBox height
```

sends the message `height` to `aBox`, and the height is returned. Messages with a colon at the end indicate that an argument is being passed, and the value follows the colon. We might set the box's height using `height:`

```
aBox height: 7. aBox height print     //prints 7
```

A full stop denotes the end of an expression. The second expression is parsed as, and may be expressed as,

```
(aBox height) print
```

where the parenthesized expression is evaluated first, returning the `Integer` object 7; the message `print` is sent to 7 and that object prints itself. Multiple arguments are dealt with using multiword messages. The message at:put: is used to insert into arrays, at is used to access them

```
aBoxArray at: 2 put: aBox.
(aBoxArray at: 2) height print.     //prints 7
```

A somewhat more conventional syntactic rendering of these might be

```
atput (aBoxArray, 2, aBox);
print(height(at(aBoxArray, 2)));
```

for the PASCAL-ish

```
BoxArray[2]  := aBox;
print(height(aBoxArray[2]));
```

and some hybrid object-oriented languages do use this kind of notion. Note that in SMALLTALK the messages are global symbols which are declared just by appearing, so that

```
aBox newMessage.
```

is syntactically correct, but will give an error at run-time if the message is not understood by the object it is sent to.

11.4.3 Instance variables

Instance variables provide local storage in an object. They are untyped—everything is just an object. For example aBox may have instance variables h, w and d for its dimensions.

11.4.4 Methods

An object has code to handle the messages it receives; each such message has a method. Thus

```
height
        ^h.
height: value
        h<- value.
```

define the two methods of aBox that we have used; here the left arrow <- indicates assignment (always to a variable) and the circumflex ^ that the following expression should be returned as the result of the methods, i.e., to the sender of the height message.

11.4.5 Class

Typically, a program deals with many similar things, for example many boxes of different sizes. The class Box provides a shared description for boxes; it describes their structure, in particular their instance variables (h, w and d), and holds their methods (such as `height` and `width:`).

Thus all instances of a class share the same methods; they differ in the values of their instance variables. Classes make instances in response to the message `new`:

```
thing1 <- Box new.  thing2<- Box new.
thing1 class print.//prints 'Box'
thing1 height: 10; width: 10; depth: 10.
thing2 height: 2; width: 5; depth: 3.
```

so that we may regard them as factories for objects. The semicolons here indicate that a sequence of messages is to be sent to an object; this is called a cascaded message. Note also that classes are objects, so that to create new classes we send messages to class `Class`. Following convention, class names begin with an upper-case letter.

Encapsulation is provided because the only access to an object's state is via messages, and these messages must be interpreted explicitly by methods which the object itself provides. There is no way to tell what an object contains or computes, so that the messsage `volume`, for example, might cause a computation, or access an instance variable, or even some combination:

```
volume          //version 1
      ^(h*w*d)
volume          //version 2
      ^v          //another instance variable
volume          //version 3
      (v=0) ifTrue: [v<- (h*w*d) ].
      ^v.
```

In SMALLTALK, signs (such as + and *) act as though they had colons, so that * acts like a binary operator. The block above is equivalent to

```
[v<- (h times: (w times: d))]
```

Thus the expression 4 + 5 indicates that 4 should be sent the message + 5, so that it is `Number` that contains the methods for arithmetic. Square brackets delimit a block (technically, a closure). Booleans have methods for messages such as `ifTrue:`. Note again that there is no direct access to the object's state. There is no way to access a `Box`'s dimensions except via messages. Note that we have not defined a message `volume:`.

Dynamic binding is required to implement the examples given, as many classes may have methods for one message, for example `print`. The binding is called dynamic just because

```
thing1 print
```

will require the activation of different code at run-time depending on the class of `thing1`. A compiler cannot know that `thing1` will be a `Box`, for it might be a `Banana`. To give a more extended example, consider the case of a CAD tool for electronic design that must deal with many parts such as resistors, capacitors, diodes, and linear ICs. It will be necessary to have collections of these components with arbitrary contents, for example a parts list, and to be able to display such a collection. Most current programming languages do not allow collections of mixed type, so that in them we have to define our own single language type to cover all the component types

```
enum ctype {RESISTOR, CAPACITOR,
    DIODE, LINEARiC ...};
struct component {ctype typeCode; ...};
```

and then the parts list can be displayed by

```
switch(thisComponent->typeCode) {
case RESISTOR:
    displayResistorData(thisComponent); break;
case LINEARiC:
    displayLinearICData(this Component); break;
...};
```

But this means that for every new type of component we must both extend the `ctype` type and also edit each corresponding `switch` statement. These statements are not localized, but are spread all over the program. Dynamic binding moves the responsibility from the client (here, the display routine) to the supplier (the component in question). The code is just

```
thisComponent displayData.
```

Of course there is no less code, since each kind of component requires a specific piece of program to display it, but the organization of that code has been fundamentally altered by putting the operations with the structure they operate on. As each new kind of component is added the extra code required is added in a single place. Dynamic binding is a general mechanism, and thus much better provided by the system than by the application programmer. Cox (1986) argues that it is the single most productive feature of OOP.

11.4.6 Subclass

In an object-oriented system, new classes are created as extensions of existing ones rather than from scratch. This extension is a subclass;

thus a subclass of a class defines a more specified object. Every class has
a superclass of which it is a subclass. These classes form a tree called the
object hierarchy; at the top is the class Object, which is its own
superclass.

A subclass can define extra instance variables, define extra methods
and redefine old methods. Objects have a form described by their class
which includes everything from its superclass, which itself included
everything from its superclass, and so on up the hierarchy to Object.
To explain the box example more fully, Box is created as a subclass of
Object. Now create a new class SolidBox describing Boxes with a
density stored in a variable rho and a method for weight

```
Box SubClass SolidBox
        instance variables rho
        methods
weight
        ^rho*(h*w*d)
```

It is important to see that a SolidBox has instance variables h, w and
d as well as the new rho; and of course it has others inherited from
Object too. These variables can be accessed directly or by message

```
weight
        ^rho*(self volume)
```

where the pseudovariable self refers to the object which is the
receiver of the weight message. This is a more powerful way of
expressing the idea, and a common OOP idiom. It means that subclasses
of SolidBox are free to define volume appropriately, but that when
objects of those classes are asked for weight they will be able to use
the inherited method defined here. As a concrete example, the class
SquareRod might describe solid boxes of square cross-section, with
method

```
volume
        ^h * xsArea
```

We have used the class Box to model boxes, but as real-world boxes,
Boxes are unconventional because their dimensions and even their
densities can be altered at will. This might be appropriate, but it is likely
that we really need to set the component values of a box when it is
created, for example

```
anotherBox<- RealBox newh: 2 w: 5 d: 3.
```

where we send a structured message to the class. Initialization in
SMALLTALK is done by class methods, described below.

Overriding can be used to modify behaviour; for example an Array
class which accepts only Integers can be defined by

```
Array SubClass IntegerArray
        methods
at: index put: value
        (value class != Integer) ifTrue:
                        [self error 'not an Integer']
        super at: index put: value.
```

where `super` is a pseudovariable whose use causes the method search
to begin with the current object's superclass. Thus

```
anIntegerArray <- IntegerArray new: 10.
anIntegerArray at: 5 put: 99
```

will indeed put the 99 in the fifth slot; after the integer check for
integrity the method from `Array` is used to actually insert the data.

These uses of `self` and `super` are key technical features in OOP,
because they allow for future flexibility, and for accessing code without
editing it. Another short example is

```
DisplayWindow SubClass BorderedWindow
        instance variables borderWidth ...
        methods
display
        self border showBits. super display.
...
```

so that a `BorderedWindow` extends `DisplayWindow` just by
having a border. There is no need to alter the code which sends the right
bits to the screen.

11.4.7 Class messages and class variables in SMALLTALK

In practice we need `Class` objects, such as `Box`, to respond to
messages other than `new`, and to be able to provide their own behaviour
for `new`. One need is for initialization of instances; another is that the
class may be a useful place to keep information common to instances.

```
Time now
Box newWithSize: #(22 34 5)
Box howManyInstances
```

SMALLTALK provides for classes to have variables, and to have
messages, and when creating a class there is access to both the instance
variables and messages, such as h and `height`, and to those for the
class, such as `numberOfInstances` and `howManyInstances`.
While such features are essential, there is a conceptual difficulty in
providing them because if `Box` were an instance of `Class`, it would

respond only to messages with methods, provided in `Class`. In SMALLTALK-80 the mechanism is for every class to be an instance of its own meta-class, which is itself a subclass of `Class`. Methods and variables for the class are defined in the meta-class. This mechanism is consistent but is complex, and is still the subject of some controversy. Usually the complexity is hidden from the programmer by the programming environment.

11.4.8 Storage allocation

Any object not referred to may be deleted and its storage returned to the common pool. This is handled automatically in SMALLTALK, generally by a combination of reference counting and occasional garbage collection

11.5 Another approach to the mechanisms

C++ is a very different language from SMALLTALK. Whereas SMALLTALK was designed from scratch as an object-oriented language, C++ is a preprocessor and library for C (Kernighan and Ritchie, 1978) that extends C and provides facilities for programming in an object-oriented style. In this section we describe how that may be done, generally following the same order as in the description based on SMALLTALK.

11.5.1 Objects in C++

C is typed, and so is C++. All variables are of a declared type; objects have a type, and basic things such as integers are not objects.

```
int x;
Box aBox;
```

Thus C++ is a hybrid system containing the mechanisms of both object-oriented and procedural programming.

11.5.2 Messages

Objects are accessed by functions, so a function `height` could be defined just as in C, allowing

```
height(aBox)+ height (x)
```

but this is not object-oriented programming. In C++ we would say

```
aBox.height()
```

which uses the height function for Boxes. The height could be set by

```
aBox.heightSet(7)
```

The dot notation here is from C and other languages with record structures; the function is essentially a component of such a structure, and so the function call is like a message send. (Additionally, and contrastingly, function names may be overloaded in C++, so that we can provide

```
int height(Box aBox){ ... };
int height(int anInt){ ... }
```

and the compiler will decide which height is appropriate, a more Ada-like style).

11.5.3 Instance variables

Objects in C++ are an extension of C structures, which have named components; methods may refer to these as variables.

11.5.4 Methods

An object's methods are functions belonging to its class

```
int Box::height(){ return(h); };
void Box::heightSet(int x){ h = x; }
```

and are called member functions. They may be defined remotely from the class definition, often in another file. The definition contains the class name so that they may be identified.

11.5.5 Class

A class is a user-defined type; the class mechanism is the cornerstone of C++.

```
class Box {
        int h, w, d;
public:
        int height ();
        void heightSet(int); ... };
```

Here the word public indicates that the following functions may be used outside the class; the instance variables may be accessed only by those functions. As in C (or PASCAL or ADA), objects may be created by declaration of a corresponding variable

```
Box aBox;
```

but are often created dynamically using the C++ operator new, and manipulated by pointer.

```
Box* aPointer ToBox;
aPointerToBox = new Box;
```

The local variables of an object are private, accessible only by the public member functions. `volume` can be implemented just as in the SMALLTALK example:

```
int Box::volume(); { return(h*w*d); };
int Box::volume(); { return(v); };
...
thevolume = aPointerToBox-> volume();
```

The $->$ here is C idiom for 'Follow the pointer and take a component of what is pointed to.'

The use of classes in C++ does not imply the use of dynamic binding; the type of the object being accessed allows the appropriate method to be decided at compile time. It was seen above how dynamic binding is needed for some applications; below will be explained how C++ provides a mechanism for it.

11.5.6 Subclass

Classes may be extended, as in SMALLTALK, to extend or redefine functionality:

```
class SolidBox:Box {
      int rho;
public:
      int weight(); ... }
```

Here `Box` is called a 'base' class and `SolidBox` is 'derived' class. C++ is much stricter than SMALLTALK about access between subclass and class, and the declaration above does not give the methods of `SolidBox` access to the instance variables (h, w and d) of `Box`, so that we cannot write

```
int SolidBox::weight()
      { return(rho * h * w * d); };
```

but must use

```
int SolidBox::weight()
      { return(rho * this->volume()); };
```

where `this` is a pseudo-pointer to the object which is the receiver of the `weight` message, i.e. whose `weight` function is being called. Even more restrictively, we cannot write

```
SolidBox aSolidBox; ...
aSolidBox.volume()
```

because although the methods (member functions) of the derived class have access to the public methods of the base class, objects of the derived class do not. However, C++ provides flexible control of such access, and in particular

```
class SolidBox: public Box { ...
```

allows

```
aSolidBox.volume()
```

11.5.7 Dynamic binding

In C++ a pointer to an object of a (public) base class may refer to an object of a derived class.

```
Box* anotherpBox; ...
anotherpBox = &aBox;
anotherpBox = &aSolidBox;
```

However, there is then no guarantee that the appropriate member function will be called. For example

```
anotherpBox>volume()
```

always uses the volume function from Box, even if the box in question is of a derived class which has redefined volume. The language provides a mechanism called a 'virtual function' which allows the programmer to declare and define a function in a base class which may be redefined in a derived class. Thus

```
class Box {
        int h, w, d;
public:
        ...
        virtual int volume(); ...};
int Box::volume()
        {return(h * w * d); };
```

allows any of Box's subclasses (derived classes) to override volume, and for

```
anotherBox>volume()
```

to work correctly. Thus C++ provides dynamic binding, but as an option which can be used where needed.

This more explicit control over access to parts and visibility of names is typical of the language; another example is that SMALLTALK's super is not provided, but an explicit call to the superclass's function is needed:

```
void BorderedWindow::display()
        { (this->border()).showBits();
          this->
            (DisplayWindow::display) (); };
```

The more explicit control can provide encapsulation which is more powerful than SMALLTALK's, and the ability to experiment with alternative styles. However, an important consequence of its careful use is that C++ code may be tightly compiled to leave only essential operations until run-time.

11.5.8 Instance initialization and storage management

A C++ class may have a constructor, which is called when objects of that class are created, and a destructor which is called when objects of that class are destroyed. The former allows initialization to be done, and the latter allows any storage referred to by the object to be deallocated or otherwise dealt with appropriately. Destruction refers to variables which go out of scope as well as those referred to by pointers and destroyed by the `delete` operator. Given that the operators `new` and `delete` may be redefined for a class by overloading, there is adequate scope for control of storage, but not the flexibility given by garbage collection.

11.6 Design and architecture of object-oriented applications

These powerful mechanisms give us expressiveness, modularity, flexibility, extensibility and modifiability. What is it like to design a system based on object-oriented software? The hallmark is in the reuse of software. Any well-designed system will be built up of modules; in an object-oriented system these will be objects. The key to a successful object-oriented design is that an appropriate hierarchy of classes is used to create these objects. This is another dimension of description from the usual dataflow diagram.

11.6.1 Designing for reuse

It is of course possible to code an application from scratch in an object-oriented language. For example, Anderson and Gossain (1988) describe the construction of a C++ program to take output from a circuit simulator and display it graphically on a plotter; the specification was provided by an already existing C program which did the job. Designing the class hierarchy, shown in Figure 11.1, was a new job and one essentially orthogonal to the process model used in the original software.

However, once this was done the coding was extremely straightforward because all the pieces of code needed (the methods) were small and the structure made it clear where to place them. It was also clearly possible to focus on reuse while designing, and indeed the

```
GraphicalObject
        Box
                TextInBox
        Division
                HorizontalDivision
                VerticalDivision
        Axis
                LogAxis
                        VerticalLogAxis
                        HorizontalLogAxis
                LinearAxis
                        VerticalLinearAxis
                        HorizontalLinearAxis
        Graph
Device
        Plotter
Dataset
PlotRequest
```

Figure 11.1   Class hierarchy for graphical presentation

final program source is 30 per cent smaller than the original and contains only 17 per cent of application-specific code; the remaining classes have been made into a graphics presentation kit. Such a kit would of course be refined as time goes on, and even on a very small scale would allow the evolution of a single program over time to be factored into incremental and conceptual changes.

11.6.2 Ready-made hierarchies

SMALLTALK-80 differs from C++ in that it is delivered with an extensive class hierarchy in place. It is in fact relatively rare for experienced programmers to make a subclass of Object, but learning to see the world in the SMALLTALK way takes time. The hierarchy is mostly fairly flat, though a nice example of depth is

```
Object-DisplayObject-Path-Arc-Circle
```

`Object` (at:put:/at:/size:)

   `Collection`   (add:/remove:/remove:ifAbsent:/includes:/do:/select:

            /collect:/detect:)

       `Bag` (no at:put:/at:)

  (no dups) `Set` (no at:put:/at:)

  (keys, associations) `Dictionary` (at:put:/at:/associationsDo:)

(integer indices,   `SequenceableCollection` (first/last/indexOf:/findFirst:

abstract)   /atAllPut:)

   (not alterable) `Interval` (from:by:to)

(ordered by add/remove) `OrderedCollection` (addFirst:/addLast:

            /removeFirst:

            /removeLast:/first/

            isEmpty/after:/before:)

   (has a block) `SortedCollection` (sortBlock:

            /no addLast:etc)

(fixed range of integer indices) `ArrayedCollection`

   (or anything) `Array`

   (of chars) `String` ($</\leq$)

Figure 11.2 SMALLTALK collection classes

A pervasive section is the group of classes used to represent `Collections`, shown in Figure 11.2. This tree illustrates the way in which subclasses are more defined than their superclasses. Note also the use of overriding—so that for example a `SortedCollection` implements the message `addLast` as an error because a `SortedCollection` determines its own order. This order is controlled by the block sent with the message `sortBlock:` to the `SortedCollection`. The block

```
[xy|(x age)  < (y age)]
```

will keep the collection in ascending order of age. The `Collection` classes also illustrate the important idea of an abstract class, a class which has no instances but is provided solely to contain the methods common to its instances. Some of its methods are required to be overriden. For example, `SequenceableCollection` is such a class, and contains the method

```
size
    self subclassResponsibility
```

to indicate that it is not defined enough to handle this message—that must be done by any subclass.

The collection classes support several messages which take blocks as arguments. For example `do: aBlock` evaluates the block for each of the receiver's elements

```
sum <-0.
#(9 99 67) do: [ :x | sum<- sum + x ].
```

puts 175 into `sum`. The hash and parentheses denote an array constant. Similarly `select: aBlock` returns a collection of the same class as the receiver but containing only those elements for which the block evaluates to `true`, as in

```
employees select:
      [ :each | each salary < 8000 ].
```

This is a powerful style of programming, familiar to users of LISP and other languages where functions are first-class objects.

It is interesting that the two most widely available areas in which stable reusable class hierarchies exist are collections and graphic interfaces. Presumably the former is the product of stable mathematics—we know that `Set` is a useful abstraction; the latter is a reflection of the current acceptance of the window–icon–mouse style. Below, the prospect for the production and sale of more application-dependent sets of classes is discussed.

11.6.3 Generic applications

Reusable software can be provided for a domain, whether conceptual like collections or concrete like graphics, by providing a hierarchy of appropriate classes. Design in that domain then has two aspects—extending the hierarchy, by subclassing and aggregation; and creating objects of those classes that are appropriate to the domain. Viewed in this way, a set of classes is like an enhanced program library, enhanced particularly because the details of representation do not need to be known. Also viewed in this way, the design process is rather bottom-up, building layers of virtual machines getting closer to the application domain.

The generic application is a radical alternative to this approach. It provides a complete and self-contained application framework, with the overall structure present and only the details missing. The system builder then subclasses the framework's classes to provide, and to connect to, the specific functionality he or she wishes to provide.

The best-known example is MacApp (1987), which implements the Apple user-interface standard on the Macintosh. It contains over 30 classes and 450 methods. The user begins with an application, which is an object (or 'Document' in Mac terminology), such as a text file to be edited or a spreadsheet, and decides on the visual appearance and the way the commands will manipulate it. Then the MacApp interface behaviour is extended to interact with the application.

The minimal application need subclass only three classes. Firstly, objects of the class TApplication do things like start up the application and display the menu bar: the only method in the class which must be overriden is doMakeDocument, which creates the object that the application is manipulating. For example, in a text editor we might find

```
TApplication subclass TExApplication
    methods
doMakeDocument: the FileNamed
    self setDocument:
        (TExDocument newfrom:
            theFileNamed)
```

Objects of class TExDocument correspond to the text in the file; in MacApp a document contains the structures representing what will be shown on the screen, called its 'views'.

```
TDocument subclass TExDocument
    methods
doMakeViews
    self setView:
        (TExView newfrom:
            (self getDocument))
```

Finally, the generic TView is subclassed to provide the behaviour which draws the images in the windows

```
TView subclass TExView
        methods
draw: viewRectangle
    // here the code to find the
    windowed text and display it
```

Altogether only three methods in these classes must be overriden for the application to execute, though three more (such as draw in TView) are required to make things actually appear. MacApp knows how the Mac user interface operates, e.g., by pulling down menus from the menu bar and selection commands, and contains the code to do and to display that. The commands are defined by the user, by creating instances of subclasses of TCommand, and must respond to the messages doIt and undoIt. The framework cannot know what the command Group does; but it knows about command objects, and that when a menu command is selected that it should send the message doIt to the relevant command object. The general undo command can be implemented uniformly—it just sends undoIt to the current command object. Dynamic binding allows the right code to be executed for the current command.

ET++ (Weinand *et al.* 1988) is a generic application providing the functionality of MacApp in a hierarchy of C++ classes on top of Xwindows.

A less structured but more flexible generic structure is the model-view-controller paradigm used in SMALLTALK's user interface (Goldberg, 1983). The internal representation of the object to be viewed is a model. The view contains the visual representation and can draw to the screen; it is updated whenever the model changes. A controller is an object that deals with inputs, sending them to the model and perhaps the view. Classes `View` and `Controller` and their subclasses such as `ParagraphView` and `MouseMenuController` are available for building with.

A generic application is a powerful way of presenting reusable software that relies on the object-oriented mechanisms of inheritance and dynamic binding to provide functionality that transcends that possible in a procedure-oriented language. The tutorial value of an accessible hierarchy of carefully designed working code cannot be overestimated—after all, the publication of UNIX and its exegesis (Lions, 1977) educated a whole generation of computer scientists.

11.7 Tools and interaction in object-oriented construction

The account of SMALLTALK given so far may come as a surprise to those who have used it or seen it demonstrated, since its most striking feature is its highly interactive programming environment. A large screen contains several windows of different kinds, and much of the interaction is controlled by a three-button mouse. The user's initial view of the system is via the 'system browser', a multipaned window that shows a part of the class hierarchy and allows selection of any method for display and editing. Classes and methods may be added and deleted interactively. When code is executed in a 'workspace' the objects involved may be investigated with an 'inspector', which gives access to all the parts. Running code may be interrupted and the 'debugger' used to investigate the state of the computation and alter it before continuation. All these tools make extensive use of multipaned windows and pop-up menus. All these tools are written in SMALLTALK and so all the classes used in their construction are available for reuse, so it is easy to produce applications with a SMALLTALK-like interface.

The notion of application is really rather alien to SMALLTALK. The work a programmer does is better viewed as augmenting his or her working environment. The job is not 'write a program to do it', but 'add the required extra functionality to the system'. Any new classes are part of the existing hierarchy. This approach is extremely productive for an individual developer, but does have two drawbacks: first, the code developed is distributed throughout the system, and can be tracked only by using sophisticated tools: secondly, different programmers may produce useful augmentations that are mutually inconsistent.

It is especially important in thinking about SMALLTALK to separate clearly the three components of the system: the language itself (what expressions mean); the class hierarchy (what code exists and how to use it); and the system (at both the screen level and the process level). For many people these three are very much intertwined, and hence the endless debates about what 'really is' SMALLTALK.

The choice of an object-oriented language would mean taking into account all the relevant factors about environments and tools; these might in fact dominate the language choice.

11.8 History and diversity

The main force behind the development of object-oriented programming has undoubtedly been the SMALLTALK project at Xerox PARC, culminating in the public release of SMALLTALK-80 (Goldberg, 1981) and its subsequent marketing and development by a spin-off company. Alan Kay was the inspiration behind this project in his struggle to realize the concept of the Dynabook, a laptop computer that would allow fluent expression and amplification of its users' ideas (Kay and Goldberg, 1977). The technical influences were from SIMULA-67, with its class mechanism and inheritance, and from LISP with its dynamic binding and interactive environment (Birtwhistle, 1971; Teitelman, 1978).

There are two main camps of object-oriented languages. The SMALLTALK group are generally interactive and interpreted, and tends so far to be used in applications that are user interface intensive. The C group generally use a preprocessor to generate C, are compiled (though perhaps using a run-time table for messaging), and are used in all kinds of applications. In the SMALLTALK group we find particularly SMALLTALK-80 itself, SMALLTALK/V (Smalltalk-V Language Manual, 1986), a low-cost system implementing similar functionality on the Macintosh and IBM PC, and Common LISP (Steele, 1984) with the Common LISP Object System (DeMichiel and Gabriel, 1987), which provides multiple inheritance. The C camp is large; many projects are using 'home-made' C preprocessors to provide some subset of C++ functionality, but the chief commercial systems apart from C++ are OBJECTIVE-C (Cox, 1986) and EIFFEL (Meyer, 1988). The producers of OBJECTIVE-C have stressed the production of class libraries and a development environment rather than sophisticated language mechanisms. EIFFEL has abandoned C's syntax, and includes both generic types and multiple inheritance. This list is by no means exhaustive, and omits even Apple's OBJECT-PASCAL (the language used to implement MacApp), which will perhaps soon be supplanted by

Table 11.1 Features of Object-Oriented Languages

Feature	SMALLTALK-80	SMALLTALK/V	C++	OBJECTIVE-C	EIFFEL	Common LISP	ADA
Dynamic binding	Yes	Yes	Yes	Yes	Yes	Yes	No
Overloading	Yes	Yes	Yes	No	No	Yes	Yes
Garbage collection	Yes	Yes	No	No	Yes	Yes	No
Initialize/delete help	Yes	Yes	Yes	No	Yes	Yes	No
Compilable	No	Yes	Yes	Yes	Yes	Yes	Yes
Interpreter	Yes	No	No	Yes	No	Yes	No
Objects only	Yes	Yes	No	No	No	No	No
Inheritance	Yes	Yes	Yes	Yes	Yes	Yes	No
Multiple inheritance	Yes?	No	Yes	No	Yes	Yes	No
Generics	Yes	Yes	No	Yes	Yes	Yes	Yes
Static typechecking	No	No	Yes	Yes	Yes	No	Yes
Commercially available	Yes	Yes	Yes	Yes	Yes	Yes	Yes
Class libraries	Yes	Yes	No	Yes	Yes	No	No
Development environment	Yes	Yes	No	Yes	Yes	Yes	Yes
Mac/Sun/PC/Vax	MSP	MP	MSPV	MSV	S	MSV	SPV

Figure 11.3 Alternative hierarchies using single inheritance

C++. Table 11.1 provides a brief comparison of some of the languages mentioned, referring to features discussed above or in the sections below.

The future of OOP seems assured, though not its precise route. However, SMALLTALK-80. SMALLTALK/V, C++ and OBJECTIVE-C are now well established in their own domains, well documented and well supported. They will probably remain the most widely known languages for some time to come.

11.9 Research directions and technical issues

OOP is an active field for research and development, where ideas are often expressed by the design of new languages, the introduction of new tools or the provision of design notations. This is not the place to survey this area, or even to summarize it, but an outline of some of the issues may indicate the kind of work being done.

11.9.1 Multiple inheritance

The inheritance described so far means that each class has a single superclass. The problem can arise of creating a class that wants to inherit behaviour from more than one superclass; in the graphics kit described above, for example, axes can be logarithmic or linear, vertical or horizontal. In SMALLTALK or C++ it must be decided which of the inheritance trees, shown in Figure 11.3, to use to describe this, where the choice seems arbitrary and both ways will require duplication of code. Multiple inheritance would allow a class to have multiple superclasses, and in cases like this with orthogonal features it looks attractive. The difficulties are that finding methods is more complex, and that some way of resolving clashes between multiple methods for a message has to be found. Current limited experience with these features indicates that serious use of multiple inheritance leads to a different programming style where small lumps of behaviour are defined, and classes created by mixing several of these. It also seems that while lack of multiple inheritance may lead to some arbitrary choices and extra code, program complexity is not usually greatly increased. Notwithstanding this, the most recent release of C++ includes multiple-inheritance; an experimental version was available for SMALLTALK-80, but is not being promoted by the suppliers. The Flavors system for ZETALISP (Weinreb and Moon, 1981) is a well-known example of the thorough use of multiple inheritance; its also provided in the recently standardized Common LISP Object System (DeMichiel and Gabriel, 1987).

11.9.2. Concurrency

The semantics of objects could be extended by allowing concurrent execution of methods; a message send would not have to wait for a reply. This can allow quite different ways of structuring systems and providing reusability. Several experimental systems work this way, notably the language NIL (Strom, 1986). It may also pave the way for concurrent execution on multiple processors.

11.9.3 Some further topics

- *Persistence*   Allowing objects to exist from session to session, perhaps in large numbers, leads to the concept of object stores and object-oriented databases.
- *Type checking*   SMALLTALK does not check types, in the sense that if an object does not understand (have a method for) a message then an error is generated at run-time. Some of these errors could be caught by having some notion of type, but the flexibility of dynamic binding is still needed. The requirements that C++ puts on the provision of virtual functions are quite restrictive.
- *Cloning*   It is possible to do without the class notion, describing new objects just by the way in which they differ from current objects.

11.10 OOP and the software life-cycle

Modern views of the software life-cycle focus on incremental delivery and the evolution of systems based on an open-ended architecture (Gilb, 1989). OOP is a promising technology for this, as it shifts the focus from the functionality of a specific application to the objects of the domain. It might then be possible to choose the classes, to make a kit, and then build up applications in an incremental way.

The first step, domain analysis, is more akin to a task in knowledge representation than to classical systems analysis, and indeed one might expect to use techniques of knowledge elicitation from the expert systems field. A comprehensive hierarchy of classes for a domain provides us not only with potential parts for software, but with a way of thinking about that domain. The reuse of code is obviously important, but more important is the reuse of this design insight.

It might be hoped that the number of classes in a developing application, or an application family, might grow only slowly after the initial domain analysis phase.

In practice this is not the case (Anderson and Gossain, 1990); the hierarchy/environment does not converge, and there is a continuous process of refinement, addition and growth. New solution strategies introduce new concepts—and this is essential if there is to be any progress! Evolutionary methods must be used for the domain kit as well as for the applications.

Thus, by taking reuse and the component view seriously we are led to a new view of the software production process, with at least three interlocking life-cycles, at the levels of components, hierarchies and applications:

- *Component life-cycle* (about goodness)   Here the interface is given. Changes involve work on the implementation of the component, perhaps to make it faster, and indeed alternative versions might be provided with different properties such as the amount of checking of the total capacity. At this level internal measurements may be made on components (e.g., cyclomatic complexity) and also the interface evaluated (e.g., degree of encapsulation).
- *Application life-cycle* (about usefulness)   By application life-cycle we refer to the sequence of software products, which may be versions of a single application, or a series of applications. We may ask which components are useful, and which need modification. We can measure the amount of reuse in the application.
- *Hierarchy life-cycle* (about reusefulness)   The really new element in the model is that the collection of components is a rich structure that is central to the software process. New classes are added and the hierarchy is reorganized. We need to track this process and to gain experience in evaluating progress. There are many questions to ask, for example about how much inheritance there is and how different classes are.

11.11 Object-oriented design and object-oriented interfaces

The phrase 'object-oriented' is used very widely in the software industry, but not always with the same meaning as in object-oriented programming.

11.11.1 Object-oriented design

There is a great deal of interest in programming methodologies at the moment—in recognizable styles of constructing software helped by guidelines, heuristics and notations. Often such methods are supported by automated tools. Some of these are promoted as object-oriented, but the objects referred to are variously abstract data types, processes (tasks), modules (packages), or just blobs on diagrams. None of these methodologies currently address the main issue of OOP, namely the design of a hierarchy of classes, and the distribution of functionality within it. The term object-based is coming to be used for systems based on objects without inheritance.

11.11.2 Object-oriented interfaces

This term is used to describe some programs that manipulate a visual representation fairly directly; in particular it is used in contrast to a bit-map interface in drawing programs. The latter maintains only a two-dimensional representation, i.e., a drawing, and so cannot support the selection and manipulation of the depicted items. It is of course quite possible to implement an object-oriented interface without OOP, and a non-object-oriented interface with OOP. However, it is easy to see that OOP is particularly suitable for creating object-oriented interfaces, because dynamic binding will allow user actions to be dealt with uniformly; a circle, a square, a menu item and a palette entry may all understand the messages `click` and `doubleClick`.

11.11.3 OOP in ADA

There is much talk of OOP in the ADA community. ADA does provide mechanisms for modularity, in particular generics and overloading, but these are not as powerful as the inheritance and dynamic binding which they echo. It is not possible to do object-oriented programming in ADA, though it can be used for object-based programming. From a software engineering point of view, the language is obsolescent. (See Meyer, (1988), for a fuller discussion of this and other comparisons.)

11.12 Conclusions

Object-oriented programming is a new approach to software construction which is becoming widely used. It aids the engineering of software by providing powerful techniques for structuring and reusability. A summary of the architectural features of OOP has been given followed by a description of the language mechanisms used to realize them, using as examples Smalltalk-80 and C++. The ways in which reusable software may be presented have been described, and the construction of generic applications explained. Finally, some current research issues and some other uses of object-oriented ideas have been discussed.

Object-oriented programming is an exciting area, still full of controversy. Research is active, with three international conferences devoted to it each year, a journal and many newsletters and bulletin boards. It is also commercially important, so that despite the immaturity of the field it is well worthwhile to develop, sell and use (and reuse!) software for object-oriented programming. All this movement is founded on some basic ideas that will continue to influence software development and software development methodology for many years to come.

References

Anderson, B. and S. Gossain (1988) 'Software re-engineering using C++', *Proceedings, Spring* 1988 *European Unix Systems User Group Conference* 213–218.

Anderson, D. B. and S. Gossain (1990) 'Hierarchy evolution and the software lifecycle', *Proceedings 2nd International Conference on Technology of Object-Oriented Languages and Systems*, Paris, June 1990, 41–50.

Birtwhistle, G. (1971) *Simula Begin*, Studentlitteratur, Lund, Sweden.

Cox, B. (1986) *Object-oriented Programming—an Evolutionary Approach*, Addison-Wesley, Reading, Mass.

DeMichiel, L. G and R. P. Gabriel (1987) 'The Common Lisp object system: an overview', *Proceedings, ECOOP '87*, Springer, Berlin, 151–170.

Gilb, T. (1989) *Software Engineering Management*, Addison-Wesley, Wokingham.

Goldberg, A. (1983) *Smalltalk-80: the Interactive Programming Environment*, Addison-Wesley, Reading, Mass.

Goldberg, A. (ed.) (1981) Issue on SMALLTALK-80, *Byte*, **6**, (8) (August).

Goldberg, A. and D. Robson, (1983) *Smalltalk-80: The Language and its Implementation*, Addison-Wesley, Reading, Mass.

Kay, A. and A. Goldberg (1977) 'Personal dynamic media', *IEEE Computer*, Mar. 31–41.

Kernighan, B. and D. M. Ritchie (1978) *The C Programming Language*, Prentice-Hall, Englewood Cliffs, NJ.

Lions, J. A. (1977) *Commentary on the UNIX Operating System*, University of New South Wales, Sydney.

MacApp Manual (1987) Apple Computer, Cupertino, Calif.

Meyer, B. (1988) *Object-oriented Software Development* Prentice-Hall, Englewood Cliffs, NJ.

Parnas, D. (1972). 'On the criteria to be used in decomposing systems into modules', *Commun. ACM*, **15** (12) (Dec.) 1053–1058.

Smalltalk-V Language Manual (1986) Digitalk, Los Angeles, Calif.

Steele, G. L. (1984) *Common LISP: The Language*, Digital Press, Bedford, Mass.

Strom, R. (1986) 'A comparison of the object-oriented and process paradigms', *SIGPLAN Notices*, **21** (10) (Oct.) 88–97.

Stroustrup, B. (1986) *The C++ Programming Language*, Addison-Wesley, Reading, Mass.

Teitelman, W. (1978) *Interlisp Reference Manual*, Xerox Corp., PARC, Palo Alto, Calif.

Weinand, A., E. Gamma, and R. Marty (1988) 'ET++—an object-oriented application framework in C++', *OOPSLA '88, Special Issue of SIGPLAN Notices*, **23**, (11) (Nov.) 168–182.

Weinreb, D. and D. Moon (1981) *Lisp Machine Manual*, MIT AI Laboratory, Cambridge, Mass.

PART IV

Usability and evaluation

12 Evaluation techniques for human–computer systems design

ANDY DOWNTON

12.1 Introduction

As will be apparent from Chapter 1 of this book, evaluation, whether formally or informally based, has traditionally been (and continues to be) a key part of effective human–computer systems design. Evaluation provides a mechanism for injecting objectivity into the process of assessing a design, and is concerned with the system as a whole, including its human component, and not just the technological components of the system. In so far as every system is different, evaluation in some form is always likely to be needed as a tool in human–computer systems design.

Evaluation in human–computer systems is the counterpart of system testing in conventional system development: it provides a methodology for verifying system performance against specified user requirements in the same way as testing involves system performance checks against technical specifications. In this chapter, an overview of all aspects of evaluation is provided—*when* to evaluate, *what* to evaluate, the range of evaluation techniques available—before considering in a little more depth the underlying basis of evaluation techniques in the formal methodology of experimental psychology and statistical analysis.

12.1.1 Classic mistakes

It is perhaps easiest to illustrate why evaluation is needed by omission: that is, by pointing out some of the more obvious pitfalls and 'HCI howlers' that are perpetrated every day in systems designs, and which would be readily uncovered even by cursory application of evaluation techniques. In contrast to the rigorous formal review procedures which have been developed for conventional engineering design, engineers continue to make all manner of false assumptions and implicit design choices, and to build erroneously based 'features' into the human–computer interface.

The following list, presented approximately in order of decreasing substance, illustrates a variety of the common problems observed.

'Common-sense' design decisions

Common sense has traditionally been the basis of human-factors design, and of course has a part to play. Unfortunately, current human-factors design issues move well beyond the boundaries where common sense can be reliably applied. Many research results contradict what 'common sense' would seem to suggest (for example, Chapanis, (1959), demonstrated conclusively that workmen in noisy environments can in fact hear speech better if they wear earplugs), while in other cases 'common sense' seems to provide no useful guidance at all. For example, much of the early research on human factors in aircraft instrument displays during the 1940s was directed to designing altimeters which were less easily misread than their predecessors (problems were detected when a number of pilots attempted to fly subterranean in poor visibility!): a variety of designs were evaluated, since no design could be selected as best by 'common sense' criteria alone.

Assuming personal behaviour is representative

This is a frequent design assumption, and is *never* the case! Even if the designer imagines himself to be an 'average' person (which would presumably require him to be a hermaphrodite!), he is still a designer, and thus usually has a very different view of the system from that of any user. As has been pointed out already in Chapter 4, the idea of the 'average' person is, in any case, a fallacy.

Handed-down truth

This problem of authority is commonly encountered by junior engineers, who are passed a design job with the words 'The boss says it must be done this way.' In many cases there may be good reasons for this, but, equally often, the reasons may no longer be relevant, or may have been superseded by subsequent changes in other aspects of the design. It is lazy to assume that something is true just because someone says so, if there is no corroborating evidence. Creative design involves a willingness to reconsider fundamental issues as part of the design process, and most of the more innovative designs have resulted from just such radical reconsideration. In this context, evaluation is essential, to provide a meaningful measure or comparison of performance.

Continuing acceptance of habit and/or tradition

A less-focused version of the problem above is where the designer is confronted with the words 'It has always been done this way before.' Accepting this statement may merely perpetuate a design error through another generation of systems. Again, corroborative evidence is required.

Implicit unsupported assumption in design

A great danger is that designers whose primary area of expertise lies outside the human-factors field will overlook fundamental issues within this field, and instead attempt to satisfy secondary issues in their own field of expertise which in fact conflict with good human-factors design. An example of this occurred in the definition of the UK level 1 Teletext display format (BBC/IBA/BREMA, 1976). The familiar style of 40-character × 24-line display was chosen principally on the basis of display bandwidth limitations (horizontal resolution) and lines per screen (vertical resolution) to maximize the displayable characters on the screen, with little consideration of human-factors issues such as desirable character aspect ratio, line spacing and general readability of the founts. As a result, teletext maximizes the amount of displayed text at the expense of poor information transfer to the reader. It is fortunate that provision also exists to display lines in a 'double-height' format, since early research on television subtitling using teletext showed that single-height captions were unacceptably illegible for most viewers (Baker, *et al.*, 1983).

Unsupported early design decisions

'Brainstorming' is a well-established technique for eliciting novel and innovative designs, but the nature of the method prevents any detailed review of the ideas elicited being undertaken at their moment of conception. As long as this more systematic evaluation is carried out later, no harm is done, but it is easy to forget the source of design ideas, and half-baked concepts sometimes become fully baked merely by the passage of time. This can be a recipe for disaster!

Postponement of evaluation 'until a more convenient time'

Like documenting a program, evaluation appears at first sight to be an 'overhead' activity, incurring costs, but with limited or unforeseeable benefits. As is shown below however, the costs of *not* evaluating an interface can be very high indeed, and progressively increase the longer evaluation is postponed.

Formal evaluation using inappropriate subject groups

It is common practice to use one's colleagues for initial evaluation. As an informal method, much can be learned concerning gross characteristics of an interface very rapidly by this means. Laboratory colleagues are extremely unlikely to be representative of the user population as a whole however, and any formal analysis should therefore always be based upon carefully chosen subjects who represent accurately the characteristics of the target user population. Failure to do this is likely to invalidate any results obtained from the evaluation.

Experiments which cannot be analysed

A primary characteristic of formal experimental evaluation is that, if correctly designed, very limited experimental effort can produce reliable evaluation results. Conversely, however, it is seldom possible to fit a set of data gathered 'off the cuff' *post hoc*. Thus although gathering experimental data can appear to have the quality of 'doing useful work', unless the design to which the data is to be fitted is known at the start, valid analysis of the data may be impossible.

12.1.2 Use of existing experience and data

Chapter 4 of this book provides a wealth of first-level guidance on human–computer interface design, and provides an initial starting point for the design process. However, guidelines are not infallible, and counter-examples can usually be quoted which contradict every 'principle'. In addition, guidelines usually have limitations (based typically upon the nature of the circumstances under which they were derived).

Evaluation work, by its very nature, tends to provide results specific to the experimental conditions chosen, and these are seldom directly relevant to other scenarios. A weakness of formal evaluation methodologies is that they do not readily cope with the wide range of variables encountered in real-life situations: a change in any variable (such as display format on a screen) thus invalidates the findings of a previous experiment.

12.1.3 Behavioural data

Since the performance of any human–computer system depends equally upon the performance of the computer and the person, evaluation of the system as a whole must include evaluation of the user using the system. Unfortunately, user response and performance are very much less predictable than those of a machine, leading to much greater difficulty in establishing unequivocal performance statistics.

A wide variety of user characteristics (experience, fatigue, training, education, motivation, skill, etc.) can all have a substantial effect on overall system performance. Balancing these effects so that they do not unduly affect measurements, and determining the appropriate mix of user characteristics which should be present in the user population selected for evaluation are skilled tasks, based in the formal methodology of experimental psychology. Thus, though it is often expedient to use simplified evaluation procedures for pragmatic reasons, the evaluator should always be aware of the compromises being made, and of the underlying theoretical principles which apply.

12.2 When and what to evaluate?

In the academic sphere of experimental psychology, experimentation has traditionally been characterized as based upon carefully crafted formal experiments with highly controlled variables, and the objective of identifying rather small differences of performance in very restricted areas (see Chapter 3). The underlying objective of such experiments has usually been to provide insight regarding some hypothesized aspect of human cognitive processing.

In human–computer systems evaluation, it is seldom possible to constrain the experimental condition in the way which is attempted in psychological laboratories, and indeed any attempt to do so would probably render the experiment insufficiently realistic. Furthermore, evaluation is not seen as a once-and-for-all exercise to be carried out at the end of system development (when it is usually too late to make any significant changes anyway), but as a set of tools ranging from the heuristic through the empirical to the theoretical which should be applied progressively throughout the engineering development life-cycle.

A basic justification for this approach comes from the well-known 'rule of 10', which applies also in other engineering fields such as testing: as the life-cycle of product development moves from each phase to the next, there is roughly an order-of-magnitude increase in the cost of correcting errors highlighted by evaluation. Thus, at the system analysis phase, design errors (perhaps highlighted by evaluation using simulation) are readily corrected simply by changes in the proposed paper design; at the system design phase, errors may involve changes to hardware or software, and may invalidate design effort which has already been completed; while at the system production phase, design errors require not only a redesign of the hardware and/or software, but also redesign of tooling and equipment involved in the production cycle. Therefore the earlier that human factors issues in the design can be subjected to informal or formal evaluation, the less cost will be incurred in correcting any errors and misconceptions.

12.2.1 System analysis phase

At the system analysis phase of the life-cycle, it may be possible to evaluate a previous design (if the proposed new design is a development from this). Such evaluation would provide direct input to the design process. Additionally, feedback can be sought from users of the previous design, from the designers themselves, from marketing and from sales, to provide indirect input to the design process. The indirect feedback is typically obtained by means of interviews and/or questionnaires (see Sections 12.3.3 and 12.3.4), and may involve projecting scenarios of technologically feasible developments and establishing their practical benefits and market appeal to users. The results of this type of informal evaluation are then combined with purely technical development criteria to determine the appropriate compromise of engineering trade-offs which should be pursued in subsequent stages of the development cycle.

12.2.2 System design phase

Where major human factors design decisions are required as part of the system design phase, small-scale experimental evaluation can be applied to these issues: with appropriately structured experimental designs, reliable results can be obtained rapidly with a very limited number of subjects. Simulation is often appropriate at this stage too, to enable users to visualize the system accurately at a stage where the full implementation is not available. The use of a modular design philosophy minimizes the effort involved in making retrospective changes.

12.2.3 Pre-production phase

Once the prototype design is complete, larger-scale evaluation can be undertaken, with more attention to detailed aspects of the design. The original specification may include human–computer performance criteria, in which case evaluation will be of absolute performance as judged by these yardsticks; however, more commonly, comparative testing (for example against a previous generation or competitor's product) is applied. Evaluation may be included as part of the beta-testing of the product, particularly where the system allows automatic monitoring and logging of users' activities. The log can then be downloaded for analysis at a later stage, providing a wealth of information about interactions in a non-intrusive way.

12.3 Evaluation techniques

12.3.1 A spectrum of options

Evaluation in the widest sense includes many different options which can be used individually or in tandem. *Analytic evaluation methods* include pencil-and-paper techniques used by HCI practitioners to apply formal models of interactions (such as Card *et al.*'s (1983) GOMS model or Payne and Green's (1983) Task Action Grammar (see Section 3.4.1)) to particular systems. Inconsistencies in predicted performance can then be used as diagnostic information identifying deficiencies of the interface.

Empirical methods, ranging from the informal (user observation) to the formal (formally designed evaluation experiments, questionnaires and interviews) are discussed in further detail below. Another possibility (not discussed in detail here) is the use of independent human-factors consultants (for example from HCI Centres set up under the Alvey programme). Such experts can provide specific expert judgement on the human interface characteristics of a product at any stage from initial specification through to production.

12.3.2 Experiments

Evaluation experiments are normally of two types. *Comparative* experiments compare the performance of the proposed system with that of some alternative system, and thus give an indication of the relative performance of the two systems. *Absolute* experiments compare performance with a pre-defined specification and establish whether or not this specification is met. In the past there have been few HCI standards to use as the bases of absolute specifications, but there is increasing interest is establishing such standards at present, and as a result it is likely that absolute performance measurement will become increasingly important in the future, particularly in respect of public sector and defence contracts.

A variety of parameters can be used as the basis of experimental evaluations.

Training time measurements

These provide an assessment of the time taken to reach a particular standard of proficiency, and thus provide useful real-world information about the ease with which a system can be learned. However, training time to achieve full proficiency for most complex systems is measured in weeks or months rather than hours, and can thus be monitored only in the context of sampled longitudinal observations of performance. Furthermore, performance is likely to continue to improve over a

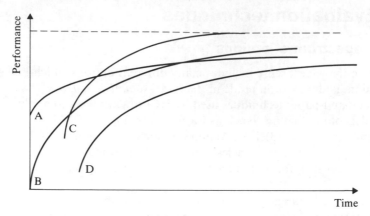

Figure 12.1 Typical learning curve variations for different users of a system

period of time according to an exponential relationship (see Figure 12.1). Difficulties therefore arise in defining both the initial standard of the user (which will vary according to previous experience, background, etc.) and the final standard achieved (has the final performance asymptote been reached?). For this reason, formal experiments are seldom based upon this parameter, though informal evaluation frequently involves its monitoring.

Time to complete specific (representative) tasks

By contrast this is frequently used as a primary parameter of performance in formal experiments, since it is readily measured either manually or by the system itself. The main difficulty in designing experiments to measure this parameter is generally the choice of suitably representative tasks which exercise the required functionality of the system, and yet can be completed within a reasonable experimental timescale—typically less than an hour per subject. A secondary problem is the influence which other parameters (such as errors—see below) may have upon the task execution time: should explicit allowance be made for errors by some normalization procedure applied to the raw execution times, or is it sufficient to assume that if performance is slowed by errors then the task execution time directly reflects deficiencies in the system which caused those errors?

Number of errors

These can be used directly as an indication of the adequacy of the system: a system which generates fewer user errors is assumed to be better than one which generates more. However, a difficulty arises in interpreting error performance, since errors can be subdivided into three classes: those detected and corrected by the user, those detected but remaining uncorrected (generally through ignorance about the system) and those remaining unobserved by the user.

User satisfaction

This is an important and additional aspect of experimental evaluation, which is generally determined as part of a 'debriefing' stage at the end of the experimental procedure. Unlike other parameters it is subjective in nature, but is an important independent check of the users' views of the system. It does not automatically follow that users' preferences will always be for the most efficient system (as measured by experimental evaluation), and if subjective assessment of users' reactions (normally by means of interviews or questionnaires) reveals this then the designer must consider carefully what balance should be struck between system efficiency and user appeal.

Regardless of the parameters being measured, a variety of data-gathering methods are commonly used.

Data logging and instrumentation

Since the system being evaluated is commonly computer-based, it is usually straightforward to arrange for data to be logged onto computer files for subsequent analysis. The data monitored consists of events such as key presses and mouse actions which characterize the user's input to the system (system output being implied by user input), together with a log of the system real-time clock to provide information about the timing of events. A disadvantage is that only direct actions on the system are monitored: no ancillary information is recorded to show other subject activities. As a result, this method is often combined with video recording (see below) in professional human-factors evaluation laboratories.

Observation

This was widely used in the past as a method of monitoring subjects but has a number of disadvantages. Most important of these is its intrusiveness, which may influence subjects' performance. A further problem is that humans are not very efficient at the monitoring process: they can be easily distracted, get bored and suffer from loss of attention, and have difficulty coping with recording sudden peaks of activity.

Commentary

Commentary spoken by the subject while interacting with the system, is often used as a way of finding out what the subject is thinking, rather than trying to infer this indirectly from their actions. Since the process of commentating can be very disruptive in relation to the primary task of interaction with the system, a popular alternative is to record the interaction on video, and then obtain a commentary from the subject as the video is subsequently replayed.

Video recording

This can have many creative uses in evaluation (see above) but has the disadvantage of generating enormous amounts of data which require painstaking and time-consuming analysis if used directly as the basis of an evaluation record.

Debriefing

Though this has important uses in correlating users' attitudes with their performance, it is a subsidiary mechanism, used in conjunction with one (or more) of the above.

Whatever parameters are measured and regardless of the method used, two problems are inherent in evaluation experiments. First is the *Hawthorne effect* (Roethlisberger and Dickson, 1939) (so called after the factory where it was first observed), which states that performance is always elevated under test conditions (as compared with normal use), owing to the interest which the experiment generates among the subjects. Evaluation experiments in general therefore tend to produce better results than might be expected among the normal user population. Second, however carefully designed, an evaluation experiment presents an artificial environment to the subject: is the experiment therefore representative of real-life use of the system, and can real-life performance be adequately extrapolated from the experiment?

12.3.3 Questionnaires

The principal advantage of questionnaires is that they can produce large databases of information concerning a system both quickly and economically. This results from the fact that subjects can be interrogated as a parallel operation rather than serially. Questionnaires are in any case often useful as a backup for objective evaluations such as experiments. Their main disadvantage is that they are only useful for evaluating attitudes and are not able to provide objective data. An additional disadvantage in the context of human–computer systems is that questionnaires are impractical unless the intended subjects are familiar with the subject of the questions: this may not be practicable if the subject is a new system which has not yet been released commercially.

Questionnaires can be either *interviewer-administered* or *self-administered*.

Interviewer-administered questionnaires

These imply the availability of trained interviewers (see below for details) and are likely to be much more manpower-intensive than self-administered questionnaires, but have a number of advantages. First, the use of interviews allows the data-gathering exercise to be better controlled than is the case with self-administered questionnaires. Where necessary, the interviewer can assist in interpreting the questionnaire, reducing or eliminating erroneous answers which might otherwise result from subjects misunderstanding the question. Second, subjects can be selected by the interviewer: this may be important in maintaining the right balance between respondents with different user characteristics.

Finally, interviews can be carried out either face to face or by means of telephone conversation.

Self-administered questionnaires

Though administratively straightforward and requiring the minimum of manpower these have a high potential for bias, because of the very poor control which the surveyor has over the respondents. The group which chooses to respond is very unlikely to have consistent attitudes and views as compared with the totality of subjects circulated with the questionnaire. Since it is common for postal surveys (for example) to have a response rate of 40 per cent or less, it is very dangerous to extrapolate trends observed among respondents to the questionnaire to the subject population as a whole. For example, in surveying user response to a new telephone service among users who have purchased the required reception equipment, one could confidently expect that the survey response would overstate enthusiasm for the service, since those people most enthused by it would be most likely to respond to the questionnaire, and all users who have invested money in the reception equipment are likely to have some commitment to it.

A final problem with self-administered questionnaires is in framing the questions: since the respondent has no interviewer to fall back upon in the case of difficulty in understanding questions, it is essential that questions be framed in an unambiguous way and thoroughly tested using a group of 'pilot' subjects before the full-scale survey is undertaken.

Whether the questionnaire is to be interviewer- or self-administered, experience and training are essential in framing questions. Bailey (1982) cites a number of commonly encountered problems, including the following:

- *Use of 'loaded' terms* Terms may have an emotional significance to the respondent which biases his or her response.
- *Suggesting the desired response* The question 'Have you stopped beating your wife?' is an extreme example of this, where it is impossible for the respondent to reply either 'yes' or 'no' without implying some fault. More commonly, questions of the type 'You do … don't you?' may make it difficult to respond anything other than 'yes'. Questions should be neutral in tone.
- *Embarrassment of the subject* Embarrassment can arise where the subject (rightly or wrongly) construes one of the possible answers to a question as implying personal inadequacy in some sphere, for example, literacy, dexterity, numeracy, job or social background, etc. A response to such a question could be expected to be biased by a desire to avoid a revealing answer, and, in the case of a self-administered questionnaire, may be refused altogether.
- *Lack of precision in questions* Precision in the formation of questions is a key element of good questionnaire design. Simple and familiar words should be used, to avoid misunderstanding by respondents, and careful consideration should be given to the range of possible responses to a question, to avoid receiving answers which cannot be analysed. Imprecise words, such as 'often', 'sometimes', 'frequently', 'seldom', etc., should not be used in questions and should be prevented from appearing in answers by wording questions to force a more explicit response (for example, the use of a multiple-choice closed question with numerically defined options rather than an open-ended question).

In general, *closed questions*, where the respondent is forced to choose between a number of defined options (which may of course include 'don't know') are very much easier to analyse than *open-ended questions*, where responses are less predictable and cannot be directly accumulated into the specified categories. However, open-ended questions may be appropriate in seeking independent opinions about a system, in soliciting suggestions, or under any circumstances where the realistic range of responses cannot be predetermined or adequately categorized.

Organization of the questionnaire is also important. An appropriate logical sequence of questions should be provided, to avoid subjecting the respondent to 'forward-referencing' problems. Questions should be presented hierarchically, progressing from the most general to the most detailed. Initial questions should be neutral and easily answered, and more sensitive issues should not be broached until rapport has been established later in the questionnaire. Questions should be ordered to avoid *sequence bias* effects, where the response to one question may influence responses in subsequent questions on related subjects.

The physical structure and layout of the questionnaire are also of importance. *Length* should be constrained by the time which it is reasonable to expect a respondent to spend in answering (typically a maximum of half an hour). *Filter questions* can be used to determine whether the responses to a subsequent group of questions should be ignored: for example an initial question regarding degree of deafness can be used to determine whether responses to subsequent questions on habits in viewing television and listening to radio are valid. Similarly, *branch questions* can be used to direct respondents to ignore irrelevant questions. Questionnaire layout is also important: not only must this layout include textual instructions to the interviewer or subject (as well as the questions themselves) but also the aesthetic style of the questionnaire should be as appealing as possible in order to attract the respondent. Figures 12.2(a) and (b) illustrate some of these points by comparing an initial draft of a survey conducted into computing facilities at Essex University with the final version actually used in the survey.

Finally, where anything other than a very straightforward questionnaire is being designed pre-testing should be carried out to check the validity of the design, and that there are no unforseen problems.

Since engineers and computer scientists seldom have the expertise to satisfy all these requirements, the best compromise is often for technical personnel to work in collaboration with human factors personnel in defining the content.

12.3.4 Interviews

Interviews are generally a high-cost evaluation option, as well as being time-consuming, and are therefore considered only for special classes of subjects who cannot be adequately accessed by other means such as self-administered questionnaires. An example might be where, to balance the set of subjects, responses are required from a group which has not responded adequately to a self-administered survey. Interviews are normally based upon a questionnaire-style set of questions to which the questioner seeks responses, but greater flexibility is possible in answering than in the self-administered case.

Interviewing for surveys is a skill which requires training, and as such is seldom undertaken by technical staff; on the other hand, the interviewer may require specialist 'peer-level' knowledge of a particular technical area to enable him or her to interact effectively with the respondent. Satisfying these conflicting objectives may present problems!

12.4 Subject selection

Almost invariably, subjects used in any kind of evaluation work are a *sample* of the full user population, hence they must be carefully chosen

PLEASE COMPLETE ONE FORM FOR EACH ITEM OR TYPE OF EQUIPMENT
(INCLUDING PERIPHERALS) CURRENTLY IN USE. A SINGLE FORM CAN
BE USED WHERE MULTIPLES OF A PARTICULAR TYPE ARE IN USE
(EG., IN UNDERGRADUATE LABS.)

SENATE WORKING PARTY ON COMPUTING POLICY—SURVEY OF COMPUTER
USE, 1987

1. HARDWARE

Name/type of equipment

How many held?

Date(s) of purchase or acquisition

Cost at time acquired (value if donated)

Source of funds

Was the equipment acquired via the Computing Service?

Usage (teaching; research; administration including word
processing; other)

Category of staff using equipment (e.g., academic, secretarial,
technical, etc.)

Maintenance arrangements (delete as applicable)

No maintenance   Computing Service   Other

2.   SOFTWARE

Major items of software used (indicate percentage in case of
split use)

Category of user (research staff, graduate student,
undergraduates, etc.)

Cost of maintenance or licensing software

Figure 12.2   (a) Original textual content of the questionnaire (part)

SENATE WORKING PARTY ON COMPUTING POLICY
SURVEY OF COMPUTER USE 1987

Please complete one form for each type of Computer currently in use

Name [   ]   Department/Section [   ]

HARDWARE

Name/Type of Computer [   ]   How many held [   ]   Financial year of purchase [   ]

Cost at time acquired (value if donated or loaned) *(Please tick box)*

<£500   £500-£1000   £1000-£10000   £10000-£100000   >£100000
[ ]   [ ]   [ ]   [ ]   [ ]

Exact cost (if known) [   ]

Was equipment: Purchased [ ]   Donated [ ]   Loaned [ ]   *(Please tick box)*

Source of funds   *(Please tick box(es) and specify percentage if more than one source)*

Departmental		Research Council		Industry		Donation		Loan		Other	
√	%	√	%	√	%	√	%	√	%	√	%
[ ]	[ ]	[ ]	[ ]	[ ]	[ ]	[ ]	[ ]	[ ]	[ ]	[ ]	[ ]

If Departmental or Other please specify [   ]

Was the equipment acquired via the Computing Service?:   Yes [ ]   No [ ]

Usage *(Please indicate percentage where usage is split)*

Teaching		Research		Administration (inc. word processing)		Other	
√	%	√	%	√	%	√	%
[ ]	[ ]	[ ]	[ ]	[ ]	[ ]	[ ]	[ ]

If other please specify [   ]

Figure 12.2   (b) Revised layout of questionnaire (part)

to be representative of the user population as a whole so as to ensure valid results in any analysis of the evaluation. Two criteria are of primary importance: the *number* of people to be tested, and their *characteristics*.

12.4.1 Numbers

In undertaking evaluation work, the first requirement is to determine the number of subjects needed to obtain reliable evaluation results, bearing in mind that a secondary objective is to minimize the cost of evaluation by using the minimum number of subjects. From these conflicting requirements it follows that there is a strong incentive to use a well-structured experimental model (see Sections 12.6 and 12.7) which allows valid analysis to be carried out using the absolute minimum number of subjects. In practice, the required numbers for any evaluation are generally determined by factors which are unknown beforehand: the *variability of the population's response*, which determines the general spread of the distribution of results obtained, and the *size of the differences to be detected*, which determines how visible differences will be when superimposed upon the overall distribution of subjects results. Without some preliminary knowledge of these factors, any initial choice of subject numbers can only be based upon the numbers required to obtained balanced analysable data: however, the design can subsequently be *replicated* for further groups of subjects if it transpires that sufficiently sensitive results cannot be obtained using a single group.

However, it should be noted that the numbers required for valid human-factors evaluation and subsequent statistical analysis can be quite small where substantial performance differences are observed: many experiments are undertaken with a few tens of subjects or less. By contrast, widely reported trials (such as those of drugs) often require many thousands of subjects because (1) the performance differences between the compared drugs are quite small, and (2) the experimenters have no control over secondary variables such as other medication, and thus require large numbers of subjects in order to be able to eliminate these factors from the analysis.

12.4.2 Characteristics

Subjects' characteristics should obviously by chosen to match as closely as possible the characteristics of the final user population. If a system is to be used by a number of non-homogeneous groups with varying needs, a stratified sampling technique can be adopted, where, for example, a 10-per-cent sample of the most important user group is chosen, as compared with only a 1-per-cent sample of the least important group.

User characteristics can be subdivided into two groups: *general differentiating characteristics* and *specific differentiating characteristics.* General characteristics include the following:

- age;
- sensory characteristics;
- responder characteristics;
- cognitive characteristics;
- motivational characteristics;
- education, training and experience.

Specific differentiating characteristics relate to subjects' training and expertise in areas of direct application to the system to be evaluated. These might include:

- specific task experience;
- computer experience;
- keyboard skills.

12.5 Experimental design

The design of formal evaluation can be subdivided into three related aspects: the *choice of experimental tests*, the *design of the experimental procedure*, and the *test sequencing for comparison purposes.* Each of these issues is considered in more detail below.

12.5.1 Choice of tests

The objective in selecting tests to be included within an evaluation experiment is to test *all important conditions* which will be encountered in the real-life use of the system. Thus the test(s) should be representative of the tasks for which the system is used in real life, including appropriate conditions and subtasks. For the test(s) to be realistic, a valid *context* must be simulated: this should include the circumstances and environment in which the system is used. Conflicting with these requirements, however, is a need to minimize the total test time, both for individual subjects (to make experimental trials practicable) and as a whole (implying the use of the minimum possible number of subjects for whom valid results can be obtained).

The initial step is to identify all *variables* which may substantially influence the experimental results. Each of these variables will, in due course, appear in one or more terms of the *statistical model* of the score obtained by each experimental subject (see Section 12.7). It therefore follows that, to minimize the complexity of the experimental design and its subsequent analysis, the evaluator should aim for an experiment with the simplest possible statistical model, that is, the smallest possible number of variables.

Clearly, the ideal would be to have an experiment with only one variable, the variable of interest, since this would produce the simplest possible analysis. Unfortunately this situation is neither realistic nor practicable. In most evaluations of human–computer systems, the real-world use of the system is in an environment where many variables exist (examples are given below); eliminating all these variables, even if it were possible, would produce an experiment which bore little relation to real-life use of the system. Furthermore, many of the commonly encountered variables are so-called *nuisance variables*. These variables (for example, variation between subjects is commonly considered a nuisance variable) are unavoidable, and must be allowed for in the experimental design so that, ideally, they cancel out in the analysis, or, failing this, they can at least be estimated.

Thus, in summary, the objective of the experimental design procedure is to produce a compromise which, on the one hand, presents a valid simulation of the use of the system in its intended real-life environment, and, on the other, uses an experimental design which has an easily interpreted analysis.

The variability of subjects has already been discussed in the previous section, and it should now be apparent that the evaluation design objective should be to select subjects who most closely match the characteristics of the intended user population. The more consistent and homogenous the subject group, the less they will contribute variation to the overall observed experimental results (although it is always the case that significant variation between the subjects should be expected in any experiment). The less the variation due to subjects (an unavoidable nuisance factor) the more visible will be any variation due to the primary variable(s) being measured.

Other examples of nuisance variables, which may or may not be able to be eliminated from an experimental design, include *environmental variables* such as ambient noise, interruption, and ergonomic issues, and *procedural variables*, which are nuisance variables inherent in the experimental procedure. Examples of procedural variables could include *learning effects* which are inherent in the way the test(s) are conducted, and may be difficult or impossible to eliminate. In this case the solution is to use a structured design which at least enables the nuisance variables to be estimated and thereby eliminated from the overall measured variation, leading to greater precision in the estimation of the primary variable(s) being measured.

12.5.2 Design of the experimental procedure

The overall experimental procedure for an evaluation often includes several different individual tests, carried out either in sequence during one session, or over a number of sessions spread over days or weeks. If more than one test is necessary, sequence limitations may be implicit for performing the tasks; for example, an experiment on computer interaction might include a test of the logon procedure, which would normally be expected to be carried out before any other function. Unfortunately, having a fixed sequence of tests may in itself introduce bias into the evaluation, and so should normally be avoided as far as possible.

Even if the evaluation consists of only a single test, it will still normally require a *prologue*, which introduces the subject to the experimental world, and an *epilogue*, which provides for debriefing and subjective comment by the subject at the end of the test.

12.5.3 Test sequencing

The general aim in arranging test sequencing for multiple-test experiments is to produce an experimental design which is simple and unbiased; unfortunately, these requirements may conflict! As is shown by the illustrative example designs in the next sections, the simplest and most 'obvious' designs have substantial biases in them which would interfere with their subsequent analysis. More complex designs are therefore often needed to eliminate these biases and allow a valid analysis.

Four general techniques are used in experimental design. They are:

- balancing;
- replication;
- randomization;
- blocking.

These techniques are introduced and illustrated in the examples of the following section, using a simple experiment concerned with comparing cursor positioning times on a VDU using a mouse and cursor keys. (A much more substantial and realistic treatment of this problem is reported in a widely cited paper by Card *et al.*, (1978).

12.6 Example experimental design

The problem, though simplified for the purposes of illustration, is a real-world issue which has been tackled in the past with the aim of providing objective data as to the relative merits of a variety of pointing devices. Card *et al.* (1978) provided much of the formal justification for the use of the mouse as a pointing device in Xerox workstation products, and subsequently it has been almost universally adopted.

12.6.1 Problem definition

In this simplified version of the problem, it is desired to compare the speed of cursor positioning using a mouse with cursor positioning using conventional cursor keys. The results of this comparison might be useful, for example, in specifying the hardware and associated text-editing software which should be provided as part of a word processor.

In the jargon of experimental psychology, the two different methods of accomplishing cursor movements are known as *treatments*, and represent the variable whose effect is of primary interest in the experiment.

12.6.2 Initial solution attempts

As a first guess, a proposed solution to this problem might be to measure the cumulative time to position the cursor for a number of cursor-positioning exercises using each of the two 'treatments' or methods. However, if different samples displays were used to define the required positioning operations for the two different treatments then it would not be possible to ascertain from the results whether any differences observed were due to genuine differences between the treatments (the variable of interest) or to differences between the displays (a nuisance variable). (These displays will hereafter be referred to as 'texts' for brevity, although they might in practice be graphically based.) To avoid this problem, the same text must be used for each treatment, to eliminate the nuisance variable. For a single subject, this might lead to the data of Figure 12.3, where A represents the positioning time required using cursor keys, and B the time required using a mouse.

At first sight, the data of Figure 12.3 appears to suggest that the pointing function is accomplished more speedily using the mouse than the cursor keys: however, further reflection reveals that the same observed effect might occur if the subject in some way 'learnt' about the cursor positioning task during the first treatment, and applied this knowledge to increase his performance in the second treatment. A

Treatment	Time (seconds)
A	45
B	28

Figure 12.3 First solution attempt—single subject

Subject	Treatment	Time (seconds)
1	A	40
2	B	30

Figure 12.4 Second solution attempt—two subjects

plausible reason for suspecting this effect would be that the subject might remember the content of the (single) text, and therefore would be able to anticipate required positioning operations on the second treatment, which is carried out after the first. Thus, elimination of the nuisance variable initially identified (variation due to different texts) is accomplished at the expense of introducing an alternative nuisance variable (the learning effect).

An alternative approach, aimed at eliminating the learning effect, would be to use separate subjects for the two treatments, as illustrated in Figure 12.4.

Unfortunately, in this case it is not possible to determine whether the differences in measured times arise from the treatments or from differences between the performance of the two subjects (or a combination of the two). Thus this second solution attempt is also unsatisfactory because a further nuisance variable (the subject) prevents estimation of any difference between the treatments.

However, if the first and second solution attempts are combined together in a design which uses four subjects (Figure 12.5) it becomes possible to make an independent estimate of the effects of the two treatments.

In this case, the following differences can be quantified:

Average of A's   39
Average of B's   31
Average difference between A's and B's   8
Average difference between subjects for same treatment   2

Since the difference between treatments (A's and B's) is substantially greater than the difference between subjects for the same treatment, it is reasonable to conclude that pointing using treatment B (the mouse) is faster than using treatment A (the cursor keys). The conclusion relies upon the fact that the difference between treatments is much larger than the difference between subjects for the same treatment: if the differences were similar or reversed it would not be possible to draw this conclusion.

Where results are as clear-cut as this, there may be no real need for more detailed statistical analysis, but nevertheless a valid design and associated statistical model are required whether or not a full statistical analysis is carried out, to ensure that estimates can be made free from

Subject	Treatment	Time (seconds)
1	A	40
2	B	30
3	A	38
4	B	32

Figure 12.5 Third solution attempt

nuisance variables. The purpose of the statistical analysis is simply to define numerically the probability that the observed result might be obtained by chance, rather than due to genuine differences between the treatments. Thus, for example, a result significant at the 5-per-cent level simply states that there is 1 chance in 20 of this result being obtained when there is in fact no significant difference between the treatments. (5-per-cent significance is in fact rather weak evidence: significance at the 1-per-cent level would typically be sought to provide strong support for a significant difference between treatments.)

An important conclusion to be drawn from comparison between these first three solution attempts is that *a single observation on each treatment is not sufficient to allow an independent assessment of variability*. The validity of the analysis in the third solution attempt rests on the fact that several different averages can be computed and compared, and, in the case of a fuller statistical analysis, estimates of variance (spread) associated with each of these averages can also be made.

Statistical significance is concerned only with the reliability of the results obtained: whether any observed difference between treatments is of practical significance is a completely different and independent question. From a practical point of view, it might be surmised from Figure 12.5 that pointing using the mouse was around 20 per cent faster than using the cursor keys. The decision as to whether this 20-per-cent speed improvement was important in practice would depend also upon other factors such as the additional cost of hardware and software to support the mouse (as compared with cursor keys only), and user attitudes towards the use of the mouse for pointing operations.

12.6.3 Replication of the experimental design

As can be seen, for gross difference effects, an analysis with only four subjects may yield sufficient information. However, more commonly the variations between treatments are much less pronounced than in these first examples, and it is under these conditions that statistical estimation of the probability of significant differences can be useful, since clearly, if differences are not statistically significant, then they may readily occur by chance. Detailed discussion of the required statistical models and analysis for the examples above is given in Section 12.7, and corresponding example calculations based upon the data quoted appear in Appendix 1.

If the observed differences are found through statistical analysis not to be significant, this does not necessarily mean that no differences exist between the treatments: it may be simply that the experiment as performed was insufficiently sensitive to reveal a rather small difference. Then the sensitivity of the experiment can be increased by *replicating* the basic design (e.g. of Figure 12.5) an appropriate number of times. For example, if the data of Figure 12.5 were such as to show an average difference between treatments of only 3 seconds (instead of 8), this result would not show a statistically significant difference, but if the sensitivity of the experiment were increased by replication so that a total of 6 subjects (instead of 2) tested each of the treatments A and B (a total of 12 subjects instead of 4), and the average difference between treatments was shown still to be 3 seconds with this larger number of subjects, then the result would be much more likely to be significant.

The principle is the same as in tossing coins; if only two coins are tossed then the chance of obtaining 2 heads is quite high, 25 per cent; but if a large number of coins were tossed then the chance of obtaining all heads would be very low. Thus obtaining 2 heads from 2 coin tosses is not a significant finding, whereas obtaining 10 from 10 tosses occurs only with a probability of $(\frac{1}{2})^{10}$ or roughly 0.1 per cent, and so is significant at the 0.1-per-cent level.

Once replication is introduced into the design, a further possible problem may arise: how should the sequence of 12 subjects be ordered in the experiment? Some sequences are clearly undesirable since they may introduce bias into the experiment. For example, it would be a mistake to sequence the 6 subjects using treatment A first and the 6 subjects using treatment B afterwards, even though this might actually simplify the practical organization of the experiment. If the tests on the 6 treatment A subjects were carried out early in the day under natural light, but the tests on the 6 treatment B subjects occurred late in the day under artificial light, a further nuisance variable, not allowed for in the experimental model, could be inadvertently introduced.

In general this type of problem is minimized by *balancing* the experiment wherever possible to avoid bias. In this case, balancing is achieved by alternating the subject sequence between treatments A and B, with the objective that any unforeseen nuisance variable which appears at any time in the experiment will have a high chance of affecting A and B equally (and therefore cancelling out in the subsequent analysis) with this particular sequencing.

However the subjects have been selected, it is possible that some unforeseen subject characteristic may also have the potential to introduce a further inadvertent nuisance variable. As an extreme example, it would obviously be unwise to allocate all male subjects to treatment A and all female subjects to treatment B, in case some unforeseen gender difference in performance affected the results obtained. To minimize this possibility, the allocation of subjects is often *randomized*. In this case, the allocation of subjects to treatments and the allocation of subject sequence in the experiment could both be random. Randomization is generally performed either by some unbiased method of selection (for example, names out of a hat) or by the use of published random-number tables, which are commonly found in textbooks on statistics (e.g. Chatfield, 1983).

12.6.4 Between-subjects vs. within-subjects designs

The principal unavoidable nuisance variable in the design above is the variation between subjects: typically this variation may be quite large, and with a design of the type shown in Figure 12.5 any differences which may exist between the treatments can often be masked by subject variation. In the jargon of experimental psychology, the design is known as a *between-subjects* design, because comparisons between the different treatments are made between different subjects. Each test result for an individual subject therefore includes not only a component due to the treatment but also an (unwanted) component due to the subject himself or herself (see Section 12.7).

An alternative approach is to use a *within-subject* design: here the aim is that the comparison between treatments is made within subjects (i.e., each subject tests every treatment, and comparisons are then made between the subject's scores for each treatment). This approach has two advantages. First, each subject acts as his own control, leading to increased precision in the subsequent analysis. Second, the design is more efficient, since each subject tests all treatments instead of only one. For a fixed number of subjects, S, and treatments, T, the design produces $S \times T$ individual test results, whereas the previous design produced only S individual test results. (Of course, the experimental procedure for each individual subject also takes T times as long, since each subject carried out T tests instead of 1.)

The within-subjects design also has a major disadvantage, however. Because each subject tests every treatment, there is a very much greater danger of introducing transfer effects (learning effects) into the experiment as a further nuisance variable. This problem is reconsidered below, after a review of the basic within-subjects design presented in Figure 12.6.

In the design of Figure 12.6, the subjects are described as a *blocking factor*, because each row of the design contains results obtained for a

	Period 1	Period 2	
	Treatment		Subject
Subject	A	B	average
1	40	28	34
2	45	30	37.5
3	38	27	32.5
4	36	32	34
Treatment average	39.75	29.25	**34.5** Overall average

Figure 12.6 Fourth solution attempt

single subject 'block'. (This would also be true if there were more than two treatments.) As is shown, with this design it is possible to calculate not only averages for each treatment, but also separate and independent averages for each subject. In the corresponding statistical analysis it would therefore be possible to make estimates not only of the effects of the different treatments, but also the effects of the different subjects, leading to greater precision in both estimates. With this design, randomization would be introduced by randomly allocating subjects to blocks.

However, as should be obvious from the figure, because of the similarity of the tasks for treatments A and B it is probable that subjects' experience gained during period 1 (treatment A) of the test will enhance their performance during period 2 (treatment B). This 'nuisance' learning effect is therefore likely to elevate scores in period 2. Unfortunately, with this design it is not possible to distinguish genuine differences between A and B from differences due to the learning effect, rendering the design invalid.

12.6.5 Final solution attempt

The solution to this problem is to perform a further *balancing* operation, by reversing A and B for alternate subjects, as shown in Figure 12.7. This produces a highly structured design for which it is possible to make independent estimates not only of the effects of the different treatments and subjects, but also of the average scores in the two periods. Since these averages are made up of equal numbers of tests conducted using the A and B treatments, statistical analysis can now be applied to show whether the differences in scores between periods are

Subject	Period 1	Period 2	Subject average
1	A 41	B 27	34
2	B 31	A 44	37.5
3	A 39	B 26	32.5
4	B 33	A 35	34

Treatment averages: **34.5**   **Overall**
A — 39.75   B — 29.25   **average**

Period averages:
1 — 36   2 — 33

Figure 12.7   Final solution attempt

significant, and, if so, allowance can be made for this in the determination of the effects of the two treatments. For this design, the subjects are a blocking factor on the rows, while the periods are a blocking factor on the columns. Again, randomization is performed by randomly allocating subjects to blocks.

(The design of Figure 12.7 is in fact a double replicate of a well-known and widely used special-case design known as a *Latin-squares* design. The basic Latin square consists of the design for subjects 1 and 2 only (3 and 4 are the replication). The term is used to describe a design in which the number of subjects is equal to the number of treatments, which in turn is equal to the number of periods. With such a design, a square grid can always be set up in which one variable forms a blocking factor on the rows and the second a blocking factor on the columns, while the third can also be independently estimated, . leading to a sensitive experiment with the smallest possible number of subjects. The basic design can then be replicated horizontally and/or vertically.)

Although the design of Figure 12.7 can detect symmetric learning effects, it would also be possible to have an asymmetric learning effect, where, for example, the learning effect due to using treatment A was very much greater than the learning effect due to treatment B. Such an effect might arise, for example, in an experiment where one treatment to which the subjects were exposed promoted much more rapid learning about the underlying functionality of the system than another. In this case, tests carried out subsequently using the other treatment might generate elevated scores as a result of the increased underlying knowledge about the system which the subject had gained during the first test, but the effect would not be balanced by a similar one where the treatments were reversed in order. This type of effect is known by statisticians as a *carryover* effect, and, although it can be estimated and allowed for, is beyond the scope of this chapter.

Thus, in conclusion, it can be seen that the 'within-subjects' design can improve precision and increase the efficiency of an evaluation by using a randomized block experiment, but that there is an increased risk of transfer or carryover effects with this type of design, and that careful analysis is therefore needed subsequently to check for these effects.

12.7 Statistical models and evaluation

In Section 12.6 the design of a structured evaluation experiment was examined, to illustrate some of the pitfalls of experimental design and some of the most common problems which must be overcome to make a valid analysis possible. The emphasis was on explaining these problems in practical terms. In this section, the mathematical models corresponding to two of the example experimental designs are introduced, with the aim of showing how the terms in the models relate directly to the practical issues already discussed, and to the methods of statistical analysis subsequently employed (and illustrated in Appendix 1).

12.7.1 Experimental models

For the experimental design presented in Figure 12.5, each subject's score can be modelled by the following equation:

$$x_{ij} = \mu + t_i + \varepsilon_{ij} \qquad (i = A, B; j = 1, \ldots, 4)$$

where
x_{ij} = observation on subject j and treatment i
μ = overall average
t_i = effect of the ith treatment
ε_{ij} = random error

Then the grand mean of all observations x_{ij}, is an estimate of μ and is given by:

$$\sum_{i,j} \frac{x_{ij}}{4} = \bar{x} = 35$$

Similarly, the mean of all observations on the ith treatment, less the grand mean, is an estimate of t_i:

$$\bar{t}_i = \sum_j \frac{x_{ij}}{2} - \bar{x} \qquad (\text{often written as } \bar{t}_i = \bar{x}_i - \bar{x})$$

Evaluating this expression shows that t_A is 4 and t_B is -4. (Note that in the expression for the subject's score, the effect of the treatment is expressed as an offset to the grand mean: alternative representations are also possible.)

For the Latin-squares experimental design shown in figure 12.7, some additional variables are allowed for and thus the following equation represents the design:

$$x_{ijk} = \mu + t_i + s_j + p_k + \varepsilon_{ijk} \qquad (i = A, B; j = 1, \ldots, 4; k = 1, 2)$$

where

x_{ijk} = observation on subject j with treatment i in period k

μ = overall average

t_i = effect of the ith treatment

s_j = effect of the jth subject (row block)

p_k = effect of the kth period (column block)

ε_{ijk} = random error

Then the grand mean of all observations x_{ijk} is an estimate of μ, and is given by:

$$\bar{x} = \sum_{i,j,k} \frac{x_{ijk}}{8} = 34.5$$

Similarly, the mean of all observations on the ith treatment, less the grand mean, is an estimate of t_i:

$$\bar{t}_i = \sum_{j,k} \frac{x_{ijk}}{4} - \bar{x}$$

and similar expressions can be derived as estimates of s_j and p_k.

12.7.2 Rival hypotheses

The aim of statistical analysis in comparative experiments such as those described above is to estimate the probability that differences between treatments are due to chance. If this probability is low enough then the result is judged significant at that level. Thus significance at the 5-per-cent (1-per-cent) level indicates that there is only 5 (1) chance in 100 that the result obtained is due to chance.

This concept leads to the postulation of two hypotheses. The *null hypothesis* (H_0) is that there is no difference between the treatments, or mathematically:

$$H_0 : \text{all } t_i = 0$$

The *alternative hypothesis* (H_1) is that there are indeed differences between two or more treatments, or, mathematically,

$$H_1 : \text{some } t_i \neq 0$$

Formally, the null hypothesis is then assumed to be true, and evidence is sought against it in the experimental data. If sufficiently strong evidence is found, then H_0 is rejected and H_1 accepted. Practically, it is often the case that the experimenter will be hoping to prove the alternative hypothesis true (for example where an experiment compares a previous and a new design), but this can be surmized only by showing strong evidence that the null hypothesis is false.

12.7.3 Statistical analysis

A variety of different methods can be used to analyse the data. The chosen method depends primarily on the number of variables in the experimental model, the number of treatments, and the assumptions which can be made about the nature of the data. If the data can be assumed to be *random samples* from a *normal distribution* then the simplest case is where there is only a single variable and only two treatments (as in Figure 12.5). In this case, the *t-test* is generally used. This is derived directly from the standard method used to estimate significance of a deviation from the mean in a normal distribution, but is intended for use where the number of samples is small (less than about 25). Where there are more than two treatments, an *analysis of variance (ANOVA)*, followed by an *F-test*, can be used to determine whether significant differences between treatments are present in the data (the ANOVA also works for two treatments, but is more complex than the *t*-test). The ANOVA method can also be extended to analyse models which contain more than two variables: for *n* variables, an *n*-way analysis of variance can be carried out.

The ANOVA and *F*-test only test the null hypothesis: if there is evidence against the null hypothesis, further tests are then required to establish exactly where the significant differences lie. The simplest approach is to use a *multiple t-test*. This is simply a variation on the standard *t*-test, which makes allowance for the fact that in the case of several, rather than two, treatments, the probability of at least one pairwise comparison between treatments yielding a spurious significant difference is increased. A more rigorous approach is to use Tukey's test (Wetherill, 1981). Examples of how all these techniques (with the exception of Tukey's test) are applied to the data introduced earlier in this chapter will be found in Appendix 1.

All the methods described above are valid only where the data can be assumed to be random samples from a normal distribution. However, these assumptions are often not true for common types of data encountered in HCI evaluation. Two other cases are commonly encountered.

The first is where evaluation data includes *frequency* measurements of some sort; for example, how many subjects fall into each of several categories, giving a *Poisson* distribution. This type of data can obviously not have values less than zero, has some positive mean, and dies away towards zero again at the top of the distribution. Separate sets of tests for analysing this type of data are available.

The second is where questionnaires or interviews produce subjective data such as ranking measurements, where it cannot be assumed that the data values are linearly distributed on a scale. In this case a variety of non-parametric analysis methods such as the *Mann–Whitney* and *Wilcoxon tests* (Gibbons, 1971) can be used. These tests make a few assumptions about the data, but do not require data to conform to specific distributional forms.

12.7.4 Statistical vs practical significance

Statistical and practical significance are two entirely different things. The only purpose of statistical analysis in experimental evaluation is to allow estimation of the probability that substantive differences exist between different treatments. A non-significant difference determined from an experiment is not necessarily the same thing as no difference: it simply means that the experiment has not been sensitive enough to allow the difference between treatments (which always exists) to be observed.

More, importantly, a significant difference is not necessarily the same thing as an *interesting* difference. Ultimately, the experimenter must decide what constitutes an 'interesting' difference and this depends entirely on the nature of the data being analysed and its application. For example, in the context of an HCI evaluation a 10-per-cent difference between two alternative designs may be found to be statistically significant in a fairly small experiment, but 10 per cent might not be enough to justify the extra cost of the 'better' design. Conversely, in a series of experiments to measure fuel consumption on jet aeroplanes, an improvement of 0.1 per cent might well be considered enough to justify the modification to the engine design which produced it, because of the very large cost of aviation fuel for the plane over its working lifetime. Of course, to determine that the 0.1-per-cent improvement was statistically significant would require a great deal of data, since the difference was so small.

12.8 Conclusions

In this chapter a review of different methods of evaluation has been provided, emphasizing the flexible approach which is required to allow evaluation to be applied efficiently and cheaply at different stages of the design cycle. The basic methodology of the more formal aspects of subjective and objective evaluation lies in experimental psychology. An introduction to experimental design methods has been presented, based upon a hypothetical but fairly typical HCI evaluation example, with the intention of illustrating the main factors which should be taken into account in evaluation, regardless of how formally the evaluation is subsequently analysed. Where a formal statistical analysis is appropriate, the models and methods used are introduced at the end of the chapter.

References

Bailey, R. W. (1982) *Human Performance Engineering: a Guide for System Designers*, Prentice-Hall, Englewood Cliffs, NJ, 509–594.

Baker, R. G., A. D. Lambourne and G. Rowston (1983) *Handbook for Television Subtitlers*, (revised edn), published jointly by IBA, Oracle Teletext Ltd and Southampton University.

BBC/IBA/BREMA (1976) *Broadcast Teletext Specification*, Winchester.

Card, S. K., W. K. English and B. J. Burr (1978) 'Evaluation of mouse, rate-controlled isometric joystick, step keys and text keys for text selection on a CRT', *Ergonomics*, **21** 601–613.

Card, S K., T. P. Moran and A. Newell (1983) *The Psychology of Human-Computer Interaction*, Lawrence Erlbaum Associates, Hillsdale, NJ.

Chapanis, A. (1959) *Research Techniques in Human Engineering*, Johns Hopkins Press, Baltimore.

Chatfield, C. (1983) *Statistics for Technology*, 3rd edn, Chapman & Hall, London, 203–287.

Gibbons, J. D. (1971) *Non-Parametric Statistical Inference*, McGraw-Hill, New York.

Payne, S. J. and T. R. G. Green (1983) 'The user's perception of the interaction language: a two-level model', *Proceedings CHI '83, Human Factors in Computing Systems*, ACM, New York, 202–206.

Roethlisberger, F. J. and W. J. Dickson (1939) *Management and the Worker—an Account of a Research Program Conducted by the Western Electric Company, Hawthorne Works, Chicago*, Harvard University Press, Cambridge, Mass.

Wetherill, G. B. (1981) *Intermediate Statistical Methods*, Chapman & Hall, London.

13 Evaluation case study I: Adaptive Intelligent Dialogues

PETER BOUCHERAT

13.1 Introduction

The Alvey Adaptive Intelligent Dialogues (AID) project was a collaborative project between Standard Telecommunications Laboratories, British Telecom Research Centre, Data Logic Ltd, and the Universities of Essex, Strathclyde and Hull. Although the project, by its very nature, concentrated on adaptive features in the field of human–computer interaction it also illustrated a variety of aspects of evaluation: the iterative design–build–evaluate cycle, formative and summative evaluation, and the evaluation of component parts of a human–computer interface system as well as the system as a whole. In addition, adaptation, with its fundamental concern with the differences between users and users' tasks, is an admirable vehicle for the study of the evaluation of user-centred systems.

Adaptation is defined as the changing, or modification, of some feature of a system, or application, to suit new conditions or needs. An adaptive system is a system which changes its interface in some way in response to certain user needs or characteristics. The theory is that an adaptive interface should be more acceptable to the individual user than a similar static system, in that it should be easier and/or faster to use and consequently the system should be accessible to a wider spectrum of potential users. An adaptive system should ideally adapt not just to the needs of a variety of users but also to the changing needs of an individual over time.

13.1.1 Background

In the early 1980s many saw adaptation as desirable. Edmonds (1982) suggested that 'Our knowledge about human behaviour is inadequate to portray correctly a typical user, particularly one whose needs change over time.' He proposed that an adaptive interface would solve this problem as the interface would change with time to suit the user's needs. Also, an adaptive system would be more suitable for a wider range of users since it could adapt to variations in users' experience (Edmonds, 1982; Larson, 1982; James, 1980), resulting in improved user performance, reduced errors, increased speed of task completion, and decreased time taken to learn how to use the system. It was also postulated that an adaptive system might be more satisfying to use since it might given the user the impression of being in control (Shneiderman, 1980).

Despite the apparent attractions of adaptation it was realized that there were also potential disadvantages to building adaptation into a system, the most obvious being the additional complexity of an adaptive system (Eason and Damodaran, 1979). The overheads required to monitor the interaction and modify this where necessary might not be compensated for by the increased ease of use. Another possible disadvantage is the potential lack of predictability of the system (Gaines and Shaw, 1983; Innocent, 1982). Traditionally, the emphasis in good systems design is on consistency, but the whole point about adaptive systems is that the interface changes to match some perceived need of the user. The interface response is not consistent as it is in a static system, but is likely to change even when the user has apparently made an identical response to the one that was made previously. Although an adaptive system may give the user a feeling of control it is also possible that the opposite may occur (Greenberg 1984). The adaptive interface necessarily has control over some aspect of the interface, but the user may prefer to retain control.

It was clear that adaptation was potentially an extremely useful property of a system but also that many unresolved problems existed. The aim of the AID project was to help resolve some of these problems.

13.2 The Adaptive Intelligent Dialogue Project

The Adaptive Intelligent Dialogue Project was divided into three phases. The first of these was to build and evaluate an adaptive front-end to the Telecom Gold electronic-mail system; the second concentrated on a study of the nature of adaptation together with the building of mini-exemplars to illustrate various aspects of adaptation; and finally, in the third phase, a multiauthor document preparation system was taken as the example vehicle. Various adaptive interface features which were considered to be of use in such an environment were built and evaluated. The underlying theme throughout the project was to address the special problems of evaluating adaptive user interfaces.

Browne *et al.* (1987) identified four requirements of an adaptive system. These were: an *objective*, a means of *identifying user characteristics*, a means of *reasoning about those characteristics*, and *flexible interfacing mechanisms* that support the user interface changes as recommended by the user model. The adaptive system must monitor the user interaction to provide the data about user characteristics with which the user modelling component reasons. Since adaptation depends upon differences in user characteristics and/or behaviour it is obviously of interest to know the dimensions along which a system might adapt. The theory upon which the adaptation is based will determine the data that has to be captured.

All adaptive systems are built on the basis of a theory regarding how human–computer interaction might be improved (Browne *et al.*, 1987). The theory may be simple or complex. A simple theory might propose, for example, that users can be categorized along a pre-specified dimension, e.g., 'novice', 'intermediate' and 'expert' and on the basis of this category error messages might be provided that increase an individual's task completion rate. Although the theory is simple the system would need to contain rules or some other principled way in which the data from the user interaction was categorized as being typical of a 'novice' 'intermediate' or 'expert' user and these rules might need to be quite complex even for a simple system. A more complicated theory might propose that the user's conceptual understanding of a system could be modelled such that the interface could introduce system concepts in a pre-defined order that would speed the user's learning of the system.

13.3 An adaptive interface to Telecom Gold

The first adaptive system to be built and evaluated in the AID project was an interface to an existing electronic-mail system. The design of the exemplar represented a practical attempt to provide an adaptive front-end to an existing application, Telecom Gold. The exemplar functioned by translating the user's requests into commands valid for the application, and translating the responses from the application into a form suitable for the particular user (Boucherat and Hockley, 1986).

As mentioned in previous chapters, the system ran on a Sun workstation, and was composed of four separate but communicating UNIX processes (Figure 13.1). Overall control of the system resided in a dialogue controller which ran under Rapid/USE (Wasserman and Shewmake, 1984). This process switched control between the various component processes, and supported the delivery dialogue. The user model was written in Prolog and POP11, and ran under Poplog (Hardy, 1984). The application expert also ran under Poplog, and was written in

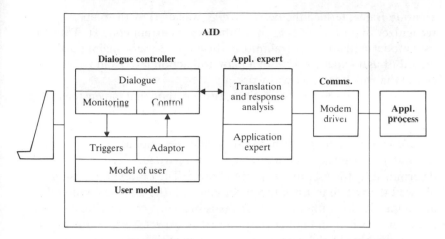

Figure 13.1   System architecture

POP11. The communication process linked the system to Telecom Gold via a modem, and was written in C.

13.3.1 Functioning of the system

On the basis of its knowledge of the application domain, and of likely consequences of user actions, the system inferred whether the user was having difficulties or not, and triggered adaptation as a result. If the system inferred that the user was performing well, the level of guidance given by the system was reduced. If the system inferred that the user was having difficulties, the level of guidance increased. Other dimensions of adaptation allowed the user to return to a task that he had not yet completed, and to use commands from UNIX Mail, an alternative mail system.

Knowledge about the user was stored in the user model, which tracked the user's task, and inferred his level of skill with that task, as represented by a count of the number of errors and help requests for that task. The user model contained a database of sequences of actions which together could be used to complete a task. Each of these sequences of actions was termed a plan. Individual users were represented as a collection of *frames*. *General frames* stored user-specified information, such as whether they had used mail systems before, whether they found the system too verbose, etc. *plan frames* stored a record of usage of a particular plan, and plan errors, determined as departures from sequence of actions stored in the plan recognizer's database. *Action frames* stored information on the use of particular actions, broken down into frequency of errors and help requests. Action errors were identified from the application expert's knowledge of legitimate commands within the application domain. A separate frame, termed the *output frame*, was used by the plan recognizer to post its assessment of the user's current context. Thus the user model contained general information about users, maintained a record of user expertise at both a plan and action level, and tracked the context in which the user was working.

The system adapted to users along three orthogonal dimensions. The *guidance* dimension was the primary dimension of adaption. For every task, there were six levels of guidance available. The levels differed in the amount of feedback given to users, and the amount of prompting the system gave. The level of guidance for a particular task was determined by the user model output frame. The *context* dimension allowed the system to track the particular task the user was undertaking and compare this with known user tasks or plans. If at any time it noted a user entry which did not correspond to an expected action (as stored in its database of valid user plans), a change in the user's task was logged. When the user finished his next task, the system would offer him the opportunity to return to what he was doing previously. Finally, the system adapted according to the user's familiarity with UNIX Mail. If the user was familiar with UNIX, as noted from an introductory logon questionnaire, the system would attempt to parse UNIX commands if they had a logical equivalent in the application.

These three dimensions were selected because they operate at a syntactic level, which reduced implementation problems. Totterdell and Cooper (1986) contains a fuller description of the operation of the system, together with examples of its operation.

13.3.2 Adaptive systems and evaluation

Static systems may be effectively evaluated by defining a dimension of performance, and then measuring this dimension under controlled conditions. Moran (1981) gives as examples:

- the range of tasks which may be undertaken on a system;
- the time taken to learn a number of tasks;
- the time taken to perform a set task;
- the number and nature of errors;
- the quality of the user's output;
- the 'robustness' of a user's performance;
- user acceptability.

In the case of adaptive systems, such measures are still valid. However, given that adaptive systems are a recent innovation, a measure of the performance of the processes supporting adaptation is also necessary. In this research the overall performance of the system was not the main interest. Instead, it was of interest to determine what is the most appropriate way of building adaptation into systems. In general, all adaptive systems make inferences to track information about the user, and then use these to perform some internal change. In addition to measures of overall performance, there are therefore two additional ways in which an adaptive system may be evaluated; these investigate its collection of information about the user, and the suitability of the changes made in response.

The first step was to assess whether the collection of information about the user was simply a logging process (i.e., was totally deterministic), or whether any degree of inference took place. Clearly, an experimental evaluation would be inappropriate in the case of a simple logging process. In the case of the system described here, user actions were logged and compared with a fixed representation of likely sequences of actions and tasks. Deviations from the system's expectations, in combination with a log of simple action errors derived from the application expert, were then taken as evidence of a lack of user expertise. The system therefore made inferences about users in the form of whether they were having difficulty or not. It was therefore decided to measure the correctness of these inferences of user difficulty. This was achieved by comparing system inferences of user difficulties directly with users' own statements of their difficulties. The assessment metrics were the percentage of user difficulties successfully inferred by the system, and the number of false positive inferences of difficulties.

The adaptations made by the exemplar embody a theory, albeit a crude one, of human performance. This theory was that experienced users needed little guidance, and were actively hindered by too much, while inexperienced users needed more guidance and support. Adaptations in the exemplar were therefore made on the basis of a rolling average of errors made for the task concerned. If an error had been made recently for the task fragment, the level of guidance was increased. If no errors were made, the rolling average decreased until it was below a threshold, when an adaptation to decrease guidance was made. To assess whether an adaptation had taken place it was therefore necessary to compare the levels called on the last occasion on which the command was used. Expert ratings were used to assess the value of adaptations, to avoid the need for directly questioning the user, as it was felt that this would draw the attention of the subject to the system's adaptivity rather than to the task in hand. Each adaptation was rated as either useful or not useful, depending on the user's declared or apparent difficulties and what the user was trying to do.

While an adaptive system may make correct inferences about users, and produce suitable adaptations based on these inferences, this is clearly not sufficient. The adaptation produced may result in a trivial increase in satisfaction and performance when considering the overhead incurred in extra processing and system development time. Alternatively, users might genuinely dislike adaptive systems, preferring something static and predictable. Therefore, in common with the evaluation of system adaptation, the overall performance of the system must be evaluated. The basic requirements for this are an experimental task, a control and some definition of what is meant by performance.

Given that the exemplar is a system for processing letters, some type of office activity was the most logical task. It was decided that subjects would play the role of a manager in a company, and would have as a task the job of processing a set number of letters. By adjusting the contents of the letters it was possible to ensure that users covered a wide range of the system's commands.

A control was necessary as a comparison, so that regardless of what it was decided to measure, some reference was available with respect to which it would be possible to interpret the results. The adaptive system was therefore modified to allow the adaptive features to be switched off, and the system, in this condition, was used as the control.

There are many different levels at which the overall performance can be addressed, ranging from the lowest syntactic level (inter-character timings), to the highest task level (business cost effectiveness). It is important that any evaluation should aim to cover a spread of these different levels, because without information from lower levels, the causes for differences in performance at the highest levels may be impossible to determine. (The higher the level, the greater the value of the measure; the use of measures at lower levels is primarily to aid the interpretation of measures at higher levels.) It was decided to concentrate on three levels of measurement, as follows.

Command entry rate

This was a low-level measure of performance, which took no account of the accuracy or value of user entries. It was simply a measure of the quantity of input that the user achieved.

Task completion rate

In this higher-level measure of performance, task completion was taken to mean any discrete, categorizable success in the application domain. Some examples are reading, writing, posting, deleting and forwarding letters, and creating a new folder.

Goal achievement rate

A still higher level of measurement, this was a measure of the user's effectiveness in terms of the task he or she had been set. For the exemplar system this was defined as letter-processing rate.

In addition to testing the performance of the system–user combination, a measure of users' opinions was desirable. There is no point in producing powerful systems if they are not pleasant to use. A

two-section questionnaire was therefore devised. The first section
assessed the user's opinions of the ease of use of the system on a variety
of functions. The second part of the questionnaire assessed whether the
user liked the system or not. In this part of the questionnaire, the user
selected from a list of adjectives those they thought applicable to the
system. An equal number of positive and negative descriptions were in
the list, and they varied in the kinds of qualities they assessed. By this
spread of descriptions it was hoped that every user would be able to find
at least some that seemed to apply to the system. From the ratio of
positive to negative comments an overall measure of the perceived
quality of the system was produced.

13.3.3 Experimental design and procedure

The experiment was designed to allow the comparison of the adaptive
exemplar with adaptation turned on with a control of the same system
with all adaptations turned off, and fixed at the default level of
guidance. There were 9 subjects. Subjects were of mixed level of
experience with computers. 6 were experienced with computers, and 3
naive. Subjects used either the adaptive or non-adaptive system. 6
subjects used the adaptive condition while 3 used the non-adaptive
condition, balanced by previous experience across the conditions.

Each subject used the system for three sessions, performing a different
scenario in each session. The sessions were separated by three days, and
the order of scenario was randomized for each subject. Each session
lasted for half an hour, timed from the first user entry after receiving the
main system prompt. The subject's task during the session was to
answer nine letters contained in their in-tray. Each session involved
working on a different set of nine letters. Answering the letters involved
performing a range of supporting tasks such as filing, deleting,
forwarding, etc. At the start of each session, subjects were given a
one-page guide to the system, a description of their task, and a list of
users to which mail could be sent. Subjects were allowed to read the
instructions until they were ready to start, and were asked to provide a
running commentary to their actions. The experimenter was permitted
to answer simple operational questions during the session, such as how
to move the cursor, or where various keys on the keyboard were. If the
subject's commentary dried up, they were prompted to continue with
the question 'What are you doing now?'.

On completion of a session the subjects were replayed a video of their
session without their commentary. They were asked to explain, on every
occasion on which they typed something, what they were trying to
achieve, and what problems they were having. Finally, subjects
completed the two-part questionnaire. A log was kept of both system
and user activity. This consisted of a time-stamped record of changes in
the user model and application expert, a time-stamped log of

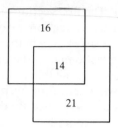

Number of difficulties stated by users

Figure 13.2 System inferences and user statements of difficulty

keystrokes, a time-stamped log of carriage returns and a recording of the screen, with the subject's commentary on one audio channel and subsequent debriefing on the other.

13.3.4 Results

A random sample of 180 user entries which could have resulted in adaptations was taken from the 24 sessions. For these 180 calls from the dialogue controller to the adaptor component of the user model (Figure 13.1), Figure 13.2 illustrates the overlap between difficulties inferred by the system, and those stated by users. The results show the system detected 40 per cent of difficulties stated by users, at the expense of a false positive rate of 53 per cent.

Figure 13.3 shows the 68 adaptations resulting from the 180 calls broken down by direction, usefulness and correctness of direction.

	Correct direction	Incorrect direction		Number useful	Number not useful
More guidance	23	4		5	22
Less guidance	26	15		0	41
Subtotals	49	19		5	63
Total	68			68	

Total calls to the adaptor = 180

Total adaptations = 68

Figure 13.3 Adaptations classified by direction, usefulness and correctness

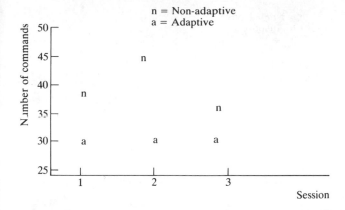

Figure 13.4 Plot of number of commands entered in each session

Adaptations were counted as useful if they either helped a user overcome a difficulty, or helped a user achieve an immediate aim. Adaptations which did not help to overcome a difficulty or achieve an immediate aim were counted as not useful. The direction of an adaptation was assessed as being correct if it matched the user's statements of his or her difficulties, and conflicted if it was in the opposite direction.

Figures 13.4, 13.5 and 13.6 show for each session the number of commands entered, the number of tasks completed, and the number of letters processed. To assess the relative effectiveness of users in the two conditions, the number of commands required for each letter processed is plotted in Figure 13.7. The lower the number of commands required for each letter, the greater the effectiveness of user operation.

User ratings of the quality of operation of the two systems, and of their acceptance of the systems, are plotted in Figures 13.8 and 13.9. In Figure 13.8 the range of possible ratings is from 0 to 135.

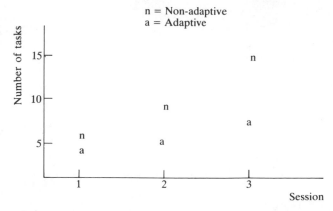

Figure 13.5 Plot of number of tasks completed in each session

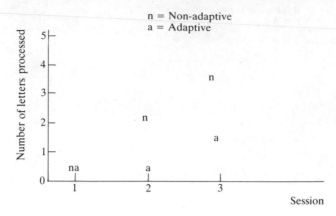

Figure 13.6 Number of letters processed in each session

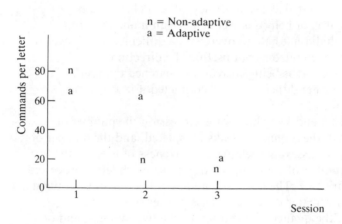

Figure 13.7 Number of commands/letter in each session

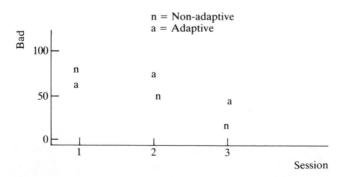

Figure 13.8 User rating of operation quality

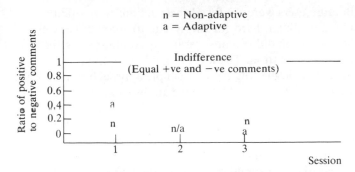

Figure 13.9 Ratio of positive to negative comments

13.3.5 Summary and interpretation

The figures illustrate that there was general performance advantage for
the non-adaptive condition, coupled with what appears to be faster
learning. This was visible from the lowest level of performance,
commands entered, to the highest level, letters processed. Examination
of expert judgements of the usefulness of the adaptations made throws
some light on this: only 18 per cent of adaptations to user difficulties
were counted as useful in overcoming the difficulty; none of the
adaptations to inferred user expertise were judged as useful. Overall
only 7 per cent of adaptations were counted as useful. This is in contrast
to the hit rate for the system's inference of user difficulties, which was
40 per cent. It therefore appears that the system's ability to infer user
difficulties was rather higher than its ability to use this information.
From the graphs of user reactions to the system, it appears that users
rated the quality of operation of both adaptive and non-adaptive
systems more highly as their experience increased, and that users rated
the adapted condition more highly than the non-adaptation condition
for the first session. However, user acceptance of the adaptation
condition appeared to polarize against the system over the three
sessions. Overall, the results indicate that adaptation as implemented
was not very successful. However, more important than differences
between the two systems is the low level of performance with both
adaptation and non-adaptation conditions. This suggests very strongly
that there are important factors at work which are unconnected with
adaptation.

   The emphasis on adaptation, and the lack of emphasis on the MMI
for both adaptation and non-adaptation conditions almost certainly
resulted in a poorer interface than was desirable. The performance of
subjects in both conditions suffered as a result. More problems were
caused in the adaptive condition than in the non-adaptive one, because
in the former the system was actively changing itself to suit the user's
level of difficulty on the basis of its understanding of what the user was

trying to do. Because users were confused their actions were often somewhat random, making it hard for the system to adapt effectively.

However, the evaluation did reveal several ways of improving the system's strategy for adaptation. The level of guidance was set individually for each dialogue fragment. A simple approach to making the system more responsive would be to have an initial strategy of allowing adaptations to propagate to all dialogue fragments. Thus, for a novice user, difficulties with one part of the system would be taken as evidence of low abilities with all parts of the system. (Inexperience is of itself insufficient grounds upon which to infer lack of ability.) As users gained in experience then use could be made of the likely structure of knowledge in the domain to increase the scope of the system's inferences. This would give the added advantage of providing a more consistent system, although still an adaptive one.

At a more specific level, the prime dimension of adaptation, the guidance dimension, proved to be questionable. Simply tailoring the amount of guidance given was shown to be an insufficient response to user dificulty. The context dimension, too, seemed a poor choice for an adaptation dimension. For example, users do not usually stop what they are doing without good reasons, but instead finish one task and then do another. Finally, the quality of the adaptation depends entirely upon the quality of the plan representations that the system contains. Any omission in the plan database will lead to unwanted offers of a context switch or inappropriate adaptation.

13.3.6 Conclusions

Although this first exemplar of the AID project did not prove to be particularly successful in terms of overall performance measures, it did succeed in demonstrating that systems can be built which can identify user characteristics and problems, and change the interface accordingly. The next step in the project was to produce further demonstrator systems which made use of the lessons learnt. The problems which were encountered were due, in large measure, to attempting to take a far too general view of what would be considered to be a successful adaptive system. The overall objectives of the evaluation were never clearly defined, and the performance measures detailed in the above description arose during the process of evaluation rather than as a requirement of meeting design objectives. In addition, it became clear that there were almost as many views of what 'adaptation' was as there were people on the project. All of this meant that the evaluators had no clear guidelines as to what was required.

A further complication encountered in this evaluation lay in the choice of exemplar, the Telecom Gold electronic-mail system, which was found to be already in some measure 'adaptive', in that its methods of carrying out some of its tasks varied according to the context in which it found itself. On a practical level, the adaptive system under test suffered from a very poor response time, commands processed locally taking in the order of 10 seconds, commands sent to Telecom Gold much longer. 3–4 minutes was typical for a 'read contents' command and a 10-minute response time was recorded for one particularly slow read command. Nor was the system completely robust; it would certainly have benefited from more time spent on the design of the user interface. This led to a suppressing of any benefits of adaptation by a dissatisfaction with the system as a whole.

Although the results of this first evaluation of the project did not reveal the hoped-for justification of adaptive interfaces they did provide a wealth of information as to how to proceed with the design and evaluation of such interfaces. The lack of clearly defined objectives at the start of the evaluation led to the realization that the process of evaluation of a system was intimately related to the design of that system, and that some form of formative evaluation, as first discussed by Scriven (1972), was necessary during the development of a system. In addition, the open-endedness of those original objectives showed the need for much more detailed examination of the processes of adaptation, which in turn led to the policy of building mini-exemplars during the second phase of the project. It became evident that the sheer volume of the data which was being collected was militating against its later analysis. Difficulties in the identification, and subsequent recall, of significant passages in the video recordings of the experimental sessions made the use of this medium very time-consuming. The use of both real-time and *post-hoc* verbal protocols, as well as being intrusive and less than wholly reliable, also make experimentation an onerous task for both the subjects and the evaluators.

This evaluation also highlighted the need for an adaptive exemplar to have an adequate user interface. Where the interface is less than adequate, any beneficial results of adaptation will be lost in comparison with the user's negative reaction to the poor interface. This means that in order to carry out a generalized summative evaluation it is necessary to spend considerble design expertise in producing a system which is developed to an extent sufficient to make it completely acceptable to the user. This may be an onerous task, and a further argument in favour of carrying out formative evaluations of individual aspects of adaptation rather than of complete systems.

13.4 Groupie: help adapted to a group of users

Groupie turned the focus of adaptation from adaptation to, and between, individuals to adaptation to suit groups of users. As with the Adaptive Interface to Telecom Gold it addressed the provision of online guidance or help. It is generally accepted that the online help provided by many systems is held in poor esteem (Viliunas *et al.* 1988); it is either too complex or incomplete, or gives help which is inappropriate because it is aimed at the generic rather than the individual user. A possible way to overcome this problem is to provide a help system which can adapt itself to the user or a group of users. Groupie is essentially an adaptive help-retrieval system which incorporates the techniques of hypertext and community support in an open-ended, multichoice help domain.

One of the problems with providing adaptive interfaces is obtaining sufficient evidence for adapting the interface in a time period which is acceptable to the user. The approach taken with Groupie was to focus on a group of users and to use the information derived from this set of users to help all users but in particular the first-time user. By taking data from a group of users, as evidence for change at the interface, there is the potential for real-time adaptation without the need for priming. For the purposes of the investigation a group was regarded as a set of users working together either as part of an organization or because they had a common interest.

One of the findings from an extensive user requirements analysis in the domain of document preparation, undertaken within the AID Project, was that groups tend to have the detailed expertise and knowledge relevant to their task distributed among individual members of the group in an unstructured fashion in what is commonly referred to as *group folklore*. It was also common for groups to have a 'guru' whose knowledge and expertise was prized and was frequently called upon by members of the group when they encountered difficulties with either the technology or the task being undertaken. Ogborn and Johnson (1982) make the point that knowledge is something that is shared by a community and is not the exclusive property of an individual, and that the perpetuation and evolution of community knowledge is effected through the sharing and learning of this knowledge. However, tapping into group folklore may not always be an easy practice. A novice to a group has first to determine who holds the relevant knowledge and has then to obtain access to that individual who may be absent or too busy. In such a case a system such as Groupie would be of benefit. The objectives of the study were to explore the notion of adaptivity in a cooperative setting, and to investigate the use of hypertext for capturing the expertise of a group.

Groupie was designed to be both group adaptable and adaptive using a taxonomic classification of adaptive systems (Totterdell *et al.* 1987). It was adaptable because it allowed users to build their own set of help into the system. Part of the responsibility for the design of the help messages was taken out of the hands of the designers and given to the users. This idea of deferred design, in which the user or system takes some control over the selection process, is central to adaptive interfaces.

It was adaptive because it altered its behaviour in accordance with an internally measured but hard-wired metric. The system based its retrieval order of help messages on a ratings metric derived from the group. Hence the system was able to adjust its behaviour by discriminating between various ratings. In this way, although the system gave the illusion of learning, it was simply using a change in the group ratings to select from a finite set of retrieval orders.

Just as it was not possible to assume users to be homogeneous in their requirements so equally it could not be assumed that a single strategy for retrieval of help would be appropriate for all groups. Groupie addressed this problem by providing different adaptive help-retrieval strategies. There were six strategies. Four of the six strategies were biased towards the community and two were biased towards the individual. The four community-biased strategies were:

- select the help frame most preferred by the group (community) as indicated by its group preference weighting;
- select the first encountered help frame whose group preference weight is above a given threshold level;
- select a help frame on the basis of its probability of being preferred by the group (i.e., if a help frame has a 40-per-cent group preference then it has a 40-per-cent chance of being selected;
- select the help frame most preferred by the group unless that help frame is not new to the individual currently using the system and there is another help frame which has a higher preference by that individual.

The two individual biased strategies were:

- select the help frame most preferred by the individual;
- select the help frame which is most preferred by the individual and whose individual preference weighting is above a given threshold level unless there is a help frame which is new to that individual and whose group preference weighting is above a given threshold level.

The strategies were selected by the designer through a pop-up menu but there was no meta-strategy for controlling the retrieval strategies. In the evaluation experiment reported in Section 13.4.1, community strategy 2 was used (i.e., select the first encountered help frame whose group preference weight is above a given threshold level).

Groupie was built up of three main components as shown in Figure 13.10. The User Interface Management System handled the display features of the interface. The Adaptor was a production rule system that generated recommendations concerning the ordering of the help messages based on current knowledge and strategies. The Analyser module managed the individual ratings of each help message produced by each user and calculated the average rating of each prompt. This module provided the adaptor with evidence for changes. These three

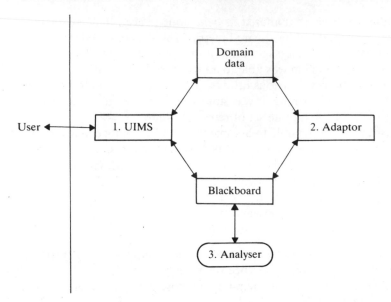

Figure 13.10   The Groupie architecture

components were implemented in Pop11 and communicated with one another via a centralized blackboard (mailbox) by using a communication protocol.

13.4.1 Evaluation

The aims of the evaluation required a task which was structured in nature, shared by a group and prone to errors in its completion. A simple form-filling task, filling a document frontsheet, was chosen. A diagram of the frontsheet used for the experiment is shown in Figure 13.11. Fields which were selectable on the frontsheet were shown in inverse video (in boldface on the diagram). On pressing a mouse over one of these highlighted fields a pop-up menu appeared, allowing the user to edit a field, view a help message, or add a help message. Windows containing the help messages appeared to the right of the frontsheet. By clicking on the 'alter' button the user could select an alternative help message, overlaid on the first, relating to the field in question. The 'hyper' button allowed the user to highlight an area within the text and attach another message to it, i.e., to create a piece of hypertext.

There was a rating scale at the bottom of each of the message windows, which allowed the user to give an assessment of the messages presented to them. This eliminated the need to employ inbuilt reasoning about the user's goals and plans when selecting information. It allowed the system to capture the user's higher level notions of good and bad,

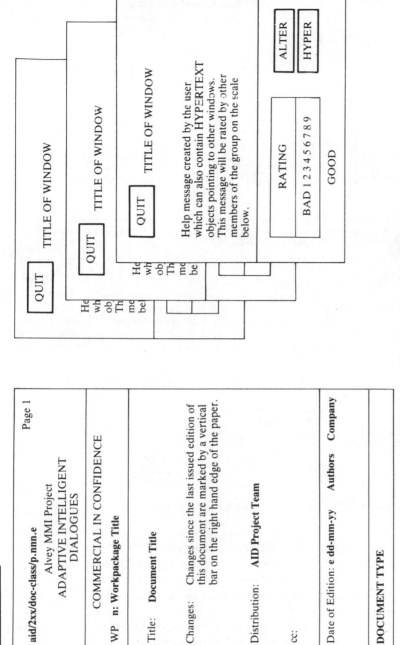

Figure 13.11 The Groupie interface

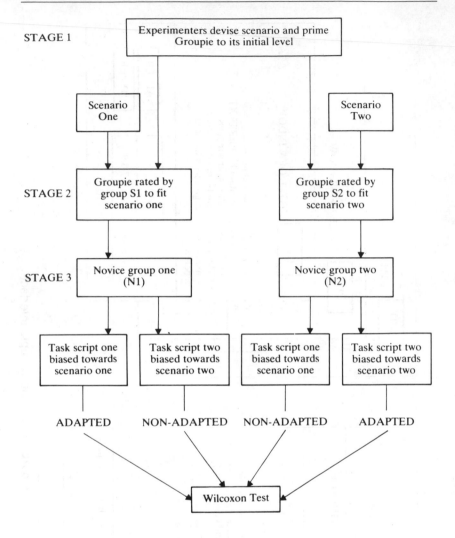

Figure 13.12 The experimental design for Groupie

which are often very subjective. These ratings provided weights which Groupie used to prioritize a set of equally plausible help texts with the hope of pre-empting the need to retrieve each one in turn. In principle the most appropriate help text for a particular user was presented to the user first.

The evaluation investigated only the capability of adapting to group practices; it did not assess whether the technique was practical. The experiment was designed to show whether Groupie, by adapting to the group's ratings, could improve the performance of a novice in the filling in of a frontsheet. The evaluation was primarily concerned with the adaptive potential of Groupie, i.e., its ability to 'evolve' with the group.

The performance measure was the accuracy with which subjects completed the task.

The experimental design is shown in Figure 13.12. The design was chosen because it was required to determine not only whether the system improved user performance but also whether any performance improvement obtained reflected the particular help requirement of a user or group of users. This was a surer test of adaptation than comparison with a non-adaptive system since it reflects sensitivity to requirements rather than functionality difference. The experiment was run in three stages. In stage one the messages held within Groupie were primed by the experimenters to hold alternative interpretations for each of the fields on the frontsheet. For stage two these messages were rated according to two given scenarios by two groups (S1 and S2) of 'experienced' members of the AID Project (i.e., subjects who had some experience of filling in a frontsheet). The scenarios described what functions the various fields on the frontsheet should fulfil. Each scenario provided a different interpretation of the frontsheet.

The null hypothesis was that a group of users using an adapted version of Groupie would not differ significantly in the accuracy with which they completed a form-filling task from a group of users using a non-adapted version. The evaluation makes the assumption that the primed help messages correspond satisfactorily to their corresponding scenarios.

In stage three 10 novices, without knowledge of the frontsheet, were divided into 2 groups (N1 and N2). N1 performed their task using the Groupie rated by S1 and N2 used the Groupie rated by S2. The alternative button was disabled so that subjects could only view one prompt per field. Each subject was given two form-filling tasks. One of the tasks was suited for the scenario presented to S1 and the other was suited for the scenario given to S2. The result of this was that for a given novice subject using a given Groupie, only one of the two tasks would be compatible with the given interpretation of the frontsheet. This meant that the Groupie being used by the subject would be adapted to one of the scenarios and non-adapted to the other. The order in which these two tasks were presented was alternated between subjects to control for learning effects.

13.4.2 Results

The completed fields were scored for accuracy producing a figure for the number of correct answers per subject per task (Figure 13.13). The resulting matched ranked data was analysed using the non-parametric Wilcoxon test (Robson, 1973). There was a significant difference between the adapted and non-adapted conditions. ($Z = 2.803$, $N = 10$, two-tailed test, $p < 0.05$). The results showed that not only did the novice groups N1 and N2 have a different view of the functionality of the

Group N1	Groupie adapted scores	Groupie non-adapted scores	Group N2	Groupie adapted scores	Groupie non-adapted scores
S1	10	1	S6	11	4
S2	9	1	S7	8	2
S3	12	1	S8	10	4
S4	9	0	S9	10	4
S5	11	0	S10	5	3

Figure 13.13 Table of correctly completed fields for each subject per task

frontsheet because of the prompts they received but also that their view produced more errors when they had to fill in the frontsheet using Groupie in a non-adapted state. The results indicate that:

- the content of the help messages was of sufficient quality to show a performance effect;
- there were differences in the help requirements of groups undertaking different task scenarios;
- Groupie was able to reconfigure its help messages to reflect those different requirements.

A number of interesting observations arose during the evaluation study. The hypertext facility was used in an unexpected manner. People use the system not only to provide help for others but also as a blackboard on which they can note comments and suggestions. Should these comments be accepted by the group, the suggestions could then be displayed to novices as established ideas in an example of group evolution. There was a problem here that although the 'established suggestion' was accepted by the group, to a novice it would still look like a suggestion and this indicated that maybe Groupie ought to be equipped with different types of messages, e.g., help, suggestions, etc., and that these differing message types should be handled by Groupie in differing ways. The study suggested that the usage of systems can undergo changes during their use by a group and that it is therefore useful to have a system which can adapt its help to track these changes. Designers cannot fully anticipate usage of the systems that they create, nor the environments in which they will operate. Groupie therefore provided an interesting method for investigating how group knowledge evolves and how this would alter the system in use.

13.4.3 Conclusion

The design of Groupie was based on some assumptions about the world in which it resided. It assumed that individuals in a community may not have common goals and interests, an assumption supported by Malone *et al.* (1987), and responded to this by providing a range of retrieval strategies, which were admittedly impoverished and lacking in meta-level control. It assumed that the rating mechanism was likely to be used quite frequently but Wilson (1984) showed that this assumption may not be justified, referring to a voting facility which was used only three times throughout an experiment on mailbox structures undertaken in a group working context. It assumed that individuals would contribute to the help database by adding their own help frames, and recent studies of groups over message-based systems (Wilbur, 1986) have shown, indirectly, that this assumption may be reasonable.

The study illustrated a method for managing the folklore held within a group of users, and showed that the method adapted successfully. There are however a number of issues still to be addressed such as whether people will actually spend the time and effort to keep their fellow group members informed. It may be that 'gurus' are very protective of their expertise. It would be of interest to see whether there are systematic differentiations in the prompts which users provide. For example, do users of different backgrounds provide different prompts and are these prompts preferred by people of the same background? These results could be used to make the adaptive strategies more sensitive. Lastly, does the success of an adaptive strategy depend on the task?

13.5 General techniques for evaluating adaptive interfaces

One of the major aims of the AID project was to develop evaluation techniques for adaptive systems. The chief outcome of the project in this respect has been to re-emphasize the importance of the iterative design–build–evaluation cycle as the most effective way of developing human–computer interface systems. The project also developed a series of metrics which greatly facilitated the design and evaluation of adaptive systems, and clearly delineated the roles of formative and summative evaluation in the overall assessment of adaptive systems.

13.5.1 Formation evaluation

Evaluation should be regarded as an ongoing element in the development of an adaptive system. At some stages, particularly early on in the development of a system, evaluation will mainly be conducted implicitly by the designer, whereas later there is a need for explicit evaluation to test quantitatively whether these objectives have been met: for instance, the objective in providing adaptation of a particular type should be clearly established early on in the system development, but whether this is being met cannot be addressed until the system has been built. One of the results of the AID project has been to encourage designers to make their implicit assumptions about the system explicit: in doing this a more structured framework or methodology for the design of adaptive systems emerged. This was encouraged by the use of 'design walkthroughs', whereby designers were asked to submit their design ideas to a group of fellow project members, including the evaluators. Such checking of the validity of assumptions under which the system is operating can give the designer confidence that the system will meet its objective.

13.5.2 Summative evaluation

Once the system has been built it will be necessary to carry out a summative evaluation. Often it will be possible to identify more than one objective in the summative evaluation of an adaptive system. The major objective of the summative evaluation of an adaptive system will usually be to establish whether subjects' performance is better with the adaptive system than it is with a similar non-adaptive system on the task for which adaptation has been provided. Before this question can be answered it will be necessary to answer some preliminary questions, as follows:

- *Does the system work as intended?*   Given the input of any hypothetical user, the designer should be able to predict the system's response.
- *Are the assumptions underlying the operation of the adaptive system valid?*   Even where the pre-build evaluation checks have established evidence in another area for the user variability on which adaptation is based it may be necessary to check that these assumptions are valid within the context of the adaptive system. It may be for instance that the adaptive system forces users to do something in a way which wipes out or modifies differences. In the AID project evaluation checks were not always carried out during the early stages of development and consequently the summative evaluation was more complicated.
- *Is the system adapting?*   It will be necessary to collect data from users to find out whether the system changes in response to user variation but not in the absence of user variation.
- *Is the system meeting the designer's objectives?*   In some cases if the system is adapting it is necessarily meeting the designer's objective, but in other cases this does not follow and an additional assessment

of whether the system is meeting the designer's objective will be required.

- *Do the users find the adaptive system beneficial?* Even if the adaptive system is superior to the non-adaptive system it may be that, for other reasons, users prefer to use the non-adaptive system. For example, users may not be able to predict the response of the system in the way that they would be able to with a non-adaptive system. This will require real users to use the system.

13.6 Conclusions

Evaluation in the AID project proved to be illuminating in many respects. Arguably the most important of these was the role of evaluation in a research project such as this. It is interesting to note that, in spite of the fact that one of the three major objectives of the project was to 'develop methods of evaluating the effectiveness of adaptive interfaces', within the first phase of the project, the Adaptive Interfaces to Telecom Gold, evaluation was only considered towards the end of the building of the exemplar. It might be argued that until there is something to evaluate it is hardly worth worrying about evaluation. All the experience of the project has amply illustrated the paucity of such a view.

Early consideration of the evaluation is fundamental to the success of a project. In fact the roles of the designer and the evaluator are certainly complementary and might almost be considered synonymous. This relationship between the two roles was utilized during the AID project by the institution of a series of 'design walkthroughs', whereby designers were required to present their ideas and the assumptions on which they were based to a panel of evaluators, also designers in their own right, for critical assessment. Of course, the final dichotomy between the roles needed to be maintained to preserve the necessary objectivity of the evaluation team. But as, in a collaborative project like AID, designers of one exemplar become the evaluators of another this is not a problem but rather a definite advantage. It ensures a broad level of expertise throughout a big project, which might otherwise become rather disparate.

The approach taken in the first exemplar was to use a comparative evaluation testing the adaptive condition against a non-adaptive control condition. This highlighted the problem of defining what the control should be when evaluating adaptive systems. It became clear that all systems, whether adaptive or static, are adapted, to a greater or lesser extent, to their user population. It would, by intuition, seem unduly biased in favour of adaptation to choose a maladapted static system for comparison; but on the other hand, any system which had been well designed to its user population was by definition adapted to that user population even though it was 'static'. Thus the success of an 'adaptive' system related more to the diversity of its user population than to the success of its user interface, which was a problem of interface design rather than adaptation.

At the start of the project there was a feeling that adaptation would provide a general solution wherever there was some sort of user difficulty and the initial studies in the AID project looked at any area where the designers or potential users of the system thought that adaptation might be useful. It became clear during the course of the project that this view was too optimistic and that adaptation was no universal panacea which could be applied to any interface to improve it. Adaptation was, rather, a possible solution in certain defined cases, where significant user differences were present, where those differences could readily be detected for use as triggers for change, and where there was sufficient understanding of the user's difficulties and of how those difficulties could best be alleviated. All of this led to the development of a set of metrics to represent the categories of data which were found to be essential elements of an adaptive system (Browne *et al.*, 1987).

The conditions which were identified by the project as necessary to make adaptation a worthwhile possibility influence the design and evaluation of an adaptive system from its earliest stages. The role of the evaluator, at this early stage, is to confirm that the necessary conditions do exist in the context, or area, to be studied. The conditions, which themselves arose from the evaluation carried out in the project, may be summarized as follows:

User difficulty or user benefit

The first condition which should hold is that there exists some sort of difficulty or problem. The idea that adaptation would be a useful feature in a system arose in the first place as a means of improving man–machine interfaces by making systems more accessible to a wider range of users, and thus more 'user friendly'. If there were no problems with the existing non-adaptive system there would be little point in investing time and money in making the system adaptive. The other side of this coin is having successfully developed an adaptive system to deal with a problem the adaptation should be of some benefit to the users. It will frequently be the objective of the evaluation to establish whether the adaptation does indeed provide some benefit to users. The proposed benefit to the user in providing adaptation is seen as central to the success of an adaptive system.

Differences between users

Another extremely important condition and the one on which the other conditions rest is that there should be significant measurable differences between users, tasks or groups along the relevant dimension. Originally, only adaptation to user differences was considered but adaptive exemplars based on differences between tasks and on differences between groups were also developed in the AID project.

Readily available triggers

The difference between users (tasks or groups) should be readily detectable from the user interaction for use as a trigger for change.

An understanding of users' difficulties and differing needs

There should be a sufficient understanding of the user's difficulty and how best to meet the differing needs of the user. It was clear that in some cases the knowledge required to make useful, meaningful adaptations did not exist.

These last three conditions provide the knowledge necessary to build a useful and appropriate model of the user and it is the conformance of these three conditions which must be established at the start of a project on adaptive interfaces.

Cost of providing adaptation

The practical costs in terms of time and money, and the system costs in terms of necessary extra functionality of carrying out adaptation, should not outweigh the benefits provided. In some cases this may be difficult to assess but generally speaking the benefits envisaged in making the system adaptive would need to be fairly large in order to justify the high expense.

In conclusion, it can be said that the AID project contributed enormously to our understanding of adaptation without really achieving any major breakthrough which can be identified as delivering outstanding user benefits. The project clearly demonstrated that there are more restrictions than previously thought on the range of applicability of adaptation and it established certain conditions which would need to hold in order to consider building an adaptive interface. Further research into adaptive systems should concentrate on providing clarification of the conditions under which adaptation is viable, with particular emphasis on understanding the needs and difficulties of users.

The AID project has been taken as a case study in the evaluation of human–computer interaction because it shows the many levels at which evaluation must take place to achieve a good user interface. These levels have ranged from the testing of design assumptions and detection of triggers, through the evaluation of small adaptive processes, to the overall evaluation of the concept of adaptation itself. During the course of the project a design-and-evaluation philosophy evolved which is fundamental to the systematic study of any human–computer interaction. Such a philosophy demands a rigorous, objective-oriented approach to design and evaluation. Each step in the design process must be subjected to close scrutiny by the evaluation team to meet closely defined objectives. Of course, such a rigourous design philosophy will inevitably lead to many cases where the design objectives will not be met. However, such studies should not be regarded as failures because, as the AID project has demonstrated, the early detection of failures can give great saving in terms of both costs and resources, and it is often the case that it is from the detailed examination of our failures that most knowledge is gained.

References

Boucherat, P. R. and A. T. Hockley (1986) 'Preliminary evaluation of the phase 1 exemplar, *Internal AID Report*, Standard Telephone Laboratories, Harlow, Essex.

Browne, D. P., R. Trevellyan, P. Totterdell and M. Norman (1987) 'Metrics for Building, Evaluation and Comprehension of Self-Regulating Adaptive Systems', in *Human–Computer Interaction—INTERACT '87*, H. J. Bullinger and B. Shackel (eds), Elsevier Science, Amsterdam.

Eason, K. D. and L. Damodaran (1979) *Design Procedures for User Involvement and User Support*, Infotech Computer Communications, London.

Edmonds, E. (1982) 'The man–computer interface—a note on concepts and design', *International Journal of Man–Machine Studies*, **16**, 231–236.

Gaines, B. R. and M. L. Shaw (1983) 'Dialogue engineering', in *Designing for Human–Computer Communications*, M. E. Sime and M. J. Coombs (eds), Academic Press, London, 23–53.

Greenberg, S. (1984) *User Modeling in Interactive Systems*, MSc Thesis, Department of Computer Science, University of Calgary, Alberta.

Hardy, S. (1984) 'Poplog: a new software environment for list processing and logic programming', *Artificial Intelligence*, Harper & Row, 110–136.

Innocent, P. R. (1982) 'Towards self-adaptive interface systems', *International Journal of Man–Machine Studies*, **16**, 287–299.

James, E. B. (1980) 'The user interface', *The Computer Journal*, **23**.

Larson, J. A. (1982) *End user facilities in the 1980s*, IEEE Computer Society Press, New York.

Malone, T. W., K. R. Grant, F. A. Turbak, S. A. Brobst, and M. D. Cohen (1987) 'Intelligent information sharing systems', *Communications of the ACM*, **30** (5) (May).

Moran, T. P. (1981) 'The command language grammar: a representation for the user interface of interactive computer systems', *International Journal of Man–Machine Studies*, **15**, 3–50.

Ogborn, J. M. and I. Johnson (1982) *Conversation Theory*, Internal report of Man–Computer Studies Group, Brunel University.

Robson, C. (1973) *Experimental Design and Statistics in Psychology*, Penguin Modern Psychology, Penguin, Harmondsworth.

Scriven, M. (1972) 'The methodology of evaluation', in *Perspectives in Curriculum Evaluation*, R. Tyler, R. Gagne and M. Scriven (eds), Rand McNally, Chicago.

Shneiderman, B. (1980) *Software Psychology*, Winthrop, Cambridge, Mass.

Totterdell, P. A. and P. A. Cooper (1986) 'Design and evaluation of the AID adaptive front end to Telecom Gold', in *People and Computers: Designing for Usability*, M. D. Harrison and A. F. Monk (eds), Cambridge University Press, Cambridge.

Totterdell, P. A., M. A. Norman and D. P. Browne (1987) 'Levels of Adaptivity in Interface Design', in *Human Computer Interaction—INTERACT '87*, H. J. Bullinger and B. Shackel (eds), Elsevier Science, Amsterdam, 715–722.

Viliunas, R. J., A. C. Wong and P. A. Totterdell (1988) *Groupie: Meeting a Group's Help Needs*, Internal AID Report, Standard Telephone Laboratories, Harlow, Essex.

Wasserman, A. I. and D. T. Shewmake (1984) *A RAPID/USE Tutorial*, Laboratory of Medical Information Science, University of California, San Francisco, Calif.

Wilbur, S. (1986) 'A study of group interaction over a computer-based message system', in *People and Computers: Designing for Usability*, M. D. Harrison and A. F. Monk (eds), Cambridge University Press, Cambridge, 235–248.

Wilson, P. (1984) 'Structures for group working in mailbox systems', in *Human–Computer Interaction—INTERACT '84*, Elsevier Science, Amsterdam, 388–395.

14 Evaluation case study II: a voice-operated database enquiry service

GARY ASHWORTH

14.1 Introduction

Funded jointly by Alvey and industry, the Voice Operated Database Inquiry Service (VODIS) was a collaborative project between British Telecom Research Laboratories, Logica UK Ltd and Cambridge University. The aim of the project was to produce a task-oriented, speech-based, man–machine interface for use by untrained, non-technical people. The exemplar application domain chosen for the project was the British Rail telephone timetable enquiry service.

Given that speech is the natural mode of communication between humans, requiring no conscious training and little effort, one reason for the project was to attempt to develop a user interface which achieved in practice the naturalness which is the claimed advantage of speech.

14.2 The system

The structure of the VODIS system is shown in Figure 14.1. The interface to the user was made up of a speech output module and a speech input module. Speech output was provided by a single-board, text-to-speech synthesizer devloped at British Telecom Research Laboratories, while speech input was recognized by speaker-independent template matching via the LOGOS connected-word speech recognizer developed by Logica UK.

The intelligent knowledge base contained a set of data structures, known as frames. Each frame contained a series of slots corresponding to particular aspects of the user's query, such as place names and

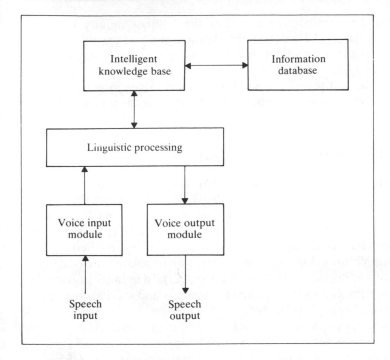

Figure 14.1   The overall structure of the VODIS system

journey times. Completed frames containing information about the
user's journey such as the departure point, arrival point and intended
time of travel could then be compared against the information stored in
the information database, which contained the necessary train timetable
information. This information was then extracted, and relayed back to
the user via the speech output system.

The interface between the knowledge base and the speech
input/output systems was provided by a linguistic processing unit,
which performed three functions, as follows:

Firstly, the unit passed text strings to the speech synthesizer, which
were converted to produce the output messages. Although initially a
simple phoneme-based text-to-speech synthesizer was used, later in the
project the synthesizer was enhanced by exploiting the context of the
text to improve intonation.

Secondly, the linguistic processing unit contained syntax graphs for
expected user responses, in order to guide the pattern matching process.
The speech recognition system worked by applying pattern-matching
techniques to each connected speech utterance rather than attempting
speech understanding; thus for the system to work, it had to have
available a set of utterance templates representing every possible (or at
least likely) phrase which might be generated as part of an enquiry. As
the dialogue, knowledge domain and vocabulary were significantly

constrained by the structure imposed on the database enquiry, it was feasible to attempt to derive complete syntax specifications for all possible responses to information requested by the speech output system (see Sections 14.3.1 and 14.3.2).

Thirdly, the unit parsed the recognition scores given to users' utterances, before passing the best interpretation of the utterance to the intelligent knowledge base.

14.3 The role of evaluation

Evaluation was necessary in order to provide data for input to the iterative design process (formative evaluation), and to assess the performance of the user interface dialogue once it had been developed (summative evaluation). Formative evaluation was explicitly used in this project to define the dialogue structure and vocabulary required for the specified application domain, rather than as an implicit check of design assumptions as in case study I (see Section 13.5). In doing this, the distinction between evaluation and task analysis and specification (as discussed in Chapter 5) is blurred.

Factors relating specifically to the recognizer and synthesizer performance were not addressed in these dialogue studies, since these could be evaluated independently of the actual dialogue used. Objective assessment of the performance of the electronic modules of a speech recognition system is straightforward, as they are consistent in their operation, and their operation is well understood. However, the human input to the system, is far less consistent. Even where the allowed vocabulary is constrained, the way humans employ language is idiosyncratic, varying from person to person in such a way that the interface must permit a large number of possible utterances in response to any prompt from the system.

Formative evaluation of the interface therefore had to identify any consistencies within this large set of possible utterances which could be used to create a regular response syntax and vocabulary applicable to all users. This information could then be used within the design process to identify ways in which the dialogue prompts could be structured in order to increase the probability of responses from any given user conforming to this syntax and vocabulary.

In practice, formative evaluation was carried out in two iterative design stages of progressive refinement of the dialogue structure and vocabulary, and a further summative evaluation stage was then used to evaluate the complete system on a realistic timetable enquiry task.

14.3.1 Study 1: dialogue structure specification

The first study involved monitoring calls to various 'information providers'. Conversations between members of the public and services

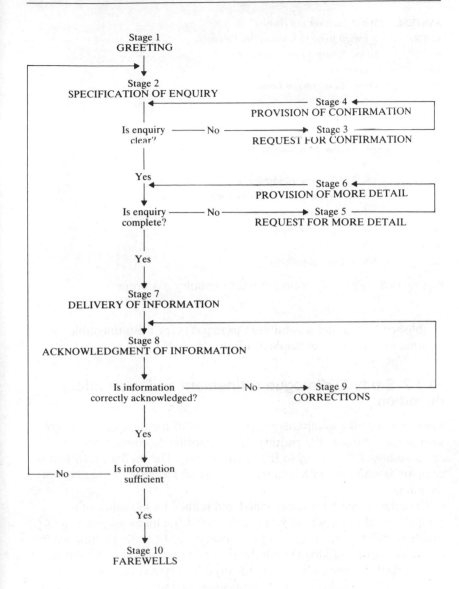

Figure 14.2 Major dialogue events in an information enquiry

providing information of various kinds were recorded in order to build up a preliminary model of the dialogues produced, highlighting the major dialogue events which were relevant to the achievement of the users' goals—i.e., receipt of the desired information. The resulting model of the dialogue events was then tailored to requests for travel information as shown in Figure 14.2.

Once a generic database enquiry dialogue structure had been

SYSTEM:	*Which train do you require?*
USER:	I want to go to London this morning.
S:	*Sorry. Where do you want to go to?*
U:	London.
S:	*From Manchester to London?*
U:	No.
S:	*Where from?*
U:	Stockport.
S:	*To London from Stockport?*
U:	Yes.
S:	*The'7:35 from Stockport arrives in London at 10:05.*
	Do you require further information?
U:	I need to arrive before ten.
S:	*The 7:00 gets in at 9:06. Is that ok?*
U:	Yes.
S:	*Thank you—goodbye.*

Figure 14.3   Example train timetable enquiry dialogue

established, the model was tailored to requests for train timetable information, as in the example of Figure 14.3.

14.3.2 Study 2: dialogue refinement and vocabulary definition

Study 2 involved a comparison of this model of the dialogue structure with genuine calls to BR enquiry agents in order to confirm the applicability of the model to the intended task. The model was found to compare favourably with genuine information requests by members of the public.

The original model was expanded and refined by inclusion of a complex vocabulary set, allowing for some of the many ways in which people can formulate a request for information. In order to enhance the naturalness of the dialogue with the system, users must be allowed to express their requests in a variety of ways. The syntax of a timetable enquiry (corresponding to the 'specification of enquiry' in Figure 14.2) will remain constant, but each syntactic construct may be expressed in a variety of ways. The enquiry will contain some or all of the following syntactic constructs:

- *preamble;*
- *fromplace (point of origin);*
- *toplace (destination);*
- *time (today, tomorrow, this morning, etc).*

If we take just the first of these constructs, preamble, there are many different phrases that users can employ to initiate a request.

Preamble vocabulary structure and content

The preamble itself can be split into two parts:

- *Request initiation* The phrases generally used when commencing a request for information.

- *Specification of enquiry* The words and phrases that identify the nature of the information required.

The following is a sample of the words and phrases which were commonly observed when initiating a request:

I want | need | would like

I am enquiring about | trying to find out about

(I wonder if you could | can you | could you) tell me | give me

After a request has been initiated, the nature of the information required was specified using the following vocabulary:

the times of trains | some times of trains | the times of departures

what time the trains go | will be going

These phrases can be employed to produce a very large number of utterances, all with the same meaning, and in natural dialogue they seem to occur at random. Each of these possible combinations was allowed for within the linguistic processing unit, in order to allow users to structure their responses in whichever way they found most comfortable.

A further refinement to the dialogue model was a guidance system, whereby help was provided by the system. Although the system could cater for a large number of different response structures, some responses will always fall outside the set of permissible vocabulary items and syntactic structures. If there was reason to believe the user was experiencing some difficulty (for instance, if after a number of dialogue cycles no valid response was recognized from the user), the system presented the user with an example of the type of response which was expected in order to allow the dialogue to progress.

Once the refinements to the dialogue had been completed, the third stage of the study could commence, which was a full-scale trial and evaluation of the fully automated VODIS system.

14.3.3 Study 3: exemplar simulation and evaluation

Study 3 was a simulation of a train timetable enquiry service carried out over 30 days at the British Telecom Human Factors Unit in Ipswich, Suffolk. 120 subjects were selected from a panel of approximately 1500 members of the public on the Human Factors subject panel. Each

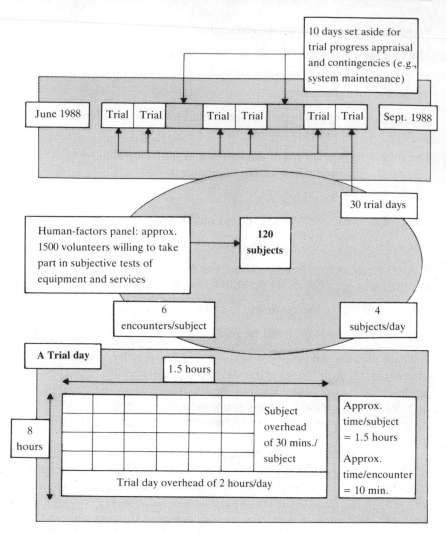

Figure 14.4   Study 3 trial logistics

subject was to make a number of calls in order to retrieve information about the times of trains for journeys described in scenarios given to the subjects at the start of the tests. The trial logistics are shown in Figure 14.4 and the layout of the text equipment in Figure 14.5.

The assessment of system performance was carried out on three levels. The first level was passive event recording. Each trial was recorded on videotape to provide a continuous objective record of the user's reactions to the trial system.

The second level was also an objective assessment of system performance, by the provision of a series of logs and objective records of system performance:

Console

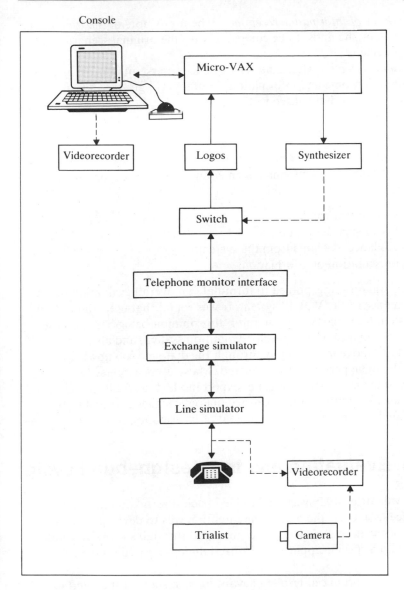

Figure 14.5 The test equipment for VODIS simulation

- *Real time log*   A log of the time taken to complete each enquiry, including detailed information on the reaction time of the user to the system, and vice versa.
- *Message log*   A log of the speech message output to the users.
- *Template score*   A record of the performance of the speech recognizer; for comparison with the video recording of the user's speech.
- *Frame activation path*   A VODIS-eye-view of the dialogue with the user. A record of how the system sees the dialogue progression.

- *Accuracy of information reception*   The user's note of the train data that he or she finds, to be compared with the original scenario requirements.
- *Training effects*   After a number of encounters, an improvement in transaction time and information accuracy will give an indication of the quality of dialogue control.
- *Informal observation*   The experimenter made a note of obvious difficulties of the users' and system performance.

The third level of assessment is subjective assessment. Subjects were asked to complete questionnaires on completion of the scenarios in order to establish users' opinions of:

- the service as a whole;
- quality of speech output;
- the guidance available from the system;
- the presentation of information.

This information was pooled to formulate an overall evaluation of the performance of the VODIS system. It was found that users did not find the system to be particularly natural, this opinion being based on the poor performance of the speech-recognition system, and also the inability to move more rapidly through the dialogue as knowledge about dialogue performance increased. Many users expressed disappointment that there was no 'expert mode' that could be employed to reduce the number of unnecessary dialogue stages that had to be negotiated in order to achieve the goal of information retrieval.

14.4 Evaluation and the design–build cycle

Each evaluation study was used to feed back information into the interface design. At the outset, the intention was to develop a generic model of the necessary dialogue events, and through successive studies to develop a specific application-centred dialogue based ·on the original benchmark.

Evaluation produced results relevant to each stage of the interface development. The first study allowed the developers to identify the key dialogue events that occur during a request for information. Once a generic dialogue model had been established, the second study confirmed that the model was applicable to a specific request type, train timetable information, by comparing the model to real dialogue events observed in authentic calls to British Rail information providers.

This study also allowed the establishment of a predicted syntax and vocabulary set corresponding to the structure of utterances in order to develop the recognition and natural language processing modules of the system. Finally, the second study allowed the developers to identify ways of enhancing the interface with the user, with the inclusion of an on-line guidance system.

The third study evaluated the performance of the interface that was developed as a result of the first two stages. The results of this stage highlighted the problems still faced in implementing an automatic speech-based system.

14.5 Naturalness of the user interface

Although VODIS was initially intended to address the issue of producing a natural language interface, naturalness proved to be difficult to achieve. One of the main problems is that people are variable, and it is difficult to allow for all the many different ways in which a person will make a request for information, however complex the internal representation of expected syntax and vocabulary.

Another problem is the fact that the system's model of how the dialogue should proceed is inflexible. Human beings are able to adapt their dialogue style over time to account for false starts, hesitations and so on. They use many non-linguistic clues to recognize the point when an interlocutor has finished speaking. The automatic dialogue controller only has a temporal clue. If no speech is recognized for a given period of time, then the system assumes that the user has finished speaking. If the user had only hesitated, however, and wanted to provide more information, then it would be unnatural to prompt the user for information which was about to be provided anyway.

Together, these two points indicate that allowing speaker-independent connected speech is not, by itself, enough to ensure a natural interface. Constraints on the vocabulary and syntax of current connected-speech recognizers still impose significant limits on the structure and content of acceptable dialogue input: users need to know exactly which words to link together, and in what order.

Coupled to this is the even greater problem of speech recognition performance. Speaker-independent connected word recognition still has many problems, producing a high proportion of misrecognized utterances. This, when combined with the unnatural synthetic speech output, has the effect of reducing users' faith in the ability of the system to understand complex utterances. Thus the quality of user dialogue styles often reduces to rather unnatural isolated word responses.

When users were able to produce responses within the limits of the predefined system syntax and vocabulary, the interface was still limited by the speech output technology. The text-to-speech synthesizer had a rather unnatural 'robotic' quality, which often made it difficult for users to understand what was being asked of them. It is impossible to make a correct response to a question that is not understood.

Another hindrance to a natural dialogue was the frequent insertion of system guidance, often when not required by the user. This proved to be very distracting, and eventually quite annoying, by increasing the amount of time necessary to complete a transaction, and highlighted the inability of the system to understand utterances that did not conform to the syntax and vocabulary required by the system.

Although in most cases interaction with the system was simple to learn and maintain, the resulting dialogues could not be described as natural. Speech is no more likely to permit humans to communicate naturally with computers than any other input method unless each is able to conduct dialogue on an equal basis. It is important that each understands the other's contributions to the dialogue, and adapts over time in order to establish a jointly agreed dialogue style; in VODIS, a rather inflexible style was forced on the user.

14.6 Conclusions

In addition to its use in summative evaluation, the VODIS project showed the value of formative evaluation as an integral part of user interface specification. The results of evaluation were fed back into the design procedure, to ensure that the dialogue developed according to fixed principles, which conformed to observations on the way natural dialogues were seen to work in the exemplar application environment. However, this did not result in a natural language interface, as the dialogue was still unable to adapt to the idiosyncratic ways in which individuals produce speech.

The need for further research in the areas of speech synthesis and recognition is obvious. Ultimately, the deficiencies (and in particular the unnaturalness) of the VODIS system could be attributed to the current limitations of speech technology. The careful analysis, appraisal, integration and evaluation of human dialogue styles appropriate to the application improved the performance of the system, but were unable fully to compensate for these limitations.

Naturalness may be impossible to attain by means of natural language dialogue control alone, given the current capabilities of speech synthesis and recognition technology. Given current technology constraints, future work on speech interactive dialogue design may need to develop ways of reducing the variability of user responses by influencing users to use specific response structures, and by careful wording of prompts designed to suggest the use of similar vocabulary in formulating responses.

Further reading

Bruce, I. P. C. (1987) 'Engineering an intelligent voice dialogue controller', *British Telecom Technological Journal*, **5**(4) 61–68.

Rosson, M. B. and A. J. Cecala (1986) 'Designing a quality voice: an analysis of listeners' reactions to synthetic voices', *Proceedings, CHI '86: Human factors in Computer Systems*, ACM, New York, 192–197.

Starr, A. F., S. M. Hudson and D. M. Jones (1989) *User Preferences and Researcher Experiences: Applications of Speech Recognition in the United Kingdom and North America*, Alvey Contract MMI-103, 29 January 1989, Report 3.

Talbot, M. (1986) 'Speech technology: is it working?', *British Telecom Technical Journal*, **4**(2), 62–68.

Appendices

Appendix 1
Statistical tests for experimental evaluation

A1.1 The t-test

The *t*-test derives directly from the standard method used for estimating the significance of a particular deviation from the mean in a normal distribution. Where the standard deviation is known, the test statistic z is given by:

$$z = \frac{\bar{x} - \mu_0}{\sigma/\sqrt{n}}$$

where $\bar{x}$ is the mean value of the test samples
μ_0 is the hypothesized population mean
σ is the population standard deviation
n is the number of test samples

when σ is unknown it is replaced by the sample standard deviation, s, to obtain the test statistic:

$$t = \frac{\bar{x} - \mu_0}{s/\sqrt{n}}$$

The distribution of t is more spread out than a standard normal distribution, and is represented by a t-distribution with $(n\text{-}1)$ degrees of freedom, assuming that the hypothesis concerning μ_0 is true. However, when n is more than about 25, the sample standard deviation is a good estimate of s, and the standard normal curve $N(0, 1)$ can be used to estimate the probability of a particular deviation.

If the observed value of t given by the expression above is denoted by t_0 then the level of significance is given as follows:

two-tailed test $P(|t| \geq |t_0|) = 2P(t \geq |t_0|)$ (for H_1: $\mu \neq \mu_0$)

one-tailed test $P(t \geq t_0)$ (for H_1: $\mu > \mu_0$)
$P(t \leq t_0)$ (for H_1: $\mu < \mu_0$)

The one-tailed test is used where we are only interested in results which depart from the null hypothesis in one direction. The two-tailed test is used where we are interested in a result which is *either* higher *or* lower than expected by the null hypothesis.

These probabilities can be found from the table of percentage points of the t-distribution given at the end of this Appendix, where the percentage point $t_{\alpha,\nu}$ is chosen so that there is a one-tailed probability α of getting a larger observation from a t-distribution with ν degrees of freedom.

In practice, for the type of evaluation experiments discussed in this book, we wish to compare two sample means rather than to compare a sample mean with a known mean μ. In this case it can be shown that the appropriate test statistic is

$$t = \frac{\bar{x}_1 - \bar{x}_2}{s\sqrt{1/n_1 + 1/n_2}}$$

where the subscripts 1 and 2 denote the first and second samples. The sample standard deviation s is then derived from the combined unbiased estimate of the variance:

$$s = \frac{(n_1 - 1)s_1^2 + (n_2 - 1)s_2^2}{n_1 + n_2 - 2}$$

where s_1 and s_2 are the separate sample standard deviations. If the null hypothesis is true, then the test statistic, t, follows a t-distribution with $(n_1 + n_2 - 2)$ degrees of freedom. The level of significance of a particular result, t_0, can thus be found as before.

Rather than evaluating s_1^2 and s_2^2 separately, it is simpler to calculate s^2 directly from:

$$s^2 = \frac{\sum x_{1i}^2 - \dfrac{(\sum x_{1i})^2}{n_1} + \sum x_{2i}^2 - \dfrac{(\sum x_{2i})^2}{n_2}}{n_1 + n_2 - 2}$$

Example 3rd solution attempt (Figure 12.5)

Sum for treatment A's: 78   Sum for treatment B's: 62
Sum of squared A's: 3044   Sum of squared B's: 1924

Estimated combined variance of A and B (s^2): 2
Estimated combined standard deviation s: 1.414

Mean for treatment A's: 39   Mean for treatment B's: 31

Test statistic t_0:   5.66

But from Table A1.1, $t_{0.025, 2} = 4.303$ and $t_{0.01, 2} = 6.965$, for a one-tailed test.

We require a *two-tailed* test, since treatment A could be significantly better *or* worse than treatment B. For a two-tailed test we therefore have significance at the 2×2.5-per-cent ($=$ 5-per-cent) level if $t_0 > 4.303$, and significance at the 2-per-cent level if $t_0 > 6.965$.

Hence, *there is evidence that treatments A and B differ: the result is significant at the 5-per-cent level.*

A1.2 Analysis of variance

If we have to compare more than two treatments, it might be supposed that this could be done simply by carrying out multiple t-tests between each pair of treatments. Indeed this can be done (and is known as a multiple t-test), but account must be taken of the fact that the overall level of significance is affected by the number of tests performed. If the significance level is 5 per cent, and there are for example four treatments, then $^4C_2$ ($= 6$) paired comparisons can be made, and the probability that *at least* one test will give a significant result if H_0 is true is $1 - (1 - 0.05)^6 = 0.26$. In a multiple t-test this effect is compensated by using a lower percentage point on the t-distribution, that is, by dividing the required percentage point by the number of paired comparisons to be made. In this case, for a measurement at the 5-per-cent significance level, a point of 5/6 per cent ($\approx$ 1 per cent) on the t-distribution would be used. (Strictly, the required percentage point, α, on the t-distribution would be chosen so that $1 - (1 - \alpha)^\nu = 0.05$, where ν is the number of paired comparisons possible.)

An alternative, more general technique is to use an analysis of variance. This technique splits up the variation in a set of observations into components ascribable to different causes including natural (residual) variation. By comparing each component with the residual variation the size and significance of the ascribable variation may be assessed. An important point to note, however, is that where more than two treatments are compared, the analysis of variance will identify any significant difference between treatments, but will not identify *which* of the treatments differ significantly. This requires the use of a further test, for example the multiple t-test or an alternative test such as Tukey's test.

The particular value of the analysis of variance technique is that it can be applied not only when a single variable is being measured (e.g., several different treatments) but also when more than one variable contributes to each score, as is the case of the Latin-squares design (final solution attempt, Figure 12.7). In this example, a three-way analysis of variance will allow the effect of the treatments and the two blocking factors (subjects and periods) to be separately assessed (assuming that there are no transfer effects).

The analysis is generally carried out by drawing up an

analysis-of-variance table, as shown below, where the nomenclature is as follows:

T is the number of treatments;
S is the number of subjects;
the number of periods is the same as the number of treatments (a requirement of the Latin-squares design);

and:

$$\bar{x} = \frac{\sum_{i,j,k} x_{ijk}}{ST}$$

$$\bar{x}_{i..} = \frac{\sum_{j,k} x_{ijk}}{S}, \quad \bar{x}_{.j.} = \frac{\sum_{i,k} x_{ijk}}{T}, \quad \bar{x}_{..k} = \frac{\sum_{i,j} x_{ijk}}{S}$$

Source of variation	Sum of squares (s.s.)	Degrees of freedom (d.f.)	Mean square (s.s./d.f.)	F-ratio
Treatments	$S\sum_{i}(\bar{x}_{i..} - \bar{x})^2$	$T - 1$	s_t^2	$\dfrac{s_t^2}{s^2}$
Subjects (rows)	$T\sum_{j}(\bar{x}_{.j.} - \bar{x})^2$	$S - 1$	s_s^2	$\dfrac{s_s^2}{s^2}$
Periods (columns)	$S\sum_{k}(\bar{x}_{..k} - \bar{x})^2$	$T - 1$	s_p^2	$\dfrac{s_p^2}{s^2}$
Residual	by subtraction	$(T - 1)(S - 2)$	s^2	
Total	$\sum_{i,j,k}(x_{ijk} - \bar{x})^2$	$TS - 1$		

The analysis hinges on two facts:

1 Regardless of whether the means of the groups differ, s^2 provides an estimate of σ^2 with 2 degrees of freedom.
2 When the null hypothesis is true, i.e., the means of the groups do not differ, s_t^2 estimates σ^2 with 1 degree of freedom. When the alternative hypothesis is true, s_t^2 is enlarged by the real differences in the means.

The ratio of mean squares with different degrees of freedom has an F-distribution, where $F_{p,q}(\alpha)$ represents the upper percentage point of the F-distribution corresponding to p degrees of freedom in the group, q degrees of freedom in the residual, and a probability of α.

In general, analysis of variance is carried out using computer analysis packages such as MINITAB, because these not only speed up the analysis but also provide the capability to perform a variety of checks on the residuals to ensure that the measured experimental results conform with the proposed experimental model. For the purpose of this experiment however, the analysis-of-variance table can be drawn up as follows:

Example Final solution attempt (Figure 12.7)

First, calculate the row and column averages, the treatment average and the overall average (already shown in Figure 12.7). In this case, $T = 2$ and $S = 4$. Calculate the overall sum of squares and correction factor

$$\sum_{i,j,k} x_{ijk}^2 \text{ and } ST\bar{x}^2$$

respectively. Then the total corrected sum of squares is given by

$$\sum_{i,j,k} (x_{ijk} - \bar{x})^2 = \sum_{i,j,k} x_{ijk}^2 - ST\bar{x}^2$$

Secondly, the treatment sum of squares is given by

$$S\sum_{i} (\bar{x}_{i..} - \bar{x})^2 = S\sum_{i} \bar{x}_{i..}^2 - ST\bar{x}^2$$

Thirdly, the subject (row block) sum of squares is given by

$$T\sum_{j} (\bar{x}_{.j.} - \bar{x})^2 = T\sum_{j} \bar{x}_{.j.}^2 - ST\bar{x}^2$$

Fourthly, the period (column block) sum of squares is given by

$$S\sum_{k} (\bar{x}_{..k} - \bar{x})^2 = S\sum_{k} \bar{x}_{..k}^2 - ST\bar{x}^2$$

The residual sum of squares can now be obtained by subtracting the treatment, subject and period sums of squares from the total sum of squares.

Each sum of squares is now divided by the appropriate number of degrees of freedom to give the required mean squares. The treatment F-ratio can now be calculated by dividing the treatment mean square by the residual mean square. The observed treatment F-ratio can then be compared with the upper percentage point of the appropriate F-distribution in order to test the hypothesis that all the treatment effects are zero. (If the subject and/or period effects are of interest, we can also test the hypothesis that these effects are zero by considering the observed F-ratios.) The values obtained for the example of Figure 12.7 are shown in the following table.

Source of variation	Sum of squares (s.s.)	Degrees of freedom (d.f.)	Mean square (s.s./d.f.)	F-ratio
Treatments	220.5	1	220.5	14.46
Subjects (rows)	27	3	9	< 1
Periods (columns)	18	1	18	1.18
Residual	30.5	2	15.25	
Total	296	7		

From the F-distribution tables, $F_{1,2}$(5 per cent) $=$ 18.51. Since the observed value is less than 18.51, we conclude that there is *no* evidence that treatments A and B differ. (It might be however, that by further replication of the experiment, substantive evidence would be revealed.)

Since the F-ratio for subjects is less than 1, there is no evidence of any significant differences between subjects. (In practice, one usually finds that there *is* evidence of such a difference!). Similarly, there is no evidence of any significant differences between periods.

Table A1.1 Percentage points of Students t-distribution

α	.10	.05	.025	.01	.005	.001
ν						
1	3.078	6.314	12.706	31.821	63.657	318.310
2	1.866	2.920	4.303	6.965	9.925	22.327
3	1.633	2.353	3.182	4.541	5.841	10.215
4	1.533	2.132	2.776	3.747	4.604	7.173
5	1.476	2.015	2.571	3.365	4.032	5.893
6	1.440	1.943	2.447	3.143	3.707	5.208
7	1.415	1.895	2.365	2.998	3.499	4.785
8	1.397	1.860	2.306	2.896	3.355	4.501
9	1.383	1.833	2.262	2.821	3.250	4.297
10	1.372	1.812	2.228	2.764	3.169	4.144
11	1.363	1.796	2.201	2.718	3.106	4.025
12	1.356	1.782	2.179	2.681	3.055	3.930
13	1.350	1.771	2.160	2.650	3.012	3.852
14	1.345	1.761	2.145	2.624	2.977	3.787
15	1.341	1.753	2.131	2.502	2.947	3.733
16	1.337	1.746	2.120	2.583	2.921	3.686
17	1.333	1.740	2.110	2.567	2.898	3.646
18	1.330	1.734	2.101	2.552	2.878	3.610
19	1.328	1.729	2.093	2.539	2.861	3.579
20	1.325	1.725	2.086	2.528	2.845	3.552
21	1.323	1.721	2.080	2.518	2.831	3.527
22	1.321	1.717	2.074	2.508	2.819	3.505
23	1.319	1.714	2.069	2.500	2.807	3.485
24	1.318	1.711	2.064	2.492	2.797	3.467
25	1.316	1.703	2.060	2.485	2.787	3.450
26	1.315	1.706	2.056	2.479	2.779	3.435
27	1.314	1.703	2.052	2.473	2.771	3.421
28	1.313	1.701	2.048	2.467	2.763	3.408
29	1.311	1.699	2.045	2.462	2.756	3.396
30	1.310	1.697	2.042	2.457	2.750	3.385
40	1.303	1.684	2.021	2.423	2.704	3.307
60	1.296	1.671	2.000	2.390	2.660	3.232
120	1.289	1.658	1.980	2.358	2.617	3.160
∞	1.282	1.645	1.960	2.326	2.576	3.090

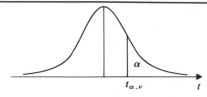

Table A1.2 Upper percentage points of the F-distribution

(a) $\alpha = 0.01$

ν_1	1	2	3	4	5	6	7	8	9	10	12	15	20	24	30
ν_2															
1	4052.2	4999.5	5403.4	5624.6	5763.6	5859.0	5928.4	5981.1	6022.5	6055.8	6106.3	6157.3	6208.7	6234.6	6260.6
2	98.50	99.00	99.17	99.25	99.30	99.33	99.36	99.37	99.39	99.40	99.42	99.43	99.45	99.46	99.47
3	34.12	30.82	29.46	28.71	28.24	27.91	27.67	27.49	27.35	27.23	27.05	26.87	26.69	26.60	26.50
4	21.20	18.00	16.69	15.98	15.52	15.21	14.98	14.80	14.66	14.55	14.37	14.20	14.02	13.93	13.84
5	16.26	13.27	12.06	11.39	10.97	10.67	10.46	10.29	10.16	10.05	9.89	9.72	9.55	9.47	9.38
6	13.75	10.92	9.78	9.15	8.85	8.47	8.26	8.10	7.93	7.87	7.72	7.56	7.40	7.31	7.23
7	12.25	9.55	8.45	7.85	7.46	7.19	6.99	6.84	6.72	6.62	6.47	6.31	6.16	6.07	5.99
8	11.26	8.65	7.59	7.01	6.63	6.37	6.18	6.03	5.91	5.81	5.67	5.52	5.36	5.28	5.20
9	10.56	8.02	6.99	6.42	6.06	5.80	5.61	5.47	5.35	5.26	5.11	4.96	4.81	4.73	4.65
10	10.04	7.56	6.55	5.99	5.64	5.39	5.20	5.06	4.94	4.85	4.71	4.56	4.41	4.33	4.25
11	9.65	7.21	6.22	5.67	5.32	5.07	4.89	4.74	4.63	4.54	4.40	4.25	4.10	4.02	3.94
12	9.33	6.93	5.95	5.41	5.06	4.82	4.64	4.50	4.39	4.30	4.16	4.01	3.86	3.78	3.70
13	9.07	6.70	5.74	5.21	4.86	4.62	4.44	4.30	4.19	4.10	3.96	3.82	3.66	3.59	3.51
14	8.86	6.51	5.56	5.04	4.69	4.46	4.23	4.14	4.03	3.94	3.80	3.66	3.51	3.43	3.35
15	8.68	6.36	5.42	4.89	4.56	4.32	4.14	4.00	3.89	3.80	3.67	3.52	3.37	3.29	3.21
16	8.53	6.23	5.29	4.77	4.44	4.20	4.03	3.89	3.78	3.69	3.55	3.41	3.26	3.18	3.10
17	8.40	6.11	5.18	4.67	4.34	4.10	3.93	3.79	3.68	3.59	3.46	3.31	3.16	3.08	3.00
18	8.29	6.01	5.09	4.58	4.25	4.01	3.84	3.71	3.60	3.51	3.37	3.23	3.08	3.00	2.92
19	8.18	5.93	5.01	4.50	4.17	3.94	3.77	3.63	3.52	3.43	3.30	3.15	3.00	2.92	2.84
20	8.10	5.85	4.94	4.43	4.10	3.87	3.70	3.56	3.46	3.37	3.23	3.09	2.94	2.86	2.78
21	8.02	5.78	4.87	4.37	4.04	3.81	3.64	3.51	3.40	3.31	3.17	3.03	2.88	2.80	2.72
22	7.95	5.72	4.82	4.31	3.99	3.76	3.59	3.45	3.35	3.26	3.12	2.98	2.83	2.75	2.67
23	7.88	5.66	4.76	4.26	3.94	3.71	3.54	3.41	3.30	3.21	3.07	2.93	2.78	2.70	2.62
24	7.82	5.61	4.72	4.22	3.90	3.67	3.50	3.36	3.26	3.17	3.03	2.89	2.74	2.66	2.58
25	7.77	5.57	4.68	4.18	3.85	3.63	3.46	3.32	3.22	3.13	2.99	2.85	2.70	2.62	2.54
26	7.72	5.53	4.64	4.14	3.82	3.59	3.42	3.29	3.13	3.08	2.96	2.81	2.66	2.58	2.50
27	7.68	5.49	4.80	4.11	3.78	3.56	3.39	3.26	3.15	3.06	2.93	2.78	2.63	2.55	2.47
28	7.64	5.45	4.57	4.07	3.75	3.53	3.36	3.23	3.12	3.03	2.90	2.75	2.60	2.52	2.44
29	7.60	5.42	4.54	4.04	3.73	3.50	3.33	3.20	3.09	3.00	2.87	2.73	2.57	2.49	2.41
30	7.56	5.39	4.51	4.02	3.70	3.47	3.30	3.17	3.07	2.98	2.84	2.70	2.55	2.47	2.39
40	7.31	5.18	4.31	3.83	3.51	3.29	3.12	2.99	2.89	2.80	2.66	2.52	2.37	2.29	2.20
60	7.08	4.98	4.13	3.65	3.34	3.12	2.95	2.82	2.72	2.63	2.50	2.35	2.20	2.12	2.03
120	6.85	4.79	3.95	3.48	3.17	2.96	2.79	2.68	2.56	2.47	2.34	2.19	2.03	1.95	1.86
00	6.63	4.61	3.78	3.32	3.02	2.80	2.64	2.51	2.41	2.32	2.18	2.04	1.88	1.79	1.70

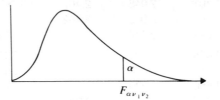

$F_{\alpha \nu_1 \nu_2}$

Table A1.2 (*continued*)

(b) $\alpha = 0.025$

ν_1	1	2	3	4	5	6	7	8	9	10	12	15	20	24	30
ν_2															
1	647.79	799.50	864.16	899.58	921.85	937.11	948.22	956.66	963.28	968.63	976.71	984.87	993.10	997.25	1001.4
2	38.51	39.00	39.17	39.25	39.30	39.33	39.36	39.37	39.39	39.40	39.41	39.43	39.45	39.46	39.46
3	17.44	16.04	15.44	15.10	14.88	14.73	14.62	14.54	14.47	14.42	14.34	14.25	14.17	14.12	14.08
4	12.22	10.65	9.98	9.60	9.36	9.20	9.07	8.98	8.90	8.84	8.75	8.66	8.56	8.51	8.46
5	10.01	8.43	7.76	7.39	7.15	6.98	6.85	6.76	6.68	6.62	6.52	6.43	6.33	6.28	6.23
6	8.81	7.26	6.60	6.23	5.99	5.82	5.70	5.60	5.52	5.46	5.37	5.27	5.17	5.12	5.07
7	8.07	6.54	5.89	5.52	5.29	5.12	4.99	4.90	4.82	4.76	4.67	4.57	4.47	4.41	4.36
8	7.57	6.06	5.42	5.05	4.82	4.65	4.53	4.43	4.36	4.30	4.20	4.10	4.00	3.95	3.89
9	7.21	5.71	5.08	4.72	4.48	4.32	4.20	4.10	4.03	3.96	3.87	3.77	3.67	3.61	3.56
10	6.94	5.46	4.83	4.47	4.24	4.07	3.95	3.85	3.78	3.72	3.62	3.52	3.42	3.37	3.31
11	6.72	5.26	4.63	4.28	4.04	3.88	3.76	3.66	3.59	3.53	3.43	3.33	3.23	3.17	3.12
12	6.55	5.10	4.47	4.12	3.89	3.73	3.61	3.51	3.44	3.37	3.28	3.18	3.07	3.02	2.96
13	6.41	4.97	4.35	4.00	3.77	3.60	3.48	3.39	3.31	3.25	3.15	3.05	2.95	2.89	2.84
14	6.30	4.86	4.24	3.89	3.66	3.50	3.38	3.29	3.21	3.15	3.05	2.95	2.84	2.79	2.73
15	6.20	4.77	4.15	3.80	3.58	3.41	3.29	3.20	3.12	3.06	2.96	2.86	2.76	2.70	2.64
16	6.12	4.69	4.08	3.73	3.50	3.34	3.22	3.12	3.05	2.99	2.89	2.79	2.68	2.63	2.57
17	6.04	4.62	4.01	3.66	3.44	3.28	3.16	3.06	2.98	2.92	2.82	2.72	2.62	2.56	2.50
18	5.98	4.56	3.95	3.61	3.38	3.22	3.10	3.01	2.93	2.87	2.77	2.67	2.56	2.50	2.44
19	5.92	4.51	3.90	3.56	3.33	3.17	3.05	2.96	2.88	2.82	2.72	2.62	2.51	2.45	2.39
20	5.87	4.46	3.86	3.51	3.29	3.13	3.01	2.91	2.84	2.77	2.68	2.57	2.46	2.41	2.35
21	5.83	4.42	3.82	3.48	3.25	3.09	2.97	2.87	2.80	2.73	2.64	2.53	2.42	2.37	2.31
22	5.79	4.38	3.78	3.44	3.22	3.05	2.93	2.84	2.76	2.70	2.60	2.50	2.39	2.33	2.27
23	5.75	4.35	3.75	3.41	3.18	3.02	2.90	2.81	2.73	2.67	2.57	2.47	2.36	2.30	2.24
24	5.72	4.32	3.72	3.38	3.15	2.99	2.87	2.78	2.70	2.64	2.54	2.44	2.33	2.27	2.21
25	5.69	4.29	3.69	3.35	3.13	2.97	2.85	2.75	2.68	2.61	2.51	2.41	2.30	2.24	2.18
26	5.66	4.27	3.67	3.33	3.10	2.94	2.82	2.73	2.65	2.59	2.49	2.39	2.28	2.22	2.16
27	5.63	4.24	3.65	3.31	3.08	2.92	2.80	2.71	2.63	2.57	2.47	2.36	2.25	2.19	2.13
28	5.61	4.22	3.63	3.29	3.06	2.90	2.78	2.69	2.61	2.55	2.45	2.34	2.23	2.17	2.11
29	5.59	4.20	3.61	3.27	3.04	2.88	2.76	2.67	2.59	2.53	2.43	2.32	2.21	2.15	2.09
30	5.57	4.18	3.59	3.25	3.03	2.87	2.75	2.65	2.57	2.51	2.41	2.31	2.20	2.14	2.07
40	5.42	4.05	3.46	3.13	2.90	2.74	2.62	2.53	2.45	2.39	2.29	2.18	2.07	2.01	1.94
60	5.29	3.93	3.34	3.01	2.79	2.63	2.51	2.41	2.33	2.27	2.17	2.06	1.94	1.88	1.82
120	5.15	3.80	3.23	2.89	2.67	2.52	2.39	2.30	2.22	2.16	2.05	1.94	1.82	1.76	1.69
∞	5.02	3.69	3.12	2.79	2.57	2.41	2.29	2.19	2.11	2.05	1.94	1.83	1.71	1.64	1.57

Table A1.2 (*continued*)

(c)$\alpha = 0.05$

ν_1	1	2	3	4	5	6	7	8	9	10	12	15	20	24	30
ν_2															
1	161.45	199.50	215.71	224.58	230.16	233.99	236.77	238.88	240.54	241.88	243.91	245.95	248.01	249.05	250.10
2	18.51	19.00	19.16	19.25	19.30	19.33	19.35	19.37	19.38	19.40	19.41	19.43	19.45	19.45	19.46
3	10.13	9.55	9.28	9.12	9.01	8.94	8.89	8.85	8.81	8.79	8.74	8.70	8.66	8.64	8.62
4	7.71	6.94	6.59	6.39	6.26	6.16	6.09	6.04	6.00	5.96	5.91	5.86	5.80	5.77	5.75
5	6.61	5.79	5.41	5.19	5.05	4.95	4.88	4.82	4.77	4.74	4.68	4.62	4.56	4.53	4.50
6	5.99	5.14	4.76	4.53	4.39	4.28	4.21	4.15	4.10	4.06	4.00	3.94	3.87	3.84	3.81
7	5.59	4.74	4.35	4.12	3.97	3.87	3.79	3.73	3.68	3.64	3.57	3.51	3.44	3.41	3.38
8	5.32	4.46	4.07	3.84	3.69	3.58	3.50	3.44	3.39	3.35	3.28	3.22	3.15	3.12	3.08
9	5.12	4.26	3.86	3.63	3.48	3.37	3.29	3.23	3.18	3.14	3.07	3.01	2.94	2.90	2.86
10	4.96	4.10	3.71	3.48	3.33	3.22	3.14	3.07	3.02	2.98	2.91	2.84	2.77	2.74	2.70
11	4.84	3.98	3.59	3.36	3.20	3.09	3.01	2.95	2.90	2.85	2.79	2.72	2.65	2.61	2.57
12	4.75	3.89	3.49	3.26	3.11	3.00	2.91	2.85	2.80	2.75	2.69	2.62	2.54	2.51	2.47
13	4.67	3.81	3.41	3.18	3.03	2.92	2.83	2.77	2.71	2.67	2.60	2.53	2.46	2.42	2.38
14	4.60	3.74	3.34	3.11	2.96	2.85	2.76	2.70	2.65	2.60	2.53	2.46	2.39	2.35	2.31
15	4.54	3.68	3.29	3.06	2.90	2.79	2.71	2.64	2.59	2.54	2.48	2.40	2.33	2.29	2.25
16	4.49	3.63	3.24	3.01	2.85	2.74	2.66	2.59	2.54	2.49	2.42	2.35	2.28	2.24	2.19
17	4.45	3.59	3.20	2.96	2.81	2.70	2.61	2.55	2.49	2.45	2.38	2.34	2.23	2.19	2.15
18	4.41	3.55	3.16	2.93	2.77	2.66	2.58	2.51	2.46	2.41	2.34	2.27	2.19	2.15	2.11
19	4.38	3.52	3.13	2.90	2.74	2.63	2.54	2.48	2.42	2.38	2.31	2.23	2.16	2.11	2.07
20	4.35	3.49	3.10	2.87	2.71	2.60	2.51	2.45	2.39	2.35	2.28	2.20	2.12	2.08	2.04
21	4.32	3.47	3.07	2.84	2.68	2.57	2.49	2.42	2.37	2.32	2.25	2.18	2.10	2.05	2.01
22	4.30	3.44	3.05	2.82	2.66	2.55	2.46	2.40	2.34	2.30	2.23	2.15	2.07	2.03	1.98
23	4.28	3.42	3.03	2.80	2.64	2.53	2.44	2.37	2.32	2.27	2.20	2.13	2.05	2.01	1.96
24	4.26	3.40	3.01	2.78	2.62	2.51	2.42	2.36	2.30	2.25	2.18	2.11	2.03	1.98	1.94
25	4.24	3.39	2.99	2.76	2.60	2.49	2.40	2.34	2.28	2.24	2.16	2.09	2.01	1.96	1.92
26	4.23	3.37	2.98	2.74	2.59	2.47	2.39	2.32	2.27	2.22	2.15	2.07	1.99	1.95	1.90
27	4.21	3.35	2.96	2.73	2.57	2.46	2.37	2.31	2.25	2.20	2.13	2.06	1.97	1.93	1.88
28	4.20	3.34	2.95	2.71	2.56	2.45	2.36	2.29	2.24	2.19	2.12	2.04	1.96	1.91	1.87
29	4.18	3.33	2.93	2.70	2.55	2.43	2.35	2.28	2.22	2.18	2.10	2.03	1.94	1.90	1.85
30	4.17	3.32	2.92	2.69	2.53	2.42	2.33	2.27	2.21	2.16	2.09	2.01	1.93	1.89	1.84
40	4.08	3.23	2.84	2.61	2.45	2.34	2.25	2.18	2.12	2.08	2.00	1.92	1.84	1.79	1.74
60	4.00	3.15	2.76	2.53	2.37	2.25	2.17	2.10	2.04	1.99	1.92	1.84	1.75	1.70	1.65
120	3.92	3.07	2.68	2.45	2.29	2.18	2.09	2.02	1.96	1.91	1.83	1.75	1.66	1.61	1.55
∞	3.84	3.00	2.60	2.37	2.21	2.10	2.01	1.94	1.88	1.83	1.75	1.67	1.57	1.52	1.46

Appendix 2
Example problems

A2.1 Short questions

1. Explain the concept and significance of 'chunks' in relation to models of the human's short-term memory.

2. Briefly explain the difference between *between-subjects* and *within-subjects* experimental designs.

3. Explain briefly how subclassing in object-oriented programming promotes the reusability of software.

4. What factors have made the mouse more popular than the light pen as an interactive pointing device?

5. Why is it desirable to provide a formal specification of a man–machine dialogue?

6. Explain the concept and significance of 'closure' in relation to models of human cognitive processing.

7. List four main advantages and four main disadvantages of raster scan CRT displays for interactive graphical tasks.

8. By means of a suitable small example, show how a state transition network can be used in man–machine dialogue design.

9. Briefly explain the advantages and disadvantages of evaluation using questionnaires compared with experimental evaluation.

10. How is data encapsulation provided in an object-oriented language?

11. Describe the characteristics of short-term memory, and explain their significance in the design of human–computer dialogues.

12. List and compare some human and computer aptitudes which should be taken into account in the design of human–computer systems.

13. Briefly describe the stages in product development at which human-factors evaluation may be applied. Explain the reasons for adopting a progressive evaluation strategy.

14. List the relative advantages and disadvantages of direct pointing devices on electronic displays.

15. Briefly discuss the advantages and disadvantages of the state transition network as a notation for dialogue specification.

A2.2 Discussion questions

1. Describe briefly psychological models of the human information processor and discuss their application to computer systems design.

2. How do man–machine dialogue styles vary? Explain how this variation can be used to match the user to the system.

3. Describe and discuss the main formal experimental techniques for man–machine system evaluation.

4. What are the important concepts in the current generation of window managers? How do these reflect differing interpretations of the design issues involved?

5. List some important dimensions of programming languages, and use them as a basis for a comparison of any two languages you have used.

6. List 10 subtasks of the text-editing task, such as cut and paste, and compare two editors on each of them.

7. Review alternative keyboard text input techniques for computers, and make a comparison with speech and handwriting input.

8. Compare and contrast flat-panel displays with raster scan CRTs for interactive human–computer dialogues.

9. What are the capabilities of current speech input and output devices for computers? Discuss the human-factors issues in their use in current applications.

10. Describe in detail a tool for designing interactive computer dialogues. What are its limitations? Make some suggestions as to how these might be overcome.

11. Discuss the use of direct and indirect pointing devices for text editing and drafting purposes.

12. Discuss in detail a proposed model of the human as an information processor and its application to computer systems design.

13. Discuss the advantages and disadvantages of dialogue systems based upon command languages, form-filling and menu systems,

with particular reference to example research implementations and current commercial systems.

14. Describe and discuss the main factors to be taken into account in the design of a formal evaluation experiment to compare several alternative dialogue systems.

15. Describe the basic data structures used to represent the graphical images displayed by a typical window manager, giving example C code where appropriate.

16. Explain the relationships between an object, its class and the superclass of that class in an object-oriented language. What is meant by inheritance? Indicate briefly how it is implemented. With the aid of examples, show how inheritance may be used to aid in the reuse of software.

17. To what extent can the user be modelled as a component of an interactive system? What limitations do models proposed in the research literature have? Discuss, illustrating your answer with suitable examples.

18. 'Direct manipulation dialogue systems require high-performance workstations with bit-mapped graphics and mouse control of the cursor.' Discuss, illustrating your answer with suitable examples.

19. Compare and contrast the use of questionnaires with formal evaluation experiments in the evaluation of human–computer systems.

20. Describe two alternative architectures for the implementation of a windowing system, drawing particular attention to any performance differences.

21. 'For text entry to word processing systems there is no better method than the QWERTY keyboard.' Discuss.

A2.3 Design questions

1. A workstation manufacturer is considering replacing the conventional command-driven UNIX interface by a menu-driven alternative which performs equivalent functions, and wishes to carry out some evaluation to determine the effect which this change might be expected to have on users' performance using the system. Discuss in detail **one** of the following:
   (a) the stages in the design at which evaluation might be contemplated;
   (b) objective versus subjective evaluation;
   (c) possible experimental designs, and potential procedural problems which might result;

(d)   appropriate experimental models and statistical analysis techniques.

2.   Suppose you are required to produce a form | menu-based interface package. A menu is a sequence of items, to be chosen from with a single keystroke. A form is a sequence of titles, with a string to be filled in for each. The system displays a menu; the user selects an entry; the system then displays a further menu, takes an action or displays a form. Describe the software you would produce, showing the data structures, and outlining the procedures included. Give C declarations for the structures, and for the headers of the procedures, but do not write more code than is needed to illustrate the design.

3.   The university has six squash courts and needs to automate the booking system for them. It is proposed to provide terminals at convenient locations for users to interact directly with the system. Discuss in detail **one** of the following aspects of the design of such a system:
   1.   The use of program generators such as *Lex* and *Yacc* to automate aspects of dialogue implementation.
   2.   The use of state transition networks to design and/or implement dialogues.
   3.   The use of UNIX tools such as shell programming and the CURSES screen manipulation package for rapid interface prototyping.

4.   Design the user interface to a database device (such as a wristwatch) which enables both textual and numeric data to be entered using a minimal set of control buttons. The design should be based upon improvements which could be made to an existing device which you have evaluated.

5.   Explain briefly under what circumstances the t-distribution should be used to estimate the significance of a particular deviation from the mean in a normal distribution. State, with justification, the expression which should be used for t where it is required to compare the means of two sets of samples.
   In an evaluation experiment to compare the speed of cursor positioning of a mouse and a joystick, the following experimental data were obtained for 10 subjects:

mouse:	55	50	80	60	70	75	40	45	80	70
joystick:	70	80	85	105	65	100	90	95	100	70

where the numbers refer to the time in seconds each subject takes to complete the task. (It may be assumed that the experiment has been designed so that the device used to position the cursor is the only experimental variable.)

    (a)   Estimate the mean speed of positioning for each cursor control device.

    (b)   What level of statistical significance can be attached to the difference in means between the data for the two devices?

    (c)   What practical significance can be attached to the difference in means between the data for the two devices?

6.   A desktop presentation is made with the help of an interactive computer system operated by the presenter but with output visible to the audience via a projector or large screen. Outline an initial design for such a system. Indicate how you arrived at this design. How would you proceed to take this design to a stage where the product was ready to market?

7.   Using a system such as Rapid/USE, how would you design a suitable system for the issuing and returning of books for a university library? Discuss in detail your approach to the design of the dialogue rather than the functional aspects of issuing and returning books.

8.   Task analysis is important in identifying the range and structure of tasks.

    (a)   A task is defined as a means of effecting a change in the domain. What is the difference between task analysis and system analysis?

    (b)   In collecting data for a task analysis when would you use the following techniques?

        (i)   Interviews.

        (ii) Questionnaires.

        (iii) Concurrent protocols.

        (iv) Retrospective protocols.

        (v) Card sorting.

        (vi) Repertory grid.

    (c)   To construct a task model the collected data must be analysed and represented. How would you analyse the following aspects of a task?

        (i)   Goals.

        (ii) Plans.

        (iii) Strategies.

        (iv) Procedures.

        (v) Actions and objects.

   Show how you would represent the results of this analysis.

9.   An evaluation experiment is carried out to compare cursor positioning speed with a mouse and cursor keys, using 4 experimental subjects. The experiment is based upon a replicated Latin-squares design and produces the results shown in Figure A2.1 (where treatment A represents the use of cursor keys, and

treatment B the use of the mouse, and the figures represent the
time to complete the task in seconds).

Subject	Period 1	Period 2
1	A 426	B 210
2	B 241	A 398
3	A 288	B 143
4	B227	A 339

Figure A2.1

(a) Use the prototype ANOVA table in Appendix 1 to determine
the treatment, subject and period F-ratios, and hence
determine which (if any) are statistically significant.

(b) Briefly discuss the value of statistical analysis for the data
given, and the practical significance of the results.

(c) When the experiment is replicated for a further 8 subjects, and
the results reanalysed for the whole group of 12 subjects, the
following F-ratios are obtained:

treatment	52.87
subject	4.53
period	8.20

Is the statistical significance of each result changed, and if so, why?

10. Task knowledge structures (TKS) provide a theoretical view of the
knowledge used in performing a task.

(a) What are the components of a task knowledge structure?

(b) Give a brief description of each of the following indicating
what aspects of a TKS they can best be used to identify:
concurrent protocols;
retrospective protocols;
sorting;
structured interviews;
rating scales.

(c) How might task knowledge structures be used to influence the
design of a computer system and its user interface?

11. Using a system such as Rapid/USE, how would you design a
suitable system for controlling a parts inventory for a garage?
Discuss in detail your approach to the design of the dialogue
rather than the functional aspects of the system.

12. How does object-oriented programming support the production of
software components, and thus of reusable software? Illustrate
your answer with short examples.

Index